'In this engaging, provocative book, Timothy Stephen argues that our current difficulties with sustaining meaningful personal identities and intimate relationships are specific to conditions of modern society that have been developing gradually, and largely unnoticed, like climate change, for several hundred years. In this process, interpersonal communication has become ever more important but also more challenging. Based on many years of research and reflection, *Self and Other in an Age of Uncertain Meaning* offers an interpretation of our current predicament that can help us to meet those challenges.'

       – **Robert T. Craig**, *University of Colorado Boulder, founding editor of* Communication Theory, *and former president of the International Communication Association.*

'Timothy Stephen offers valuable insights on daily life that will resonate with any living person. He constructs thought-provoking arguments for why things are as they are. The historical analysis and cultural commentaries are interesting and persuasive. The work is readable and compelling and will appeal to scholars and educated non-specialists alike. I feel confident that even those who disagree with Stephen's conclusions will find value in this book.'

       – **Matthew Clemente, PhD**, *Boston College.*

'The "self" has become a very enigmatic category: who exactly is the "I" and how is our identity shaped by our social environment? Even more perplexingly: who and what is the modern self? Lucidly and consistently well-argued, *Self and Other in an Age of Uncertain Meaning* addresses these questions in the context of intimacy and marriage. You will understand far better than you ever did what makes an intimate talk so supremely modern.'

       – **Eva Illouz**, *author of* The End of Love *and Professor of Sociology at the Hebrew University in Jerusalem and the School for Advanced Studies in the Social Sciences in Paris.*

Self and Other in an Age of Uncertain Meaning

Self and Other in an Age of Uncertain Meaning explores the nature and origins of widespread problems of self in modern societies. It examines the paradoxical interplay between the modern world's many benefits and freedoms, and its mounting social challenges and psycho-emotional impacts.

Over time the character of consciousness has shifted in concert with societal trends. The experienced world has become more nuanced, fragmented, and uncertain, as well as increasingly personal and intimate, reshaping social relationships. Chapters analyze the interdependence of language, mind, intimacy, the self, and culture, arguing that as the coevolution of these five factors produced the modern world, many features of contemporary culture have become disruptive to security of being. The book explores the importance to the vital sense of self in constructing relationships based in mutual recognition of moral and intellectual equality between partners.

Rich with examples from everyday experience, this text offers profound insights for those interested in sociology, psychoanalysis, psychology, communication, history, and culture.

Timothy Stephen, PhD, is professor of communication at University at Albany (SUNY), specializing in the interrelationships of language, mind, culture, the self-concept, and intimacy, and, particularly, in the way in which communication in intimacy produces shared mind.

The Psychology and the Other Book Series

The *Psychology and the Other* Book Series highlights creative work at the intersections between psychology and the vast array of disciplines relevant to the human psyche. The interdisciplinary focus of this series brings psychology into conversation with continental philosophy, psychoanalysis, religious studies, anthropology, sociology, and social/critical theory. The cross-fertilization of theory and practice, encompassing such a range of perspectives, encourages the exploration of alternative paradigms and newly articulated vocabularies that speak to human identity, freedom, and suffering. Thus, we are encouraged to reimagine our encounters with difference, our notions of the "other," and what constitutes therapeutic modalities.

The study and practices of mental health practitioners, psychoanalysts, and scholars in the humanities will be sharpened, enhanced, and illuminated by these vibrant conversations, representing pluralistic methods of inquiry, including those typically identified as psychoanalytic, humanistic, qualitative, phenomenological, or existential.

Recent Series Titles Include:

Lacan and Race
Racism, Identity and Psychoanalytic Theory
Edited by Sheldon George and Derek Hook

Self and Other in an Age of Uncertain Meaning
Communication and the Marriage of Minds
By Timothy D. Stephen

Fanon, Phenomenology and Psychology
Edited by Leswin Laubscher, Derek Hook, and Miraj U. Desai

Madness in Experience and History
Merleau-Ponty's Phenomenology and Foucault's Archaeology
By Hannah Lyn Venable

For a full list of titles in the series, please visit the Routledge website at: https://www.routledge.com/Psychology-and-the-Other/book-series/PSYOTH

Self and Other in an Age of Uncertain Meaning
Communication and the Marriage of Minds

Timothy Stephen

LONDON AND NEW YORK

First published 2022
by Routledge
2 Park Square, Milton Park, Abingdon, Oxon, OX14 4RN

and by Routledge
605 Third Avenue, New York, NY 10158

Routledge is an imprint of the Taylor & Francis Group, an informa business

© 2022 Taylor & Francis

The right of Timothy Stephen to be identified as author of this work has been asserted by him in accordance with sections 77 and 78 of the Copyright, Designs and Patents Act 1988.

All rights reserved. No part of this book may be reprinted or reproduced or utilised in any form or by any electronic, mechanical, or other means, now known or hereafter invented, including photocopying and recording, or in any information storage or retrieval system, without permission in writing from the publishers.

Trademark notice: Product or corporate names may be trademarks or registered trademarks, and are used only for identification and explanation without intent to infringe.

Library of Congress Cataloging-in-Publication Data
Names: Stephen, Timothy, 1952- author.
Title: Self and other in an age of uncertain meaning : communication and the marriage of minds / Timothy D. Stephen.
Description: New York, NY : Routledge, 2021. | Includes bibliographical references and index.
Identifiers: LCCN 2021008549 (print) | LCCN 2021008550 (ebook) | ISBN 9780367445041 (hardback) | ISBN 9780367445065 (paperback) | ISBN 9781003010234 (ebook)
Subjects: LCSH: Communication--Social aspects. | Identity (Psychology)—Social aspects. | Self—Social aspects. | Interpersonal communication. | Interpersonal relations. | Intimacy (Psychology)—Social aspects.
Classification: LCC HM1206 .S741426 2021 (print) | LCC HM1206 (ebook) | DDC 302.2—dc23
LC record available at https://lccn.loc.gov/2021008549
LC ebook record available at https://lccn.loc.gov/2021008550

ISBN: 978-0-367-44504-1 (hbk)
ISBN: 978-0-367-44506-5 (pbk)
ISBN: 978-1-003-01023-4 (ebk)

DOI: 10.4324/9781003010234

Typeset in Times New Roman
by Apex CoVantage, LLC

Our changed and mingled souls are grown
To such acquaintance now,
That if each would resume their own,
Alas! we know not how.
We have each other so engrost,
That each is in the union lost.

Katherine Philips
To Mrs. M. A. at Parting, 1667

Contents

Preface	xi
1 Interpersonal climate change	1

PART 1
Language, mind, and intimacy — 21

2 A change of mind	23
3 Signals to symbols: the awakening of intimate experience	45

PART 2
The origins of uncertainty — 65

4 Through the rear-view mirror	67
5 Recipe for existential crisis: step 1: undermine certainty and truth	88
6 Recipe for existential crisis: step 2: weaken neighborhood ties	116
7 Recipe for existential crisis: step 3: foster isolation	131

PART 3
The shape of the modern self — 153

8 Selfie nation	155

x   *Contents*

9 Self from the inside out: language, mind, and the
   sense of self   166

10 From the basement up: modernity, the self, and the
    unconscious mind   188

11 And from the outside in: influences of work,
    technology, and societal institutions   210

12 We are each other: the dawn of the interpersonal self   228

13 Multi-Me: self, intimacy, and loss   241

14 Mini-Me: wrong ideas about communication, self, and
    intimacy   262

References   292
Index   312

Preface

The subject of this book is the fascinating story of the interdependent evolution of language, mind, the self-concept, culture, and intimacy, which are the five principal components of the system in which humans manage meaning. I began researching this subject 30 years ago and started writing this book in the spring of 2012. The project has occupied virtually every day since then. Suddenly, on the cusp of the book's publication, the psychological, social, and economic order of the world I aimed to describe and analyze has been turned upside down by the COVID-19 pandemic. Now, the world over, as much as public discussion is about the disease, the economy, and politics, people are also clamoring to understand the extensive impacts of disrupted social connection caused by lockdowns and shelter at home orders, and by fear that normal social contact places people at risk of death. Students can't meet in classrooms, lovers can't touch, people can't even attend the funerals of their family members and friends. The understandings around which many have built their lives have been called into doubt. In this book, I demonstrate that social isolation and uncertainty have long been on the rise, but so slowly and incrementally that, even while their impacts on our psychology and our intimate practices have been profound, generally this has gone unnoticed by most people. Not anymore. Suddenly, everyone is isolated, the future has exploded with uncertainty, and the impacts of this are universally apparent.

This book isn't about biological disease or pandemics. It is about human communication, the mind, and the socio-cultural impacts of a set of historically changing conditions collectively referred to as "modernity." These conditions affect how people live, think, and relate to each other. It is important to understand that modernity does not refer to a point in time; rather, modernity is a process of historical change, moving slowly but with overwhelming force, that has been gradually reordering the world during the last 400–500 years. Key areas of change include the shift of populations from the country to cities, declines in the influence of religion and tradition, increases in diversity, social mobility, and social equality, the rise of the mass culture, and the revolution in high-speed communications. Because modernity has greatly increased the frequency and speed of global trade and travel, it has long been understood that its risks include the heightened possibility of pandemic disease. However, aside xii *Preface*

from specific impacts of diseases such as SARS and COVID-19, or of those of any of the other individual factors of modernity, collectively, at its core, modernity increases uncertainty. This makes social relationships much more important (but also more fragile) and threatens psychological well-being. Ironically, it is in the experience of COVID-19 – in our universal and highly amplified restriction of access to normal interpersonal contact – that the way that this happens has been made especially vivid. I expect that most readers will have suffered in this unanticipated experience of isolation and, in consequence, will have a profoundly personal appreciation of the connection between reduced social contact and psychological malaise. I regret that this has happened to anyone, but, in fact, we have been edging in this direction for a long time: over the course of generations, we have been moving ever further into a world of increasing social disconnection and uncertainty of thought. This trend has tended to undermine faith in the continuity and coherence of our sense of who we are and has colored many lives with a subtle but chronic low-grade jitteriness, and a tendency toward inner focus, withdrawal, and solo activity. Tracing this is the central purpose of this book.

1 Interpersonal climate change

Man's search for meaning is the primary motivation in life.
Victor Frankl, *Man's Search for Meaning*:
An introduction to logotherapy[1]

The best and worst of times

During the last decades of the twentieth century, scholars with expertise spanning the humanities and social sciences were engaged in intensive analysis of the consequences for America of a number of worrying trends, trends that have continued and, indeed, have increased in intensity and visibility. These include political fracturing and polarization, and gradual decay in the quality of public discourse; changing patterns of intimacy and marital and family life that have rendered intimate involvements more vulnerable to disruption; Americans' withdrawal from meaningful community interconnection into what appears to be obsessively individualistic pursuits; growing disillusion with traditional roles and distrust of institutions; and, commonly, a subtle but stressful psychological fragmentation as economic tensions have chipped away the boundaries between work and home, and between one job and another, forcing many Americans to enact multiple roles simultaneously, to be in one place physically and somewhere else psychologically. In particular, alarm was raised over evidence of increasing absorption in problems of personal identity. Indeed, by the end of the twentieth century, "finding yourself" had become an exceptionally common concern, as it remains today.

These problems are all part of a common package, whose roots are historically deep. As long ago as 1953 – decades before the invention of earbuds, the selfie stick, the Game Boy, ADHD, or the Oculus Quest – drawing from a literature that had been accumulating for decades before him, eminent Berkeley sociologist Robert Nisbet proclaimed that America had become a country of "distracted multitudes and of solitary, inward-turning individuals."[2] Though nearly 70 years old, this description ought to sound familiar to even the most casual observer of America today. And whatever of this was apparent in Nisbet's time is far more prominent now. In his day, the social column of the small-town local paper listed the names of those who came into town on the weekend to shop or go to the movies, and, before the feature film, audiences

DOI: 10.4324/9781003010234-1

2 *Interpersonal climate change*

in the town's crowded theater sang together, following the bouncing rhythm ball on the screen. So, if Nisbet could say in 1953 that America was "inward-turning," what language remains for us to use to express our situation, where local newspapers are battling extinction, and not only is singing in a public movie theater unthinkable, but theaters have been downsized, chopped up, and multiplexed, the short subjects, newsreels, and sing-alongs replaced with relentless advertising. And, anyway, most families stay at home, everyone watching something different on their tablet or smartphone. Small wonder that, by the end of the twentieth century, social scientists were becoming alarmed about what was going on.

The internet arrived in the midst of this discussion like an EF5 tornado stepping up to the podium at an otherwise languid college debate over the reality of weather extremes. In the two decades since the launch of the World Wide Web, and one since the widespread adoption of smartphones and texting, there's been a dizzying range of impacts of digital technologies on the lives of Americans, with important consequences for the manner in which self-identity – our sense of who we are – is established and maintained, and the ways in which we involve ourselves with others, in intimate relationships, families, communities, and at work. And, although there have been many welcome innovations, there's also growing cause for concern. Comparing the impacts of digital life on interpersonal process to a vast, unauthorized and uncontrolled social experiment, the nation's leading commentator on digital culture, MIT psychologist Sherry Turkle, asserted recently that, "the unhappy findings are in: we are connected as we've never been connected before, and we seem to have damaged ourselves in the process"[3] – and this before the tragic and unsettlingly iconic death of Mexico City's Oscar Aguilar, who accidentally pulled the trigger instead of the shutter release while pointing a loaded pistol at his temple, posing for a cool selfie to upload to his Facebook page.[4]

With the recent arrival of so many new technologies of communication, "the digital age" provides a possible label for this period, but the impacts of digital technologies, visible as they are, aren't the only prominent hallmark of this era. This is also a time in which previous notions of what it means to be human – including our powers of conscious will, our volition in matters of moral responsibility, and the basis for emotional response – are being vigorously challenged in some areas of science, where, in its extreme (but hardly uncommon) form, there's a view that we are more the robot slaves of our brain chemistry and our DNA than the conscious masters of our own lives. At the center of this perspective is a depleted understanding of the nature and function of language – its role in creating and sustaining mind and connecting one mind to another and, beyond, to the broader circumstances of interpersonal life and the surrounding culture, which, as we will see, have been in a state of ongoing change throughout history.

Generally, the direction of this change has been toward an ever-more prominent role of communication in the management of inner experience and personal identity (where, especially in the last 100 years, expanded freedoms of choice have increased the need for consultation and social support), greater

Interpersonal climate change 3

recognition of communication's importance in navigating America's expanding diversity, a broadening (and often unnerving) recognition that a great deal of knowledge and truth are not fixed and timeless but relative to changing context and social experience, and that, critically, in these circumstances, communication has become both the means for creating structures of shared meaning that bridge increasingly separated minds and the essential glue that keeps social relationships together and the sense of self in place.

Yet, in contrast to this, today, evolutionary psychologists promote the idea that subjective experience (for example, of being attracted to your partner) is mainly biological ("chemistry"), and that thoughts and preferences aren't the products of consciousness and imagination, but are produced in the service of our genes in their effort to steer behavior so as to increase the odds they will be reproduced and proliferate in the gene pool. Language, mind, and culture have virtually no role in this mechanical vision of relationships formed and controlled by hard-wired processes of the body. (If you buy into this, it might make sense for you to sign up with the company GenePartner, which proposes to find your best intimate partner based on DNA samples swabbed from your cheek.) Others in cognitive neuroscience take this even further, contending that your essential consciousness, your sense of self and other, is just an illusion of your body and your computer-like brain. Why take up ideas from evolutionary psychology and cognitive neuroscience in a book on language, mind, culture, and intimate experience? One reason is that it's easier to appreciate the strengths of one set of ideas if there's a clear alternative point of contrast. If this was an early geography book arguing that the world was a sphere, it would be useful to take a look at what the flat-earth model does and doesn't account for.

There's another reason for taking up interpersonally relevant ideas from evolutionary psychology and cognitive neuroscience. It's not unusual to find controversial hypotheses like theirs batted back and forth across the corridors of university departments, where new, experimental strains of thought usually don't escape and do the public any real harm. But *this* fracas has spilled onto the street with immediate and concrete consequences for many in modern societies. Having recently shed its former expertise in the arts of talk and interpretation to take cues instead from evolutionary psychology and neuroscience, medical psychiatry now tells us the fidgety person is no longer as he once was: a fully conscious and agentic person who, perhaps, needs to be supported in his struggle with the stresses of complicated contemporary life and, moreover, who needs to understand and control impulse through conscious acts of self-restraint. Now, he's ever more likely to be regarded as the victim of the controversial new medical condition popularly referred to as ADHD, which, postulated as a neurological disease, would be unreasonable to expect anyone to control through an exercise of will. Never mind though, the doctor has a pill.

In fact, according to reports in the *New York Times*, doctors are now prescribing those particular pills (e.g., Adderall, Concerta, Ritalin) to more than 3.5 million American children,[5] including as many as 10,000 toddlers younger than 3,[6] generating more than $7 billion per year in sales revenues for

4 Interpersonal climate change

pharmaceutical companies.[7] As we'll see in a later chapter, the number of areas of psychological and interpersonal experience redefined by psychiatric authorities in this way, as diseases of the material brain often addressed with drug treatment, has vaulted from about 100 in Robert Nisbet's time to more than 350 today (that averages about four new mental disorders proclaimed by the psychiatric authorities every year for the last 60 years). As a result, the number of Americans with a diagnosable psychiatric disorder has risen from a rate of approximately 1 in 1,000 at the beginning of the twentieth century[8] to today's level of 1 in 5, if one can believe the National Institute of Mental Health.[9]

In 2016, American doctors wrote 594 million prescriptions for just the top 25 psychiatric drugs,[10] compounds designed to regulate the moods, cognitions, and emotions that shape and color our core interpersonal experiences: happiness, sadness, love, elation, anxiety, and so on. If these prescriptions were spread evenly across the population, this works out to 1.8 scripts for a psychiatric drug for every man, woman, and child in the United States. In actuality, the prescription rate for psychiatric drugs is reckoned at one in six adult Americans, with 80 percent of those on psychiatric drugs using them long term.[11] It's estimated that a new prescription for the popular anti-anxiety drug Xanax is written at a rate of one every second of every day (which means that some 30 Americans received a prescription for their anxiety disorders in the time it took you to read this paragraph), that one in ten Americans has a prescription for an antidepressant drug (e.g., Zoloft, Prozac, Paxil), and that this rate stands at a stunning one in four among middle-aged American women. Here is evidence that something troubling is happening in modern American life

In America's past, someone experiencing psycho-emotional difficulties might have gone to an analyst to start a course of talk therapy. The presumption was that inner experience was linked to processes of mind – especially, dysfunctional ideas of self – which ongoing intimate talk with a therapist could expose and gently nudge into a happier configuration. But, today, medical psychiatry has largely abandoned talk therapy and exploration of mind in favor of drug therapies tenuously linked to ideas from neuroscience and evolutionary psychology. In part, in psychiatry, these ideas reflect an optimism that neuroscience discoveries will eventually succeed in grounding psychiatric practice in material science. But they also appeal, in part, as they do to some in areas such as politics and marketing, because they promise significant new efficiencies in managing people. The hope is to be able to bypass the mind and talk (obviously, talk is slow, and what we say is subject to intentional and unintentional distortion), and instead get readouts on our values, motivations, and thoughts in the biomechanical traces of blood flow in the brain, in measures of skin conductivity, or pupil dilation, or blood chemistry, or the pulse, or in patterns of response on countless scales and measures of abstract traits and dispositions cooked up by psychologists in the service of their theories and absorbed into the broader culture as though they were real (e.g., Type A personality, IQ, introverts and extroverts, etc.). Here, the conscious mind is regarded as an accidental artifact, and communication a kind of expressive sideshow.

Interpersonal climate change 5

An extension of this type of approach into the realm of intimate relations would propose that you solve your marital problems by taking a pill – psychologist and psychopharmacology advocate Lauren Slater suggests MDA.[12] Others have suggested surreptitiously spritzing your partner with aerosolized oxytocin to pump up their warmth toward you,[13] or even spiking the public water supply with lithium as a solution to burgeoning suicide rates.[14] If this strikes you as bizarre or far-fetched, consider the blockbuster drugs Miltown and Equanil, marketed in the mid-twentieth century on claims that they would help women better manage the stresses of their notoriously subordinated and alienating marital roles.[15] Miltown and Equanil (the original "mother's little helpers" made famous by the Rolling Stones) proved to be runaway commercial successes, but also alarmingly addictive, and they were withdrawn from the market. However, pharmacologically speaking, the game was on. Today, the formulary of interpersonally relevant drugs contains names so common they have entered into the everyday parlance of pop culture. Many readers will recognize Xanax, Valium, Ativan, Wellbutrin, Concerta, Celexa, Abilify, Paxil, Adderall, Prozac, Ritalin, or Zoloft. There is no other category of prescription pharmacological agents with this breadth of name recognition.

As an index of how far the trend to bypass communication has gone, Pizza Hut recently began experimenting with electronic menus with built-in eye-tracking sensors that allow customers to order "subconsciously" (the picture of the item your eyes spend more time on is the one automatically selected and auto-ordered). According to the Pizza Hut corporation,[16] the benefit in this is that it saves customers the time and effort of actively thinking or talking about what to order, and so they end up with what they *really* want rather than what they only think they want (which is an idea that surely would have put Enlightenment philosopher René Descartes off pizza for good, no doubt sputtering angrily on his way out of the Pizza Hut shop, *cogito ergo ceno – I think, therefore I eat*).

But, make no mistake, our language-based communication practices are the vital center of modern human experience, the nexus at which mind, culture, and self meet and come into being. As sociologist Liah Greenfeld argues, mind is culture internalized, and culture is the externalized product of many minds.[17] Both mind and culture are produced in talk, both constituted from the common stock of symbolic meaning that we make use of to express ourselves in conversation. The difference between mind and culture is that, while mind struggles for simplicity and internal consistency, culture, as a construction of many communicating minds, is loaded with ever-greater contradiction and diversity. So much so, these days, that its unfiltered flow back into the minds that produce and sustain it is potentially overwhelming. When this occurs, it may result in various forms of psycho-emotional distress, ranging from anxiety disorders and depression to full-blown psychosis.

Here, exactly, is where personal identity comes into play.

Personal identity is an historically recent invention of mind that functions as a protective system for filtering culture. The self-concept consists of ideas,

6 Interpersonal climate change

preferences, and values related to core being which provide a sense of distinction and individuality. Most importantly, the self-concept provides a basis for prioritizing, moderating, deflecting, and integrating diverse and contradictory cultural meaning. When you know who you are, you know what to think and how to act. And, when you don't know who you are, you're in trouble. The sense of self as distinctive and individual – utterly familiar to most people – wasn't always part of the human experience (it is far less prominent in other, non-modern cultures today), and it didn't just appear by accident. Self-identity is a purposeful mental adaptation that only came into evidence about 500 years ago in response to newly emerging cultural stresses that were beginning to be experienced in the opening years of Western modernity.

Unfortunately, self-identity has become more difficult to sustain as modernity has gained momentum. Ever more likely to find their connections to family, neighbors, community, and tradition weakening, Americans are increasingly presented with more options, greater diversity of opinion, more contradiction, more sham, faster change, and less certainty. It is a mistake to attribute the widespread psycho-emotional disorders of modern America to problems of the mechanisms of the material brain. They stem from the increasingly difficult character of our cultural circumstances, which have rendered personal identity less secure and less stable and, therefore, less effective in filtering the backflow of inconsistent cultural meaning.

To effectively address this, it is important to encourage social practices relevant to creating and sustaining a strong and secure sense of self. The chemistry of the brain is far less relevant. A psychiatrist's pill may be able to deaden anxiety or, in some cases, mask depression, but there's no pill or medical procedure that can repair a damaged self-concept or a distressed moral narrative. It takes talk to come into being, to establish direction and purpose, and to sustain virtue in the face of life's normal flow of challenges and crises. The sense of personal identity is a social accomplishment that results from ongoing dialogue within our deepest social relationships. There are voices in the current neuroscience literature (Thomas Metzinger provides a particularly vivid example)[18] claiming that the self-concept, the tendency to see yourself as a coherent entity with particular past experiences, and a vision of yourself in the present and future linked to those experiences, is like a puddle you might see on a sizzling Arizona highway: just a mirage, an accidental byproduct of the workings of the physical brain. But that's only an academic proposal, a purposefully provocative one that utterly ignores the historical record of culture's dramatic impacts on communication practices, psycho-emotional experience, and the sense of self. No one should mistake such views for uncontested fact.[19]

The field of cognitive neuroscience captures attention with articles showing colorful fMRI scans of brains in which one or another area "lights up" under various experimental stimuli, implicitly suggesting, in the manner of the phrenologists of the nineteenth century who tried to argue that character was biologically determined by the shape of the skull, that there are biological prerequisites for virtually all human experience, that what we do and say is built in to the computer-like structures of the brain. In the extreme, for some authors, it's as if the brain operates independently of culture, and the mind, the self, the spirit, and the soul have been thrown out of the brain, which is seen as itself a sufficient account of human consciousness, decision making, and all the passions. For those who take this view, mood disorders are caused by flawed regulation of neurotransmitters. But, at this time, despite all the excitement about these ideas among popular authors, there is no support for such a conclusion. There is no blood test for anxiety. In fact, studies exploring the leading biological theory of depression – that it results from depletion of the neurotransmitter serotonin – have failed to find any reliable difference in levels of serotonin between depressed and non-depressed people.[20]

Without doubt, the brain and the rest of the material body play a part in shaping the sense of self, but their contribution isn't enough and pales against the immediate and visible relationship of the self to the acquisition of language in the context of social experience. Again, as Greenfeld argues, mind is culture-in-the-head. But culture doesn't simply float in and settle. It's interpreted, amplified, distorted, and selectively channeled in the myriad interpersonal transactions that pattern our days and lives. No brain acquires language on its own, encounters culture on its own, evolves mind on its own, or creates a self on its own. Beginning with the infant's grasp of the separation of her experience in the world from the experiences of others around her, and in her growing ability to use language and symbols, the child develops, in interaction with others, a sense of unique being. This understanding of self is created initially in the communication that transpires in the deeply intimate parent – infant relationship. But it continues to evolve throughout life in the context of communication within our other important social relationships. It's in these relationships that we construct with others a meaningful world, a sense of personal coherence, a moral compass, and an appreciation of the possible courses a life may take. As we'll see, it is this critical structure, the socially constructed sense of self-identity, that provides the ultimate protective filter against the stresses that follow from life in societies characterized by rapid change, high diversity, and deep contradiction. For many, and especially for the isolated, self-identity is not sufficiently well formed or supported, and for this reason many a modern American brain is now the site for a great deal of anguish and anxiety, which spill out to color interpersonal experience and have visibly transformed political and public life.

As yet, there's been insufficient time to fully comprehend the impacts of our era on our psychological and interpersonal situation, but what's already visible has reinforced fears about the continuation of trends that, 30 years ago, Christopher Lasch famously characterized as a growing American "culture of narcissism."[21] Lasch wasn't the first person to warn about wrenching changes in the nature of modern life, and narcissism is only one dimension among these changes. But his analysis struck a particularly deep chord that continues to resonate. The ongoing question of the extent to which isolation and self-focus

8 *Interpersonal climate change*

have become hallmarks of life in America has been fueled by a variety of data that have come along since Lasch.

Hold on to your hat. There's quite a dramatic pattern, including signs in college students of increasing levels of narcissism[22] and insecure interpersonal attachments,[23] and of diminishing levels of empathy;[24] among Americans more broadly, there are diminishing trust in others,[25] downward-trending personal happiness, especially in comparison with the 1970s[26] and particularly for women,[27] elevated rates of suicide across virtually every segment of the U.S. population, including children between 10 and 14,[28] sometimes in conjunction with drug overdose,[29] a rising age of first marriage and a growing proportion of people who forgo marriage even when having children,[30] a tendency for marital couples to spend less time interacting with each other and sharing activities[31] (indeed, even the frequency of sex is in decline),[32] a world-leading pace of relationship disruption,[33] ongoing decline in the rate of remarriage,[34] increasing rates of divorce among older Americans with long-term marriages,[35] disconnection from interaction with neighbors,[36] a sharply increased rate of solo living,[37] decreased involvement in church activities and social organizations,[38] and the highly visible tendency of digital technologies to allow people who are surrounded by others to nevertheless withdraw from each other and become psychologically remote.[39]

The breadth and consistency of this pattern of data are striking, but it's important to understand that it's not that recent generations of Americans have been born with bad DNA or had their personalities damaged by inadequate parenting, or that some environmental contagion has been screwing up our neurotransmitters, or that digital devices inevitably poison social practices. There's a much bigger story: the root causes of the psychological and social difficulties of modern American society are structural and historical. And among these causes lie the reasons it has become so important now for those in highly modern societies to form deeply intimate relationships characterized by meaningful, self-sustaining discourse, the reason that that has become an imperative of our time, though it wasn't before. The social behavior and inner experience of anyone growing up in America today are influenced by the unique conditions that define *this* period of American life, which in their combined impacts have tended to undermine ontological security – our faith in the continuity and coherence of our sense of who we are. This colors many an American life with a subtle but chronic, low-grade jitteriness, a little edginess in outlook, and, without doubt, leads to withdrawal and self-focus, and a lot of prescriptions for drugs such as Ritalin, Xanax, and Zoloft.

Narcissism, as philosopher Charles Taylor points out, isn't a flaw in personality, much less a problem in the workings of the brain. It is a condition of anxious uncertainty about personal identity: who you are, what you stand for, and your basis for moral behavior.[40] In one type of response to this problem, we turn inward to work through these questions of self, a potential explanation for the patterns of social withdrawal and self-focus that are so evident today. Digital culture has made this particularly easy. Turkle believes that the cultural

Interpersonal climate change 9

impacts of smartphones, texting, and social networking sites have amplified the problem, creating social anxiety and a "flight from conversation," even in the context of intimate life where conversation could be doing its most important service.[41] This type of reaction feeds back and has negative consequences because avoidance tends to perpetuate problems of connection and self-identity, not resolve them. An alternative type of defensive response is projective instead of avoidant. Some go on the offensive, but it's still about quashing self-doubt and anxiety. According to Hobson, this type of strategy (e.g., manipulation of others, bullying, hostility, aggressive confrontation) tends to have highly unpleasant consequences and, rather than resolving problems of self, this too feeds back, perpetuating the underlying difficulties.[42]

Uncertainty about self-identity and the trademark interpersonal dynamics that people employ to cope with the anxiety it breeds are so prominent today that it could be said that this, rather than the proliferation of digital technologies, defines the times. But, clearly, it would be a mistake to attribute the interpersonal challenges of our era to a single factor. And, at any rate, whether we call this the age of doubt and anxiety, or the age of distrust and isolation, or the digital age, or something else, much more important than the label of our era is the understanding that it didn't just blink into being, perhaps in result of the introduction of new social policies, or a particular new genre of communication or entertainment technology such as the smartphone or Facebook. Ours is a frame in a flowing stream of slowly changing historical circumstances that have had consequences for the stability of the sense of self, our psychological experience, our connection with each other, and our communication practices. Because the evolving circumstances of American culture are unique, we interact with each other in ways that are unique to our times. Our times pose particular problems related to constructing and maintaining self-identity and to connecting with others meaningfully and sustaining those relationships. Our emotional lives reflect these problems. What's happening in intimacy has nothing to do with "chemistry" or the neural circuits of the brain, and there is nothing but confusion and futility in store for those who take that perspective.

Where we've come from

Yi-Fu Tuan, who is one of America's most insightful students of the impact of modern life on individual consciousness, wrote that, "Modern man and woman, believing that they live in a fragmented and impersonal society, have periodically yearned for the greater social cohesiveness of people living in distant times and places."[43] That was in 1982 and, even then, was a dramatic understatement. Today, the manufactured past is all around us, central in film, television, and political campaigns. The journalist Kurt Andersen contends that America has gone haywire in a cultural-level retreat from our immediate problems into fantasies of the past.[44] What might once have looked like periodic longing for bygone days now appears as a compelling thirst for escape from the present, or, more accurately, escape into a projected, sanitized alternative to

10 *Interpersonal climate change*

the present, scrubbed clean of psychically inconvenient details such as shortened life spans, widespread poverty, high rates of infant death, gender and racial inequality, the exploitation of children, bad sanitation, the absence of effective anesthesia, unsafe working conditions, and epidemics of unchecked family violence.[45] What attracts such flights of fantasy?

Consider *Victoria Magazine*, introduced in 1987. As it still does today, its first covers depicted opulent nineteenth-century estate houses with manicured lawns, rooms filled with vases of roses and sewing baskets, family portraits and mementos, decorative china, formal dinner settings and tea servings, and tapestry-covered wing chairs adorned with lace comforters, all strongly suggesting a place where a woman was at leisure, her life comfortable, intimate, domestic, and under control, and where her identity and range of social powers were understood and secure. Historically, it's a gross distortion, but, at least in imagination, a white woman of means in the Victorian era knew who she was and was at peace with that. *Victoria Magazine*'s introduction was so successful it shocked its own publisher. A record-setting 80 percent of the first run of *Victoria Magazine* was sold without promotion or advertising, just by copies being placed in newsstands and grocery-store checkout aisles.[46] Tellingly, the magazine's debut occurred at just the same time American women were struggling to cope with stressful issues of self-redefinition resulting from their recent mass entrance into the workforce in the 1970s and 80s. Attractions similar to *Victoria Magazine*'s are frequently visible in media programming that distorts the past to offer viewers fantasy experiences free of the intractable complications of modern life. The past is a kind of virtual-reality experience, a refuge of the imagination. The ways we construct it tell us something about the psychic difficulties at play in the here and now (as do related media such as *Self* magazine, with its feature stories promising greater control over physical image, sandwiched between ads for Botox, plastic surgery, and prescription antidepressant medications).

For many, an attraction of the fantasized past is a promise of secure self-identity and moral clarity, a relieving sense of confidence about who you are and what you need to do: personal identity unchallenged and, in a simpler culture, unthreatened, free of anxiety, defined in stable and satisfactory terms. Stereotyped gender and class roles in historical dramas are attractive because they populate a world so unlike our own: one in which identity was less conditional, less burdened with uncertainty and doubt. Then, more so than now, people's lives were limited by the conditions of birth, which meant that, more than now, they knew who they were and, so, had less anxious work to do in chiseling out and sustaining a life narrative. Whatever else the past held, and however it is distorted in fantasy, the idea that former times provided greater security of self is not a fantasy or a distortion.

As we'll see in the second part of this book, in America's Colonial period, people tended to be situated in smaller, less diverse, and more cohesive communities and were more likely to be guided by tradition and religion. To a greater degree, self-identity tended to be defined in external circumstance and

Interpersonal climate change   11

a more consensual appreciation of the moral and good. Information flows were then so much slower that truth and knowledge appeared more solid, steady, and reliable. In this type of environment, the emotional, intellectual, and social requirements of life were reduced in contrast to our current situation. It may have been more difficult in those days to heat one's house, but it was considerably easier to feel you were a clearly defined person, living correctly, leading a fulfilling life (especially if you were male).

Though America can no more return to its past than any of us can return to our own childhood, as we all know, knowledge of the past can be of great value in coping with problems in the present. Analysis of the difficulties confronted in personal development can lead to insights into the issues currently at play in our lives, and, so too, focused examination of the major dimensions of change in American society can help to clarify the sources of some of the dilemmas of identity and intimacy commonly faced today. Indeed, in some cases, knowledge of the past can indicate strategies we might pursue to improve the positive qualities and stability of our sense of self and our intimate relationships.

And as for nostalgia, it's important to underscore that the consequences of modern life are in no way universally negative. As one example among a host of others that would surely include improvements in longevity and material security, new freedoms to pursue highly creative and personalized lifestyles, and reductions in family violence and the exploitation of women and minorities, sociologist Rose Coser argued that, as a result of the circumstances of modern society that compel us to pull back from complete immersion in our occupational, social, and familial roles, we may develop a more agile and cosmopolitan perspective.[47] Our standpoint isn't that of the person invested in a single, all-encompassing role or identity, but that of one who has a little piece of self invested in a range of identities and roles. This may result in a greater capacity among modern Americans for adaptation and creative response, as each role involvement, no matter how partial, brings with it exposure to the perspectives of the distinct groups of people who share that context. In contrast, members of non-modern cultures are more likely to be perceptually constrained by their immersion in simply structured roles, able to place their lives in only one frame.

Notice that I said that members of non-modern cultures *are* more likely, not that members of non-modern cultures *were* more likely. It's important to understand that "modernity" doesn't refer to a point in calendar time, or to a nation's state of technological sophistication, or to its political organization, but to a set of socio-structural forces that tends to produce characteristic ways of relating to the world and each other, of sensing and thinking, especially as regards notions of self. As we'll see, in most cases, the further back in historical time one looks, the less people were possessed of the signature traits of modern consciousness. But, there are groups in America today, such as the Old Order Amish, who are not as invested with modern consciousness as the rest of the country, and there are areas throughout the world, such as China and the Middle East, where the development of modern consciousness is coming

12   *Interpersonal climate change*

on so quickly that it constitutes a significant threat to national stability. The development of modern consciousness is a social-psychological game changer. If the societal conditions that foster it evolve too quickly, it leaves people dislocated in time, stressed and anxious, their bodies located in the present, with their methods of thinking and relating no longer adequate for coping with the stresses of the age.

As historian Peter Laslett described, in former historical periods, a person's life was totally invested in a small number of lifelong, harmonious roles and fenced in by the limited perspectives that those roles afforded.[48] A seventeenth-century baker could see the world as a baker sees the world and as a father does, and that might be all. But, to grow up in America today is to acquire a more complex awareness of the perspectives of an expanded and diverse range of interpenetrating roles, none of which comes close to encompassing an entire life, and in many of which we perform a slightly different version of self. This is part of why self-identity has become an increasingly complex issue in American life, and authenticity an increasingly difficult problem.

To illustrate this contrast, Coser juxtaposed two newspaper articles from the late 1970s reporting parallel incidents in which a family member had fallen down a well and become trapped. On April 1, 1979, the Dutch newspaper *Het Nieuwsblad* reported that,

> Twelve members of one Pakistan family were asphyxiated in a well last Monday. This family drama took place in a village a hundred kilometers west of Rawalpindi. The first victim had gone down into the well in order to fix a broken pump. When he did not come up again, number two went to look. He didn't come back either. This went on until the twelfth family member had gone down into the well. Then a fellow villager hit on the idea that the motor might be exuding toxic gases. He alerted the police.[49]

On December 15, 1979, according to the *New York Times*, an 8-year-old boy in Illinois responded to his 4-year-old brother's fall into a 40-foot well by throwing two life preservers into the well, calling the telephone operator for help, and then running for assistance. The conceptual world of those in a non-modern culture, the features of which may well have been evident in rural Pakistan in the 1970s, may be restricted and rigid in comparison with those growing up in America today. But, as we'll see, cosmopolitan consciousness comes at a price.

As regards intimate life, in Colonial America, family experience was notoriously lacking in affectionate bonds between husbands and wives. Marriage was often the result of economic convenience, and there was a significant imbalance in power between men and women. This made it difficult for partners' discourse to meld minds in structures of interdependent thought and perception. Couples formed and stayed with each other for reasons independent of existential being, because, to a much greater extent than now, existential being was untroubled. Meaning was more consensual, and self-identity was more likely to be determined by the larger culture and the circumstances of

Interpersonal climate change   13

birth. Factors such as religion, community, gender, race, and ethnicity pre-populated minds with moral values and notions about self and world. For most Americans, this is now mainly in the past. New conditions of American life have rendered men and women much more equal, but have also reduced the influence of external sources of meaning that previously structured the world and one's sense of self. This has created new freedoms of thought and being, but it has also left many vulnerable to anxiety, depression, and other forms of psycho-emotional distress.

In adaptation, many men and women now turn in one of two directions. Some struggle to shore up hierarchical structures of the past. This response represents a retreat toward traditional ways of relating, ways that do confer self-identity (albeit formulaically) and that avoid exposure to the particular risks and vulnerabilities that occur when long-term intimate partnerships are founded on full equality. Social hierarchy enables cooperation between people of different categories, bypassing any need to know each other deeply as individuals.[50] The sources of risk in being known deeply include that one cannot control how this will turn out, which may trigger anxiety. Second, one's center of being and vision of the world become interdependent, subject to the influences of a co-equal partner. That requires trust, a commitment to dialogical discourse, and a surrender of power, which, for some, may be too much. So, the structures of the past may remain attractive. But, increasingly, others sense the possibility of true communion and now expect their intimate partnerships to exploit the benefits to self-identity and psychological balance that are possible between those who recognize each other as intellectual and moral equals. In the best circumstances, their discourse gradually coordinates the fields of meaning that constitute the substance of their minds, generating a uniquely protective private culture jointly supportive of each other's vision of self and world. Confronting the world jointly, their interior life stabilizes, and their sense of purpose and being sharpen and blend.

Today, intimate talk provides a potential for higher levels of satisfying and meaningful connection than has been available to Americans in any previous period. This type of intimate bond, an interdependence of the symbolic worlds of intimate partners (to turn Shakespeare's phrase around: a true marriage of minds), is constituted of the private culture that members of long-term relationships spin together in their ordinary and routine conversation (if they have the psychological prerequisites and interpersonal skills). Because Americans' sense of self and world have become disconnected from previously influential external sources, for many, intimate talk has become the new existential center of being. If we're good at talking with each other and we regard each other as equals, we create a kind of micro-community, populated of moral and factual assumptions that are distinctively ours. This sustains, nourishes, strengthens, protects, and stands in for a great deal of what has been lost in modern life. On the other hand, as we will explore later, if a relationship like this ends – and, to be sure, the challenging circumstances of modernity have greatly increased that risk – it may generate unprecedented levels of trauma.

14 *Interpersonal climate change*

Linking the past and the present

The origins of modern interpersonal experience are traceable to long-running processes of cultural change that sculpted the present and are so deeply rooted and powerful that it is certain they will continue to influence the future. These processes, ten of the most central of which are discussed in Chapters 5–7, brought problems of identity and interpersonal connection to full boil by the end of the twentieth century, but it took hundreds of years for that to happen. There's only minor evidence of concern about problems of personal identity or interpersonal life before the twentieth century and virtually no generally recognized concern before the nineteenth. This is not to say that there weren't some early signs of trouble. There were, but, in earlier times, these problems were far less evident. Greenfeld documents early indications of difficulty in self-identity in the increasing frequency of suicide and the appearance of depression, schizophrenia, and other forms of psycho-emotional trouble in the dawning of modernity in sixteenth-century England, but with comparatively low frequency, affecting only certain groups, and without even a broadly shared vocabulary that permitted recognition and discussion of these conditions.[51]

Like our modern understanding of the operations of the unconscious mind, difficulties of psycho-emotional life, self-identity, and interpersonal relations became widely visible in the dramatic and accelerating changes of modern secular/urban/industrial life in the nineteenth and twentieth centuries. Those writing about interpersonal experience today often fail to appreciate that interpersonal practices evolve as adaptations to the shifting circumstances of culture (or, when they do, it's usually without bigger-picture awareness of the interdependencies that link many interpersonal phenomena and make them sensible in terms of each other). John Hewett observed that those writing about self-identity typically do so oblivious to culture and history, working under the delusion that they will discover human universals that apply in all times and places.[52] This is similar to the neuroscience-oriented psychiatrist's faith that the cause of elevated levels of anxiety and depression will one day be traced to treatable flaws in the organic processes of the brain. Good luck with that. Human experience, what we think and do and feel, is neither universal nor timeless, but a product of cultural conditions that are ever on the move (but systematically, not randomly).

Surrounded by a cascade of new communication and entertainment technologies and new patterns of economic and family life that have contributed to a dramatically shifting social landscape, commentary on contemporary interpersonal life focuses almost exclusively on phenomena occurring in the present or within recent memory (hooking up, online bullying, sexting, marriage delay, epidemic appearance of ADHD, social isolation, high rates of relationship turnover, political fracturing, helicopter parenting, and so on). But the root causes of many aspects of contemporary interpersonal and psycho-emotional experience are deeply historical and, as such, could never be detected in the short span of analysis of most social science research projects or, of course,

Interpersonal climate change   15

at all in a neuroscientist's brain scan. The underlying historical factors are irresistible and massively influential. Sociologist Anthony Giddens famously described modernity as "the juggernaut" – a relentless and overwhelming tide of social change that, for the last 400 years, has gradually built in intensity, reconfiguring the world inch by inch.[53]

The trouble is that, generally, the impacts of modernity come on slowly and in tiny increments, and often influence in abstract or indirect ways, so that they don't create effects that are easily noticed and linked. We see, for example, that the population is concentrating in cities, that social diversity is increasing, and that information flows have radically increased in speed and variety, but we don't realize that these external changes also change us internally, creating new psycho-emotional pressures and compensatory interpersonal practices. And many of the changes are so gradual they escape notice. Just as global warming, potentially among the most transformational phenomena of all human history, isn't visible in even a year's worth of climate data, evidence of the steadily increasing importance of personal relationships (discussed in Chapters 3 and 4), the loosening of meaning (discussed in Chapter 2), or the fragmentation of self-identity (discussed in Chapters 7, 11, and 13) – three key effects of America's historical process that have challenged existential being and changed the interpersonal climate – is virtually undetectable in studies that focus only on people alive today. To get a sense of the subtle and slow incrementalism that characterizes this process, go to YouTube and cue up a version of Maurice Ravel's *Bolero*. This is the soundtrack of the juggernaut. When this familiar 15-minute standard is performed competently, it's nearly impossible to point to any particular moment at which the music has become more intense. But there's no question that, somehow, by the end, the gentle tones and rhythms that introduce Bolero's brief, ever-cycling theme have, in imperceptible increments, become strong enough to blow the cat out of her chair. That there has been change is suddenly obvious, but we can't see how we got there. In modern societies, interpersonal life transforms in this way too: the gradual shifts tend to go unnoticed and can seem discontinuous and mysterious until one takes the long view, which reveals the links and patterns. The trouble is that those who write about current interpersonal life tend to focus on one issue at a time and rarely take the long view.

Without big-picture awareness of the historical ecology of interpersonal experience, it's easy to regard deficits in a partner (inattentiveness, withdrawal, unsupportiveness, philandering, poor listening, lack of affection, self-absorption, erratic behavior) as moral lapses originating in flaws of personality or brain function, or weakness of character or will. And there we stop, wondering if we should go back to Match.com and try to find somebody else. And, perhaps, that's what we do, only to experience additional difficulties in the relationship with the new partner. This leaves one wondering if there's not some general problem with (wo)men today. But behavior becomes erratic and self-oriented – in other words, will weakens, and one becomes caught up in oneself – in consequence of difficulties in personal identity. These difficulties are broadly at

16 *Interpersonal climate change*

play in our time, but they weren't so much at play in the deep past. Modernity makes such a precarious business of the sense of self that virtually no one escapes some impact, and many suffer persistently. This issue bleeds out into political life, into the workplace, and into our intimate relationships. Personal identity is the vital organizing principle of existential being, the blueprint that directs activity and imparts a sense of purpose. It's the master plan that provides a basis for choice and willful action.[54] When identity isn't secure or stable (borderline personality disorder represents an extreme version of this), one becomes centrally preoccupied by this problem, and interpersonal relationships are likely to suffer. The fluid circumstances of modern life require more frequent adjustments to self-identity, and, as this happens, the basis for willfully directed activity is reduced. With one's life heading in unknown directions, it becomes harder to determine any particular course of action's relevance to future goals. And so, life is likely to become somewhat blown about rather than purposefully focused and self-directed. Frequently, and at varying levels, this is accompanied by anxiety, depression, impulsive behavior, defensiveness, relationship strife, and narcissism. Here, it is important to state again, so as not to lose sight of Taylor's vital point: narcissism, so much in evidence today, doesn't result from a flaw of personality or character, much less from an organic condition of the brain. It is a signal manifestation of uncertainty about who you are, a condition that modernity has amplified and made common.

Greenfeld documents that, as modernity has come on more intensely in the West, so have problems of self. They appeared first in places where modernity took root earliest, beginning in England in the sixteenth century and then spreading to other parts of Europe, including France, Germany, and Russia, as those societies transformed into modern secular nation-states whose citizens gradually became free to pursue their own ambitions, and to drive themselves crazy doing so.[55] In this, today, the United States is ground zero. Modernity's psychological and interpersonal impacts are widely distributed throughout the world, but not in equal proportion. They are more dramatically visible here than anywhere else. In areas less influenced by modernity, rates of psycho-emotional distress are lower. For example, linguist Daniel Everett describes the Pirahãs of Amazonian Brazil, who, at the time of his tenure with them, remained untouched by modernity and completely free of anxiety, depression, grief, loneliness, and psychotic disorders. There, despite their materially hard lives, community was exceptionally strong, self was not at issue, and the Pirahãs lived happily, without need of psychiatrists or psychiatric medications.[56]

Failure to appreciate the magnitude of the correlation between external culture and internal experience has led to a crisis of credibility for medical psychiatry as it continues to champion the scientifically unsupported idea that psychiatric problems such as depression, anxiety, and psychosis originate not in the circumstances of modern society, but in diseases of the material brain. As we'll take up again in Chapter 14, the epidemic-level psycho-emotional difficulties of our age are quite real, but they aren't due to problems in the

Interpersonal climate change 17

workings of the brain or any other structure of the body; they're rooted in the difficulties of creating an effective personal identity in modern society and then sustaining it. Psychiatric medications may sometimes be effective in controlling symptoms, but the ultimate solution to these problems requires new awareness and new social and cultural choices.

There are strong historical blinders biasing what many scientists and popular writers tell us about interpersonal and psycho-emotional life, akin to what Peter Burke once referred to in the field of sociology as a "parochialism of time."[57] We don't see the influence of history until "we make generations our persons and centuries hours,"[58] and that isn't the habit of most who write about interpersonal and psycho-emotional experience. However, just as tomorrow's history is created out of conscious action occurring in the present, interpersonal behavior occurs within the constraints of historical precedent. To try to understand today's dilemmas of being and relating without knowing what those precedents are is to lose track of their ultimate origins and the directions of the evolving process in which our modern lives are embedded, often creating problems that we mistake as ours alone. This era's widespread alienation and anxiety, its loneliness and insecurity, its difficulties in sustaining intimate relationships, and its rising tides of psycho-emotional distress are consequences of modernity that belong to the times. Looking backward helps us to understand that the problems we experience in communication, intimacy, emotion, and self-identity are rooted in a set of powerful trends that have structured the present and will continue to shape the future. Looking backward, in other words, enables us to look forward to glimpse the outline of where our lives and our children's lives are headed, and then, perhaps, to do something about it: to live deliberately.

Notes

1 Frankl, *Man's search for meaning: an introduction to logotherapy*, 105.
2 Nisbet, *The quest for community: a study in the ethics of order and freedom*, 16.
3 Turkle, *Alone together: why we expect more from technology and less from each other*, 293.
4 Mosbergen, Man posing for gun selfie dies after firearm goes off: report.
5 Schwarz, The selling of attention deficit disorder.
6 Schwarz, Thousands of toddlers are medicated for A.D.H.D., report finds, raising worries.
7 Smith, Inappropriate prescribing.
8 Davies, *Cracked: the unhappy truth about psychiatry.*\
9 National Institute of Mental Health, Any mental illness (AMI) amomg adults.
10 Grohol, Personal communication.
11 Moore and Mattison, Adult utilization of psychiatric drugs and differences by sex, age, and race.
12 Slater, *Blue dreams: the science and the story of the drugs that changed our minds.*
13 Friedman, Infidelity lurks in your genes.
14 Fels, Should we all take a bit of lithium?
15 See Coontz, *A strange stirring: The Feminine Mystique and American women at the dawn of the 1960s*; Herzberg, *Happy pills in America: from Miltown to Prozac.*

18   *Interpersonal climate change*

16   Henderson, Eye-tracking technology aims to take your unconscious pizza order.
17   Greenfeld, *Mind, modernity, madness: the impact of culture on human experience.*
18   Metzinger, *The ego tunnel: the science of the mind and the myth of the self.*
19   See, for example, Midgley, *Science and poetry*; Robinson, *Absence of mind: the dispelling of inwardness from the modern myth of the self*; Tallis, *Aping mankind: neuromania, Darwinitis, and the misrepresentation of humanity.*
20   Slater, *Blue dreams: the science and the story of the drugs that changed our minds.*
21   Lasch, *The culture of narcissism: American life in an age of diminishing expectations.*
22   Twenge et al., Egos inflating over time: a cross-temporal meta-analysis of the Narcissistic Personality Inventory.
23   Konrath et al., Changes in adult attachment styles in American college students over time: a meta-analysis.
24   Konrath et al., Changes in dispositional empathy in American college students over time: a meta-analysis.
25   Pew Forum on Social and Demographic Trends, *Millennials in adulthood: detached from institutions, networked with friends.*
26   Lane, *The loss of happiness in market democracies*; NORC, General social survey: trends in psychological well-being, 1972–2014.
27   Stevenson and Wolfers, The paradox of declining female happiness.
28   Curtin et al., Increase in suicide in the United States, 1999–2014; Hedegaard et al., Suicide mortality in the United States, 1999–2017; Tavernise, Sweeping pain as suicides hit a 30-year high.
29   Kolata and Cohen, Drug overdodes propel rise in mortality rates of young whites.
30   Pew Forum on Social and Demographic Trends, *The decline of marriage and the rise of new families.*
31   Amato et al., *Alone together: how marriage in America is changing.*
32   Julian, *Why are young people having so little sex? Despite the easing of taboos and the rise of hookup aps, Americans are in the midst of a sex recession.*
33   Cherlin, *The marriage-go-round: the state of marriage and the family in America today.*
34   Kreider, Remarriage in the United States.
35   Ellin, After full lives together, more older couples are divorcing.
36   Dunkelman, *The vanishing neighbor: the transformation of American community.*
37   Klinenberg, *Going solo: the extraordinary rise and surprising appeal of living alone.*
38   Halpern, *Social capital.*
39   Conley, *Elsewhere, U.S.A.*; Gergen, *The challenge of absent presence*; Turkle, *Alone together: why we expect more from technology and less from each other*; Turkle, *Reclaiming conversation: the power of talk in a digital age.*
40   Taylor, *Sources of the self: the making of modern identity.*
41   Turkle, *Reclaiming conversation: the power of talk in a digital age.*
42   Hobson, *The cradle of thought: exploring the origins of thinking.*
43   Tuan, *Segmented worlds and self: group life and individual consciousness*, 14.
44   Andersen, *Fantasyland: how America went haywire, a 500-year history.*
45   Coontz, *The way we never were: American families and the nostalgia trap.*
46   Charmody, Hearst finds unexpected success in a magazine for dreamers.
47   Coser, *In defense of modernity: role complexity and individual autonomy.*
48   Laslett, *The world we have lost: England before the industrial age* (3rd ed.).
49   Coser, *In defense of modernity: role complexity and individual autonomy*, 75–76.
50   Harari, *Sapiens: a brief history of humankind.*
51   Greenfeld, *Mind, modernity, madness: the impact of culture on human experience.*
52   Hewett, *Dilemmas of the American self.*

Interpersonal climate change 19

53 Giddens, *The consequences of modernity*.
54 Greenfeld, *Mind, modernity, madness: the impact of culture on human experience*.
55 *Ibid.*
56 Everett, *Don't sleep, there are snakes: life and language in the Amazonian jungle*.
57 Burke, *History and social theory*, 2.
58 Jaynes, *The origin of consciousness in the breakdown of the bicameral mind*, 445.

Part 1

Language, mind, and intimacy

2 A change of mind

Fully human consciousness is inconceivable without language. Indeed, inconceivability is itself inconceivable without language.

Merlin Donald, *A Mind So Rare:*
The Evolution of Human Consciousness[1]

How many times have you heard that the universe began with a big bang? It didn't, of course. A bang is a sound, and, although there may have been an explosive event of inconceivable proportion, that particular blast was stony silent, as are all things that take place in the empty vacuum of space. Until that explosion dispersed matter across the universe, nowhere was there a medium to convey sound – no material of any kind. So there couldn't have been an audible bang. It would be more accurate to name the beginning of everything something else: perhaps the Big Start or the First Thing. However, as every student of rhetoric knows, one of the consequences of the fact that the human mind is built of language is that it's a pushover for the alliterative flourish that's the sport of advertisers and headline writers ("March Madness," "Romney Routed," "Cannibal Cops Find Killer's Kit," "TikTok Teens Troll Trump in Tulsa"). So "Big Bang" breezily bested the bunch.

Call it what you will, that event only marked the beginning of the material expansion of the universe, and, as Buddha taught, our relationship to material being, though indisputably important, is overrated. Madonna famously sang that living in the material world was all that mattered. The song was catchy, but, as one of pop culture's master manipulators of psychologically charged symbolism, Madonna knew far better than most that the material world shrinks to insignificance compared with the world of mental representation – the world of inner experience, thought, motive, feeling, and association, in short, the world of symbols. For us, the universe of consequence is constituted of images, propositions and ideas, stories and emotions, of morals, motives, and ideals – all constructed with symbols and linked in various ways, much of it without any objective connection to the "real world." Because we're users of a language constituted of symbols, we're conscious beings whose sense of ourselves and the world is wholly built in our minds. Knowledge of the physical universe is only correlational. In Plato's familiar allegory, what one

DOI: 10.4324/9781003010234-3

24 *Language, mind, and intimacy*

knows of the outside, the physical, or real world, are only like the shadows of objects cast on the walls of a cave by the light of a fire. We know the world, not directly, but through models and approximations formulated and expressed in the associational flicker of symbolic meaning. The emergence of our immensely consequential inner universe isn't rooted in the Big Bang, but in the gradual shift from more primitive methods of signal-based communication to the use of symbolic language and the accompanying evolution of culture. It was the symbolic character of language coupled to the growing complexity of social experience that slowly gave rise to the modern mind and our historically particular ideas of self and other.

No one knows exactly when symbolic language got started, but it certainly wasn't before our hominid ancestors had evolved into socially sophisticated beings, well along the evolutionary pathway, and our forebears, *Homo sapiens*, had become dominant. This was perhaps just some 50,000–70,000 years ago. That may sound like a long time, but it's instructive to put this in scale: for a moment, try to imagine the full, colossal range of cosmic time, beginning with the origin of the universe in the Big Bang, 14 billion years ago, and extending to this moment right now. If this span of time were mapped onto a 24-hour clock, with now being midnight, each hour on the clock would represent about 580 million years, each minute about 10 million years, and each second about 170,000 years. On this cosmic scale, *Homo sapiens* acquired speech barely half a second ago. When that happened, *Homo sapiens* pretty much severed direct interaction with the material world, a world of triggered action controlled by DNA and reflex – a world controlled by signals rather than symbols – and entered a world increasingly crafted in discourse with others, shaped, indeed, by the evolving quirky proclivities of language itself. Linguistic culture has its own preferences, and those preferences influence consciousness. Its tropes and clichés steer minds toward some perceptions and away from others. As every speech writer, novelist, poet, song writer, or advertiser knows, some ways of expression have a kind of gravitational pull that make certain forms of experience more likely than others, regardless of the actual state of the world.

Myriad clever psychological experiments have shown how difficult it is to get people to see the real world when it presents itself in ways that contradict cultural expectations. A recent book by psychologists Christopher Chabris and Daniel Simons details their now well-known study in which 50 percent of those shown a video of people passing basketballs back and forth and asked to count the passes didn't notice when a woman wearing a gorilla suit appeared in the action.[2] In the video, the gorilla walks into the middle of the ball-passing basketball players, stops, turns to the camera, and thumps her chest. The reason this wasn't noticed was simply that we don't expect to see gorillas in the midst of basketball warmup activities. And so, we don't. Expectations like this are just half the story, the other half being about broadly influential shared cultural visions (as philosopher Charles Taylor calls them, "social imaginaries"), grand systems of belief that structure our thought, our feelings, and our choices ("Christianity," "the American dream," "feminine mystique," "patriarchy").

A change of mind   25

Carl Jung believed that we formulate our sense of self under the guidance of a set of deeply rooted characterological templates ("the trickster," "the hero," "the wise old man"), so powerful in their influence that they may become our destiny. But Jung's archetypes aren't a product of our DNA; they are deeply rooted cultural stories, conventional ways of thinking about what kinds of people there are, so powerful that they shape our behavior, thought, and expectations, possibly producing exactly those kinds of people. Culture is a byproduct of language-equipped minds. It's a set of ideas, visions, presumptions, and requirements of being that humans produce together that then act back on us, influencing what we see, what we think, what we talk about, and how we conceive of ourselves. And, as we'll see, there's strong evidence that, in highly modern societies such as ours, culture has been evolving in ways that undermine personal security, fostering anxiety, depression, and other difficulties of being – the problem that is a central focus of analysis in this book.

Although the Big Bang may be of little immediate relevance to us, the revolutionary event that created our world most certainly began with sound. The beginning of human thought, meaning, and symbolic culture, and of our increasingly complicated and abstract inner life – what is sometimes referred to as "the cognitive revolution" – began to develop as human vocalization evolved into fully symbolic language. Although this process was gradual and played out over a huge span of time, speech became increasingly sophisticated, eventually reaching a point at which the utterance of sounds with fixed meanings – signs or signals – was replaced by the utterance of sounds with arbitrary and conventional meaning – fully symbolic language.

Here, it's important to emphasize that the meanings of words are ever-shifting (consider, for example, the dramatic evolution of the words "masculine" and "feminine" in recent decades). We acquire language and then must continuously reacquire it in encounters with culture and discourse with others. For the most part, the ideas language affords us are what mind and culture are made of. There is some controversy about whether symbolic language is the vehicle of *all* thought, but without doubt it is the vehicle of all abstract thought. *Homo sapiens* is Latin for "wise man," but the human capacity for sagacious thought isn't built into our DNA. Wisdom is the result of our capacity for the social negotiation of meaning in symbol-based discourse. Here, mind is formed, modified, and linked up to the cultural net. And, as for the "man" part of "wise man," as the world has modernized and ideas about gender have continuously evolved, it's no longer just males who speak with authority and consequence. So now, a better name than *Homo sapiens* might be *animalis loquentes*: we are the talking animal – male and female. Our communication practices are the foundation of all higher-order conscious experience. It is true, however, that our symbolic practices are overlaid on a deeper, species-level facility for more primitive, sign-based communication, one that we continue to make good use of.

There's been a great deal of circumstantial argument, but no one knows how speech first appeared. There's no record or direct evidence. And, anyway, just as there would have had to have been a preexisting matrix of wave-transmitting

26 *Language, mind, and intimacy*

matter for the beginning of the universe to have been announced in a loud bang, any eye-witness account of the invention of symbolic speech would presume the existence of language to formulate and express those observations. Without language, no one had the capacity to see language invented, for we can't analytically address that which we have no means of representing, no vocabulary that permits description and contemplation. In modern societies, intimate conflict often originates as partners' ideas of self are forced to undergo change such that they may eventually find themselves confronting in each other what may feel like a kind of breach of contract: one's partner is no longer the same person on whom one had banked one's future. Unfortunately, it's exceptionally difficult to work through such conflict when partners lack vocabulary that permits accurate description of the dilemmas of interdependent self-construal that are common in modern intimate life. It's impossible to talk about something for which you have no words.

Until the invention of modern recording technologies, unwritten speech left no traces. However, for better or worse, the lack of hard data didn't keep early scholars from armchair theorizing about how language came about: the bow-wow theory (language developed in the imitation of natural sounds); the tata theory (language developed as people used sounds, like tongue clicks, to substitute for physical gestures), the yo-he-ho theory (language began with rhythmic utterances people used to regulate physical labor), the pooh-pooh theory (language originated in vocalization of pain or surprise), and more. Darwin theorized in this way too, proposing that language evolved in the imitation of natural sounds expressed in rhythmic, song-like cadences that infused them with emotion and reinforced their continued expression.[3] Early speculation about the origins of language never resulted in a productive scientific consensus. In fact, owing to frustration over the absence then of any evidence that might provide a basis for judging one theory against another, in the mid-nineteenth century, papers on language origins were formally banned from scientific journals and scholarly discussion. The area of inquiry didn't pick up again for many decades. Recently, however, advances occurring across a range of relevant sciences have provided a better picture. Today, much more is known about the evolution of the larynx and the speech centers of the brain, and how to place these critical prerequisite events on the timeline of early human history.

So let us back up a bit and recognize that, long before the invention of language, there was communication among early men and women. Language isn't necessary for many forms of interdependent activity. For our hominid ancestors, life was socially coordinated and productive of rudimentary culture, music, and art. Many animals engage in elaborately organized social behavior and create tools, and some occasionally learn signs from each other. So, the modern development of symbolic language in humans was likely preceded by primitive exchanges of vocalized signals of fixed meaning. Here, you might think of the mating calls of birds or the frenzied warning chirps of the sentinel prairie dog that spots an approaching snake. This is communication, but it isn't

A change of mind 27

symbolic. The signal has a single, invariant meaning. As we'll take up in detail in the next chapter, modern language is a system comprised not of signals with fixed meaning, but of symbols with fluid, nuanced, and complex associations, many of which may be idiosyncratic to particular social groups (especially groups of intimates, such as families, couples, or close friends). The vocalized communication of our primitive ancestors was a system of sounds with relatively specific and unchanging external reference. This type of utterance is pre-symbolic and functions more like gesture. For example, a particular vocalization can signal the perception of threat, or anger, or sexual interest, just as this can be done with gestural movements of the body. Although it's possible to coordinate sophisticated social activities with gesture, the limitations of gestural representation are severe. In particular, gestural communication can't support complex narrative.[4]

And, so, until language advanced from the transmission of sounds with fixed meaning and became fully symbolic, the world of our ancestors was not a world of abstract propositions or elaborately linked ideas or stories. It was not a world where people could reflect on the quality of their lives, on whether they had been treated by others unjustly or with adequate respect. It was not a world where people retreated into themselves, contemplating the question of who they were or whether their life had value. Nobody engaged in discussion of goals or motives or ideals. In fact, until humans adopted symbolic language, there was no possibility that they ever experienced guilt or shame. These advanced social emotions require appreciation of the concept of the negative (of what you might have done but didn't, of what you did but should not have, etc.). The negative is a wholly symbolic idea that is impossible to express in a primitive, signal-based communication system.[5] But this idea – of what isn't, of what we are not, of what might have been, of what we didn't succumb to, of what is missing – is a hallmark of modern consciousness and the basis of all ideas of moral behavior.

Before we dwelt in the house of language

Cognitive psychologist Merlin Donald has proposed that human prehistory moved through stages delineated by changes in the nature of conscious awareness.[6] His argument draws from recent work on the cognitive capabilities and social behavior of animals, on the archaeological and anthropological record of early human life, and on the historical record's suggestions of changes in the presence and relative size of structures of the brain, which are now understood to correlate with different capabilities of mind. Donald's is an unusual account of the progression of early human life. It's common to see cultures classified according to their differential use of various materials (Stone Age, Bronze Age) or methods of organizing authority or inheritance (matrilineal, patrilineal), whether the society was warlike or pastoral, and so on. But, in light of recent advances in several scientific fields, it's become possible to differentiate eras in human prehistory in terms of differences in capabilities of the

28 *Language, mind, and intimacy*

physical brain, capacities for different types of communication, and the nature of mind and conscious experience. Doing so, we see that changes in communication practices co-evolved with the emergence of new modes of mental experience. I'm going to take a few moments to describe this because a central argument of this book is that, fueled by profound socio-cultural changes, particularly in the circumstances of modern communication, human consciousness continues to evolve in our time, more and more quickly, and with dramatic consequences for our sense of being and the nature of social experience. To understand the changes happening now and how they relate to problems of mental and social experience, one must appreciate that the nature of human consciousness isn't fixed, but has undergone continuous evolution throughout history, leading, in modern societies like ours, to new problems of being and new difficulties in intimacy, but also to new potentials for social relationships. Donald recognizes two distinctive eras in pre-linguistic hominid history separated by a period of rapid and radical change. The predominant feature of the first of these eras, which he refers to as a period of "episodic culture," is that during this time human awareness was fixed in the moment, limited to appreciation of what is happening in the present, a state of selfless consciousness that is exactly what millions today struggle to reacquire in meditative practice.[7] Episodic consciousness is not the consciousness of the frenetic, analytic, language-equipped modern mind, and it is a major struggle to achieve it. To do so, meditators try hard to master techniques to shut down internal speech so that their mental experience can become unmediated and centered in the unfolding present, as it was for our distant ancestors. The goal, of course, is to retreat from the implacable burden of stress imposed by the contradictory conditions of modern culture to which our minds are networked through the medium of language. The mind is an outpost of complex culture, and, all things being equal, to the extent that the culture in which your mind is embedded is troubled, so are you. Episodic culture is the culture of primates and other animals who have rudimentary capacity for social organization, but, because they are severely restricted in their ability to encode and store information, they're limited in their ability to recall, link, and sequence memory. And so, compared with modern culture, episodic culture is simple and untroubled, and so is the psycho-emotional situation of minds that are linked to it.

Anyone who has lived with a pet dog or cat appreciates that they're capable of acts of signal-like communication, can recognize their position in the social system of the household, and frequently engage in actions that reinforce their emotional attachment to people and other animals (for example, calling to draw attention to their needs or engaging others in play or mutual grooming). Vocalization in lower animals (snarls, moans, chirps, calls, etc.) is controlled by the limbic system, an area of the brain responsible for emotion that evolved long before the appearance in humans of the brain's speech centers. We retain this basic system for controlling emotional sound production. Its independence of our system of normal speech is demonstrated in that "limbic speech" (the utterance of sounds related to emotional arousal – high-pitched gasps

A change of mind   29

accompanying surprised delight, screams of people on roller coasters, cries of sexual passion, the sobs and moans of grief, etc.) often remains intact in aphasia victims.[8] The episodic mind, therefore, supplies a platform for rudimentary social connection, built on a foundation of perception in the present moment that has been shaped by instinct (see squirrel, chase squirrel). Additionally, the episodic mind is fully capable in terms of primary emotions (pleasure, pain, fear) and, through conditioning, associates positive and negative feelings with particular members of the social group, or other stimuli. Humans have retained these capabilities. In myriad social encounters, our emotional attachments are deeply sedimented in positive and negative association. This runs underneath our verbal-analytic mental process, which is why, under normal circumstances, regardless of one's naive intensions of detached nonchalance, repeated sexual contact with someone results in emotional attachment. Emotional attachments draw on the brain's primitive, pre-linguistic capacity for sociality and evolved to facilitate survival and reproduction. Our emotion-based social capabilities developed during the vast span of time before our species acquired symbolic language and higher mental functioning.

Donald calls the second phase of hominid history "mimetic culture." Its key feature was the development of the ability to reenact events through imitation and mime, which created a foundation for a much more elaborate level of culture. This moved human culture from the level of the apes to the level of *Homo erectus*, whose culture featured the use of fire, music, art, tool-making, and advanced social organization. Concurrent with the transition to mimetic culture, the brain grew in size and acquired areas whose functions are now associated with language. The distinctive social feature of mimetic culture is the development of communication through intentionally representational activity. Mimesis provides a way of modeling and conveying the impressions of episodic experience, and this capacity provided a revolutionary boost to the sophistication of culture. Donald offers covering the face or holding the heart to indicate grief as examples of mimetic expression. Mimesis continues to play an important role in modern human societies. Pantomime and ritual dance are purely mimetic. During the period of mimetic culture, the innate vocalizations of episodic culture were likely to have been deployed mimetically as well – the voice began to be used intentionally to signify and recall events. Just as modern humans reap a number of emotional and physiological benefits by acquiring the meditative discipline that permits reentering the here-and-now consciousness of episodic culture, we are also strongly drawn to the simpler sociality characteristic of our mimetic ancestors. Mimesis provides for advanced social coordination, allowing people to feel bonded and securely embedded in the human group. Participation in shared rhythmic activity, especially music and dance, provides respite from the challenges of modern culture, replacing psycho-emotional stress with a sense of social integration and security. This is one of my favorite methods of escaping the strains of modern being. Having trained for several decades as a classical musician, but finding few opportunities to perform with others, a few years ago I took up hand

30 *Language, mind, and intimacy*

percussion and began sitting in with a drumming group that meets in a public space in a local town center. Typically, it attracts an ad hoc collection of 10–25 drummers, plus participation from dozens of tourists, children, dancers, and others of varying interest and skill who may show up with all manner of instruments and costumes, or who pick up an extra drum and beat along. There's practically no talk among the drummers. A different type of social connection is accomplished in long stretches of shared rhythm. Typically, and more or less randomly, someone beats out a short, prominent pattern, and others join in. The patterns go where they will without negotiation or direction. Usually, after 10–15 minutes, the group stops, and then, after a short pause, someone beats a new rhythm. Participation in the communal groove is mesmerizing and provides relief from stress in a kind of primal, pre-linguistic social connectivity that lies in our mimetic heritage. It produces a sense of selfless social connection that transcends normal divisions of symbolic culture. Drummers, dancers, and onlookers from the full spectrum of races, ideologies, ethnicities, ages, and economic conditions coordinate together in an untroubled sense of common humanity – at least until the session ends, and they start talking to each other again (as T. S. Eliot so nicely put it, "Till human voices wake us, and we drown").

Donald estimates that the era of mimetic culture may have lasted 1 million years. It gave way as *Homo sapiens* gradually acquired symbolic language and the capacities for mental modeling and abstract thought that language confers. This wasn't a sudden acquisition. Just as it takes years of sign-based vocalization and mimetic interaction with caregivers to gradually prepare the mind of the preverbal infant for the acquisition of speech and, then, eventually, conscious awareness and the sense of self, the mimetic culture of our ancestors prepared the way for a gradual shift from the exchange of vocal signals to the use of language comprised of vocal symbols. With this, in time, came the capacity for narrative that symbolic language confers and, with that, eventually, the cultural acquisition of myth and the shift from mimetic culture to "mythic culture," Donald's third era. As with Charles Taylor's social imaginaries, myths are narrative visions that allow people to model and tie together their experience, reach beyond the here-and-now, placing them in systems of shared belief that provide guidance for right living.

In the end, the evolution of symbolic language spurred a revolution of mind because it provided the means for recognizing and preserving the connections between episodic events to create time-spanning narrative. Symbolic language takes the human experience out of the flow of the here and now and into the world of history, imagination, and the future. But these new capacities – for imagining and for comparing outcomes against expectations – came with a cost. They gave birth to the secondary emotions of anxiety, which comes from being fearful of things we imagine might happen, and depression, which may have a range of origins but often results when outcomes fail to meet expectations. Minds with and without symbolic language share episodic and mimetic capability, but the language-enabled mind is so differently equipped, so much more capable (but also, as we can now see, so much more vulnerable), that we have to keep reminding ourselves that underneath our verbally formed consciousness are other systems of social connection, sedimented over vast spans of time. The fact that so many people invest so much time and energy attempting to reduce stress and anxiety by reentering the simpler mental situation of episodic and memetic culture provides a strong clue that the origins of modern psycho-emotional problems are not biological but cultural, and are related to the co-evolution of language and mind.

For Donald, the final mind-and-culture-reshaping transition occurred in the move from the era of mythic culture to the more advanced capacities of mental experience that we recognize in ourselves and our culture today. This was largely spurred by the development of writing and its revolutionary impacts on memory, rationality, and narrative. Writing not only advances social coordination, it permits the preservation and analysis of large sets of data, which is vital for the systematic advance of intelligent action. Of course, the communication revolution didn't end with writing, and, centrally relevant to the arguments of this book, neither did the evolution of mental experience. And so, we turn now to trace what we can of the evolution of communication and mental experience that has occurred since the advent of written history: roughly the last 5,000 years. Many assume that psycho-emotional experience has been more or less constant, but now we can appreciate why this was unlikely to have been so.

Bicameral being: when language functioned as signal

Psychohistorian Julian Jaynes is the best source for imagining what mental life was like during the earliest period of symbolic language use, when some limited range of words and other symbolic objects had become available to provide signification, but meanings were still largely fixed.[9] This is Merlin Donald's mythic period, which began as symbolic language came into being and lasted, according to Jaynes, until about 1000 BCE, there being some variation in different parts of the world. A remarkable feature of early writing is that it appears that the written word was never used as a vehicle for any form of self-reflection. In fact, there were no words describing mental states in early texts. Our forebears didn't use writing to record or reflect upon their inner experience, to fabricate stories, or extend their powers of imagination. Early writing was used almost exclusively for the administration of government, for keeping account of trade transactions and tax records, or conveying government edicts. In other words, this system of communication was something like what you can accomplish with modern computer code. You can't write your diary or reflect existentially in FORTRAN or C++, but you can use computer directives to store information, keep accounts, and establish the limits of what you can and cannot do with your stored data. In Jaynes's appreciation, the minds of early language users were actually not conscious in our modern sense of active self-aware reflection; rather, the mind then was still predominantly

32   *Language, mind, and intimacy*

signal-based, not consciously self-aware, perhaps operating within the limited range of capabilities that computers have. The transformation of language from signal to symbol had begun but was not far enough along to permit the inner self-reflective awareness that is the simultaneously liberating and stress-inducing natural condition of those living in today's modern societies.

Jaynes believed that early language users' vocalized sounds were not experienced reflectively and assigned meaning, as they are for us, at arms' length after consideration of the possibilities in play. Your partner says, "I love you," which could mean practically anything, including "I find you silly but tolerable," "I want to have sex with you," "I'm going to stay with you and have no intention of leaving," "I'm having an emotional experience of oneness with you," and so on, through myriad other possibilities including mere ritual expression along the lines of "amen" at the end of a prayer or "over and out" at the termination of a military radio transmission ("Love you!" – "Love you too!"). Hence, modern humans contend in conversation with a highly inexact, loose quality of meaning and come to hypothetical understanding of what the other intends to convey on the basis of stored experience and best estimate, as well as some reflection on who we are and how we differ in perspective from our conversational partner and what we think of his or her motives. This analysis occurs in consciousness and may be accomplished almost instantaneously, but, alternatively, it may pull us up short and require a great deal of active reflection. The point I wish to strongly underscore here is that, in deep human history, meaning once was considerably less variable and more exact. In modern cultures, meaning has become more and more uncertain, and this has stimulated new operations of mind and new states of being, including, especially, an appreciation that self and other are independently agentic beings, each possessed of idiosyncratic motives and ideas that often run beneath conscious awareness. This has become ever more the case in the increasing diversity of modern society. As this uncertainty of meaning has intensified, it has ushered in new difficulties of relationship and problems of being.

Leaving aside the fact that the phenomenon of romantic love is a relatively recent historical development which would have been wholly outside the experience of early humans – none of them would have ever said "I love you" – Jaynes's argument is that early language users did not perceive the words and other symbols they encountered as objects of potentially variable meaning, but rather experienced them as internal commands, in the manner of the hallucinated voices that are experienced today by some people (an occurrence that is not as rare as we tend to think).[10] This is the era of human development characterized by Jaynes as the "bicameral mind." As this describes a state of mental operation that existed before the development of modern consciousness, it can be challenging for modern minds to appreciate.

Jaynes's central proposition is that most waking activity was conducted automatically, behavior occurring without reflection – for example, as happens much of the time as one drives a car. We don't think, "now I should brake slightly," "now I should steer left a little" – we simply do so. Because,

A change of mind   33

as we'll see, the idea of the self as autonomous and distinctly separated from others didn't come along until much later in historical time, when early speech occurred it would have been experienced in the same manner as a hallucinated voice might be experienced today – a voice, as if from an external source – perhaps as if of a god – giving directives or signaling some occurrence. Perhaps this is something of the way a pet dog or cat experiences its owner's voice – not reflectively, but as an external signal. Thus, Jaynes believed that there were two chambers of mental activity that were reasonably separate from each other, one processing the stimuli of sentient experience rather automatically and the other processing the vocalizations of other people. This is the sense in which he refers to the deeply historical mind as "bicameral." These separated chambers of mental experience couldn't become integrated without the development of an internal model of self-being, which, the evidence suggests, did not emerge until about 1000 BCE. Here, it's important to note that Jaynes was not referring at this point to the emergence of the modern sense of personal identity, the autobiographical/narrative self, which, in the circumstances of modernity, has become a centerpiece in the success of intimate relationships and critically important to mental well-being. Rather, Jaynes was referring to the gradual development of a sense of one's own distinctiveness among the other objects in the mind's analog representation of the experienced world. This appreciation may not come easily for modern readers because we take for granted our internal model of self. We see ourselves as distinct and highly individuated, but in earlier times this would not have been the case. Just as there must have been a time before language when our hominid ancestors perceived the physical world, not as a catalog of differentiated objects (trees, water, sky, etc.), but as a continuous fabric (after all, they did not have language which is the means by which people make and label such distinctions), the sense of the autonomous self had to be carved out from a more global and undifferentiated episodic consciousness that likely perceived the social group as a collective unity. Jaynes believed that the initial awareness of self, which he referred to as the "analog I," did not appear as a feature of modern consciousness until necessitated by rapid changes in sociological conditions, especially in the increasing frequency of encounters with strangers that occurred during the period of the Bronze Age collapse, about 1250–1000 BCE.

The autobiographical/narrative self, the sense of self-identity as we experience it, didn't emerge until much later. The autobiographical/narrative self is a phenomenon of the modern world, which began to take shape only about 400–500 years ago in response to the changing conditions of Western societies described later in this book. Even today, the sense of self is not expressed in all places to the same extent or in the same way, because the social-psychological conditions of modernity are not uniformly in play everywhere in the world. And so, the circumstances of mental experience are not the same everywhere today. My baseline point is that the modern mind is not a given of biological existence. It is shaped by our interconnection with others through language and

34   *Language, mind, and intimacy*

culture, and so, as culture and language change, it is appropriate to expect to see changes in the common situation of psycho-emotional and social experience.

The mind – language – culture connection

The science fiction film *Arrival* depicts the strong version of the Sapir – Whorf hypothesis. In the film, aliens come to Earth with the intention of boosting human evolution by teaching us a new language. The aliens' language contains constructs that enable speakers to see into the past and the future. This strong version of Sapir – Whorf – the notion that language determines reality – tends to be discounted today. However, there is support for a softer version of Sapir – Whorf: language doesn't determine reality, but it may reflect it and it can certainly influence how we deal with it. Not all scholars agree with the soft version either, but, as linguist Daniel Everett wryly points out, even linguists who disagree with Sapir – Whorf tend to support the American Linguistic Association's policy requiring that its members use gender neutral language in the organization's journals.[11] The idea that language has some influence on how we relate to the world and each other has a great deal of common-sense appeal. Reciprocally, language is influenced by external reality, evolving to accommodate new phenomena. Most readers are probably aware of the old Sapir – Whorfian canard that the Eskimo sense of reality is exceptionally snow-oriented because the Eskimo vocabulary sports more than 50 words for the textures of snow – the Eskimo world is a snow-world. Consider now that the current edition of the diagnostic manual for medical psychiatrists (*DSM-5*) currently provides terms for distinguishing between more than 350 types of mental disorders (more than tripling the size of the inventory from just 60 years ago). Here, perhaps, is an indication that the modern world is a world burgeoning with interior stress.

If you were born in Massachusetts in the seventeenth century, you would not speak as you do today – the language was different. But you also would not think as you do today. Obviously, you wouldn't credit the same truths, assume for yourself the same authority, recognize the same range of distinctions, be vexed by the same doubts and concerns, find the same things funny, or experience the same range of emotional responses. Moreover, however, your mind wouldn't work the same way. A seventeenth-century mind was not a twenty-first-century mind with different content; it was a mind that existed in a different linguistic – cultural matrix in which the sense of self, the basis of personal will, and ideas of unconscious motivation were fundamentally different than they are now. Mind is not a biological process; it's an expression of culture. And culture is an expression of mind at the group level.[12]

Mind and culture exist in reciprocal relationship, built of the same symbolic materials, with language the common matrix in which both are expressed. So, there's no question that culture and language have a lot to do with how we think and behave.

Culture, mind, and language create each other and are all built of symbols, but they are not the same thing. In the first place, although a lot of culture is comprised of ideas expressible in words, culture consists of other kinds of symbols too, including visual images, musical phrases, gestures, and physical objects. More importantly, culture is comprised of *systems* of meaning and significance, which may for the most part be constructed and expressed in language, but are not language itself. In culture, symbols are arranged into meaningful patterns, which make some ranges of behaviors and perceptions sensible and discourage others, solve some problems of being and give rise to new ones. A language might be described as an inventory of word types coupled to a system of grammatical rules, but culture places linguistic symbols in connection and assigns them different priority, yielding propositions, visions, ideas, traditions, myths, ways of behaving, ideals, moral values, and so on. Without question, the most important difference between culture and mind is that, whereas culture has an almost infinite capacity for inconsistency, complexity, sham, and self-contradiction, the human mind does not. For this reason, as modern culture has become more complicated, inconsistent, multivocal, and unstable, it has resulted in accelerating increases in the frequency of diagnosis of psycho-emotional disorders.

Even while the mind searches for consistency, truth, and stability, culture doesn't stand still. Culture is dynamic, and, as it changes, interior life changes too. Cultural change disrupts normal life trajectories, introducing new problems of being and relating. Without doubt, among the most important culture-induced change for the operation of the mind and the organization of social relationships has been the development of the modern self-concept, which emerged as a defensive response to mounting psychological challenges created by the advent of modernity in Western societies.[13]

The modern sense of self-identity, which scholars believe only began to be broadly visible about Shakespeare's time, emerged as a protective response to the cultural complexity that by then had begun to become manifest in Western societies as they gradually became more secular, nationalistic, and cosmopolitan – less held in place by religion, tradition, and obligations to family and local authority. Mind is culture-in-the-head, but, as modern culture began to provide increasingly more choice, contradiction, and varied meaning (to become more symbol-like and less signal-like), encountering it without some type of protective filter could be psychically overwhelming, fostering anxiety and uncertainty about how to act. The self-concept is precisely that protective filter. It is, in essence, a collection of ideas about who we are and what we believe and value. We use it (1) to filter and organize perception (attending to this but not that, believing this and discounting that, behaving in this way rather than that way) and (2) as a basis for the expression of choice – that is, as a basis for will. When you're sure of who you are, you know what to think and how to act. When your sense of self is poorly formed, you may become anxious and impulsive. Some believe that, should a sense of self fail to form at all, it may result in schizophrenia,[14] which may be what happens to the mind in modernity when the protective filter of the self is absent and the mind is awash in unfiltered perception and unanchored reflexivity.

36 *Language, mind, and intimacy*

Here is one reason that, in modern societies, late adolescence can be a difficult developmental epoch, why roughly half of all major mental disorders are first manifest in the mid-to-late teens.[15] This is the time of life during which young minds begin to awake to the inconsistencies and hypocrisies of complex culture. The self is a protective shield, but, in the teen years, identity is not yet strongly formed and socially supported, and so it can't yet do its work. An inadequately protected adolescent mind may collapse under anxiety or buckle into distortion, or it may retreat in any of a hundred ways, becoming easy prey for utopian causes, the military recruiter, the cult leader, or the drug dealer. Similarly, one might conjecture that, among the reasons that mental disorders occur more frequently and more severely among women than men, is that, within the current conditions of modern societies, the hurdles women confront in forming a strongly rooted and internally consistent sense of personal identity are more formidable.

Of course, when life is well embedded in religion, tradition, family, and clan, the creation of a strong sense of self isn't such an emergency matter, because the required filtering is accomplished by these external frameworks of belief, and correct choice is dictated by their doctrine. Difficulties of personal being came about an inch at a time as those external frameworks receded in influence, and the fabrication of self-identity became a critically important project. And so, historically, the psycho-emotional disorders that follow for those whose sense of self is not strongly constructed (borderline personality disorder, eating disorders, narcissism, anxiety disorder, and so on) also came on an inch at a time. The shift was gradual. People didn't walk into the sixteenth century religious and selfless and walk out of it godless and with minds like ours. The changes were slow and went unnoticed, until recently, when the pace has accelerated to such an extent that it's hard not to see.

Intimacy

What about intimacy? What does intimacy have to do with the evolution of symbols, minds, growing cultural complexity, and psycho-emotional risk? Actually, a lot. The intimate landscape of former times was nothing like ours. Here are two key points to keep in mind. The first is that neither culture nor mind forms on its own. They are both the outcome of interpersonal discourse in ongoing social relationships. No baby ever learned to talk without help from other humans, and, in all of cosmic history, no hominid ever developed the symbolic capacities of mind except through interaction with others. And as for culture, no culture ever sprang up independently of human discourse either. Culture is the outcome of the buzzing interconnection of a society full of symbol-processing minds using language to bootstrap each other and connect. So, the first point is that it's all social. The second point is that, as discourse has gradually become more and more a matter of symbols and their variable meaning, and less of signals and fixed meaning, meaning has become ever more pliable, nuanced, and personal, and this has had some important

A change of mind 37

consequences – especially that it has introduced a general sense of uncertainty and increased the potential for psychological isolation.

Thus, intimacy has become a vitally important phenomenon of the modern world. Like romantic love, intimacy wasn't a feature of earlier times. However, unlike love, which is a condition of the heart, intimacy is a condition of the mind. To be intimate is to connect with someone else in a framework of privately understood meaning. Your intimates are the people who understand your particular slant on things and share your secrets; in fact, they are usually the people who have co-constructed those understandings with you. In some friendships, this may occur to such an extent that partners generate a level of culture of their own, a little bubble of shared, personalized understandings that functions as a haven, shielding them against the psycho-emotional challenges inherent within the larger culture. The preconditions for intimacy are privacy and individualism, but these traits, which are now widely recognized hallmarks of modern Western culture, are ever less visible in the world the further back we look. Both privacy and individualism had to be in place for the emergence of the sense of strongly autonomous self-identity, which, for most of us, has become an essential structure of being.

Each of us has a story of self, a story of who we are and how we came to be. For modern Western minds (and more and more, as well, in other parts of the world) that story assumes the central character to be an autonomous individual whose life course has been self-determined, his or her will acting against circumstances of birth and fate. The stars that guide us are of our own selection. The voice in our head is our own voice, not the voice of the gods, or our parents, or our tribe or clan, or some other collective. Our dreams are a reflection of our desires and anxieties, not, as in Homer's *Iliad*, instructions sent from the gods on Mount Olympus directly to the mind of the sleeping King Agamemnon informing him that it's time to send his armies to attack Troy. We behave as we do because it is *our* will to behave as we do. This historically unique conception of ourselves as completely autonomous beings enables us to think we can write our own story, to become, through our own intelligent action, the person we imagine is our best expression of our essential being. In this we sense the opportunity to fill our life with meaning. But, of course, in multivocal modern symbolic culture, where meaning isn't fixed, but greatly in flux, it is exceptionally difficult to sustain personalized meaning that you create on your own, including the story of who you are.

You might take a moment to try this experiment: create four new words that represent states of your experience or yourself that you otherwise find difficult to represent. Record these words on a slip of paper and put it aside for a week. Then, try to remember the words. I predict that you won't be able to. Symbols are instruments of social connection and, if they aren't used socially, they don't work. A symbol that isn't shared is like a bridge that goes halfway across the Chesapeake Bay and stops. Meanings that you make up on your own and don't bring to others for validation have minimal staying power and fade quickly. Your new word or idea or vision has to be expressed in conversation

38 *Language, mind, and intimacy*

and reacted to so that it functions for those in the conversation as a point of mental intersection. You must regard that person as your equal (and the more significant and central that person is for you, the better) and see them react to your meaning as sensible and valid. They need not agree with you. They may see your idea as crazy. They may quickly modify it and toss it back to you. But, at the least, they must understand you and treat your expression as a valid token of meaning. When that happens, your meaning becomes a living part of the social fabric, doing its work to connect your mind and its fields of meaning to your conversational partners and to the larger cultural net.

Likely, most people aren't used to thinking of symbols as little mind-bridges, and, if this seems in any way mysterious, the bottom line is this: you can't have a self on your own because the meanings for the symbols out of which you construct it are always socially determined. There is no such thing as an autonomous self. The meanings you attach to yourself all must be connected (and periodically reconnected) to other people in discourse or they become unstable and fade. The more autonomous you are, the more disconnected, the more isolated, the more your sense of being will become distressed and likely infused with anxiety. If you become sufficiently isolated, your mind will begin to decay into hallucinatory states. It is a cruel irony of modern life and its relentless valorization of autonomy that we are in no way autonomous selves. We must validate and revalidate our sense of self, as we do all our other meaning, in discourse, discourse that itself will act back upon and influence our original meaning. No discourse, no self – and, taken far enough, no mind. We are the selves that our social relationships allow us to be. We craft each other. And, without rich connection, we come apart, mind first.[16]

To make this important point more vivid, let's retreat once more along our historical timeline to see how our situation, the situation of people in modern cultures, compares with the situation of earlier eras. This time, we'll roll back the timeline about 500–600 years, which takes us to the period when the modern world was just beginning to take shape in Western Europe. As we've seen and will explore in chapters ahead, the pre-modern world was one of relatively fixed meaning. Certainly, people connected through language comprised of symbols, but the range of variation in meaning was highly limited in contrast to our time. One minor take on this is that, at least in English, there weren't as many words. It's estimated that the English language of the fourteenth century contained about 70,000 words, as compared with some 470,000 words available today from which we can choose in making distinctions between things.[17] However, much more important than the size of the available vocabulary, meaning in the world of the past was held in place by the powerful influence of broadly accepted visions of the universe and its proper order. These are those "social imaginaries" of philosopher Charles Taylor that were referred to a few pages back. Towering among these in influence were Christianity and patriarchy.

Choice was severely limited. You might easily have been born into a family that had been tied to a particular location or occupation for so many

A change of mind 39

generations that it was reflected in your family name. Your marriage may have been arranged by your family and was likely to have been undertaken for economic purposes. You shared the common belief in a universe governed by a god worshiped by everyone in your society. There was little information about the world outside your own household and its small number of social and economic connections. You were unlikely to move. The house you lived in probably afforded no privacy at all (it was not uncommon for an entire family to live in one or two rooms), and, without privacy, there are no secrets; without secrets, there is no intimacy.

Your few external contacts were almost all with like-minded people (similarly educated, similar religious beliefs, similar economic means, same race, locally born) from the immediate vicinity. The day was regulated with reference to the natural world as it was manifested locally (the tides, the seasons, sunrise and sunset, the movement of the stars) and the requirements of religious observance. The clothing you wore and the material objects you purchased may have been restricted by sumptuary laws that functioned to make sure everyone remained slotted within their proper social position – for example, to make sure no one born into the trades could attempt to dress like an aristocrat and pass as someone beyond their social station. The idea of universal social equality, especially the intellectual and moral equality of men and women, lay far in the future, which meant that, if you were a husband seeking support for your private point of view from your wife, because females were not regarded as the intellectual equals of males, she would be unable to provide the confirmation required for your meaning to be sustained. In short, you were born into a highly local and consensual world that afforded little control in your life, no exposure to diverse belief, limited opportunity to create your own belief, and virtually no choice with regard to self-definition.

To the average modern Westerner, this probably sounds awful, but, consider that in these circumstances questions of self simply don't come up. Angst is much reduced. Existential dread doesn't exist. No one need fret, like Robert Frost, over paths not chosen (indeed, in the world of the pre-modern past, Yogi Berra's famous advice, "If you come to a fork in the road, take it!" comes close to making sense). Choice means freedom of expression, and, in the abstract, we welcome it because it fuels the illusion of the autonomous self. But, as Sartre argued, too much choice brings anguish and immobility of action and risks exhausting the spirit.

Can there be too much choice? You need only try to select rationally among the pages and pages of table salt available through Amazon (pink Himalayan, Hawaiian black or red lava, Celtic light grey sea salt, flaked salt, Kosher salt, kala namak, fleur de sel, smoked salt, iodized or non-iodized, potassium chloride-free, etc.); or choose just the right college major from among the 2,000 college degree programs offered by the U.S.'s 5,300 universities and colleges; or pick the right shampoo and conditioner among the 80 types for sale at your grocery store. Or go to OkCupid, Match.Com, or Eharmony and start searching through their bottomless catalogs of possibility for your perfect

40 *Language, mind, and intimacy*

life partner. If this creates a little decision stress, treat yourself with just the right cookie by selecting among the 250 brands at the store, or divert yourself by selecting the best film to watch among the 6,000 on Netflix. Or work out with one of 18 distinct styles of yoga. Or you can seek spiritual guidance by selecting among the 140 distinctive religious denominations Americans associate with. The examples could go on for pages.[18] We often think that choice conveys freedom. And it does. But the absence of choice conveys a different and equally important kind of freedom.

Boats against the current

It should now be clear that, in the best circumstances, the deep cognitive interconnections of intimacy shield against threats to private ideas of self and nurture the formation of personally fulfilling belief. This is important in the exceptionally difficult cultural conditions of our time. People who manage to embed their minds in enduring, high-quality intimate relationships are much better protected against psycho-emotional distress. Beliefs or attitudes that come into doubt in the blurred confusion of the larger culture can be reenergized by a trusted and credible partner. Unfortunately, there are many factors now in play that make it difficult to sustain deep friendships. Among these are economic pressures resulting from stagnating and declining wages, employment insecurity, and rapid job change (the gig economy); high rates of geographic mobility (nearly 10 percent of Americans change residence each year, many moving far enough away to disrupt existing networks); and the mass adoption of digital communication services that, despite their many benefits, encourage social withdrawal and narcissism by subverting empathy and rich face-to-face contact. It is unlikely that we'll see improvement in these factors any time soon. And, anyway, even if all this did change, it wouldn't solve our problems. The twenty-first century's lightning-speed communication flows have turned mass culture into a churning semiotic slurry fed by many streams, including commercial advertising, spam, fraud, hucksterism, corporate hype, and political deceit. Factual data are often so diverse, contested, inconsistent, fast-changing, and distrusted that they tend to undermine the idea of truth. This places many people in a condition of more or less permanent doubt and cynicism.

The result is a low-grade but pervasive sense of threat with psycho-emotional consequences that range from mild uncertainty and despair to full blown anxiety and depression. Again, as noted, the rate of mental disorders at the end of the nineteenth century is estimated to have stood at about 1 in 1,000 Americans. Today's rate is 1 in 5. And these estimates are based on the formal reports of conditions that were sufficiently severe that they motivated somebody to consult a health authority, and so the negative consequences of modern life are likely far more widespread. They show up in many disguises, impacting the sense of well-being and interpersonal behavior through underground routes. As we'll explore later in this book, the secular/scientific idea of the unconscious

A change of mind   41

mind did not emerge much before the middle of the nineteenth century. But, at that time, which was also the time that America was starting to feel the stresses of rapidly increasing population diversity and urbanization, people began to sense the disparities creeping in between their publicly presented selves, their ideal self, and the self within (often each of these representing a conflicting set of moral priorities).[19] Here began the late-modernity-induced problem of reconciling disparate versions of self. Who I am on the job is not quite the same as who I am at home (much less the various personae I maintain on the internet), and, perhaps, none of these is the person I would desire to be seen to be in the eyes of my children. One of the strongest conclusions of twentieth-century social psychology is that the mind strives for internal consistency. Because of the historically unprecedented segmentation of social experience in modern societies, it may now take some artful mental gymnastics to manage that.

One option is to bury some of this conflict in the structure of mind identified by the psychoanalytic theorists of the late nineteenth century that has come to be known as the unconscious mind. The relatively recent historical recognition of the influence of the unconscious in modernizing societies reminds us that the evolution of mental life that has been ongoing since the time of episodic culture hasn't concluded, and likely never will. No doubt there was unconscious mental experience in earlier periods of history, but, as we'll see, such was rarely understood in secular terms and not, as it is now, as a function of a common structure of mind. Today, the idea we are each possessed of an actively influential unconscious process is widely accepted and influences the way we understand and relate to each other. But this has come about recently. Modernity squeezes existential being, making life more contradictory, meaning less certain, and the self ever more important, but also more difficult to sustain. Different periods of history pose different problems of being, which has led some to speculate that different cultural circumstances have encouraged distinctive defensive operations of mind,[20] making sense of the otherwise puzzling sudden appearance of a spectrum of conditions of post-nineteenth-century mental experience. At the extreme are a range of conditions that reflect the fragmentation of self: multiple identity disorder, PTSD, borderline personality disorder, and possibly ADHD in children. And then, far more commonly, the mechanisms of psychological defense and perceptual distortion that virtually everyone employs to cope with difficulties of self – denial, projection, regression, splitting, and others identified by the psychoanalytic theorists.

It's been noted that, increasingly, Americans seem to be seeking escape in fantasy (live-action role play, historical reenactment, pornography, pseudo-military activities, etc.) or aligning with fantastic and contrarian ideas: UFOs are real, crackpot medical cures, creationism, government conspiracies, made-up religions, spiritualism, immigrants are running amok murdering and raping, Satanism, the Holocaust never occurred, COVID-19 infections are spread by 5G cell-phone towers, the imminent end of the world, reincarnation, Barack Obama wasn't born in the United States, the Clintons are running a child sex trafficking ring out of a pizza shop in Washington D.C., vaccinations cause

42 *Language, mind, and intimacy*

autism, global warming is a fiction, the moon landings were faked.[21] At the same time, others have noted the degree to which addictive behaviors seem to be ever on the increase, which shows up in compulsive work, alcohol consumption, sex, eating, drugs, gambling, shopping, smoking, exercising, and now internet gaming.[22] The common thread connecting all this is that these responses are driven by anxiety related to the precarious situation of self-identity in highly modern society, where consensual structures of belief – the last vestiges of mythic culture – have lost most of their former authority. This has rendered the construction of a protective shield of personal identity much more important, but also more difficult. The problem is simply too much for a substantial number of people.

And so, they seek escape from the anxiety that accompanies an inadequately formed sense of personal identity. Of course, drugs, alcohol, sex-related behavior, and endorphin-generating exercise can directly deaden existential pain, at least temporarily. But addictive behavior can also be attractive because repetition, even the repetition of exercise or work, re-embeds personal identity in routine, and routine stabilizes the self by removing anguish-of-decision about what to do. In this way, routine may become neurotically compulsive. As for those who identify with flaky ideas, here the attraction is similar to the boost to one's sense of personal being that many experience when embroiled in intense conflict. In the passions of hostility, anxiety and doubt are put aside. During conflict, for as long as it lasts, we know exactly who we are and what we stand for. We see ourselves illuminated in the strong light of opposition. Those who identify with contrarian ideas may do so for this benefit. The strongly improbable and defiant character of the positions they take relieves anguish-of-being by bringing the sense of self into the vivid light of contrast and opposition. For psychologist Louis Sass, the individualism of modern societies paradoxically encourages "a radical contrariness, in which freedom from constraint is declared through unconventional behavior."[23]

In another take on this, some attempt to escape their problems of being by advocating for the return to an overtly religious, patriarchal, or race-privileged society. This too becomes sensible when you consider that, in the days when these structures of belief were dominant, you knew who you were because self-definition was imposed externally, and so it was far easier to maintain self-identity. So, here, it's important to recognize that it's not necessarily the privilege that people seek; many women also support a return to patriarchy. Rather, for many, it's the relief from the anxiety inherent in an inadequately protective sense of self.

One must feel compassion. The loss of self represents a cataclysmic level of trauma. So, it should come as no surprise that so many in modern societies engage in magical thinking or other seemingly irrational behavior in their attempts to dodge the threats to the sense of being that come about when the self is cast loose from its historical moorings. Cultural change that threatens personal identity can be expected to result in desperately defensive reactions.

A change of mind   43

But cultural change cannot be stopped. Regardless of what some public figures may advocate, modernity's clock won't be turned back. Nor will the medical profession be able to supply a solution. The self-concept, which is the center of our trouble, is a social object, not a biological one. You can't fix a damaged self-concept by taking a pill. We must encourage other ways to shore up the self and protect fragile fields of meaning.

In an era during which it's been established that social isolation is on the rise and is a major contributor to both physical and mental health problems, it's vital to appreciate the way that who we are is constituted in our discourse; our sense of being – our foundational mental process – requires ongoing communication. Structures of personal meaning can only be sustained in ongoing exchange of private views among those who regard each other as equals. Unfortunately, recent sociological changes make this difficult. Even though increasing numbers of Americans find themselves living in densely populated urban environments, their range of social connection has been shrinking.[24] However, one hopeful sign derives from the steady rise of gender equality in modern societies. Today, there is a new and historically novel possibility of real friendship between men and women involved in long-term intimate relationships. As we'll see, until recently, true friendship was never possible in cross-sex relationships because men and women did not see each other as moral and intellectual equals. Of course, in many cases, they still don't. However, for those who've seen the logic and the benefit, and who have the strength of character and have been able to adapt, the payoff is the possibility of obtaining a vital source of ongoing support for private meaning and personal identity at a level without historical precedent.

Notes

1 Donald, *A mind so rare: the evolution of human* consciousness, 275.
2 Chabris and Simons, *The invisible gorilla: how our intuitions deceive us.*
3 Donald, *Origins of the modern mind: three stages in the evolution of culture and cognition.*
4 Donald, *A mind so rare: the evolution of human consciousness*
5 Burke, *Language as symbolic action: essays on life, literature, and method*
6 Donald, *A mind so rare: the evolution of human consciousness*
7 Clarke et al., *Trends in the use of complementary health approaches among adults: United States, 2002–2012*
8 Donald, *Origins of the modern mind: three stages in the evolution of culture and cognition.*
9 Jaynes, *The origin of consciousness in the breakdown of the bicameral mind.*
10 Division of Clinical Psychology, *Understanding psychosis and schizophrenia.*
11 Everett, *Don't sleep, there are snakes: life and language in the Amazonian jungle.*
12 Greenfeld, *Mind, modernity, madness: the impact of culture on human experience.*
13 Greenfeld, *Mind, modernity, madness: the impact of culture on human experience*; Baumeister, *Identity: cultural change and the struggle for self.*
14 Sass, *Madness and modernism: insanity in the light of modern art, literature, and thought.*
15 Kessler et al., Age of onset of mental disorders: a review of recent literature.

44 *Language, mind, and intimacy*

16 The British government recently inaugurated a new Ministry for Loneliness in recognition that isolation is the key factor in many contemporary problems of mind and culture: Yeginsu, U.K. appoints a minister for loneliness.

17 Alexander, Patchworks and field-boundaries: visualising the history of English.

18 Schwartz, *The paradox of choice: why more is less*.

19 Kasson, *Rudeness & civility: manners in nineteenth-century urban America*.

20 Grotstein, *Splitting and projective identification*.

21 Andersen, *Fantasyland: how America went haywire, a 500-year history*.

22 Giddens, *The transformation of intimacy: sexuality, love & eroticism in modern societies*; Giddens, *Runaway world*.

23 Sass, *Madness and modernism: insanity in the light of modern art, literature, and thought*, 75.

24 Klinenberg, *Going solo: the extraordinary rise and surprising appeal of living alone*.

3 Signals to symbols

The awakening of intimate experience

> The function of symbols as symbols must be taken into account whenever we discuss social relationships in any context of experience.
>
> Hugh Dalziel Duncan, *Symbols in Society*[1]

The symbol-using animal

People talk a lot about each other's communication, but usually without any particularly deep appreciation of what actually happens in interaction: what discourse accomplishes, and why it's important. We communicate more or less continuously, and so we think we know something about how talk works, and obviously we do to at least some superficial extent. But we so often talk about our communication using ideas based on immediate experience, fashion, and untested generalization that it leaves a lot of this armchair analysis, at best, really just catharsis and, at worst, an unsorted muddle that can itself perpetuate needless conflict and relationship distress. So, this book zeros in on a set of ideas about how, in the conditions of the modern world, communication builds intimacy and a sense of self-identity; about how this process shields against stresses inherent in modern culture; and about how this has been undergoing revolutionary change in recent history as modernity has rendered culture increasingly diverse and contradictory, and self-identity much more difficult to sustain and more dependent on our interaction with each other.

As we've seen, theorists commonly distinguish between two modes of communication: communication as signal (or sign) versus communication as symbol. This distinction is essential for understanding social experience in this era, especially how isolation has become more dangerous, and what ties intimate relationships together or makes them unravel. As discussed in the previous chapter, the historical shift from signal to symbol in the way humans communicate has been responsible for changes in the experience of self, making something that had been relatively untroubled into what is now of such complicated and deepening concern that it's become a signature feature of the modern interpersonal landscape. Communication-as-symbol is a hallmark of modern America, but not Colonial America, and it's generally true that, the further back one looks, the more one sees a world of signal communication, and the less evidence there

DOI: 10.4324/9781003010234-4

46 *Language, mind, and intimacy*

is that people were caught up in issues of self. On the time scale of recorded civilization, the American experience began relatively recently and spans only a small portion of the total; nevertheless, much movement in the signal-to-symbol shift is visible in a comparison of the more religious, communal, integrated, gender-differentiated, and hierarchical world of early American settlement with the present, secular age of super-diversity, social equality, privacy, unprecedented freedom of belief, and choice; of urban life, strangers, and distrust; and of subjective identity, vivid inner experience, and anxiety over the ever-present possibility of becoming isolated from others in what we make of ourselves and the world and what we value (a world much more of symbol).

To speak of communication as signal is to speak of efficiency and accuracy of information transfer in an ordered, linear system of components with fixed characteristics. The computer is an excellent example of such a system. To speak of communication as symbol is to emphasize the problem of separated minds struggling to coordinate meaning in the culturally fluid situations in which people now find themselves. The signal/symbol distinction is vital to understanding of the history of human consciousness and the migration of morality's foundations from external sources to processes of conversation in close relationships. And it helps explain the way in which separation and loss have become increasingly traumatic experiences. The signal/symbol distinction goes to the heart of the modern sense of self-identity. We are, as Kenneth Burke said, "symbol using animals,"[2] and the modern world is more obviously one of symbols – of fast-changing, private, and contested meaning. From this flows many of the joys and difficulties of contemporary social experience.

So, consider the communication that occurs between a home thermostat and the heat pump. The thermostat is a sensor that detects temperature change and then sends an electronic pulse to a switch on the heat pump that causes it to turn on or off. The communication system consists of components that we may refer to as a sender, a message, a communication channel or medium (through which messages are transmitted, in this case a wire), and a receiver. The electronic pulse has a fixed meaning that's unambiguous – turn on or turn off. In such a system, it makes sense to speak of communication failures and breakdowns. They could be caused by an electrical interruption, a faulty sensor, a cracked wire, or a broken receiver. In each case, the "communication" problem is solved by repair or replacement of the bad part. This is communication as signal: invariant meaning and components with fixed functions interacting in a linear and mechanical fashion. It is the communication system used by bees to report back to their colony the location of distant resources, by birds to attract mates, and by prairie dogs to alert the colony to danger.

The function of communication in affectionate relationships was indeed more signal-like in the past, but, in our era, communication in important relationships is not signal-like, and describing it using inappropriate concepts and metaphors makes an already complicated matter even more murky. Communication between intimates occurs through mutual participation in systems of symbols, which are objects or actions (words, gestures, behavior) whose

Signals to symbols 47

meanings are not fixed, but rather are loosely understood in common ways by those who, insofar as they do this, may be said to share a common culture. Whereas the pulse of electricity has an invariant meaning, which makes it a signal, human language is symbolic, which means that it is comprised of elements whose meanings are flexible and idiosyncratic. The *Oxford English Dictionary* describes a symbol as something that "stands for, represents, or denotes something else (not by exact resemblance, but by vague suggestion, or by some accidental or conventional relation)."

The meanings that words take on are acquired through a process of conventional rather than fixed relation. For example, as symbols, the words "mother," "father," "child," "husband," and "wife" can have an extensive range of private meanings and potentially potent associations. There's no invariant, correct definition for any of them. They acquire their meaning in "conventional relation," which is to say, in the way that we choose to understand and deploy them in use. In this way, the marital relationship and the parent – child relationship are not invariant experiences, but in every case are uniquely negotiated and privately meaningful for the people involved. One may speak of marriage as though it is a category of life experienced commonly, but this is misleading. Increasingly, as modernity has intensified, each relationship has become a private creation, experienced uniquely, each the site of particular qualities and conflicts. As Betsy Rath said to her husband Tommy in *The Man in the Gray Flannel Suit*, a film that famously dramatized and focused discussion of the growing tension between conformity and individualism of mid-twentieth century America: "The way I think about marriage, it ought to be a kind of secret between two people, just between them and nobody else in the world." In our day, it always is.

Symbols populate fields of associational meaning. A newly acquired symbol may have a relatively sparse network of links, but, as the symbol is deployed in use, the net will grow denser and more nuanced. The symbol may be linked to other conceptual tokens as well as to emotional states, imagery, sounds, and other sensory data. Any symbol can occupy a position in more than one field of meaning, in which case it may be useful to consider that the network of associations may be complexly multidimensional. For me, the word "Brandenburg" has strong presence in three relatively distinct associational nets: one related to trips to Berlin, where Brandenburg is an adjoining suburb; one related to Johann Sebastian Bach's masterpiece, the Brandenburg Concertos; and one related to pets – Brandenburg is the name of one of my cats. To enter into discourse with someone is to have the opportunity to explore aspects of these associational networks, perhaps to bring additional nuance by introducing new associations (the fact that you and I spoke about the Brandenburg Concertos now links the symbol "Brandenburg" to memories of you – that is, to the symbols that I use to represent you – and for you it links to memories of me) or add new meaning or alter existing meaning. As our conversation exposes various fields of meaning, they are reenergized, which gives them greater subjective presence and inhibits the normal tendency for them to fade gradually from

48 *Language, mind, and intimacy*

availability. Of course, conversation always involves some degree of restructuring of the meaning fields for all involved, because language is the primary social vehicle for the formation of semantic links, and engaging an area of meaning in conversation will inevitably affect its configuration of associations, creating complex multidimensional nets of linked symbols that connect the minds of conversational partners. In the course of their ongoing discourse, significant partners themselves become master symbols within each other's consciousness, each new encounter with the other calling to presence the myriad arrays of interconnected meaning that the pair have co-generated over the course of their history of communication.

Nothing like this is the case in signal communication, such as occurs between computers, or across the neuronal synapses of the brain. There, appraisal of communication quality would address questions of fidelity, efficiency, reliability, and speed of transmission. On the other hand, the appraisal of quality in communication between humans in modern societies involves consideration of the manner in which social partners engage in the construction or coordination of the various fields of meaning relevant to aspects of the world they have in common, including their understanding of each other's past, fantasies about the future, orientation to the material and spiritual worlds, understanding of their friends, neighbors, family, and other social relations, and, these days especially, for their joint understanding of each other's self-narrative and sense of personal identity, which, like all other meaning, is represented in complex fields of symbols arrayed in terms of their strength of association. In signal communication, there's no question of the identity of each component of the system: a thermostat is forever a thermostat, and a drone bee will remain a drone bee all his life. Unlike the human symbol user, the bee will never find itself transformed into some new understanding of self through its discourse. Thus, because bee brains run on signals rather than symbols, if you married a bee, you'd never have to worry that your spouse will suddenly upend your relationship, abruptly fancying himself a great lover, an agent of God, a hero, or a queen bee trapped in a drone's body.

In signal communication, messages are unidirectional, flowing from an origin to a destination, as occurs when one computer transfers data to another, or, perhaps, when an ascetic prophet hears the voice of God issuing commandments. However, in systems of symbolic exchange, discourse tends to simultaneously influence the source as well as the receiver. You've probably noticed that, in the act of speaking or writing, we often discover our values and beliefs. They aren't static articles that we carry in the brain, uncrate, and reveal: they're fluid elements of subjectivity – of mind – that are formulated in discourse (even when we speak to ourselves or an imaginary audience in private, perhaps while driving, or in prayer, or in recording daily experience in a diary). In signal communication, messages are discrete and antiseptic, but, in symbolic communication, each utterance has a tendency to pull meaning along with it, to reconfigure the past and contaminate the future, paving the way for related beliefs and values. When someone you're hoping to end up going

Signals to symbols 49

home with mentions how strongly she feels about animal protection, simultaneously as you attempt to hide your lucky rabbit's foot deeper in the recesses of your pants pocket, you apprehend the strategic value of an emphatically sympathetic response. However, despite this initial insincerity, you may in fact wind up genuinely sympathetic. Philosopher Jean-Paul Sartre had something of this in mind when he wrote that the future drags us along from in front of us.[3]

In signal communication, messages are unidimensional, conveying only content. In communication with symbols, in the context of modernity, in addition to their content, messages simultaneously convey information about the relative status of the interactants. For example, it is possible to send quite a variety of status messages in the statement, perhaps said to one's boss, "You're some kind of woman," depending on which word is stressed, what tone is employed, whether the message is muttered or spoken clearly, what emotion the face conveys, and other aspects of context. It's so difficult to sidestep this that it's reasonable to say that, to all intents and purposes, *all* human symbolic communication conveys both content and relationship information simultaneously and continuously. In this way, the negotiated identities of the "components" in symbolic communication are active issues in every modern social encounter, encoded in the deep structure of discourse. However, this was likely not so much a part of the discourse of Americans in the distant past because, then, to a greater degree, identity was externally defined and relatively fixed.[4] Now, personal identity tends to be far less stable, and so questions of who's who are perpetually present in the deep structure of talk, and this issue ever holds the potential to rise to the surface and swamp every other aspect of an exchange. And because, in the circumstances of modernity, the sense of self-identity has become so much more free-floating and precarious, it often does. Questions about how each participant understands who the other is, how self and other are to be regarded and addressed, and what obligations, responsibilities, rights, and powers each has with respect to the other are ever present on the table (or just under it).

In the schematic descriptions of communication commonly encountered in textbooks, messages originating from senders are encoded and transmitted through some more or less noisy channel or medium and then decoded by a receiver or listener who might react in some way with feedback. As a description of human communication in conditions of modernity, this is misleading in that it reduces a conscious symbolic process to mechanical terms originally proposed by Bell Labs engineers to describe signal communication occurring between machines. But even there it misleads, perpetuating a serious error of reasoning that Raymond Tallis has called "thinking by transferred epithet,"[5] in which a metaphoric description of some new phenomenon in the terminology of something familiar sows and then perpetuates the idea that the two are similar to the point that we lose track of their distinction and begin to look to the properties of the new phenomenon as a way to illuminate new aspects of the old one. For example, it would be a fair enough description of the process of program-to-program communication in computer systems to say that software

50 *Language, mind, and intimacy*

modules constitute the senders and receivers, which are loaded and continually active, programmed to "listen" on a particular "channel" (or "port" – for a web server, it's usually port 80). When a web server program located at some internet location receives data, it does in fact decode the stream of binary information and extracts the internet address of the sender and other data. It acts on the content of the message (perhaps to return a web page).

However, this manner of describing machine communication draws its concepts from the human realm. Computer programs don't listen, or send, or have ports (or think). Program-to-program communication is strictly a process of flipping bits back and forth between zero and one and copying streams of digits from one place to another. To conceptualize this as "listening on a port" or "reading," "writing," or "transmitting" "messages" between "senders" and "receivers" is a convenient metaphor that makes designing computer software immensely easier by thinking of the programs as though they're little human beings that interact with each other as we do. But it doesn't describe what actually happens. Having drawn from the language of human communication to describe signal communication in the realm of computers, our mistake occurs when we lose track of the fact that the machine was being described, not in terms unique to it, but by loose analogy to us. Then, as though we didn't already have adequate terms of self-description, we remap the characteristics of the machine back onto us, using the computer as a metaphor for understanding our own experience – speaking perhaps of our being "wired for love" or concocting a "life hack," or of our capacity for "multitasking" or "networking" or "wiping our memory" or being "online" or "offline," or "crashing" or "syncing" or, lately, "rebooting" (as in "I went with Jinna to Montreal for the weekend to try to reboot our relationship"). What was originally an act of anthropomorphic generosity – describing machines in human terms – has paid back in a philosophically disastrous tendency to conceptualize ourselves as machines.

This mistake is the essence of Tallis's "reasoning by transferred epithet," and, in this case especially, it's an important error because machines are signal-based rather than symbol-based. To think of computers and humans as similar in their manner of communication is to start down a pathway to a philosophical muddle that makes it impossible to properly understand human culture, intimacy, and self-identity. Outside of the confusion generated by science fiction movies, a computer-driven robot – little more than an adding machine on steroids – will never experience an existential crisis. The odds aren't so good for the rest of us. The modern mind is comprised of idiosyncratic fields of symbolic meaning, which, in this historical period, have broken free of their external anchors and so are easily blown about and subject to challenge and shifts in relevance as social partners come and go – a particularly dangerous situation for the isolated.

The conceptual confusion perpetrated by the source → message → receiver model can be particularly harmful when this wheezing old donkey of freshman communication theory is hitched up to describe communication processes in

Signals to symbols 51

interpersonal life, as it often is. For example, read carefully cognitive psychologist Louis Cozolino's recent comparison of the communication that occurs between neurons in the brain with human social communication:

> Individual neurons are separated by small gaps called synapses [which] are inhabited by a variety of chemical substances engaging in complex interactions that result in synaptic transmission . . . When it comes right down to it, doesn't communication between people consist of the same building blocks? When we smile, wave, and say hello, these behaviors are sent through the space between us. These messages are received by our senses and converted into electrical and chemical signals [which] generate chemical changes, electrical activation, and new behaviors that, in turn, transmit messages back across the social synapse . . . people, like neurons, excite, interconnect, and link together to create relationships.[6]

As we'll see in the final chapter, misconceiving of human social exchange as though it consists of mechanical transfer of energy from one component to another – as though it were signal – is not uncommon among biologically oriented scientists. This is unfortunate, because to come to terms with the role of communication in human affairs requires an appreciation of the symbolic nature of mind, the manner in which our language system functions as an organ of perception,[7] and the way in which symbolic discourse leads to the construction of shared meaning and a sense of intimacy with conversational partners. Mechanical transfer is the stuff of Rube Goldberg machines, computers, and the central nervous system, not human communication, mind to mind.

Biologically oriented scientists aren't alone in making this type of mistake. We all do in moments of intimate conflict when we raise our voices, as if the trouble was that our message wasn't being heard; when we continuously repeat the same accusation, as if our partner's receiving unit was broken; or when we angrily demand to know if something is wrong with our partner's ability to comprehend what we say, perhaps on the presumption that her decoding unit is on the blink. Conflict styles become dysfunctional when they are grounded in the presupposition that our communication is a process of signal exchange. Within that frame, when things go wrong, humans typically take any of a number of steps that would be perfectly reasonable if their partner was a malfunctioning heat pump.

Unlike the situation of signal-based machines that exchange data, in human communication, the medium is more than just a passive conduit through which messages are transmitted. Those who get their news from TV have a different experience of a story from those who read the story in a newspaper. As much research has demonstrated, those who watch television have a characteristically different vision of the world they live in, often a world that seems scarier and full of greater risk.[8]

The media (the set of mediums through which we communicate) and their often unanticipated and sometimes insidious influences on our lives continue

52   *Language, mind, and intimacy*

to proliferate. Now, texting structures many people's relationships, connecting them superficially to distant others while disconnecting them from those they are with. The 280-character limit to tweets creates in one way a kind a soundbite world of self-advertisement and announcements without detail or nuance. The time-shifting character of telephone answering machines and email eroded barriers between work and private life, putting everyone on perpetual call and sometimes fostering so much stress and burnout that one now hears recommendations that corporations implement "digital detox" policies, limiting times when employees can be accessed by email. The cell phone has amplified these effects, ironically undermining the possibility of rich personal contact by frequently interrupting face-to-face interaction to place people in comparatively superficial connection with distant others.[9]

In the high-speed feedback loops of this era, where campaigning politicians commonly issue instantaneous retractions for statements that surprise them by proving unpopular, the distinctions between sender and receiver and between message and feedback aren't clear. It all happens so fast that these roles and functions become intertwined: Is the politician creating public opinion? Or is public opinion creating the politician? This happens as well in the interpersonal realm, where pages on social network sites may sometimes function as a sort of barometer of external opinion about qualities of the self.[10] Am I the person I describe on my Facebook page, or is it more that the conventions of expression on Facebook are shaping the person I'm becoming? The question has frequently been raised as to whether the possibility of meaningful discourse has fallen victim to the proliferation of new systems of mass communication and their unintended but potent consequences. In the visions of postmodern theorists, sender, message, receiver, and medium all dissolve into one. The medium isn't just the message; in our age, it also profoundly shapes us: our lives, our sense of ourselves, our relationships. This vision probably exceeds the boundaries of common experience, but it's relevant in conceptualizing the problems many people experience today in forming a comfortable, stable, and psychologically protective sense of self-identity. We'll take this up in more detail later. For now, it's sufficient to underline the distinction between communication as signal and communication as symbol and recognize that, if ever it was before, the source → message → receiver model is no longer applicable and is, in fact, a significant hindrance to understanding communication in modern times.

A little culture of secrets

So, to get anywhere in understanding social experience in this era, it's important to conceptualize communication correctly. Betsy Rath was on the right track: in deep, intimate relationships, interpersonal discourse is a matter of creating secrets, a continuous process of establishing and confirming private understandings that bridge and bind the fields of meaning that comprise partners' minds. Betsy may have been referring to a type of marital secret that's commonplace: views we share that we keep hidden from others, such as that we both think that the ham pie Aunt Sadie makes each Easter is disgusting, or that we regard the intelligence of the neighbors across the street with the loud cars and attack dogs as somewhere just beneath the level of Canadian geese. Of course, there's more. Intimacy depends on "particularized knowledge," which includes awareness of each other's personal vulnerabilities, potentially embarrassing failures, private dreams, wishes, hatreds and passions, and physical defects[11] (and this underscores the extent to which intimate relationships are these days held together by bonds of trust formed between people whose thoughts and emotions are idiosyncratic and intentionally masked from others).

These types of shared secrets are a vivid part of intimate life, but the kind of private meaning that is created in long-term relationships is also deeper and more general. This is so because language is itself an inherently intimate medium. A symbol is a social instrument of potentially limitless form and significance, a malleable vehicle of meaning that both have to orient to in similar ways in order for it to be used in communication. For partners to have a talk about the joy of personal accomplishment, they must discourse to the point where they are comfortable that both have pretty much the same things in mind in talk about ambition, effort, reward, setbacks, frustration, success, and so on. Some scholars have suggested that intimates rely upon each other's minds for storing particular kinds of information, and, indeed, such a process would produce mental interdependence.[12] Here, however, I am speaking of something more fundamental: the fields of meaning that constitute the minds of intimates are mutually cultivated, becoming more similar over time. The more partners talk to each other, and the greater the breadth of their talk, the more they enter each other's minds, apprehending idiosyncratic meaning, sowing their own, and, generally, rearranging what they find and charging it with new significance. In result, both walk away transformed to some degree by shifts of perspective and forever dependent on each other for reconfirmation of the structures of meaning they created together. This is an inescapable process that is intrinsic to symbolic communication. It results in the construction of networks of shared symbols that function as mind-bridges, forming an important kind of social glue that binds minds to each other.

Everyone participates in cultural-level systems of loosely shared symbols that have the effect of dividing the experienced world into constituent and communicable parts. Objects are carved out of the undifferentiated experience of the natural world and given arbitrary names, attributes, and other qualities. Language allows us to parse and organize the world. As Nobel poet Wisława Szymborska asserts in her View with a Grain of Sand,"[13] there's nothing inherently "grainy" in a grain of sand, and the substance referred to is not "sand" except that we named it so. Says Szymborska, "it does just fine without a name." And there's nothing inherently "wet" about water, or "sunny" about the sun, or "beautiful" about a beautiful view from a window except that we have agreed to think that there's structure that we call a "window" that has something in it we choose to call a "view" that has a quality we call "beautiful" and

54 *Language, mind, and intimacy*

say so. Words are conventionalized mental constructs. To say the sun is setting in the sky is to force-fit the continuous fabric of the natural world into concepts of "sun" and "sky" and "setting." Quite literally, the sun never rose or set until there was language. In fact, before language, though it surely could be sensed, the sun could never have existed as a distinct object and a subject of abstract human contemplation. Reflecting culture, language is the brush that creates the world, which is why the acquisition of vocabulary in children is a critical and ongoing process of development. A child who is slow to build vocabulary can't conceive of or work with the concepts that those missing words could supply (and neither can an adult who fades from education and the effort to expand his or her repertoire of language and distinction – there is no more certain way to disempower oneself).

The names and qualities of things and their boundaries and definitions are matters of convention, artifacts of the process of communicating through symbols. And they must be established for communication to occur. Experiences are segmented off from the flow of life, named, and given significance. Today one is "single" and tomorrow "married," concepts that, for all their importance and drama in American culture, may mean nothing similar in some others. A culture is a vast skein of distinctions and significances that condition and constrain perception. Conversation creates it and sustains it, and it acts back upon us. We experience it as the given world and, with small exception, take it for granted. Culture, therefore, is the mother of all boxes that are difficult to think outside. Like the air we breathe, culture is the unseen substance of all communicable meaning. Its precepts set the directions and limits of our sense of what's possible and sensible and communicable, of the moral, and of the important versus the trivial. However, it doesn't enter our minds directly. It comes to us in discourse with others.

Culture changes through time. In highly modern societies, culture becomes more diverse, complex, multivocal, and contradictory. Currently, the media speak of "culture wars" in the United States, which refer to intense and ongoing struggles over such matters as how to parse moral behavior, especially family-related obligations, and the relative attributes and status of members of social categories, such as gays and straights, men and women, and people of differing ethnicity. Such categorical divisions themselves are, in all cases, matters of arbitrary convention. Racial composition isn't discrete but a result of blending, and, in the U.S., categorization by race is more about tradition and convention, a system that may be doing an increasingly poor job of representing America's diversity.[14] Here, you might recall the national controversy during the summer of 2015 over Rachel Dolezal, the biologically white woman who identified herself as black and assumed leadership in the Spokane, Washington chapter of the NAACP, until outed by her parents. Is race a state of mind, a matter of language, or a state of your DNA? What about gender?

Male and female may be biologically demonstrable categories, but divisions of gender identity and sexuality are not at all clearly separated, but matters of degree and history and culture. By the early 1980s, psychologist Sandra

Signals to symbols   55

Bem's research had made clear that it is reasonable to speak of femininity and masculinity as cognitive schema that exist independently of biological sex.[15] How quaint that seems in hindsight. By 2016, Facebook was providing users with 56 options for declaring their gender, including "pangender," "transfeminine," "transsexual male," "non-binary," "neutrois," "gender questioning," "genderqueer," "cisgender," "bigender," "MTF," "intersex," "gender fluid," "transperson," "transgender woman," "androgyne," "transsexual man," and "two spirit." By 2019, Facebook had given up trying to maintain this ever-expanding list, allowing users to simply write in whatever they want.

All this matters very much. Consider the Catholic priest of many years' service to the upstate New York parish that serves my town, who, after a sex change operation, was prohibited from performing professionally because "he," a biological male who had long understood himself to be female, had become "she."[16] What imaginable difference could a change of genitalia make in anyone's ability to minister to the spiritual needs of parishioners? The trouble results because there's no language that permits the sensible conceptualization of people with this experience that does not also run afoul of issues of power and hierarchy, and the distinction, like that between an embryo and a human being, is saturated with political consequence. That the culture war's conflicts are often bitter and protracted underscores the felt importance of the way that conventional distinctions are established in language, and their importance to our sense of self and morality. As sociologist Hugh Duncan noted, "much blood is spilt in our world over the control of names."[17]

But we do not participate in cultural-level systems of meaning exclusively. When we form relationships, through talk and common experience, they accrete their own structures of meaning. This is especially important in modern societies where culture has become so full of diverse and conflicting ideas that significant psycho-emotional distress may result for those whose sense of self is inadequately formed or supported, leaving them unable to filter this effectively. So, one seeks to build a protective community – a private culture that includes support for one's primary fields of meaning. This occurs gradually as we put particular spins on existing concepts. For example, as a result of many conversations between us, I know that, when I talk to Vincent using the word "bureaucracy," he will understand that I refer to a kind of creeping evil that makes good teaching increasingly difficult, and I will understand that Vincent generally regards bureaucracy in the context of government regulations that impede innovation and good business. The critique of bureaucracy is one of ten thousand discourses that have ever more deeply connected us. But, while Vincent and I have created our particular field of association for bureaucracy, the word may not carry this framework into discussion with someone else.

We may also concoct new concepts that have no meaning at all to relationship outsiders – an "idiolect."[18] In relationships between social equals, ordinary conversation tends to generate a reasonably large array of private distinctions, significances, and interpretations of self and world, shared understanding of history and morality, and a set of privately meaningful actions, concepts, and

56   *Language, mind, and intimacy*

gestures – sometimes even a private vocabulary[19] (what linguist Basil Bernstein called a "restricted code").[20] Intimacy often gives rise to private jokes and a unique historical calendar that allows relationship partners to "date events in relation to significant incidents in the history of the relationship (e.g., 'It was right after our trip to Yellowstone')".[21] In writing about the extent of idiosyncratic language that bound her to her husband, Paul West, author Diane Ackerman noted that, "we lived in a house made of words. Our personal vocabulary had ranged from the word 'flaff,' which meant utter nonsense, to 'mrok,' a plaintive cry often uttered by one of us hoping to locate the other."[22]

In this way, intimate partners come to inhabit their own sub-universe of particularized meaning – a microculture – and the fields of meaning that constitute their minds become interdependently bonded to each other in result of this process. As their communication conditions them to make much the same sense of the world they see, and as this places them in distinction from others, partners increasingly rely on each other for confirmation of the uniquely held points of view that they generated together, and as well for their sense of themselves as particular types of people. Self-definition is involved in this because, after all, all thought is symbolic, and no symbol – and, therefore, no idea of self – can have meaning except in being shared with others. This is how the self-concept – personal identity – is produced in intimate experience, and it is why no one will never be quite the same person in two different relationships. Identity is crafted in the unique discourse of each relationship and exists only in that relationship's interdependent fields of meaning. To enter a new relationship is to begin becoming a different person. Thus, when an important intimate relationship ends, it often has dramatic consequences for self-definition. Similarly, this is the reason it is difficult to describe the experience of an intimate relationship to outsiders in satisfactory terms: you can only relate global features and feelings. The relationship experience is ineffable to outsiders, who can never understand it because they have not participated in its uniquely intertwined fields of meaning, its specialized symbols and gestures, its private language, and the unique constructions of the world and each other that that language affords. There's no dictionary, no Google Translate, that allows one to express Ian-and-Brittany in terms of Kaitlin-and-Brandon.

But this hasn't always been the case. This process has taken on unprecedented importance in the historical changes of the last 100–200 years of American history as strong external frameworks for understanding self and the world have eroded, and as women and men have become social equals. Once strongly defined externally, personal identity has become one of the symbolic objects of the world that's now defined and sustained in primary relationships. Gradually, these relationships have become important not only for the accomplishments that marriage, family, and friendship enable, such as reproduction, enhanced economic productivity, and mutual care, or even for the emotional fulfillment they bring. According to philosopher Charles Taylor, intimate relationships have become "the crucibles of inwardly generated identity."[23] Today, we're defined within the interpersonal process of our personal relationships

Signals to symbols 57

more so than from external cultural sources that once figured larger in this process, such as occupational life, community, tradition, and religion. Unfortunately, at the same time that this has become a prominent hallmark of our era, and our intimate relationships have become more important, they have also become more fluid and fragile.

That has happened because virtually all former external barriers to relationship dissolution have eroded in the historical transformations of modernity. Now, nothing much keeps intimate partners together beyond the sense of satisfaction, personal meaning, and confirmation of self experienced in interaction. We've exited historical times, when relationships were held together externally through law, tradition, religion, and economic necessity, and entered an era of what sociologist Anthony Giddens calls "pure relationships": a shift from "for better or for worse" to "let's see how it goes."[24] Now, it's the quality of our discourse, our ability to mutually create and sustain a satisfactory sense of self, that matters to the survival of our intimate relationships. Looking back to Colonial America of the 1600s and 1700s, this was reversed: in that era, there were many external forces providing meaning, defining and securing self-identity, and keeping relationships bonded. More so than now, knowledge of the world was absorbed from sources outside of self. Intimate communication, as a process for the shared construction between relationship partners of a vision of the world, definition of each other, and a shared morality, was almost without contribution. The process of discourse in marriage was less about establishing an intimate, private culture and was somewhat more like a signal type of communication system, more about coordinating information and following directives. To a great degree, this was so because of the unequal social status of men and women. For communication to function as an engine of intimate culture that bonds and stabilizes the minds of participants, it must occur in the context of social equality.

Here, then, is one contributing dynamic in the explanation of Americans' apparent growing reluctance to commit easily or fully to intimacy,[25] of the rising numbers of people choosing to live as singles,[26] of the increasing age of marriage and the growing number of people who forgo it even when having children,[27] of the number of people now opting for the emotional safety of hooking up in place of the risks of involved sexuality,[28] and of the substantial decrease in the rate of remarriage following divorce.[29] In the past, when personal identity was more strongly defined externally, struggles over self-definition, over who the relationship lets you be, who you want to become, and how this meshes with your partner, were not so common. And, in those days, the end of a marriage wasn't as likely to precipitate a crisis of self-definition because less of self was defined within the marriage and threatened in its termination. In today's era of fragile relationships, should a primary partnership fail, the blow to the self-concept may represent a level of trauma many would like to avoid.

It's true, however, that protection of the self isn't the whole story. It's also the case that commitment is difficult in modern conditions of abundant choice,[30]

58   *Language, mind, and intimacy*

and, as well, for some, intimacy may be influenced by the rationalities of modern consumer culture, where one doesn't commit strongly to much of anything as objects or experiences tend to be regarded as disposable and valued in terms of changing fashion. Daters may hold back from commitment because continuous access to attractive and interesting people may foster a sort of "upgrade mentality" about intimate life,[31] where low commitment makes it relatively easy to shift partners when more attractive options pop up on dating apps. Yet the heart of the trouble is the difficulty of sustaining an adequately strong and stable structure of self in the circumstances of modernity.

The fact that intimate relationships have become the primary site for securing personal identity produces a complex web of tensions and contradictory impulses that have the combined effect of leaving people yearning for the critical supports of self-identity that come with deep connection, but sensing the risk and complexity of the problem and so holding back from commitment. Yet failure to invest sufficiently in an intimate relationship to allow it to become transformationally self-defining will certainly contribute to its risk of termination.

Symbolic interdependence

Thus, summing up the above, in our time, what constitutes quality in interpersonal interaction is properly understood, not in the terms of signal communication: not as efficiency of message transfer from senders to receivers, or avoidance of breakdowns, or failures of components to perform up to spec. Rather, quality in the interpersonal realm inheres in one's skillfulness in participating with significant partners in exploring the myriad associational links that constitute each other's fields of meaning – and in cultivating new ones. This process creates a condition of symbolic interdependence, bonding minds and consciousness by blending, augmenting, and prioritizing the ways in which each construes the world and each other and understands what's moral, what's important or trivial, what's exciting or dull, and so on. The principal cause of successful intimate bonding isn't that initially similar minds match up and link like puzzle pieces, drawn to each other by some mysterious process of attachment (think here of the models that drive services such as EHarmony, Match.Com, and OkCupid); it is rather that, as we spend time in each other's company, we mutually cultivate shared beliefs, attitudes, and values in our discourse, and this ends up conjoining our minds.

This process coordinates emotion too. When partners have constructed their world together, they're more likely to react to it in similar ways and with similar feeling. They're more likely to find sadness or joy in the same places, humor in the same jokes, beauty in the same vistas. This is so because they've come to share the conceptual frameworks that make things happy or sad, funny or not, beautiful or ugly. Partners are not copies of each other, but they tend to share knowledge, epistemology, morality, aesthetic preference, humor, memory, and feeling. This sharing is constitutive of intimacy and generates a sense

Signals to symbols 59

of solidarity, a feeling of "at-homeness" with each other, of being understood. In most important relationships, this is an interdependent process insofar as significant change in one person's construal of aspects of this shared culture will likely result in pressure to change for their partner too (or conflict). Such change – especially in ideas about self-identity – can be a significant source of relationship difficulty.

The paradox of autonomy

It is an unfortunate irony that, in modern cultures, autonomy is widely regarded as an ideal quality of character, reflecting one's ability to live a self-determined life free of external constraint, choosing for oneself what to value and how to act. Researchers documented a shift in the mid-twentieth century in the traits most desired in American children, with those related to autonomy and independence replacing those related to obedience to institutional and parental authority.[32] Psychologists reified this idea, converting it into a measurable feature of personality and, recently, coining a new term to refer to the opposite trait – "sociotropy."[33] Sociotropy is a tendency to become overly socially oriented, to lack what these days is regarded as healthy independence. Autonomy has become a modern uber-value.

The trouble with this is that humans are symbol users and, thus, unable to be completely autonomous of thought. As we've seen, symbols, which are the foundational elements of all conscious thought, are social objects whose associational meanings are established and sustained in discourse. In former times, some vectors of belief were so strongly and universally held that they didn't require the type of continuous reconfirmation that is now obligatory in the free-for-all circumstances of the modern mind, and so, then, a life of independence and autonomy was easier than now. But now, in the modern world, the isolated mind risks degenerating.

It is true that the meaning created in intimate relationships brings definition and stability to the sense of self, but never to the point of providing completely secure self-definition – a problem that's become increasingly difficult in modern societies. For self-definition to be truly secure, it would have to be arrived at independent of all the varied and shifting points of view that comprise the swirling cultural matrix in which modern minds are situated. This may have been easier in the past, when information wasn't as diverse and didn't flow or evolve as quickly, but is now impossible.

Yet, unaware of the philosophical contradictions inherent in this, we strive to live autonomously. Psychoanalyst Ernst Becker believed that, universally, we search for essential self-definition independent of others (he called this the "*causa sui* project"), but he saw this as a quest that can't succeed. We're interpersonal beings.[34] We have consciousness of self only because we use language, and language is inherently social and connective. No child learns what words mean on her own, and, as our lives go on, the meanings of the words we use change, their senses established and altered in discourse with others. And

60   *Language, mind, and intimacy*

we must continue to deploy these meanings in discourse so that their validity may be recertified; otherwise, they fade.

As we falter in the quest to establish ourselves as autonomous, sensing the extent to which we depend on our social connections and, also, the limitations that being social places on us, it may trigger feelings of unease and a desire to reassert independence. And so, in intimate experience, it's not uncommon for there to be a kind of pulsation: the one pulse stimulated by fear that one has become overly dependent, an awareness of the threat to autonomy that's implicit in deep intimacy (I find the perception threatening that I need you as I do; in my dependence, I fear I've lost my ability to confront the world on terms of my own definition). The other pulse is unease at the possibility of isolation that resides in the backwash of living truly independently, the discovery that, without strong personal relationships to confirm and validate our meaning, the contents of mind degenerate. For Kenneth Burke's symbol-using animals, this is unavoidable. Just as there's no sound of one hand clapping, there can be no absolute autonomy, because, in the modern world, where, for a majority, previously authoritative, cultural-level sources of meaning have lost influence, we're defined in the unique symbolization established in our social experience. No social experience, no us.

Why men and women experience intimate connection differently

It may also be true, however, that some people are better equipped to participate in symbolically interdependent bonding than others. Among other qualities, this requires an openness to influence and a capacity for dialogic conversation, and some people don't have enough of either one. For some, life may be so infused with insecurity of self – in other words, the symbols that comprise self are so tenuously held – that they draw back from occasions that might induce further change, lest the whole structure of being come apart. As well, symbolic interdependence requires interpersonal equality. This is an egalitarian era, but many relationships have been caught in the turbulence generated by the gradual reconfiguration of domestic power relations between men and women that began in earnest in the mid-twentieth century. The shift from patriarchal forms of relationship prevalent in previous eras to our time of companionate marriage, or, more abstractly, "pure relationships," has required psychological and emotional realignments for both men and women. According to Giddens, some men, whose orientation to interpersonal life still reflects previous historical periods, may not be capable of "loving others as equals, in circumstances of intimacy, [though] they are well able to offer love and care to those inferior in power." Similarly, for some women whose consciousness continues to reflect issues rooted in the past, "The demand for equality may jostle psychologically with the search for a male figure who is emotionally remote and authoritative."[35]

Signals to symbols 61

Why? For psychoanalyst Nancy Chodorow, a contributing factor in the persistence of the problem of men and women having difficulty connecting dialogically originates in America's historically deep pattern of sex-differentiated parenting, a pattern more resistant to change than other factors that have promoted gender inequality in intimacy in the past but have been changing recently (e.g., more equal access to employment and education, voting rights, etc.).[36] According to Chodorow, the problem originates in the common case in which parenting is more a matter of infants interacting with mother (or other outsourced female caregivers) than father, a situation that Chodorow views as global and pan-historical.

In this context, a girl's sense of herself as female arises in an uninterrupted flow of identification with her primary female caregiver. But the boy's gender identity is born, and remains forever bound up, in the dynamics of separation and differentiation from his opposite-sex caregiver (think of the common sight of a young male walking alone, hands in pockets, head cloaked by a hoodie, or iconic figures of masculinity such as James Dean, Clint Eastwood, Batman, James Bond, and countless stone-faced policemen in mirrored sun glasses or dark-clothed biker-guys – masculine identity expressed in rejection of others, or confrontation, or withdrawal). At an early point, every little boy learns that he's different from his mother in where he can go, how his body works, and what he can do, and in this he awakens to his identity as male. For sociologist Lillian Rubin, "when a boy who has been raised by a woman confronts the need to establish his gender identity, it means a profound upheaval in his internal world."[37] For boys, masculine identity is established in acts of differentiation, but this is not so for girls.

In result of this asymmetry, it may be difficult for males to feel comfortable in deep connection with others, especially with a female intimate partner, as this may challenge their sense of themselves as masculine. And women, more likely to feel comfortable with continuous psychic connection, may have difficulty relating to their partners within the framework of loosely bounded independence that feels more comfortable to men. Men may try to cope with the anxieties intimacy produces for them by seeking to sustain patriarchal structures of inequality in their relationships. This provides an illusion of greater control, and, is confirming of their masculinity, which is a core component of personal identity. Here, then, is an explanation for the sustaining power of patriarchal marriage in an otherwise increasingly egalitarian age.

Here, too, is another factor contributing to that pulsation of ego boundaries in intimate connection related above to Becker's discussion of the lifelong struggle with autonomy. Men, fearing a threat to their sense of self-as-differentiated, a foundational plank in their gender identity, attempt to exercise control and impose distance. Women, fearing a threat to their sense of self-as-connected, a foundational element of *their* gender identity, struggle to establish greater intimate contact. Females' bids for intimacy may encounter silence, or the language of rationality, distance, and control.

62 *Language, mind, and intimacy*

And then the opposite pulse: men who move too far from their partner, who create too much distance for their relationship to solve the problem of the instability of meaning in fluid modern life, may fruitlessly pursue intimacy elsewhere, never able to establish it satisfactorily as the underlying psychological dynamic will carry from one relationship to the next. For some women, the problem is reversed: at its extreme, if they succeed in establishing continuous psychic connection with their partner along the lines of their childhood relationship with their mother, it can threaten their autonomy in the same way that their intense childhood closeness with mother may have generated an anxious sense that their personal identity was indistinct or smothered by their mother, ultimately propelling them to dissociate from meanings that their intimate relationship could provide. In result, they may turn away emotionally and take steps to assert their independence. The tension often experienced between autonomy and connection is a consequence of cultural changes that detached the question of self and its value ("Who am I?", "Am I good enough?") from secure anchors in pre-modern community, religion, and tradition, driving these issues into interpersonal relationships.[38] The cultural imperative to live autonomously runs foul of the need for social reassurance about self-identity and worth, which must be negotiated in personal relationships. We fear explicitly requesting commitment from an intimate partner (which would address the need for reassurance about self and its value) out of the recognition that this may be seen to encroach on our own or our partner's autonomy, compelling one or both of us to pull away. This is one of several dynamics that destabilize modern relationships.

These problems aside, assuming that the relationship has been established under the presumption that partners are intellectual and moral equals, and the process of symbolic interdependence is moving forward, the transformations that it creates most often occur without awareness. The realignment of beliefs is "almost automatic in character."[39] By millimeters, our intimate relationships shape our understanding of who we are, our values, and the ways that we interpret and respond to the world. This realignment of consciousness may be visible to others but invisible to us. We don't see this in ourselves, and yet most people can speak, sometimes with great regret, of a former close friend whose values and behaviors changed following involvement in a new intimate relationship. However, we may sense that this process has occurred when we're away from our partner and feel a loneliness, not so much for physical companionship, but for her or his ability to appreciate the world as we do and to understand our reactions to it; for her or his ability to see the sense in our behavior and our feelings; for her or his ability to relate to the humor or the tragedy we see around us, to comprehend, as we do, the qualities and nuances of the world as we experience it. A co-evolution of consciousness occurs as minds of intimates are linked in structures of meaning that they cultivated together, and, when this happens, their relationship becomes a haven, and their discourse becomes the means for keeping their minds coordinated.

Signals to symbols 63

Outside of significant interpersonal relationships, those traveling abroad for an extended period may experience something a little like this after initial enchantment with the novelty of a foreign culture is gradually offset by a nostalgic glow about the U.S., a glossy, false fantasy that, there, most understand concepts in the same way and orient to the same broadly shared cultural experiences. After a couple of weeks overseas, any American happened upon may seem like a cultural comrade, and there may be a marked tendency to warmly overidentify. In modern America, in a symbolically interdependent relationship, one may experience this feeling of camaraderie reconnecting with one's partner after a day away at work, especially if work involves extensive contact with people of diverse backgrounds and values. However, unlike the overseas situation, this is less likely to be a false fantasy: linking back up with a symbolically interdependent partner reunites us with a primary collaborator in the formation of significant beliefs and values.

Without intimate connection, whether romantic or not, modern life can be unbearably lonely. Loneliness – the want of society – is the downside burden of the intense individuality of modern culture. Disconnected from family, neighbors, tradition, and religion, which formerly provided confidence about what to believe and how to live; actively preyed upon by politicians, marketers, and advertisers who attempt to promote insecurity of self and then market solutions to it; awash in commercial hype and the fast-changing and contradictory information flows that destabilize belief; isolated by the very technologies that promise global interconnectivity; one may well despair. Part 2 traces how the modern world has become such a lonely place.

Notes

1 Duncan, *Symbols in society*, 152.
2 Burke, *Language as symbolic action: essays on life, literature, and method.*
3 Sartre, *Being and nothingness: a phenomenological essay on ontology.*
4 See Baumeister, *Identity: cultural change and the struggle for self.*
5 Tallis, *Why the mind is not a computer: a pocket lexicon of neuromythology*; Tallis, *Aping mankind: neuromania, Darwinitis, and the misrepresentation of humanity.*
6 Cozolino, *The neuroscience of human relationships: attachment and the developing social brain* (2nd ed.), xiv – xv.
7 See Jaynes, *The origin of consciousness in the breakdown of the bicameral mind.*
8 Shanahan and Morgan, *Television and its viewers: cultivation theory and research.*
9 Turkle, *Reclaiming conversation: the power of talk in a digital age.*
10 See, for example Yurchisin et al., An exploration of identity re-creation in the context of internet dating.
11 See Davis, *Intimate relations*; Zelizer, *The purchase of intimacy.*
12 Wegner et al., Cognitive interdependence in close relationships.
13 Szymborska, *View with a grain of sand: selected poems.*
14 Prewitt, *What is your race? The census and our flawed efforts to classify Americans.*
15 Bem, Gender schema theory: a cognitive account of sex typing.
16 Gardinier, Priest told parishioners of plans for sex change.
17 Duncan, *Symbols in society*, 23.

64   Language, mind, and intimacy

18 Taylor, *The language animal: the full shape of the human linguistic capacity*.
19 Berger and Kellner, Marriage and the construction of reality: an exercise in the microsociology of knowledge.
20 Bernstein, Elaborated and restricted codes: their social origins and some consequences.
21 McCall et al., *Social relationships*, 16.
22 Ackerman, *One hundred names for love: a memoir*.
23 Taylor, *The ethics of authenticity*, 49.
24 Giddens, *The transformation of intimacy: sexuality, love & eroticism in modern societies*; Giddens, *Runaway world*.
25 Illouz, *Why love hurts: a sociological explanation*.
26 Klinenberg, *Going solo: the extraordinary rise and surprising appeal of living alone*.
27 Pew Forum on Social and Demographic Trends, *The decline of marriage and the rise of new families*.
28 Freitas, *The end of sex: how hookup culture is leaving a generation unhappy, sexually unfulfilled, and confused about intimacy*; but also see Monto and Carey, A new standard of sexual behavior? Are claims associated with the "Hookup Culture" supported by General Social Survey Data?
29 Kreider, Remarriage in the United States.
30 Schwartz, *The paradox of choice: why more is less*.
31 See Ansari and Klinenberg, *Modern romance*
32 Alwin, From obedience to autonomy: changes in traits desired in children, 1924–1978.
33 For example, Sato et al., Individual differences in ego depletion: the role of sociotropy-autonomy.
34 Becker, *The denial of death*.
35 Giddens, *The transformation of intimacy: sexuality, love & eroticism in modern societies*, 131.
36 Chodorow, Oedipal asymmetries and heterosexual knots; Chodorow, *The reproduction of mothering: psychoanalysis and the sociology of gender*.
37 Rubin, *Intimate strangers: men and women together*, 55.
38 Illouz, *Why love hurts: a sociological explanation*.
39 Berger and Kellner, Marriage and the construction of reality: an exercise in the microsociology of knowledge, 16.

Part 2

The origins of uncertainty

4 Through the rear-view mirror

> If we would diagnose our own age we had better do so historically, for history is the essence of human culture and thought.
>
> Robert Nisbet, *The Quest for Community: A Study in the Ethics of Order and Freedom*[1]

> We forget how quickly things that only yesterday seemed bizarre have become the norm today.
>
> Arlie Russell Hochschild, *The Outsourced Self: Intimate Life in Market Times*[2]

If you wanted to understand how the United States came to be settled as it was, it's worth consulting an atlas and taking in North America's geography. Major waterways such as the Connecticut, the Hudson, the Mohawk, the Susquehanna, and the Mississippi provided natural pathways for expansion, flowing people and goods into the interior of the country and to the west. It takes just a topographical map of the U.S. and a little historical imagination to see the population flows heading out from the Colonial coastal cities of Boston, New York, Philadelphia, Baltimore, and Charleston. The migration patterns were shaped by the river valleys and the waterways. Mountain ranges, such as the Rockies and the Adirondacks, had the opposite effect, blocking transit and commerce and isolating people on either side. You can clearly see these patterns in the seventeenth-century map of Northern America's settlements in Figure 4.1. Of course, different regions have different climates, are more or less favorable to the concentration of the population, and are better suited to different types of farming and industry. This affected how people lived in these areas.

The history of interpersonal life the United States can similarly be described with reference to significant features of the *social terrain* that had this type of prominence and impact. These features didn't flow people into geographic places; rather, they led them into particular patterns of consciousness, culture, and intimate behavior, and this affected how people thought of themselves and related to each other during different historical periods. But, unlike the country's physical terrain, the social terrain doesn't stay still for long. The structural conditions shaping the social and psychological circumstances of

DOI: 10.4324/9781003010234-6

68 The origins of uncertainty

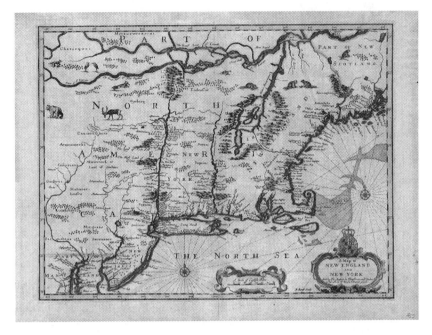

Figure 4.1 Patterns of Seventeenth-Century Settlement along Waterways
Source: Map image courtesy of the Norman B. Leventhal Map Center at the Boston Public Library.

the interpersonal world transform over time, sometimes quite quickly, and so, in America's history, the nature of social and psychological experience where people settled became distinctively different as times changed.

Table 4.1 lists ten areas of dramatic change in mainstream American society, operating since the Colonial period of the 1600s and 1700s, that each had far-reaching impacts on psycho-social experience. As these features have changed, interpersonal life changed too, quite profoundly, bringing many new freedoms and opportunities, but also new emotional and psychological challenges, and new difficulties in connecting with others. These great areas of change are grouped into three sections. The first, "disembedding processes," are factors of American culture that once more strongly attached the self-concept – ideas about personal identity – to external frameworks of belief. In the shift from the Colonial period to now, many formerly important external anchors of belief were largely eroded, leaving the self comparatively free of cultural-level sources of definition and requiring everyone to take care of the problem of establishing identity on their own and in coordination with the points of view of others within their circle of significant personal relationships. The second, "differentiating processes," are factors of change that have tended to heighten awareness of diversity and, consequently, of difference between self and other – differences not only in such external matters as race and ethnicity, but in outlook – in attitudes, beliefs, and values. Diversity

Through the rear-view mirror 69

Table 4.1 Areas of Change that Have Transformed Interpersonal Life

Colonial Period	Contemporary United States
Disembedding Processes: The Decline of Certainty and Truth	
Hierarchical society	Egalitarian society
Religious society	Secular society
Tradition-centered society	Individual-centered society
Local economy	Mass culture
Differentiating Processes: The Weakening of Community Ties	
Unicultural/consensual	Multicultural/pluralistic
Stationary population	Mobile population
Rural	Urban
Isolating Processes: The Atomization of Experience	
Intensely public	Intensely private
Linear information flows	Self-reflexive loops
Unified world & self-concept	Segmented world/fragmented self-concept

increases awareness that one's particular orientation to the world is distinct, that all belief is tentative, that there may be few overarching truths that are equally valid for everyone. The third, "isolating processes," are dimensions of change that have tended to create a sense not only that experience is uniquely segregated, but that, ultimately, one is responsible for finding one's own meaning in life.

Although it's important to keep in mind that there have been many variations in the American experience, depending on factors such as race, gender, ethnicity, sexual orientation, education, religion, and wealth, the ongoing influence of the processes in Table 4.1 have shaped the nature of interpersonal experience for most Americans today. The ten trends represent substantial directions of change in American society and, though they won't necessarily capture the experience of all people or of particular individuals, they're validly descriptive of American experience in the aggregate. Although no one would think it controversial to say that, in 1863, America was caught up in the Civil War, that wouldn't have been true of all Americans and, of those who were, it wouldn't have been true of everyone to the same degree; people's involvement might have taken many forms and would have varied by factors such as race, gender, ethnicity, education, and wealth. Still, we say without hesitation or thought of controversy that, in 1863, America was caught up in the Civil War. Our discussion of the changing circumstances of interpersonal life in American society is pitched at this level of abstraction. Unfortunately, this masks variation and glosses over some important exceptions, but the payoff is that it brings into focus trends of change that are broadly influential in the social-psychological experience of life in America now.

It is important to emphasize too that, while these trends do sometimes run on the surface in plain sight, often their consequences are more subtle and elusive, impacting beneath awareness. So, in consideration of the various ways in which some of the trends have tended to foster existential anxiety, you should

70   *The origins of uncertainty*

not imagine that I'm proposing that America's cities are now teeming with incapacitated Edvard Munch *Scream* people, but rather that America has come under the influence of a general but diffuse current of restlessness, an unrecognized tendency toward social disengagement, and a subtly deepening and more automatic distrust of others and institutions (yet, recall that prescriptions for the anti-anxiety drug Xanax are currently being written at a rate of one every second). While social scientists see these trends in their data, at the personal level, this anxiety may be suppressed or sublimated, misidentified as a consequence of an individual personality deficit rather than a common trend in the culture, and so on, and, therefore, generally unrecognized for what it is. Be this as it may, the fact is we're now living in a period in which anxiety and depression are being diagnosed and medicated at epidemic levels in modern societies. It's important to keep in mind that, like climate change, the shifting currents of interpersonal life often become manifest so gradually that they escape notice. And so, the trends may be hard to reconcile with our own experience, except, perhaps, when looking back over long periods or when looking across our extended family network, or the range of people we work with, and noting the typical distribution of human suffering that occurs in the membership of most people's social networks (substance addiction, divorce, interpersonal disorders – the narcissistic, the inexplicably shy, the overly controlling and manipulative – disrupted employment, clinical depression, and so on).

Godfrey Reggio's visually innovative film *Koyaanisqatsi* examined modern city life by switching between time-lapse and slow-speed photography. The time-lapse sequences dramatically expose the extensive degree to which modern urban experience involves lockstep patterns of behavior so vivid that they call free will into question. Though, like everyone else, we mindlessly participate in these patterns, normally we don't do so from a vantage that allows this to be noticed. On the other side, the slow-motion sequences of *Koyaanisqatsi* permit the viewer to hover at length over a few seconds in a person's face. This technique dramatically exposes emotional and spiritual impacts of urban life that are otherwise too fleeting to register in awareness. Like this, this book zooms in and out between sociological and psychological levels to much the same purpose, but, because we don't experience our own lives at high speed or in slow motion, this may mean that we have an easier time seeing the effects of modernity in others than in ourselves.

Finally, it's important to understand that these ten great dimensions of change aren't independent of each other but are mutually influential. The shift in modern societies from being strongly religious to predominantly secular overlaps substantially the abandonment of tradition. The shift from public to private overlaps the shift from a rural/stationary to an urban/mobile population. And so on. In fact, all of the processes listed in Table 4.1 have tended to overlap and synergistically fuel each other. And, vitally, they've all been important in changing the manner in which people in modern societies develop their sense of personal identity: from a process in which the self was largely derived from external sources and relatively fixed for life, to one in which self-definition is

Through the rear-view mirror   71

now a matter of personal priority and ambition, addressed internally and in discourse in interpersonal relationships, more or less constantly challenged and in flux, and in need of active support from friends and intimates – a high-stakes process in which there is no finish line and no guarantee of success.

Table 4.1's dimensions aren't an exhaustive list of modernity's features. For example, increases in globalization, reliance on systems so abstract and technically dense that most people don't have the expertise to understand them (e.g., electronic banking, global air traffic control, medical technology), the growth of a surveillance society (where the daily behavior of Americans is tracked by the NSA; by E-ZPass; by Facebook; by Google, Yahoo, and Microsoft; and by an ever-growing web of security and traffic cameras),[3] and the management of new types of risk that accompany modernity (e.g., world financial collapse, the pandemic spread of disease, global warming) are prominent among other factors receiving a great deal of attention. However, the ten areas in Table 4.1 define our focus because they've been of particular importance in reducing the stability of meaning, undermining certainty and the taken-for-granted, and repurposing the nature of personal identity and the function of discourse in interpersonal life.

Communication and courtship in Colonial America

Direct evidence of interpersonal practices in Colonial America is not available. There are no records of everyday conversation, and there were no researchers on hand studying the psychology and social practices of the times. Some colonists left diaries, but writers weren't concerned with recording their thoughts and experiences about discourse in their social relationships. Still, enough is known about the day-to-day lives of settlers in America in the 1600s and 1700s to render an informed sketch from which it's possible to make some reasonable deductions about the nature of daily interaction between these people in their significant personal relationships. This is a useful exercise because it helps establish the magnitude, range, and nature of changes that have occurred since those times and the impacts that these changes have had on the social-psychological situation of our day.

So, let's imagine a young man living from the mid-1600s to 1700 in Northampton, Massachusetts, a town located about midway in the Pioneer Valley of western Massachusetts, which extends along the Connecticut River between Springfield in the south and Deerfield, 35 miles north. Most likely our young man spent his days on the family's agricultural plots growing crops and tending livestock for the family's own sustenance and trade with others. For nearly the first 200 years of American history, only 1 person in 20 lived in a town of more than 2,500 people.[4] As of 1790, there were only 24 towns in the United States of that size.[5] At its founding, Northampton's population numbered fewer than 100 and, like populations of other settlements of the era, it was relatively immobile.[6] In Colonial America, "few sons moved farther than 16 miles from their paternal home during their father's lifetime."[7] Thus,

72   *The origins of uncertainty*

many people lived in sparsely settled rural areas and were likely to stay there, embedded in stable social relationships comprising neighbors and the members of their family of origin.

Northampton was settled in 1654 by deeply committed religious exiles, and so it's reasonable to assume our young man and a majority of the other settlers living in the area around him were oriented to more or less the same religious ideas. Though disputes over church doctrine occasionally led to social division and splintering within the colonies, and over time people's interest in religion waxed and waned, it's likely that most of the European settlers in Massachusetts in the mid-1600s were similarly oriented to core Christian beliefs. Most settlers in Massachusetts could also read and write and had much the same educational background. Imagine that our Northamptonite has decided to try to locate a woman to marry. Leaving aside the possibility that the goal for marriage for someone at that time was not as much for companionship as to obtain the economic wherewithal to establish oneself as an adult,[8] and leaving aside as well the possibility that a marriage might be brokered by parents for their children, by today's standards, our young man's options for a marital partner were drastically restricted; in fact, it's likely that he had no meaningful choice at all.

The range of potential partners he could conveniently seek out for consideration was limited to those within reasonable walking distance – that is, those within about a 5-mile radius. Even allowing for travel by horse, the range of potential partners was not greatly expanded. Thus, the practical options for a marital partner likely consisted of a tiny number of nearby women, virtually all of whom could be assumed to have lived their entire lives under much the same circumstances and educational influences, with the same core values and political and spiritual beliefs, more or less the same material wealth, and all with a common understanding of who they were and what type of future they might expect (which, because social and technological change was then almost too slow to notice, was much like the present they were then inhabiting). Mate selection in these circumstances was possibly a little like the restaurant in the Monty Python sketch in which one can order a wide variety of meals, but they're all made with spam.

The formation of marriages was made somewhat easier by the fact that the institution wasn't principally based on expectations of affection or of a partnership of friends (these could come later), but was often more like forming a unit for work. Today, it is common to speak of the search for a soulmate, but, in former times, colonists found it sensible to speak of the search for a "yokemate" (yoked to your spouse like oxen connected together to pull a plow – note that we still speak of people getting "hitched"). According to Morgan, for the Puritans it wasn't uncommon for a man's decision to marry to be made without thought of a particular woman.[9] The man desired to acquire a woman to occupy a helpful role with the expectation that affection might come later. Arthur Calhoun's history of early American family life has been challenged over its sources, but he reported that it was not uncommon that, "a lonely

Through the rear-view mirror 73

Puritan came to the door of a maiden he had never seen before, presented credentials, told his need of a housekeeper, proposed marriage, obtained hasty consent, and notified the town clerk, all in one day."[10] (If you think this sounds far-fetched, consider the problem of making sense of speed dating or the Tinder app for a seventeenth-century settler.) The determination of the suitability of a marriage often involved bargaining between parents over financial aspects of the union, and frequently a match was impossible without parental consent. Of the 13 colonies, 8 had laws requiring parental approval for marriage, and, even among those that didn't, few children risked marrying without parental approval because the social and economic consequences could be severe or even ruinous.[11]

More generally, the mate selection process occurred within highly enmeshed frameworks of kin relationships and community. The period of courting was not, as it is now, a time of discovering and appreciating unique selves and particular outlooks on the world and morality and beginning to build a distinctive couple culture, but rather one of gauging the degree to which the male suitor's attitudes and behavior were aligned with the values and standards of the community group that the woman represented.[12] A little later in American history, in his mid-nineteenth century courtship of Olivia Langdon, Samuel Clemens (Mark Twain) was required by his future wife's family to submit letters of reference for their evaluation, as though he was applying for a job. The courtship period was not yet a time of long talk in which the couple began to weave a private, transformative culture and shared morality (the possibility of which, as we've seen, has become a hallmark of the emerging egalitarian relationships of our era), but rather focused on establishing that the suitor's values were consistent with and reaffirmed those of the surrounding community. Those seeking mates did not, as now, view the problem of couple formation as one of sifting cautiously through an ocean of candidate partners, but rather, they exercised a "pragmatic rationality," settling for "the *first available* satisfactory *good-enough* marriage prospect."[13] With the grounds for marital choice external to the prospective couple, embedded in the social systems in which they were situated, it's likely that premarital discourse was different in nature and function than it is now and, without doubt, far less important than it has come to be.

Panning forward to our time, imagine a similarly aged man living in Queens, New York, who commutes to Manhattan to his job in a media company. Surrounding him, within a 5-mile radius, are thousands of available age-appropriate candidates, and indeed there's an almost limitless set of additional possibilities available through social sites and dating services on the internet. Leaving aside the difficulty created in committing to any particular selection when a decision is highly important and the barrel of options is almost bottomless,[14] such an abundance of potential partners might seem to offer considerable advantage – indeed, a luxury of choice. However, members of this population are likely to have highly variable backgrounds and levels of education, diverse ethnic origins, a wide-ranging set of points of view and

74 The origins of uncertainty

commitments as regards religion, varying political ideas, unpredictable social and personal interests, and a significant array of possible visions of themselves and their desired future, driven by their own imaginations, media experiences, education, family, encounters with others, and so on, rather than by shared community standards or traditional knowledge.

It has to be anticipated that any possible partner today might have already moved sufficiently within the country or the world to leave a trail of geographically and culturally dispersed involvements and may at any time need to relocate within the U.S. or abroad for work or education. And, to add to the burdens that all these factors introduce in appreciating how each potential partner might affect one's own future, our contemporary world has been almost completely drained of potent cultural-level customs, traditions, and rituals that, in former times, increased predictability about people's values and how they were likely to live. According to a recent *New York Times* analysis, growing up in America's denser urban areas can reduce the chance of marrying by age 26 by as much as 12 percentage points (see Figure 4.2).[15] Diversity and abundance make choice more difficult.

Whereas the majority of Americans once lived in small communities where anonymity and privacy were rare to absent, today, most Americans live in relatively dense urban areas, where anonymity, privacy, and diversity permit – indeed, even encourage – the adoption of eccentric points of view, interests, and values. In the Colonial period, Americans' lives were enmeshed in community with their neighbors. On the one hand, this tended to limit the sort of self one could construct; on the other, it minimized uncertainty about each other's character, beliefs, and values. In contrast to this, in modern city life, we

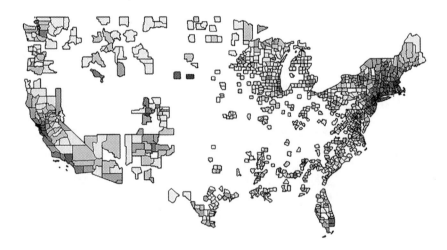

Figure 4.2 Modernity, Urbanization, and Intimacy: Counties where Marriage Tends to be Delayed (darker shading = greater delay).

Source: Map based on data from Chetty and Hendren.[16]

Through the rear-view mirror 75

never really know what the people around us believe or value, are capable of, or are likely to do. And so, the reduction of uncertainty has become an active issue in modern interpersonal encounters.

As sociologists George McCall and J. L. Simmons noted, when two people encounter each other for the first time, they "face the problem of identification in its purest and most agonizing form. Who is the other person? Who am I in this situation? Who *could* I be? What do I *want* to be? Who does *he* want me to be?"[17] And, in the digital age, with a growing number of relationships conducted online, where self-presentation may be heavily edited and separated from any verifiable real-world presence, the range of possibilities for self-presentation has become hyperinflated,[18] and so has the problem of authentication ("What is the likelihood that this person actually will turn out to be who she represents herself to be?"). This is so of the age we live in, but it was ever less the case as we retreat into historical America, where problems of personal identity and authenticity that loom large today were far less relevant.

Thus, unlike his Colonial-era counterpart from Massachusetts, a young New Yorker lives in a world in which "trust is not pre-given but worked upon" and is confronted with a problem of partner selection that requires a great deal of time, energy, and, most of all, interpersonal sophistication to address. The skills required include the ability to attract and engage people of unknown character, diverse background, and unpredictable beliefs in conversation targeted toward discovery and verification of who that person claims to be, while at the same time engaging in a tentative and gradual disclosure of progressively less superficial and more intimate information about one's own self, testing for the possibility that this partnership might form the basis for constructing a meaningful, conjoint understanding of the world. This work of trust is performed as "a mutual process of self-disclosure."[19]

As partners get to know each other, the slow dance of self-revelation performs the function of testing for mutual interest and affection in small, safe increments. As they talk, they screen each other for authenticity and for compatibility of beliefs, values, interests, and character, sustaining the possibility of freezing their depth of intimacy or abandoning ongoing contact. Success in this process requires a degree of flexibility in self-conception and an openness to influence. To the extent that they see a future for their relationship, they may adapt their self-stories for each other, emphasizing points of similarity and downplaying or avoiding points of difference, eventually, perhaps, yielding to their partner's subtle invitations to view self a little differently than they had: suggesting that they have potential that they hadn't before imagined, perhaps that they are more attractive than they had thought, wittier, or more noble. In this way, self-identity isn't fixed, but over time is expressed at least a little differently within each important social relationship.

This slow process of incremental, self-disclosing communication represents an adaptation to life in modern times. It would not have operated in Colonial America (or any other similar historical context) where, by today's standards, the individual was a member of a comparatively tiny community of similarly

76 *The origins of uncertainty*

minded people with little variation in their beliefs and backgrounds and with self-concepts not created reflexively and in cooperation with members of their network of close personal relationships, but strongly related to the beliefs and values of the external community, to tradition, to one's relatively invariant position in an accepted social order, and to religious precepts.

Of the language of courtship in the distant past, Richard Sennett, who believed that there was a significant difference in the nature and functions of talk in intimate relationships in former times, wrote:

> the idea that a lover must find a unique language for talking about his feelings for a particular woman, a language of love specific to two particular people, was . . . unknown. The phrases carried from one affair to the next to the next.[20]

Indeed, the conversations of husbands and wives in eighteenth-century Spain were conventionalized to such an extent that no personal meaning may have *ever* been exchanged between them.[21] Sennett argued that our modern view, that interpersonal discourse functions to unite the private perspectives of intimates in shared symbols of negotiated meaning, was not descriptive of intimate discourse in the past. In prior eras, the process of communication in intimacy was more like an exchange of signals between individuals whose sense of self was fixed by their gender and social position than what it is now, a process of negotiating a shared understanding of each other and the larger world.

Social interaction in former times was to a greater degree constrained by rules of form that, more often than now, served to signify the relative social status of participants.[22] The optional features that distinguished a superior conversation from a lesser one were rather like the sophisticated structures and embellishments that comprised the tool kit of composers and musicians of the Baroque era of the seventeenth to mid-eighteenth centuries: for composers, the fugue form, the sonata and concerto forms, the dance forms, and, for performers, the trill, the turn, the mordant, the appoggiatura, and so on. Individual musicians demonstrated their excellence in their facility to apply these standardized embellishments within the set of formal musical structures. Composers such as Johann Sebastian Bach, Georg Telemann, and Johann Quantz rarely notated their scores with these embellishments; it was understood that the performer would add them according to personal discretion. An accomplished organist or cellist might play ad lib from an incomplete bass part written in a form known as "figured bass," in which a score contained not a fully articulated part but a series of single notes annotated with numbers that suggested the intended type of harmony to the performer, who then improvised within the confines of the musical form. Thus, as in expressive forms of music of the seventeenth and eighteenth centuries, to have a conversation was not today's free exploration of personal meaning as much as a social exercise in which people showed their understanding of sophisticated social rules and their facility at rhetorical methods of constructing arguments and embellishing speech. Conversation was not

Through the rear-view mirror 77

as personal, as full of subjective meaning, as it is now. More than now, it was an exercise of rule-governed performance.

In music, many delight in the preservation of the externally structured, complex, rule-bound practices of former periods; however, outside of courtrooms and college forensics teams and debating clubs, this manner of verbal conversation has largely been rendered obsolete in the social-psychological transformations of modernity. This is not to say that conversation in our time is absent of structure and predictable, rule-like sequences ("Hi, how are you?" – "Fine. And yourself?"; "Love you!" – "Love you too!"), but to note the passing from an era in which expression was more likely to be engaged as an exercise in form. In dance, this might be analogous to the shift from the era of the minuet, the rondo, and the passepied to today's free-form style of the nightclub dance floor. The change from language-as-signal-constrained-by-structure to more free-form language-as-private-symbol is a critical factor that has influenced the psycho-emotional and social dynamics of interpersonal life and is a consequence of the set of changes in society that we'll discuss below. For now, it's important to point out, in this exercise of comparing the circumstances of the present with those of the past, that these timeline differences are not just a matter of structural changes in society: in the distant past, the social and psychological circumstances of life, and the functions of communication, were so profoundly different than today that it's almost impossible to imagine successfully transplanting people from one age to the other. Hollywood does a major disservice by producing historical dramas populated by people who dress in different costume, but appear to reason, speak, and experience in the same manner as modern Americans. Viewers are often quick to notice anachronisms of technology, but fail to appreciate glaring anachronisms of psychology, consciousness, and interpersonal life, errors that foster the impression that psychological and interpersonal experience is now as it has always been. Nothing could be further from the truth.

Modern theories of intimacy don't work in historical times

In his work on French cultural history, Robert Darnton cautions about how easy it is to assume that, centuries ago, people thought and felt just as we do today, warning that, "We constantly need to be shaken out of a false sense of familiarity with the past, to be administered doses of culture shock."[23] Of course, as we have seen, at its core, all thought is social, and so to say that people thought differently in the past is also to say that they related to each other differently. And so, the further back one looks, the less likely it is that the psychological principles that figure in today's social relationships were present.

It's a commonplace in the modern literature of the psychology of intimate relationships that partner happiness and relationship stability are a function of two dimensions. First is the extent to which the relationship provides rewards at a level consistent with desire. In Thibaut and Kelley's social exchange theory, this factor is called the "comparison level." Second, there's the extent to

78   *The origins of uncertainty*

which the social milieu appears to provide possibilities for reward in alternative intimate relationships. This is referred to as the "comparison level for alternatives."[24] Thus, in our era, social science teaches that a relationship is happy and stable when partners feel rewarded beyond their expectations and there are no perceived alternative relationships from which greater reward might be obtained. This conceptualization has achieved status as an established standard in theorizing about intimacy and has been taught to generations of university students.

For our purposes, it's instructive to consider these ideas historically. To begin with, the context of comparison has certainly changed. Today, the mass media surround Americans with models of unrealistic perfection in virtually every dimension: physical appearance, economic success, athletic prowess, musical talent, romantic appeal, graceful aging, and so on. So, it's possible to speculate that our internal standard for comparison has been on the increase since the beginning of media saturation in the early twentieth century (and, as sociologist Eva Illouz argues, the advent of the cosmetics industry and its promotion of a cult of physical perfection and sexiness).[25] Why settle for less when one appears to live in a world of abundant flawlessness? Why settle for a partner who appears to have a jouncy one-pack when the media suggest we're surrounded by crunch-crazy sexy people with chiseled six-packs?

Added to this, as we've seen, urbanization and the internet have substantially increased real and perceived access to alternative partners. These factors not only destabilize existing relationships but likely keep many from committing in the first place. The media promote the impression that Americans live in a kind of boundless gourmet food court, and, in a period of history that accepts nibbling between meals, non-committed grazing is rational. With urbanization and internet dating, the arena of selection has become impossibly large, governed by a logic of rational choice that may make it seem like an error of judgment to commit to any normally flawed person, as thousands upon thousands of other candidates are immediately at hand.[26] Tellingly, it's our era that's seen the rise of a popular advice literature admonishing women and men to stop holding out for perfection and settle for whomever is at hand, exemplified by the columnist Lori Gottlieb's *New York Times* bestseller, *Marry Him: The Case for Settling for Mr. Good Enough.*[27] But this may be a hard sell in an age of individualism and increasing isolation, when four in ten Americans believe that the institution of marriage is becoming obsolete,[28] and, reflecting this, the proportion of never-married Americans has been on the rise, now reaching a record 20 percent of the adult population.[29]

But it's not just that these contextual factors have changed. Though they are important, it isn't only a matter of urbanization and the media. As Sennett asserted, there is a particular social psychology rooted in American capitalism, and the modes of perception and judgment that capitalism encourages were likely not functioning during America's pre-capitalist, rural agrarian Colonial period. In other words, our modern idea of intimate attraction being based on

Through the rear-view mirror   79

the framework of an economic cost – benefit analysis may not represent the psychology of earlier periods of American life.

The roots of our present exchange-based orientation can be traced to nineteenth- and early twentieth-century industrialization, which occurred on a massive scale, generating intensive interest in maximizing output in the factory. Resulting from this was the recognition that the management of human emotional relationships in the workplace (parties take a neutral stance toward each other, control their emotional expression, make good eye contact, listen carefully, acknowledge each other's points of view, etc.) enhanced productivity. This encouraged a gradual understanding of the self as an object: manipulable, and even fungible (searching for workers with "excellent communication skills" is common in job advertisements).[30] In the same way that an actress may trade on her skill at portraying particular personality types and characters, so in America's service economy people trade on their skill at human relations, and, by gradual extension, intimate partners have come to trade on their relationship skills, seeing making-a-successful-marriage as a kind of labor,[31] the success of which requires interpersonal skillfulness similar to that employed by therapists, counselors, and other human relations specialists.

Historian Beth Bailey analyzed American courtship norms and practices between 1920 and 1965 and is worth quoting on this subject:

> As it emerged in the twentieth century, courtship largely was constituted and understood in models and metaphors of modern industrial capitalism. The new system of courtship privileged competition (and worried about how to control it); it valued consumption; it presented an economic model of scarcity and abundance as a guide to personal affairs. The rules of the market were consciously applied; the vocabulary of economic exchange defined the acts of courtship.[32]

For Western capitalist societies, the mid-twentieth century marked a shift from a production orientation to a consumer orientation, and that shift *within* American capitalism has further influenced how we orient to our social relationships, casting them along consumer lines – tracked in terms of a continuous cost – benefit assessment, but also disposable and valued in terms of stylishness and novelty, and so on.[33] The internet's smorgasbord of online dating sites, one of the most profitable areas of internet enterprise, represents the ultimate expression of this.[34] And profitable these sites should be, as their existence adds a significant boost to the number of people who *don't* commit but rather keep searching endlessly for partners. For every marriage Match.com, OkCupid, and EHarmony claim to have facilitated, the existence of their boundless catalogs of possibility has likely kept dozens of others continually filtering, fantasizing, and rejecting each other.

When we examine the situation of intimate relationships in early Colonial America, Thibaut and Kelley's exchange theory appears out of place, a better fit to modern America where, by the late twentieth century, the economic

80   *The origins of uncertainty*

and bureaucratic world had become the dominant model for personal life, and where decision making in the interpersonal realm may more likely be driven by minds used to thinking of the world through the lens of marketplace considerations of gain and loss.[35] Indeed, even the norm of reciprocity (I reward you, and you reciprocate by doing something rewarding for me; I disclose to you at some level of depth and breadth, and you disclose back to me at the same level; etc.), a conceptual keystone of the social psychology of interpersonal life, was not in play in the heterosexual love relationships in the nineteenth century and earlier. In European courtly love, to give all for love without requirement of return – the abandonment and dissolution of self in the worship of the other – was the ideal experience, but one that might land you in a psychiatrist's office today.[36] In Colonial America, and for those groups in our time that have resisted the influences of modernity, such as the Old Order Amish, our modern economic method of reasoning about our intimate lives would likely be bewildering.

It's a similar case for other twentieth- and twenty-first-century theories that address the psychological dynamics of intimacy. Like exchange theory, Walster, Walster, and Berscheid's equity theory postulates that relationship satisfaction is a matter of economic assessment: a function of perceived justice in the distribution of relationship rewards and costs.[37] The "bank account model" conceptualizes positive and negative relationship outcomes as though they were transactions in a financial institution.[38] The "investment model"[39] views intimate dependence in terms of assessments of rewarding and costly outcomes in a couple's interaction. Resource theory[40] grounds attraction and commitment in the "commodities" partners bring to the relationship. Altman and Taylor's social penetration theory is grounded in the norm of reciprocity and assumes a degree of personal privacy and of hidden aspects of self, and of wariness and distrust in others that were not as characteristic of life in the 1700s and earlier as they are now.[41] Attachment theory, as applied to adult romantic relationships,[42] rests in assumptions about the psycho-social dynamics of childhood that are fixed in the historically specific practices of childcare in modern Western societies. Yet modernity brought with it a substantial extension of the period of childhood (now, in many cases, more than two decades) and, moreover, change in the very idea of what having a child (or being a child) is all about.

Children were once welcomed for their ability to enter the family's agrarian workforce, kept at arms' length emotionally until it was clear they were likely to survive diseases of childhood, and then ushered into productive labor as quickly as possible.[43] The child passed from infancy to young adulthood with almost nothing in between,[44] as reflected in family portraiture of the Colonial period. The portrait of the Grymes children in Figure 4.3 provides a good example of the common tendency to portray children with little physical differentiation from adults. In sharp contrast, today, for many Americans, the child is a unique "object of emotional consumption," brought into the world for the pleasures of the heart that define the new function of modern family life: not as

Figure 4.3 The Grymes Children: Lucy, John, Philip, and Charles.
Source: Attributed to John Hesselius, Virginia, 1750. Courtesy of the Virginia Historical Society.

a site of team-based production, but rather as an emotional and psychological haven. For others, the child is an accessory of the self, brought into the world in a desperate effort by the parent(s) to secure their own identity and achieve a sense of personal purpose. This is such a radical change that it's worth considering the possibility that attachment theory too describes dynamics unique to our particular historical circumstances.

If a twenty-first-century young urban American were somehow beamed to Northampton, Massachusetts, in the 1650s, he would not lose his churning troubles of self-definition; his sense of anxiety about the precarious nature of economic life, in which either a wrong move or bad luck can lead to a drastic drop in socio-economic status and disruption in self-identity; his caution about the authenticity of the people around him; his suspicion that all truths for living are relative and tentative; his twenty-first-century valuation of self and others in terms of standards of sexiness and physical perfection; his tendency to seek affection, personal meaning, and emotional expression in his personal relationships; or his desire for privacy and autonomy. But the people around him

82   *The origins of uncertainty*

wouldn't share these characteristics or understand them. The changes in social practices and patterns of consciousness that have occurred in America during its history have, until recently, come on gradually and often without notice or comment, but their cumulative effect has been momentous.

Modern American children may sometimes perform in a school's Thanksgiving play imagining themselves as colonists, anticipating differences in technologies and costume. However, the extent of change is vastly greater and includes fundamental differences in consciousness of self and intimacy and their relationship to communication practices. It is not simply a matter of swapping a diesel tractor for a horse and plow, or a baseball cap for a Pilgrim hat. People from early and contemporary America would find each other's consciousness incomprehensible. It's worth underscoring the possibility raised by Sennett that language itself worked differently in the past than it does today. When a twenty-first-century American speaks, it's with the implicit understanding that she represents the point of view of an isolated individual in a world of relative knowledge, a world teeming with alternative perspectives. When a seventeenth-century American spoke, it was to reference some item of information within a world of manifest truth, the majority of which could be assumed to be shared by the people of the surrounding community, or at least of one's own social position. Naturally, there would have been differences of opinion, creativity of expression, divergent loyalties, interests in varying doctrine, and so on. The people of the era were not clones, even if, by our standards, their lives were similar. However, it's important for our purpose to appreciate the extensive degree to which diversity of thought, behavior, and experience has increased. This has fundamentally altered the function of discourse in interpersonal life. The more people's bases of experience and knowledge are similar, the more talk tends to be expositional rather than exploratory, informational rather than transformational, and the more it functions as a means of coordinating activity rather than as a method of creating social bonds and private culture. In other words, discourse in earlier periods tended to resemble more a system of signal transmission than our modern process of symbolic bonding.

Communication and partner equality in heterosexual marriage

And now, returning to our exercise, what of a young woman in Colonial Massachusetts as compared with a young woman from twenty-first-century New York City? Colonial marriage was not a question of affectionate collaboration between equals. The legal status of a married woman in Colonial Massachusetts was bound by the principle of "coverture," which meant that, upon marriage, a woman essentially lost all independent standing in the courts. Her identity was "covered" by her husband.[45] According to historian Edmund Moran,

> The proper conduct of a [Puritan] wife was submission to her husband's instructions and commands. He was her superior . . . and she owed him an

Through the rear-view mirror 83

obedience founded on reverence. He stood before her in the place of God; he exercised the authority of God over her.[46]

For all intents and purposes, in the eyes of the law, on marriage a woman became her husband's property, unable to sign contracts, pursue an education, start a business, or own property independently. Colonial society was, thus, patriarchal. Puritan religion imagined a "great chain of being" in which God's authority was administered through male church leaders to male heads of household and, through them, down the chain of authority to their children and wives.[47] Indeed, not only were women of lesser standing in the eyes of the law and the church, there's evidence that they were regarded as psychologically and intellectually inferior beings. The diary of John Winthrop, governor of the Colony of Massachusetts, mentions the case of a colonial woman thought to have gone insane as a result of overwhelming her inferior female mind with too much reading and writing.[48]

As we'll see in the next chapter, the social standing of women improved gradually, although through a route with some twists and turns that are important to understand. Tracing historical change in the relative legal and social standing of women and men is essential for understanding the dynamics of intimate communication today. As we've seen, the way that communication holds modern relationships together is through participants' mutual creation of a private culture – a fabric of shared understanding and interdependent meaning that may impart a sense of purpose, defines us to ourselves and to each other, and binds us in shared beliefs and moral precepts. This can only occur between partners who regard each other as intellectual and moral equals and as friends, conditions not as likely to be satisfied in heterosexual relationships in mainstream American society until recent years. Note that this book's epigraph, a poem from 1667 attesting to the author Katherine Philips's deep symbolic interdependence ("We have each other so engrost, That each is in the union lost"), is addressed to another woman, not to a man.

Writing of marital couples in the 1970s, sociologist Lillian Rubin noted the common experience of solitary co-habitation between working-class husbands and wives, whose time together at home was typically isolated from each other and "filled with silence."[49] This was all the harder for some couples at that time who were becoming aware of new, egalitarian models of relating and new possibilities and requirements for communication in intimacy, but had not succeeded in establishing that type of companionate connection in their lives together. The famous "Middletown" studies of family life in the twentieth century in Muncie, Indiana, revealed that, just 100 years ago, in many cases discourse between husbands and wives was not a process of friends building meaning together, but was instead mostly functional, a restricted matter of aligning activities rather than creating shared beliefs and values or forging and then shoring up each other's self-concepts. Communication was used primarily for coordinating activities of the household.

84 *The origins of uncertainty*

Rather than engage in activities together, the 1920s Middletown husbands and wives tended to participate in separate social and recreational pursuits. And, as for the time those couples spent at home,

> [it] does not appear to have been filled with pleasant or stimulating conversation. Decisions about the children, the house payment, and the food budget were quickly dealt with in a bickering fashion, and, with those problems disposed of, couples often lapsed into apathetic silence.

Further,

> the limited communication between husbands and wives and the trivial nature of their conversation left many of them isolated in their separate worlds, his pertaining to work and friends and hers to the children and the home. In many marriages, they shared a house, each other's bodies and little else.[50]

Writing of couples in the nineteenth century, historian John Gillis described the domestic lives of American husbands and wives as strongly separated, hardly the lives of friends and partners: "The lives of middle-class husbands and wives were quite unconjugal. Men's lives . . . revolve[d] around an exclusively male world of work and leisure. In their careers, they rarely encountered women except as subordinates."[51] So, while there may have been affection and cooperative partnership between spouses in earlier times, it hasn't been until recently that the survival of marriage has come to depend on partners functioning for each other as co-equal friends – co-constructors and sustainers of each other's self-identity, beliefs, and values.

Co-equal is important because equality is a precondition for the kinds of mutual influence and communal support of self-identity that are at the heart of interpersonal intimacy. Sociologist Jessie Bernard noted long ago that the shift in marriage from paternalism to a fully companionate model required spouses to regard each other as equals.[52] And this equality has to be the genuine item, not just the mouthing of an egalitarian ideology. There's a kind of friendship we can have with pets or children or those who work for us, and it may be so deeply affectionate that you might regard the promotion of your child's, or your subordinate's, or your pet's well-being as even more important than your own. Positive emotional bonds like this may, in fact, be easier to build and preserve under conditions of social inequality.[53] YumYum the cat is much more easily an object of constant and committed love than is the spouse of equal standing to you whose views and preferences have to be integrated with your own and whose elaborations of meaning will inevitably influence yours. However, socially unequal relationships can't supply the kind of friendship in which we become profoundly bonded in an *interdependent* construction of the world and each other's sense of self, because one partner's contributions will not be as influential. Mutual influence – even mutual comprehension – is

Through the rear-view mirror 85

virtually impossible between occupants of different status positions in a social hierarchy.[54]

Though the shared mind that results from intimate discourse has become a primary bond, there have always been other types of social bonds. Among these are attachment, which some believe occurs as a result of habituation and familiarity and in infants may have a genetic basis; identification, which occurs when you see someone else as an ideal; and, of course, kinship. As well, in former times, restrictive divorce laws kept marriages intact, as did the proscriptions against divorce of some religions. Marriages were also tied together economically in a variety of ways that are now obsolete, or nearly so. A Gallup poll from 1936 revealed that fully 82 percent of Americans then believed that a wife shouldn't work outside the home if her husband had a job,[55] and such employment prospects as existed for women in the mid-twentieth century were grossly unequal.[56] Until recently, owing to gender discrimination in hiring and education and the closed-door employment policies of some professions, women were often unable to leave a marriage without facing economic calamity. Looking further back, marriage has sometimes functioned as well as a means of creating economic advantage in the alliance of two extended families, which may create strong family pressures on couples to stay together.

Discourse isn't central or necessary to the operation of any of these bonds and, in some cases, it may be completely absent (your kin are your kin, and you're bound to them legally in various ways regardless of whether you have any contact). Yet, as we'll see, as America has evolved, bonds based in law, religion, and economic dependence have dropped away. At the same time, as gender equality has increased, the shared culture that may now be created in heterosexual intimate discourse can step up and function as a primary bonding factor in high-quality relationships. But here there's difficulty because, among the factors that sometimes tie people to each other, bonds created between close intimates in their discourse are relatively fragile, susceptible to erosion in the fast and shifting currents of modern culture.

These bonds are also unique in the degree to which they are based in a voluntary process that requires psychological and social sophistication. The necessary skills include a capacity for empathy, for seeing self and the world as seen by one's partner; for negotiation, which requires an openness to being influenced and the ability to place the needs of your partner on the same plane of priority as your own; for mental flexibility, so that you can allow your views to shift to accommodate your partner; and for delaying personal gratification so that outcomes for your partner may be pursued with the same degree of priority as outcomes for yourself. This is a heavy load, particularly in the circumstances of modernity that make an ongoing life problem out of self-identity, which, as we've seen, fosters anxiety, self-focus, and narcissism and suppresses empathy. And there's growing concern that all this may be made worse by new communication technologies that tend to disrupt good dialogical contact between intimates.[57] Here, then, may lie a major portion of the explanation

86 *The origins of uncertainty*

for the precarious state of intimate relationships in America, which, as noted, is now the world leader in the rate of relationship turnover.[58]

The next chapter begins detailed exploration of the large trends listed in Table 4.1, trends that, in their collective impact, changed the world from one of shared belief and stable meaning to an ever-more anxious one in which meaning has become so uncertain and unstable that it has disrupted the basis for common sense (beliefs shared so widely that, while they prefigure the given world, they fade from awareness). This has elevated the importance of discourse in interpersonal experience, making relationships far more important and more deeply intimate. And so, now we will begin to explore the changes brought on by modernity that so altered the nature of social and mental experience as to open the door to existential crisis.

Notes

1 Nisbet, *The quest for community: a study in the ethics of order and freedom*, 71.
2 Hochschild, *The outsourced self: intimate life in market times*, 225.
3 See Turkle, *Reclaiming conversation: the power of talk in a digital age.*
4 Larkin, *The reshaping of everyday life 1790–1840.*
5 Bushman, Family security in the transition from farm to city, 1750–1850.
6 Mank, Family structure in Northampton, Massachusetts, 1654–1729.
7 Mintz and Kellogg, *Domestic revolutions: a social history of American family life*, 16.
8 Main, *Peoples of a spacious land: families and cultures in colonial New England.*
9 Morgan, *The Puritan family: religion and domestic relations in seventeenth century New England.*
10 Calhoun, *A social history of the American family from colonial times to the present: Volume 1 colonial period*, 57.
11 Coontz, *Marriage, a history: how love conquered marriage.*
12 See Illouz, *Why love hurts: a sociological explanation.*
13 Illouz, *Why love hurts: a sociological explanation*, 178 (original emphasis).
14 See Illouz, *Why love hurts: a sociological explanation*; Schwartz, *The paradox of choice: why more is less.*
15 Leonhardt and Quealy, How your hometown affects your chances of marriage.
16 Chetty and Hendren, The impacts of neighborhoods on intergenerational mobility: childhood exposure effects and county-level estimates.
17 McCall and Simmons, *Identities and interactions: an examination of human associations in everyday life* (revised edition), 179 (original emphasis).
18 See Turkle, *Life on the screen: identity in the age of the internet.*
19 Giddens, *The consequences of modernity*, 121.
20 Sennett, *The fall of public man: on the social psychology of capitalism*, 102.
21 Gaite, *Love customs in eighteenth century Spain.*
22 Burke, *The art of conversation.*
23 Darnton, *The great cat massacre and other episodes in French culture history*, 4.
24 Thibaut and Kelley, *The social psychology of groups.*
25 Illouz, *Why love hurts: a sociological explanation.*
26 See Schwartz, *The paradox of choice: why more is less.*
27 Gottlieb, *Marry him: The case for settling for Mr. Good Enough.*
28 Pew Forum on Social and Demographic Trends, *The decline of marriage and the rise of new families.*

Through the rear-view mirror 87

29 Wang and Parker, Record share of Americans have never married as values, economics and gender patterns change.
30 Illouz, *Cold intimacies: the making of emotional capitalism.*
31 Celello, *Making marriage work: a history of marriage and divorce in the twentieth-century United States.*
32 Bailey, *From front porch to back seat: courtship in twentieth-century America*, 5.
33 Bauman, *Liquid love: on the frailty of human bonds.*
34 Illouz, *Cold intimacies: the making of emotional capitalism.*
35 Bellah et al., *Habits of the heart: individualism and commitment in American life*; Triandis, The self and social behavior in differing cultural contexts.
36 Illouz, *Why love hurts: a sociological explanation.*
37 Walster et al., *Equity: theory and research.*
38 Smith, Bank account model.
39 Rusbult and Righetti, Investment model.
40 Foa et al., *Resource theory: explorations and applications.*
41 Altman and Taylor, *Social penetration: the development of interpersonal relationships.*
42 Fraley and Shaver, Adult romantic attachment: theoretical developments, emerging controversies, and unan swered questions.
43 Bauman, *Liquid love: on the frailty of human bonds*; Darnton, *The great cat massacre and other episodes in French culture history.*
44 See Calvert, Children in American family portraiture, 1670–1810.
45 See Zelizer, *The purchase of intimacy.*
46 Morgan, *The Puritan family: religion and domestic relations in seventeenth century New England*, 44–45.
47 Mintz and Kellogg, *Domestic revolutions: a social history of American family life.*
48 Demos, *Past, present, and personal: the family and the life course in American history*; Morgan, *The Puritan family: religion and domestic relations in seventeenth century New England.*
49 Rubin, *Worlds of pain: life in the working-class family*, 123.
50 Caplow et al., *Middletown families: fifty years of change and continuity*, 118.
51 Gillis, *A world of their own making: myth, ritual, and the quest for family values*, 147.
52 Bernard, *The future of marriage.*
53 Illouz, *Why love hurts: a sociological explanation.*
54 Zeldin, *An intimate history of humanity.*
55 Degler, *At odds: women and the family in America from the Revolution to the present.*
56 See Coontz, *A strange stirring: The Feminine Mystique and American women at the dawn of the 1960s.*
57 Turkle, *Reclaiming conversation: the power of talk in a digital age.*
58 Cherlin, *The marriage-go-round: the state of marriage and the family in America today.*

5   Recipe for existential crisis

Step 1: undermine certainty and truth

> We are historical products of a period that has developed an increasingly wide-spread and increasingly penetrating cult of individuality.
>
> Randall Collins, *Interaction Ritual Chains*[1]

The disembedding processes

Supertrend 1: hierarchical to egalitarian

> *Hierarchically structured societies, including those that privilege one gender over the other, confer self-definition at birth. In such circumstances, because of their unequal status, symbolically interdependent bonding is impossible between men and women. Emotional bonding is possible, but people perceived to have different moral and intellectual qualifications cannot be equally influential. In egalitarian societies, self-identity is freer but also less secure. Yet, where partners consider each other equals, intimate dialogue can be mutually influential, generating support for ideas of self and a measure of community that is well adapted to the requirements of fluid modernity.*

In the early 1830s, an aristocratic French scholar and politician named Alexis de Tocqueville toured the United States recording his observations. His remarkable treatise, *Democracy in America*, published in 1835, stands as one of the most frequently referenced studies of American political and social history.[2] Much of the work is concerned with analysis of the new American democratic political system. However, de Tocqueville's commentary also includes observations on some of what he considered to be democratically inspired features of American social life that set the United States apart from the old European aristocracies. His attention was drawn to the institution of marriage. In de Tocqueville's view, American marriages were more stable and of higher quality than those in Europe, and he offered a novel theory to explain it. De Tocqueville wrote that the rigid hierarchical divisions that characterized European societies made it impossible for people of different social positions who were attracted to each other to come together in marriage. He believed that this resulted, in Europe, in a higher rate of distressed and estranged

DOI: 10.4324/9781003010234-7

Recipe for existential crisis: Step 1 89

marriages and more extramarital hanky-panky (high Euro-panky versus low Yankee-panky). De Tocqueville theorized that America's principled commitment to social equality meant women and men were able to form marital unions as they wished, and so they were more rewarding and stable.

Equality under the law is understood to be a bedrock principle of democratic life in the United States. But, because the struggle for universal civil rights has been ongoing and has frequently been visible in recent times, most people are aware that the achievement of true equality for all citizens has been a long-running, incremental, and incomplete process. Its history extends from Colonial times, where there were many disenfranchised groups, including blacks, American Indians, and women, to our era, where struggle is still apparent. However, even as the equality bestowed by the 14th and 15th Amendments to the U.S. Constitution has gradually been extended more effectively, this equality refers only to matters in public and political life, such as the legal rights to due process and equal protection, and the right to vote. And it should be noted that these amendments, which were passed at the end of the Civil War and extended the right to vote to former slaves, did not extend the right to vote to women. Women's suffrage wasn't established until the passage of the 19th Amendment in 1920, only 100 years ago (and, as an index of how contemporary these dynamics are, even in modern Western societies, it should be noted that women didn't get to vote in Switzerland at the federal level until 1971).

The extension of equal suffrage, legal equality, and nondiscrimination in matters of gender is of particular relevance in the context of interpersonal relations in family and intimacy, because this has gradually established a presumption of equality between partners in heterosexual marriages. In Colonial America, no such expectation existed.

Hierarchy and self-identity

In some societies, there is a clear hierarchical order: people born to different social positions grow up with different expectations of their behavior and different levels of authority, privilege, and obligation. These expectations can be so widely held and well blended into the deep assumptions of the culture that they actually become part of the common sense and difficult to notice. For example, sometimes people of different social position are subject to legally enforced requirements of dress.[3] This was visible in U.S. state and municipal laws (many remaining on the books until recent times) that made it a criminal offense to be found wearing gender-inappropriate clothing in public.[4] In such situations, there may be consensus about the duties and powers of different categories of people: in some cases – as de Tocqueville observed of early nineteenth-century America – that men will act with greater authority in public matters and women with greater authority in the home, or that women will take primary responsibility for socio-emotional aspects of family life and men for instrumental aspects. De Tocqueville's observations were not of a system in which husbands and wives related as equals, but rather of an American

90   *The origins of uncertainty*

social system that was somewhat novel at that time insofar as men and women were freer to marry without regard to their social/economic origins. In fact, de Tocqueville took note that, during his era, some Europeans were beginning to advance the idea that men and women were each other's equals and similarly capable. He regarded this as faulty thinking and noted that, "this is far from being the American view."[5] Increased free choice in American marriage did not signal that the sexes regarded each other as similarly empowered, similarly privileged, similarly authoritative, or even similarly capable.

With America now still in the midst of change, most movement in the direction of true gender equality has come much more recently, but has faced continual resistance from both men and women. The source of this resistance is clear when it's recognized that hierarchy confers the benefit of security of self to people at every level. Hierarchy provides relief from the burden of determining one's own purpose and position, which, as argued throughout this book, is a modern freedom that brings with it existential risk. As we have seen, failure of personal identity is a key cause of psycho-emotional distress, one increasingly in play in the modernizing world, and the fluid conditions of modern life tend to render personal identity less secure. Without a strongly formed vision of self to shield against the diversity, contradiction, and sham of modern culture, the mind becomes vulnerable to anxiety and depression.

In the face of insecurity of self, people cling to whatever sources of identity they can, even personally limiting or morally unsupportable hierarchical ones. By the nineteenth century, white American males were increasingly free to pursue their own ambitious notions of self, but, because America was still hierarchically structured with respect to race and gender, no matter their experience, white males could always fall back to their baseline position of privilege in the social hierarchy. And a female married to a white male could also fall back to her given status, enjoying relief from the stress of crafting self from scratch. However, by the end of the first decade of the twenty-first century, America had an African American president, and there was every expectation that his successor would be a woman. In response, significant numbers of white voters, particularly those in segments of society experiencing difficulty of ambition (through loss of economic power, lack of education, etc.) reacted to this as an existential threat, a challenge to foundational aspects of their sense of being. According to data from a national study of sexism in post-2016-election America, in sharp contrast with the views of the country as a whole, Republican males were significantly more likely to believe that it was a better time to be a woman than a man in America.[6] The collapse of racial- and gender-based hierarchy threatened to upend primitive notions of personal identity still in play. As we'll see, equality can lead to highly positive outcomes, but it requires more of us socially and psychologically and places the self at risk.

There are two points about social equality that are central to the arguments of this book. One relates to the possibility created by social equality for discourse to function as a bonding force in personal relationships of depth. The other relates increases in social equality to our ability to shape self-identity relatively free of

Recipe for existential crisis: Step 1　91

external constraint. With regard to the first point, the ability of dialogue to create shared structures of mind is limited in the face of differences in social power.[7] While there's ample opportunity for relationships between those who initially regard each other as equals to self-differentiate with respect to dominance and authority, perhaps as one person demonstrates clear superiority over the other in some area of activity (e.g., although we regard each other as equals, there's no doubt that you're a better cook, but you would concede that I know more about music), it's considerably more difficult for those defined by the larger culture as inherently unequal to regard each other otherwise. It's only been in relatively recent years that a presumption of moral and intellectual equality between men and women has become a broadly accepted idea (though one still visibly resisted by some who prefer the security of self-identity that accompanies hierarchy and tradition – again, to be freer is not necessarily to be happier).

As regards the second point, to the extent that a society is hierarchical, it may be simpler to form a self-concept because options are more limited. Consequently, less of this task is played out in talk in our deeper relationships. We're guided and limited in the types of stories we tell about ourselves by consensually held beliefs about what is possible and proper for a person of our social position. This information is part of the unexamined background of our lives and incorporated without conscious reflection in foundational ideas we have about who we are (in part, certainly, about what it means to be a man or a woman, and what powers, obligations, and responsibilities that involves). The limitations to behavior and opportunity in a hierarchical society narrow the possibilities of who we can aspire to be but also supply a clearer recipe for a successful life than that in a society where we can become anyone we imagine (at least in principle). So, while an egalitarian society is clearly desirable on moral grounds, egalitarianism contributes to the critical difficulties experienced in our time by those attempting to figure out their life story, character, purpose, duties, and moral responsibilities. We turn to our interpersonal partners for help in this.

Literary critic and communication philosopher Kenneth Burke claimed that one of the defining qualities of the human condition is that we are "goaded by hierarchy," obsessed with issues of empowerment and social position,[8] and, unquestionably, modern America reflects this. We may be a society grounded in assumed social equality, but everywhere people scramble to place themselves favorably in one type of status hierarchy or another. As anthropologist Mary Douglas pointed out, the hierarchies in modern Western societies, "enterprise cultures" as she called them, tend to be meritocracies, based mostly on economic success. One rises or falls on the basis of accomplishment and luck. But, because economic success can shift abruptly, social position is rarely felt to be secure, often leaving people haunted by a sense of economic vulnerability: "tormented by the possibility of their own decline."[9] Anxiety stemming from this vulnerability may be projected externally, channeled into efforts to protect self and family from sources of threat (perhaps by moving into a gated housing development, taking self-defense courses, buying guns, outfitting the house with security cameras, never letting the children out of sight, driving a

92 *The origins of uncertainty*

military-style vehicle, or obsessing about health, diet, exercise, or fantasies of marauding immigrants).

For those in meritocratic enterprise cultures, social position is felt to be one's own responsibility, but, in traditional hierarchical, non-enterprise cultures, everyone participates communally in maintaining each other's position in the social order and collective well-being, which includes people at the lowest levels. There, the group rises or falls together, and personal identity has greater stability. One can't so easily fall on one's own, but, unfortunately, one can't easily rise on one's own either. The sense of identity is more limited, but also more stable and less likely to be experienced anxiously or taken to one's intimate partners for a tune-up.

Philosopher Charles Taylor described a feeling of "terrifying emptiness" that may befall those who fail to construct or sustain a satisfying self-identity.[10] This is particularly well illustrated in Coontz's description of the malaise broadly experienced by American women in the 1940s, 50s, and 60s.[11] These were the women who were the audience for Betty Friedan's highly influential 1963 analysis of this situation, *The Feminine Mystique*. Despite the increasingly affluent circumstances of post-World War II America, many women struggled to create a sense of personal significance. The culture devalued their contributions within the home, limited their opportunities outside of it, made it difficult to divorce, and, until Friedan's book was published, largely invalidated their resulting distress. This situation provides an almost perfect example of a phenomenon known in psychotherapy circles as a "double bind," which was once thought to play a role in destabilizing the foundations of self-identity sufficiently to result in major mental disorders.[12]

This was also the starting period of the mass infusion into middle-class culture of new anti-anxiety and anti-depression medications such as Miltown and Equanil. The depressed and anxious middle-class housewife provided a target of opportunity for the manufacturers of these drugs to exploit.[13] But, it wasn't just women who were struggling in this period. These new tranquilizing drugs (really mild sedatives) were marketed to men too on the promise that they could provide relief from commonly felt stress and anxiety related to the pressures of modern work life, enabling them to return to their gender-stereotyped status as economically competitive alpha males.

By the mid-twentieth century, erosion in the degree to which Americans could link their sense of who they were to stable external sources had led to a state of "permanent identity crisis,"[14] which tends to direct attention inward in contemplation of one's life situation and subjective experience. The transformation away from a more hierarchical society with stable traditions and institutions – even unfair patriarchal or racist ones – was a significant part of this. It contributed to a disconcerting feeling that foundational aspects of the world, including the sense of self, may be uncertain, impermanent, subjective, and, to an extent, floating free of any larger defining reality. This was the mid-twentieth century, a time of far-reaching and accelerating social and technological change.

Recipe for existential crisis: Step 1   93

Indeed, under the influence of psychoanalytic theory, which became broadly influential at the start of the twentieth century, we've come to understand that sometimes our views of the world are projective reflections of our inner being (e.g., the threats we imagine to health, safety, family, and security may be amplified by the degree to which we feel vulnerable in our own life circumstances, economic or otherwise). Hence, in this era, because of the assumption that one is subject to the dynamics of the unconscious mind and the defenses of the ego, difficulty in creating a firm and stable sense of personal identity is compounded because, apart from everything else, it's not always easy to fully trust the reality of one's own impressions. (More on this in Chapter 10.)

In former times, a person born to a particular station in life (e.g., a Colonial-era farmer's wife in rural Massachusetts) may have understood that she had limited options for self-definition and may have accepted her circumstances as an exercise of fate or divine will. However, for those struggling with unfulfilling lives in twenty-first-century America, it's difficult not to direct blame inwardly because, in the popularly held assumptions that frame this era, we recognize few externally imposed limitations to our lives and so perceive ourselves and each other to be responsible for our successes and failures. In general, Americans today are much less likely than in the past to see their lives as limited by their situation in the social order, and, as discussed in the next two sections, we're also much less likely to attribute our fate to God's will, or to use tradition to justify choices made about how to live or to conceive of self.

In result, inward attribution of responsibility for an unsatisfactory life can be hard to avoid, leading to some degree of disappointment, a feeling of incompletion, perhaps a sense that life has been wasted, or other forms of psycho-emotional distress including anxiety and depression. Adding greatly to this problem are the dark communications industries – particularly marketing and advertising – that, on the whole, effectively amplify and trade upon this widely experienced malaise, marketing apparent solutions to it in the form of identity products of all sorts, designed to appeal to those searching for self-definition.

To sum, as American society has become increasingly egalitarian, it's brought both positive and negative consequences. On one hand, equality has brought greater freedom of opportunity and choice. However, on the other, rising equality dropped the burden of crafting a fulfilling life on the shoulders of people who, in previous eras, might have accepted that their situation, if not perfect, was satisfying enough and functionally sensible in the commonly accepted precepts of the social order. As historians point out, in the twentieth century's history of women's struggle for equality, there's a substory of significant resistance, not just from men, but from women too.[15] Freedom of choice imposes costs as well as benefits.

Patriarchy and shared mind

Regardless, on many measures, women's social equality has significantly advanced since the mid-twentieth century, and this has had important

94 *The origins of uncertainty*

consequences for social experience today, especially in the increasingly important context of intimate exchange. Understanding the path from paternalism to egalitarian models for marriage is especially important in this, because equality is a precondition for conversation to function as a force bonding partners through their participation in the creation of a private culture that provides support for each other's self-identity and a shared sense of morality. Uniquely, a relationship in which partners regard each other as equals has the power to supply the benefits of the kind of stable community that has otherwise been in decline in modern experience. For those who have the psychological and social prerequisites, and are fortunate and find a good enough partner, the benefits conferred by this type of highly personal and intimate community may be superior to what used to be obtained in church and village, and better suited to the fluid demands of the era. As Giddens put it, "Intimacy is above all a matter of . . . communication . . . *in the context of interpersonal equality*" (my emphasis).[16] In other words, in former times, a man and woman might have married, but, because the presumption of equality between spouses has only been established recently, it's unlikely that their communication functioned as it does now; that is, it's unlikely that husbands and wives influenced each other in their discourse to the same degree.

Although it's true that women's legal and social status is now considerably elevated over what it was in Colonial times, it's not true that this has been a linear process of increase. Gender equality advanced along a route that included some twists and turns. Looking back to Europe in the sixteenth century and earlier, Coontz notes that, "marriage was an authority relationship as much as a personal one," and that, "no one disputed the principle that a wife must be subordinate to her husband."[17] Indeed, wives were advised not to be too familiar in the mode in which they spoke to their husbands, not to use nicknames, but rather to address them as "sir" and sign their letters to their husbands with assurances of obedience. This is the heritage that European settlers brought to the American colonies.

Within the colonies, John Winthrop, governor of the Colony of Massachusetts, wrote in 1645, "A true wife accounts her subjection [as] her honor and freedom and would not think her condition safe and free, but in subjection to her husband's authority."[18] De Tocqueville's writing attests that this belief continued to form the basis for social practices in America 200 years later. He observed, that Americans have

> [never] supposed that democratic principles should undermine the husband's authority and make it doubtful who is in charge of the family. [In the view of Americans] . . . the natural head of the conjugal association is the husband. They never deny him the right to direct his spouse.[19]

In America, prior to the Revolutionary War, married women had virtually no legal status in the public sphere independent of their husbands. They could neither vote nor own property. Inside the domestic sphere of the family, their status was also subordinate. Historians believe that this power relationship changed with the coming of the Industrial Revolution and the advent of factories. Industrial work paid more reliably than agriculture and so drew men from their farms for steady wage-paying employment. As men increasingly spent time away from their homes at work, in their absence, women gained authority in the home, as de Tocqueville noted. Reflecting the beginning of this shift, future president John Adams wrote in 1776 that,

> [females'] delicacy renders them unfit for practice and experience in the great businesses of life, and the hardy enterprises of war, as well as the arduous cares of state. Besides, their attention is so much engaged with the necessary nurture of children, that nature has made them the fittest for domestic cares.[20]

The medical profession of the early nineteenth century reinforced this type of self-serving blather. Coontz quotes the eminent nineteenth-century obstetrician Charles Meigs as stating that a woman "has a head almost too small for intellect and just big enough for love."[21] In other words, the sphere of industry and public affairs is for men, and home and family are for women. Even in the utopian sex-role equality of the Oneida community of the mid-nineteenth century, where it was held that, "by nature woman in her understanding and spirit is a *smaller pattern* of man" (emphasis in the original), the business activities of the Oneida community were handled by men, and the care of children was left to women.[22] Even Freud perpetuated this type of thinking, remarking in his 1930 *Civilization and Its Discontents*, "Women represent the interests of the family and of sexual life. The work of civilization has become increasingly the business of men ."[23] These views persisted well into the mid-twentieth century, and doubtless there remain closeted believers today. Thus, from the advent of the Industrial Revolution to the powerful social restructuring of the mid-twentieth century civil rights movement and the economic downturn of the 1970s, in a kind of domestic apartheid, in the home men yielded authority and women gained authority,[24] while in matters outside the home, in the public sphere, men retained authority.

This period is referred to by historians as "separate spheres" (a public – male-dominated sphere versus domestic – female-dominated sphere). This system, exemplified in a range of TV shows of the 1950s and 60s (e.g., *The Jetsons, Leave it to Beaver, The Dick Van Dyke Show, My Three Sons*), was on the way out by the 1970s owing to a cluster of developments that included: (1) the expansion of manufacturing in the face of labor shortages during World War II, which prompted the government and industry to undertake campaigns to persuade women to imagine themselves in non-domestic roles (famously, the Rosie the Riveter campaign); (2) advances in civil rights and women's rights legislation that reduced barriers to employment; and (3) the availability of the birth control pill in the early 1960s that, for the first time, gave women the ability to effectively time their pregnancies to permit educational

96 *The origins of uncertainty*

and career attainment (however, it's worth noting at this point that, as late as 1963, 17 states still restricted women's access to contraceptives,[25] and the use or even the sale of *any* form of contraception was illegal in Connecticut until 1965, when the U.S. Supreme Court intervened).

Of particular importance as well, beginning about 1970, inflation and the diminishing performance of the post-war American economy led to declining wealth in many American households and created pressure for women to step outside the domestic domain to join the workforce outside the home. Of course, two-paycheck homes now predominate, and the arrangement is taken for granted.[26] A consequence of this is that women who have their own incomes are less likely to see divorce as an economic calamity, and this weakened another of the external forces that formerly kept couples together (for better or worse).

However, as women gained economic and political power, as they gained power in the sphere of public affairs, this enabled them to engage their relationship partners on more equal footing, permitting the possibility, for the first time in American history, for heterosexual marriage to be based on a fully egalitarian model in which spouses communicate with each other within the presumption of moral and intellectual equality and equivalent social power. With this equality came the possibility of truly mutual influence and symbolic interdependence. Thus, as one external bonding force declined in influence, it enhanced conditions in which the bonding potential of interpersonal dialogue could come to the fore.

Rising egalitarianism had consequences for intimate communication in a second way. Historian Kristin Celello has noted the increase in the use of "communication" as a catchword in discussion of marital relationships during the mid-twentieth century.[27] Before this, "emotional immaturity" was assumed to be the primary basis for marital dysfunction, but, by the end of the 1960s, this had given way to a conceptualization of marital problems as an outcome of "communication breakdowns." According to Celello, psychiatrist Bernard Green, who had tracked the most common marital complaints over a 10-year period, noted that, in the early 1960s, communication was only in seventh place on his list; however, by 1972, it headed it. One can make sense of this change by recognizing that, when people complain of "communication problems," frequently they mean that there are conflicts in the area of relational power and decision making.

By the end of the 1960s, the rising tides of the civil rights and the women's movements were causing many areas of wrenching restructuring in the distribution of power in American society. In this context, with the assistance of a psychotherapy industry rapidly broadening its influence throughout American culture,[28] women were openly questioning their traditionally subordinate positions at home and demanding greater influence, sensitivity, and equality from their husbands. When a couple in conflict in the 1970s sought expert advice about communication problems, often what may have motivated this was a wife seeking equal influence in the construction of the couple's little culture in the face of her husband's resistance. However, to reiterate, equality between

Recipe for existential crisis: Step 1   97

spouses opened the door to the possibility of a new form of interpsychic bond to take root, one ideally suited to help shore up the increasingly important but fragile sense of self-identity. In deeply personal egalitarian relationships, whether appreciated or not, the mutual maintenance of self-identity often occurs at the core of conversation.

It's important to emphasize that, in the context of this discussion, an "egalitarian" relationship is not necessarily a relationship in which partners participate equally in household chores, child rearing, or household economics. In scholarly and popular discussion of heterosexual intimate relationships, the question of "egalitarianism" often does refer to this type of issue, which has often been in focus in recent years. But that aspect of egalitarianism is another matter. In the context of our discussion, egalitarianism refers to the degree to which partners recognize each other as *equally credible sources*, which is the critical prerequisite for mutual persuasion and the growth of shared mind. There's no necessary relationship between the proportional contributions of relationship members to household labor and their ability to influence each other's minds. They don't even have to live in the same country, much less the same household, to do so. But they absolutely do have to regard each other as moral and intellectual equals.

Supertrend 2: religious to secular

> *Religion confers self-definition and prescribes moral behavior. It stipulates gender roles and the requirements of marital and family life. In a secular age, these central matters become subject to individual negotiation.*

Among modern Western nations, the United States may appear more energetically religious than many others. More Americans claim affiliation with one or another religion than Europeans, more state that they believe in God, and more report attending church regularly.[29] A significant portion of Colonial America was settled by people seeking freedom for religious expression, and, particularly in recent decades, there's been a resurgence of the visibility of religion in politics and public life. Today, 72 percent of Americans believe in miracles.[30] From televangelism to mega-churches to the political empowerment of conservative religious groups, religion seems to be more a matter of public life than ever, and, indeed, the population of the United States is now more religious than at some points in the past.[31] Hence, it may seem strange to speak of the U.S. as having moved from a religious society to a secular one.

But this shift has been dramatic. In the West, the world of yesterday was animated by religious ideas to a vastly greater extent than now. To bring this point to life, take a minute, go to the Google Images database, and try a set of searches for "fourteenth-century art," "fifteenth-century art," and so on through "twentieth-century art." As Greenfeld notes, in early periods, the common vision of the world was bursting with religious symbols.[32] But, starting in the 1600s, with each new century, the Madonnas, crucifixes, prayerful

98 *The origins of uncertainty*

people, angels, and cherubs are progressively replaced by portraits of wealthy and august people, domestic and village life, commerce, and images of nature and warfare.

By the nineteenth century, the angels are completely gone, replaced by romantic visions of nature and impressionist explorations of sensual experience. By the twentieth, there are Picasso's abstract shapes, Dalí's surrealist landscapes, and Munch's *Silent Scream*. Psychologist Louis Sass argues that modernist art, characterized by an anxious disassociation of symbols from conventional use, reflects the schizoid quality of life in modern societies.[33] Trends in the visual arts reflect the changing condition of the self – increasingly turning inward, increasingly fragmented, increasingly caught up in private meaning – as the stabilizing influences of hierarchy, tradition, and religion faded. This is apparent as well in literature and music.

Charles Taylor contends that there are three senses in which secularism is evident in the Western world today.[34] In the first, the contexts for religious expression have greatly contracted. Over the past 400 years, a growing secularity is evident in people's conceptions of the forces shaping their lives and in their understanding of the domain of spiritual influence. There's been a progressive increase in the authority of science for the explanation of the natural and social worlds and an accompanying decrease in the authority of sacred traditions. There have been a separation of the affairs of church and the affairs of state and a rise in the rule of secular law. In the world of the Puritan settlers, religion, family, and government were not distinctly separated as they are today. For the Puritans, religion encompassed both work and government, and government was directly involved in the management of families – even to the point of enacting laws that required single adults to live within families.[35] Cherlin quotes a 1636 law from Connecticut that dictated that, "no man that is neither married, nor hath any servant . . . shall keep house of himself without the consent of the Town where he lives" – no solo-living there.[36]

John Winthrop famously wrote in 1637, "A family is a little commonwealth, and a commonwealth is a great family,"[37] to which it might reasonably have been added that they were both integrally extensive of the church. The Puritan minister Cotton Mather described the family as "the Mother Hive, out of which both those swarms of State and Church issued forth."[38] What actually issued forth from what might have been more complexly causal than that, but what matters here is appreciation of the extent to which the daily experiences of Americans in work, public life, education, and family, which were formerly infused with religious and spiritual concepts, are now guided by ideas derived from secular sources such as science and law, or those derived from the internal rationalities of the various areas of activity in which people engage (organizational life, sports, etc.).

Looking even further into the past, at the extreme end of this progression is the kind of animistic spirituality associated with some Native American religions, a view of the natural world as infused with spiritual forces – trees, the weather, rocks, the sun, dreams, water, all divinely invested. It's perhaps not so large a step from this to the thinking, frequently evident in the letters and diaries of Americans in former times, that invoked "divine providence" or "God's will" or "the hand of God" in explanation of myriad natural phenomena that, today, would be explained with reference to secular concepts derived from science or medicine. For example, of the cholera epidemic that swept New York City in 1832 killing more than 3,000 out of a population of 250,000, Henrietta Wilson wrote to her sister, Elizabeth Meads, "The Christian God is undoubtedly the God of cholera, and it goes nowhere but where he sends it."[39] This type of expression was common, at least until science determined that cholera was caused by microbes that breed when city water mixes with sewage, after which citizens stopped looking to God for relief and started lobbying the mayor's office and the bureaucrats in the Department of Public Health. Max Weber referred to this change as the end of enchantment. There was an old world of mysterious forces, now replaced by a new world of rationality, science, and human will.

Historians note the considerable evidence for Colonial Americans who believed in occult and magical explanations for everyday events and in witchcraft, astrology, and alchemy,[40] and even the evil eye.[41] Surprising numbers of modern Americans do as well. According to a recent Harris poll,[42] 40 percent of Americans believe in ghosts, 26 percent in witchcraft, 36 percent in UFOs, and 24 percent in reincarnation. And, if not in witchcraft or alchemy, or the curse of the *malocchio*, modern Americans may sustain belief in other forms of supernatural influence such as magical systems they concoct on their own for winning at the track or picking numbers for state lotteries. However, in the main, with regard to natural phenomena, the credibility of the supernatural and religious has given way to science and other secular systems of thought (the Harris organization found that the number of Americans who believed in the existence of God dropped more than 10 percentage points between 2003 and 2013, while belief in the accuracy of Darwinian evolution increased 5 percent).

Taylor's second sense of secularism occurs when a society decreases its investments in practices of church and faith. This is evident in most Western societies, though not as obvious in the United States. Still, despite a vigorously visible presence of religion in America's public life, there's also been a falling-off of participation in many aspects of religious practice. Church membership fell an average of 10 percent over the last three to four decades, church attendance has dropped at least 20 percent, and participation in affiliated religious activities (e.g., study groups and church social activities) has dropped between 25 and 50 percent.[43] Recent analyses by the Pew Forum on Religion and Public Life found that the number of Americans stating that they had no religious affiliation increased from 14 percent to 20 percent between 2007 and 2012 and then to 23 percent in 2014.[44] The bulk of the defections occurred among Protestant denominations. This would have been as evident among Catholics as well, and more severe overall, except that Catholicism has been more strongly represented among recent immigrants who have brought their religious values with them to the U.S. On top of this is mounting evidence that Americans

100　*The origins of uncertainty*

may dramatically exaggerate their reports of church attendance and religious involvement when surveyed,[45] so that the actual amount of decline may be greater overall than reports have indicated.

Taylor's third sense in which secularism has come to dominate modern societies occurs as religious belief changes from more or less universal to becoming one option among a set of options for understanding the self in its relation to the cosmos and morality. This third expression of secularity is strong today. While one may maintain an active and traditional Catholic faith, one's neighbors may easily be Baptists, agnostics, or believers in New Age precepts, or atheists, Hindus, mystics, or any of a wide variety of others.

The village on the Mohawk River where I live, with a population of just 900, hosts a Catholic church, a Protestant Reformed church, and an evangelical congregation. Nearby is a major Chinese Buddhist retreat, which is bordered by a 600-acre Catholic shrine that abuts the town of Glen, New York, which is home to a growing community of conservative Old Order Amish. As you drive the short trip to the Buddhist retreat, you pass two Jewish synagogues, a meeting house for Jehovah's Witnesses, an Eastern Orthodox church, and, according to Churchfinder.com, 36 churches in Amsterdam, NY (population 18,000) that cater to Catholics and various Protestant sects.

In the past, many nation-states were religious organizations as much as political organizations, and a central pillar of this was often a single state-supported church. The proportion of the U.S. population with religious affiliations now divides into more than 140 religious denominations that encompass a diverse and contrasting set of beliefs and practices.[46]

In a theme that will be taken up again in several places ahead, the presence of a diversity of belief has a tendency to make all knowledge appear relative: in a society characterized by an extraordinary range of options for faith and spirituality, all options lose a degree of authority. In a world increasingly experienced as consisting of relative knowledge (meaning no knowledge is particularly privileged), interior being is more complicated. In such a world, for a life to be experienced as meaningful, one must to a greater degree engage in an active sorting through of competing possibilities in order to make decisions about what to invest and believe in. And the belief is not likely to be as deep. Of course, it's still possible to be a devoutly religious person in America, but this no longer happens automatically, and, because of this extraordinary diversity, religious belief may be held a little more tentatively than in the past.

In addition to Taylor's three senses of rising secularity in American society, we may add a fourth: segmentation. For many Americans, the activities of day-to-day living – once a blend of government, family, economic, and religious activity – have become compartmentalized.

In most cases, worshipful practice has been relegated to discrete locations and scheduled into particular days and time slots. In contrast, for those unusual subgroups that have resisted modernity, such as the Old Order Amish, practices of spirituality tend to infuse virtually all aspects of daily experience. For the Amish, congregational services are not held in a separate church building but

Recipe for existential crisis: Step 1   101

in rotation in members' homes, to reinforce that there's no distinction between daily life and spiritual life – religion is not something that happens once a week in a particular building.[47]

America's strong shift to the secular has contributed to the set of changes in which many have come to experience their lives as isolated and disembedded: free of the constraints of external systems of belief, the mythic structures that once imparted direction and meaning in common-sense precepts held throughout a community. In modern secular society, self-definition is more of an individual production and so may become a preoccupation, even to the point of narcissism. Participating in spirituality embeds self-definition in external systems of belief, connecting us to others in a common vision of the past, and to ideas of how to conceive of self and our purpose in the universe. Religions tell how to live morally and, often, how to live as a man or a woman and the requirements of family roles. This has sometimes created tension between religious values and America's growing cultural commitment to social equality (e.g., as in the nineteenth-century drama of the Mormons' forced repudiation of the practice of polygamy). The notion advocated by some religions that a wife should subordinate herself to her husband's authority has become an increasingly hard sell in modern Western societies because it directly conflicts with legal commitments to social equality. Whether Christian, Hindu, or Islamic, the more a nation is religious, the greater its gender inequality.[48]

In modern America, significant erosion of the force of religion has weakened the extent of social interconnection within neighborhoods, leaving many to work out personal meaning and moral definition without the benefit of formal community. In result, people more frequently turn to interpersonal partners to work out issues of self and questions of right and wrong (sometimes, too, we turn to our proxies for those relationships: our therapists, life coaches, marriage counselors, etc.). Certainly, some Americans do turn to religion in this quest, and, of course, there remain many deeply religious people and vital religious communities in the United States. Service activities of many American community churches interpenetrate the lives of the congregation and its surrounds, facilitating meaningful social encounters, in many cases organizing charitable care for the needy who might otherwise go without, and so on. But, in general, this has scaled back, or the congregational activities themselves exist a little less as manifestations of faith and doctrine and a little more for the secular purpose of community care. The domain of religious influence has contracted, and its force has diminished. In this, intimate relationships have acquired greater importance in defining and supporting the sense of self.

Supertrend 3: tradition-centered to individual-centered

> *Like religion, tradition embeds people within a seemingly deep and tested basis of cultural experience, an unseen and unquestioned common sense, much of which is relevant to personal identity. But modernity tends to render tradition irrelevant and upend common sense. In its absence, doubt, uncertainty,*

102 *The origins of uncertainty*

and anxiety are more common, as one is forced to contend with the world as an endless flow of unprecedented situations. Some believe that an increase in compulsive and addictive behaviors has resulted from the declining influence of tradition in modern societies.

Leaving tradition behind runs all the way through our tradition.[49]

No life is constructed from scratch, but rather is informed by practices and knowledge handed down from preceding generations, not only from parents, teachers, and grandparents, but as well from the store of rituals, customs, routines, and generally accepted ways of behaving and thinking that have informed the culture in prior times. Tradition is protective and sustaining. As the novelist Jeanette Winterson put it, "the past . . . comes with us like a chaperone."[50] Tradition eases the burdens of doubt and indecision that are hallmarks of modernity, whose freedoms confer greater opportunity, but at the same time make it difficult to ever really settle issues of self-identity and purpose.

Of course, it's impossible to say exactly what proportions of behavior and outlook come from traditional sources, but, clearly, some cultures are more strongly traditional than others. Generally, these are rural – agrarian, with non-industrial economies (the Old Order Amish, for example). There, life tends to be centered in family and embedded in local communities, and the functions of government, religion, and education may intermingle with family and community to a greater extent. To the extent that a culture is tradition-centered, there's likely to be greater consensus of thought. Beliefs are more likely to be derivative of a shared sense of the past and future and perhaps of a shared understanding of social hierarchy. Customs and rituals are more likely to be widely honored and may serve to reinforce a common identity and moral code. There may be a sense that orthodox ways of behaving form a connecting highway between generations, or beyond to earlier times and ancestral wisdom. Traditional cultures are less likely to be egalitarian, leaving people with less uncertainty about who they are, but also with less freedom to be who they want.

Some traditional practices are visible in modern times in certain professions that remain tradition-bound. For example, in performances of multi-movement chamber music – sonatas and concertos from the Baroque era – even though the performing group stops between movements, by convention, applause is held until the completion of the whole work. When there is one, the group will tune to the oboe. The first violinist is the lead player. Tempo and dynamics are usually noted on scores in Italian using terms of inexact meaning (*allegro ma non presto, poco vivace*), many of which could be more precisely specified in modern, quantitative terminology (beats per minute, relative decibel levels), but are not because they function to embody and convey the force of history in orienting and organizing the musicians in the present. These practices sustain a musical culture with roots extending hundreds of years into the past, and those who engage in them tend to gain not only whatever expertise they

Recipe for existential crisis: Step 1 103

represent, but also a sense of personal identity, oriented within a community of thought and practice and united with others by esoteric language and symbols and agreed-upon definitions of correct action.

The practice of classical musicianship is likely to impact the self-concept. This is true in other professions with particularly visible ritual and customary practices, including the military and, of course, religion. Beyond these traditional professional practices, tradition bridges generational differences in pastimes such as karate and judo, in ethnic dance, and in children's games – such as hide-and-seek, jacks, or hopscotch – whose origins stretch far back into the mists of time. Certain micro-rituals and communication practices are traditional, such as the sequences involved in greeting ("Hi, how are you?" "Fine thanks. And yourself?") and leaving, or saying "gesundheit" or "bless you" following a sneeze. The origins of these practices are not found in conscious choice or in adaptations to contemporary life. They are simply passed down.

Some traditions that function as rites of passage are more visible. Secular ceremonies, such as weddings, school proms and graduations, birthdays, funerals, and retirement celebrations, and those of religious significance, such as baptism, first communion, or the bar mitzvah, are powerful because they usher in a new chapter in the story of self-identity, linking participants to what may seem to be preexisting and almost timeless shared wisdom about how to conceptualize self in the progression of life's stages. The traditional practice of a new husband carrying his bride across the threshold has this type of transition symbolism at the literal level.

However, although we may hang on to some traditional practices, many of them have lost a great deal of their former significance and relevance to self-definition. America is no longer a society in which modes of thought and activity from the distant past structure lives to the extent visible in other cultures and times. Rather, what's remarkable about America today is the rapidity of social change, the fluid nature of social institutions, and the extent to which behavior and self-definition are disconnected from tradition, shaped instead in conscious activity occurring in the present.

The modern era is inherently generative of novel situations (the sudden appearance of new technologies of communication, sudden shifts in family forms and norms, sudden changes in the employment outlook for various industries, and the sudden emergence of new categories of economic activity).[51] Modern society has become so fast-changing, the situations confronted so unprecedented, that traditional practices often can't sustain their relevance. In the absence of prior experience, one must find one's way through the world reflexively – in the present, through conscious, active reasoning or, especially, in conversation with others. In the absence of tradition, the need to reason one's way along is forced on us all.

Today, we're all confronted more or less continually with decisions over matters that no prior generation has dealt with, with job-related roles that have never before been performed, in corporations that can quickly merge, morph, and migrate, serving changing industries based on fast-evolving technologies

104 *The origins of uncertainty*

and economic circumstances. Sociologist Zygmunt Bauman regards this period as characterized by "liquid" institutional and social forms, so transient that they "cannot serve as frames of reference for human actions and long-term life strategies."[52] And, with the dropping away of solid institutions and traditions as a source of orientation, not only economic life, but also core ideas of self must be constructed on the fly, without the benefit of traditional scripts. That modern life is not constrained by tradition creates freedom and opportunity; however, this also generates anguish and anxiety, for one may often see no clearly correct course of action and find oneself in the midst of possibility without a clear basis for choice, always tempted to imagine that the path not taken might have been the better choice.

In communities guided by tradition, social practices have the character of objective necessity. One does what's required, not through conscious reasoning or selection among options or negotiation with others, but because the correct form of behavior simply appears to be self-evident: in traditional cultures, "meaning is manifest in things, people, and activities; it is not a point of view."[53] This stands in contrast to contemporary America where, because of the operation of many of the processes described in this chapter and the two to follow, meaning is more likely to be manufactured internally, within us, and in discourse with close intimates: the world is no longer objectively given, nor is knowledge of it transmitted from generation to generation through traditional practices. In modernity, meaning almost always *is* a point of view, a personal interpretation. While this has been a frequent subject of discussion, what has been less often appreciated is that this has elevated the importance of interpersonal relationships, which is where we go to sort our experience, find our stance, and receive support for the meaningful world co-constructed in those relationships. Absent those relationships, what may remain is insecurity, indecision, and psycho-emotional instability.

Traditions change or fall away when the circumstances to which they refer change.[54] The marriage ceremony loses meaning when it's widely recognized that the union is likely to be a life-long commitment only about half the time. The baptism loses meaning in a predominantly secular culture. The retirement ceremony loses meaning as jobs are no longer for the long term in stable businesses. In particular, technological changes can spell the end of traditions, and even the most cursory glance at the last 200 years reveals a frenetic pace of technological change impacting virtually all areas of modern societies. Although people may still carry forward practices of the past, the United States is long beyond a tradition-centered culture. Commonly, younger generations eschew the authority of older generations and look inwardly for guidance, to each other, or to secular sources such as science or advertising and consumer culture. The latter eagerly exploits the anxieties produced by the erosion of tradition by slapping the word "traditional" on myriad ordinary products. A search for items described as "traditional" on the Walmart website yields more than 900 products, including "traditional soup," "traditional picnic tables," "traditional dumbbells," and even "traditional underwear." (Hoping to

Recipe for existential crisis: Step 1   105

fend off the juggernaut of modernity by wrapping yourself in the security of tradition? It could make sense to start at the bottom!)

Particular traditions are eroded – ways of behaving, methods of accomplishing work, pathways through the course of life. More generally, a traditional society stands distinct from a modern society in the degree to which individualism is absent. The focus in a traditional society is on the group (family, village, clan) and the preservation of its ways of behaving and lines of authority. Communication practices there are more signal-like. The meaning of the self isn't fluid, but held in place through communally held precepts. Dialogue isn't creative of private culture, but serves to reinforce and preserve group culture. In contrast, modern American society valorizes autonomy and is intensely atomized, which leaves each individual the problem of finding interpersonal partners sufficient to help establish meaning and purpose. And, of course, success is not guaranteed. An isolated person may defend against the anxiety that accompanies atomized modern life by routinizing behavior – in essence, by developing private traditions and rituals that help keep anxiety under control by providing predictable structure. A personal routine may originate in some sensible sequence of action, but then, sometimes, repetition becomes compulsion, and an irrational personal ritual takes hold.

Giddens has discussed the extraordinary extent to which modern societies have become concerned with addictive behavior, finding it now in almost every area of life: work, alcohol consumption, sex, eating, gambling, shopping, purging, smoking, use of the internet, hoarding, pornography, exercising – the list of addictive concerns keeps growing.[55] In a society in which one must navigate without benefit of tradition, the problem of managing anxiety may be reduced by the self-reinforcing security of compulsive routine. Repetitive behavior, which may morph into personal ritual, provides a self-generated structure of predictability that armors against the anxieties that accompany the difficulties of holding on to meaning in modern life, the ever-present risk of social or economic failure, and the difficulty of constructing a satisfactory personal identity. This is an age of uncertainty about the world's future, diminishing social connection, diminished consensus, and weakened community. All these contribute to insecurity and stress. Neurotic ritual can develop as a coping strategy.

Professional sports provide many examples of players' ritualized behavior. Vivid among them is the batter's preparation ritual of former All Star baseball player Nomar Garciaparra, which, before every pitch, required him to step back from home plate and strap and re-strap both of his batter's gloves, touch the brim of his helmet, and tap his bat to his toe. This type of compulsive routine can become a sort of personal micro-tradition and may structure individual consciousness and, therefore, help manage anxiety, but, because it isn't social in nature, because there's no aspect of the behavior that bridges self and other, it lacks the ability of communal traditions to place one in a framework of accepted wisdom and so foster a sense of security and meaning. (On the other hand, such was the influence of Garciaparra that his compulsive batting ritual was widely copied and may now serve as a means of group identification for

106 *The origins of uncertainty*

many young players who stand at home plate strapping and re-strapping their batter's gloves.)

In our time, everyone must find the interpersonal skills and resources to create and maintain with family and intimate others a sustaining and meaningful life, one that provides security in its structure and predictability. Ulrich Beck and Elisabeth Beck-Gernsheim believe that, "As traditions become diluted, the attractions of a close relationship grow,"[56] because intimate relationships can restore a portion of the stability that has been lost in the decline of tradition. At their best, ongoing relationships evolve their own micro-traditions that contribute to a sense of interpersonal solidarity (the family always eats at six following the ringing of a cow bell; everyone in the car enthusiastically yells "choke on it!" as coins are tossed in the toll baskets at the pay stations along the Garden State Parkway; we have chocolate chip pancakes every Sunday and always pronounce pancake as "pahncake"; we use food coloring to dye the poodle something striking every Easter; we say grace at every family dinner, even though no one is religious).

The micro-traditions generated in intimate relationships become important tokens of interdependence, reaffirming partners' continuing commitment and shared mind. Each time one of a couple's quirky micro-traditions is enacted, it serves as an efficient shorthand for a discussion reconfirming that partners honor their connection and the culture they've built together: in other words, in an era of instability at the personal level (high rates of divorce, low rates of commitment, etc.), private rituals and traditions reconfirm and sustain the couple's identity as a couple, the family's identity as a family.[57] When lives are embedded in these connections, sustained in micro-traditions, the jittery insecurity that stems from the relatively rootless quality of modern society is reduced, and the possibility of security and fulfillment increases.

Supertrend 4: local economy to mass culture

> *The mass culture substitutes diffuse global forms for those that reflect and reinforce local meanings and traditions. It forces the conception of the self using meanings that may seem unsatisfactory because they are transitory, insubstantial, shallow, and ephemeral – often tied to commercial enterprise – and not related to local, immediate, and authentic experience.*

The Industrial Revolution, which started to become visible at approximately the time of the American Revolution, led to rapid advances in communications, manufacturing, and transportation. It scientized the processes of production through the creation of efficient factories of mass production that replaced cottage manufacturing. Work life became regulated by technique and the demands and values of economic growth: efficiency, economy, and rationality.[58] Gone was the sense of personal meaning that accompanies the act of creation of the individual artisan working in his own home or shop, selling his products to his neighbors. Gone too was the sense that work was a means of having

Recipe for existential crisis: Step 1 107

contact with sustaining traditions and values. Work became, instead, something abstract, with reduced importance for self-definition: labor and time are traded for money, and, in many cases, the connection between personal identity and work performed has diminished or vanished altogether. There are still professions where the connection between self-identity and work is sustained, but, for many, as long as there's some job, what job that is has relatively little consequence for identity.

As the factory replaced the home workshop, work was divorced from the family, a context especially hospitable to tradition and, through that connection, to the definition of self. Increasingly, people (at first, males only; wives were left behind) worked outside the home on some part of a product that might be irrelevant to their own life, the purpose of which they might not understand or care about, in exchange for money, which is perhaps the most impersonal and abstract social invention of all time. (For an object lesson in the strangely abstract and impersonal nature of money, next time you're on a date, after the good night kiss, try offering your partner a $50 bill as a token of your affection.)

It was not just the rise of industrialization that was so transformational. Coupled with it was the development of transnational markets, of "the American economy," as it is now called.[59] In prior eras, people went hungry when their crops failed from bad weather. But, as modernity came on and America transformed into an interconnected mass market, people no longer necessarily suffer when their own crops fail; they go hungry when the national economy falters and markets fall, as happens from time to time in cycles of economic recession or depression. This represents a start point in the process in which local experience was subordinated to a sense of regional, national, and now global interconnection. In the distant past, the village or town was the center of both economic and existential experience, but this has now changed, leaving most people with a much thinner connection to location. And now, for some, modernity's press toward globalization has begun to be felt as a threat to that aspect of personal identity that comes from national identification. This has recently become evident throughout the West in the reactionary assertion of populist political movements, which have been fueled by the anxiety generated in the replacement of local norms and sensibilities in favor of global trade, open communication, and the equality of race and gender required of a globalized, post-national politics. The wall many on the political right want to construct on the U.S.'s southern border (or, in the UK, the Brexit movement) is best understood as a metaphor for a broadly felt need to reassert identity by people for whom core aspects of self have been threatened in the impacts of the global mass culture on local experience.

As more and more goods have become mass-produced (including information products such as books, newspapers, film, and television) and distributed broadly throughout the United States and the world, they've often replaced goods produced locally, which are more likely to reflect and sustain local variations in culture and tradition. In contemporary times, in much of America, local businesses have been replaced by national and international chains.

108　*The origins of uncertainty*

MacDonald's and Walmart provide examples of the power of this process that tends to edge out smaller, community-oriented businesses.

As this process gains force, local businesses, which are more likely to reflect the traditions, tastes, ideas, and cultural quirks of a particular community, may not be able to compete with the cheaper and powerfully marketed artifacts of the mass culture. In a familiar pattern, America's mass economy has stripped away the local and, in substituting mass-produced products, has in some cases stripped away authenticity and meaning too. Everything becomes the same (and, in so doing, becomes closer to signal than symbol). According to Robert Kaplan,

> Crossing America in the early twenty-first century . . . You are like a mouse on a treadmill. Each Best Western or Holiday Inn Express is made as if out of the same machine mold, with the same juice machines and same dispensers and styrofoam bowls for Kellogg's cereal in the morning. You feel as though you wake up each morning in the same room, even as you are covering more than 100 miles a day.[60]

The mass culture has produced visually perfect but relatively tasteless fruit and vegetables (strawberries, apples, tomatoes, bananas); limp triangular bread audaciously labeled "croissant," which, to make authentically, with "its holy balance of buttery heft and feathery flake,"[61] requires the most delicate expression of baking skill; uniform styles of dress; and countless hotels, malls, restaurants, and office buildings without local or regional variation in style or construction. Even local newspapers may be unable to compete with national newspapers designed for mass consumption (e.g., *USA Today*).

Franchise operations have invaded many sectors of the marketplace, driving out local businesses: food services, tax preparation, real estate, home building supplies and hardware, home health care, office supplies, automobile parts and repair, funeral services, computer and electronic sales, clothing retail, education, medical services, and so on. Generally, religious services have not been affected in this way; however, according to sociologist Arlie Hochschild, in some cases the American Catholic Church passes requests for special prayers to a department in the Vatican where they are relayed to Catholic priests in southern India and conducted there.[62] Recently, the extent of mass production and "MacDonaldization"[63] has progressed to such a point that it has fostered a backlash in the movement for "locatarian" food. Though a laudable trend in the eyes of many, it is of insufficient size to offset the juggernaut force of the mass culture.

The mass culture is the enemy of local culture, if not of the meaningful world altogether. Luckmann refers to the "half-real, half fictive" world of the mass culture,[64] while Bauman describes mass culture as "a collective brain-damage caused by a 'culture industry' planting a thirst for entertainment and amusement."[65] But it isn't just about the degree to which entertainment has pervaded everything, the degree to which Angry Birds, Disney characters, or

Recipe for existential crisis: Step 1 109

James Bond films have become universal tokens of experience. As Becker and others have argued, the functional causes of the pursuit of distraction and trivia are existential anxiety and insecurity about the stability of self-identity, which, to a great extent, have resulted from the disconnection of the sense of self from traditional and religious ideas shared within a close community.[66] This is a loop, in other words, in which the mass culture thrives upon the social-psychological circumstances that it itself fosters.

In the cynical world of marketing and advertising, the self-serving Alice-in-Wonderland world that created such gems as the "pre-owned car," the "starter home," and, that bizarre masterpiece, the "training bra" (each little more than a mindset designed to encourage consumption along particular lines by persuading you to a particular vision of yourself), an industry where poet Wendell Berry's lament over "public meaninglessness preying on private meaning"[67] couldn't be more apt, the separation of concepts from any traditional signification they may have once had and from their referents in external reality has spread far. There's no shortage of examples. Indeed, the *New York Times* carried a report on September 23, 2013, detailing the extent to which online product reviews are forged on sites such as Amazon and Yelp. Investigations of travel sites by the New York State Attorney General revealed "a web of deceit in which reviewers in Bangladesh, the Philippines and Eastern Europe produced, for as little as a dollar a rave, buckets of praise for places they had never seen in countries where they had never been."[68] Or try the websites boostlikes.com or buy-cheap-likes.com (among many others) where you can bulk purchase "likes" for your company's Facebook, Twitter, YouTube, or Instagram sites for as little as $120.00 for 10,000 likes. When you need to boost the appearance of support for your candidate or political agenda, hire a "buzzer team" from Indonesia who will manufacture buzz by tweeting and posting online from hundreds of social media accounts.[69]

The commercial corruption of meaning is evident in other cases as well, including the creation of housing developments with evocative marketing names of empty or even ironic significance such as "Avon Crest" in Niskayuna, New York, presumably for those with aristocratic fantasies, or "The Great North Woods" for an apartment complex in the midst of an area of dilapidated strip malls in Columbus, Ohio, where the trees were cut down long ago as commercial interests expanded. Or try "The Meadows at Glenwyck," which, sounding like someone's nostalgic fantasy of rural Wales where bunnies from the *Wind in the Willows* idle on summer days, is actually a newly constructed elder care facility located on a scruffy lot in a commercial development zone in Glenville, New York, next to a Walmart and the end of a runway at the county airport. Or try "The Bluff at Buckingham Summit" or "Falcon Abbey," which, as far as I know, are not actual places but meaningless selections from the bottomless barrel of candidate names generated by the web app "Real Estate Subdivision Name Generator."

Then, there are the exotic claims of the dietary and health supplement industry where such outcome research as there is most often suggests the potential

110   *The origins of uncertainty*

harm of the substances marketed, or their irrelevance. A recent investigation by the New York State Attorney General revealed that 80 percent of dietary supplement samples from major U.S. retailers GNC, Target, Walgreens, and Walmart did not contain *any* of the herbs listed on their labels, comprising little more than fillers such as powdered rice, asparagus, and house plants.[70] Or consider the case of the Volkswagen Corporation, which stealthily outfitted more than 11 million of its diesel cars with software systems that were capable of detecting when the vehicle was undergoing routine government emissions tests. During the test, the engine would adjust itself so that it would be found to comply with government requirements. But, detecting that the test was over, the car would cease strictly controlling its engine emissions, providing the higher standards of mileage and performance Volkswagen advertised to buyers of these supposedly eco-friendly diesel cars, all the while spewing illegal toxins and damaging compounds into the air.[71] A 2012 VW Golf TDI put out as many environmentally damaging pollutants as a 18-wheeler truck, but not when government inspectors were looking.[72] Volkswagen is only the latest in a spate of automobile manufacturers recently found by the U.S. government to have hidden life-threatening defects or to have defrauded consumers with false claims about mileage and performance. Then, there's the giant banking firm Wells Fargo, which for 6 years defrauded as many as 2 million of its customers by creating bogus bank and credit card accounts in their names and charging service fees on the accounts.[73]

Or consider the recent trend of relabeling mass-produced grocery chain foods as "artisan." The "artisan" bread sold at Walmart and in your local large grocery store arrives in cardboard boxes on a refrigerated truck and is baked in the store by an hourly worker whose artisan skill set consists of opening the box and putting the factory-made dough into the oven at a specified temperature for a designated period of time. The artisan part of this has nothing to do with the bread: it's in the marketing fantasy. In its semantic connection to a bygone world, "artisan" sounds good and helps to sell products. So do false claims about environmental benefits. Manufacturers have now been outted for engaging in that practice with such frequency that a new word to describe the process, "greenwashing," was added to the *Oxford English Dictionary* in 2002.

Then there's the widespread relabeling of fish for commercial gain. According to the Oceana Research Group, as much as one-third of the fish sold in supermarkets and restaurants in the United States today is fraudulently labeled. As many as 84 percent of white tuna samples they analyzed were found to be a different fish entirely.[74] In subsequent research,[75] the group found that more than 40 percent of U.S. salmon was fraudulently labeled (e.g., as being wild when it was actually farmed, or being a completely different fish such as rainbow trout), and about the same for shrimp. Over half of the "Chesapeake Bay" blue crab cakes served in the metropolitan Washington D.C. area contained crab harvested in Indonesia or on the Pacific coast of Mexico from species flagged with "avoid" warnings on seafood watch lists. And consider the

Recipe for existential crisis: Step 1   111

marketer's magic in which a fish previously known to the world as the "slime-head" was rechristened "orange roughy" to make it more palatable to shoppers.

Philosophers of language have long taught that our humanity inheres in the separation between symbols and the objects to which they refer, as this gap allows us to create unique meaning and share it to form communities of thought and expression. But, when the relationship between symbol and referent becomes excessively stretched for purposes of commercial or political exploitation, it may instead contribute to cynicism, depression, alienation, and a sense of anxiety.

To the extent that a town fails to resist the mass culture – as the Walmart or Target big box store leads to the closure of small local shops, as chain hotels such as Marriott, Red Roof, and Hampton Inn edge out the town's own historic hotels, as Amazon displaces the book stores, as their local newspaper goes out of business – communities lose their unique character and history, and whatever traditions they may have hung on to are more likely to fall away, or to become thin and insubstantial. In sports, quickly, unapologetically, and unceremoniously, the local/historical has been commercialized: Albany, New York's Knickerbocker Arena, named originally in honor of the seventeenth-century Dutch settlement of the region, became the Pepsi Arena and then the Times Union Center, advertising a newspaper. Shea Stadium, named to honor a man's accomplishment, was replaced by Citi Field, advertising a bank. Today, half the Major League Baseball stadiums in the U.S. have been renamed to advertise corporations or their products. And this trend continues to spread. The Disney corporation offered $1,000 prizes and a trip to London to pastors who mentioned its film *The Chronicles of Narnia* in their Sunday sermons,[76] the U.S. National Park Service has started selling the naming rights to buildings in Yosemite National Park, and public schools across the country have sold naming rights to buildings, sports fields, and educational programs.[77] To be sure, the progressive gobbling up of the local by the mass economy isn't the only factor contributing to the flattening of local identity. As we'll see, others include high levels of social mobility, urbanization, and changes in the nature and speed of communication flows.

The net effect is an erosion of the traditions and symbols associated with particular places. One urban space begins not only to look like any other, but to feel like it too. And so, it becomes difficult to connect self with location, which may undermine civic involvement and contributes to the destabilization of the population. In a remarkable display of co-dependence, in recent years, many American towns have looked to the mass market for help, hiring public relations firms to "brand" the town with marketing slogans and visual symbols. And so, street post flags now hang in many American towns as if to persuade visitors that there's something distinctive about them after all, something perhaps otherwise easily overlooked. Mass marketers and advertisers are well aware that America has no shortage of people dislocated in semiotic space, struggling to construct and sustain a rooted sense of self. Consequently, many products are pitched for their ability to brand the person, especially in product

112 *The origins of uncertainty*

categories such as cigarettes, clothing, cosmetics, pickup trucks and up-market cars, travel, beer and hard liquor, and so on. Often, these products are marketed not as much for their merits as for their ability to assist with self-definition in our relatively rootless times.

Sadly, even government-sponsored gambling operations and military recruitment campaigns seek to capitalize upon Americans' insecurities about self, suggesting, for example, that a lottery ticket in a draw in which the odds can easily top 150,000:1 might become a quick route to a desirable self-identity (New Jersey's "Give your dreams a chance"), or that the dangerous and notoriously depersonalized life of a military recruit might pay off in self-definition ("Be all you can be," "The few, the proud, the Marines"). On occasion, universities enact this strategy too, promoting educational programs not by detailing what will be learned, but by pitching to prospective students that by enrolling they'll obtain attributes of an attractive vision of self. An MBA program at Rensselaer Polytechnic Institute advertises that it's designed "for fast track professionals"; the University of Akron declares, "we're young agile bright and on the rise, just like you"; and, at universities across the country, the most common advertising appeal hits this pitch directly: "Find yourself at [fill in the blank with: University of Arizona, James Madison University, University of Kentucky, University of Alaska, Northeastern University, Boston University, University of Alberta, Ursuline, or any of many others]." Obviously, they don't mean that you can expect to open your eyes one morning and see that you're located at University X. They mean that, in exchange for 4 years of study and somewhere between $80,000 and $200,000, you'll find yourself – that is, you'll obtain a sense of self-identity, stability, and direction in your life narrative.

Virtually all clothing companies pitch to self-identity, but the J. Peterman company set a sort of high watermark and trades on its notoriety for this. The company's website, among a multitude of other examples, pictures what appears to be an ordinary polo shirt and describes it with this text:

> Diplomat. Polo player. Race car driver of considerable stamina (did the 24 hours at Le Mans twice). He also had something of a reputation as a playboy. Two of his six wives were French movie stars. I made this polo for personalities in life that have a quality of being unstoppable.

The shirt is virtually irrelevant to the purchase. Like much of the mass economy, J. Peterman sells self-identity in a society where that's something much in demand.

According to Giddens, "Consumption addresses the alienated qualities of modern social life and claims to be their solution."[78] Indeed, it's not uncommon for people experiencing stress or anxiety to try to cope by going shopping,[79] sometimes becoming so driven about it that the psychotherapy industry has recently declared "compulsive buying disorder" to be another form of addiction.[80] But this is a cruel move in a society so artful at promoting consumerism that designers of shopping malls consciously craft their spaces to create what they call "the Gruen effect," an environmentally induced sense of disorientation that makes people more susceptible to impulse buying. The ultimate origin of much of our stress and anxiety is not psychological flaws or dysfunctions in brain chemistry, but the precarious nature of disembedded life made worse by commercial culture. To suggest that the problem is internal, something treatable by pharmacists or psychotherapists, mystifies the situation and distracts from the pursuit of effective solutions.

To sum up, the mass culture affects self-identity through the manufacture and promotion of fantasies that may to some degree operate as standards against which one understands and judges experience, and around which we organize our goals for the future. The screen projects heroic characters confronting moral crises and demonstrates how different responses lead to different consequences for self-definition. The commercial advertisement uses highly condensed tropes to associate products with laudable attributes of character. Mass culture organizes and institutionalizes certain visions of self (and intimacy) through "well-trodden narrative formulas and visual clichés."[8][178] The fact that this happens at the global level further detaches people from symbols and meanings that are local and personal and that, in other times, might have been central in constructing a more secure and stable sense of self.

Notes

1 Collins, *Interaction ritual chains*, 372.
2 de Tocqueville, Alexis, *Democracy in America.*
3 See Sennett, *The fall of public man: on the social psychology of capitalism.*
4 For example, Weigel, *Labor of love: the invention of dating.*
5 de Tocqueville, Alexis, *Democracy in America*, 601.
6 PerryUndem, The state of the union on gender equality, sexism, and women's rights: results from a national survey conducted by PerryUndem.
7 Hermans and Gieser, History, main tenets and core concepts of dialogical self-theory.
8 Burke, *Language as symbolic action: essays on life, literature, and method.*
9 Ehrenreich, *Fear of falling: the inner life of the middle class*, 56; Conley, *Elsewhere, U.S.A.*
10 Taylor, *The ethics of authenticity.*
11 Coontz, *A strange stirring: The Feminine Mystique and American women at the dawn of the 1960s.*
12 Bateson et al., Toward a theory of schizophrenia.
13 Herzberg, *Happy pills in America: from Miltown to Prozac.*
14 Berger et al., *The homeless mind: modernization and consciousness*, 78.
15 For example, Demos, *Past, present, and personal: the family and the life course in American history*; Coontz, *A strange stirring: The Feminine Mystique and American women at the dawn of the 1960s.*
16 Giddens, *The transformation of intimacy: sexuality, love & eroticism in modern societies*, 130.
17 Coontz, *Marriage, a history: how love conquered marriage*, 121.
18 Quoted in Coontz, *The social origins of private life: a history of American families 1600–1900*, 96.

114 *The origins of uncertainty*

19 de Tocqueville, Alexis, *Democracy in America*, 601.
20 Taylor, *The Adams Papers, Papers of John Adams*, 208–213.
21 Coontz, *The social origins of private life: a history of American families 1600–1900*, 222.
22 Klaw, *Without sin: the life and death of the Oneida Community*.
23 Freud, *Civilization and its discontents*.
24 See for example Lantz et al., The American family in the preindustrial period: From base lines in history to change.
25 Coontz, *A strange stirring: The Feminine Mystique and American women at the dawn of the 1960s*.
26 Wang, For young adults, the ideal marriage meets reality.
27 Celello, *Making marriage work: a history of marriage and divorce in the twentieth-century United States*.
28 See Illouz, *Cold intimacies: the making of emotional capitalism*.
29 Butler, *Awash in a sea of faith: Christianizing the American people*.
30 The Harris Poll, *Americans' belief in God, miracles and heaven declines: belief in Darwin's theory of evolution rises*.
31 Fischer, *Made in America*
32 Greenfeld, *Mind, modernity, madness: the impact of culture on human experience*.
33 Sass, *Madness and modernism: insanity in the light of modern art, literature, and thought*.
34 Taylor, *A secular age*.
35 Morgan, *The Puritan family: religion and domestic relations in seventeenth century New England*.
36 Cherlin, *The marriage-go-round: the state of marriage and the family in America today*, 41.
37 Bender, *Community and social change in America*.
38 Quoted in Morgan, *The Puritan family: religion and domestic relations in seventeenth century New England*, 133–134.
39 Meads/Wilson Collection, Correspondence.
40 Butler, *Awash in a sea of faith: Christianizing the American people*.
41 Jones, The evil eye among European-Americans.
42 The Harris Poll, *Americans' belief in God, miracles and heaven declines: belief in Darwin's theory of evolution rises*.
43 Halpern, *Social capital*.
44 Pew Forum on Religion and Public Life, "Nones" on the rise: one-in-five adults have no religious affiliation; Pew Forum on Religion and Public Life, A closer look at America's rapidly growing religious "nones."
45 Cox et al., *I know what you did last Sunday: measuring social desirability bias in self-reported religious behavior, belief, and identity*; Presser and Stinson, Data collection mode and social desirability bias in self-reported religious attendance; Smith, A review of church attendance measures.
46 Pew Forum on Religion and Public Life, U.S. religious landscape survey: religious affiliation: diverse and dynamic.
47 Kraybill et al., *The Amish*.
48 Schnabel, Religion and gender equality worldwide: a country-level analysis.
49 Bellah et al., *Habits of the heart: individualism and commitment in American life*, 75.
50 Winterson, *Why be happy when you could be normal?*, 145.
51 Archer, *The reflexive imperative in late modernity*.
52 Bauman, *Liquid times: living in an age of uncertainty*, 1.
53 Tuan, *Segmented worlds and self: group life and individual consciousness*.
54 Shils, *Tradition*.

Recipe for existential crisis: Step 1 115

55 Giddens, *The transformation of intimacy: sexuality, love & eroticism in modern societies*; Giddens, *Runaway world.*
56 Beck and Beck-Gernsheim, *The normal chaos of love*, 32.
57 See Bruess and Pearson, Interpersonal rituals in marriage and adult friendship; Wolin and Bennett, Family rituals.
58 Ellul, *The technological society.*
59 Ehrenreich and English, *For her own good: two centuries of the experts' advice to women.*
60 Kaplan, *Earning the Rockies: how geography shapes America's role in the world*, 65.
61 Strand, Is the world's best croissant in Australia?
62 Hochschild, *The outsourced self: intimate life in market times.*
63 Ritzer, *The MacDonaldization of society* (revised ed.).
64 Luckmann, Personal identity as an evolutionary and historical problem.
65 Bauman, *Liquid modernity*, 19.
66 Becker, *The denial of death.*
67 Berry, Window poems.
68 Streitfeld, Give yourself 5 stars? Online, it might cost you.
69 Lamb, "I felt disgusted": inside Indonesia's fake Twitter account factories.
70 O'Connor, New York Attorney General targets supplements at major retailers.
71 Ewing and Davenport, Volkswagen to stop sales of diesel cars involved in recall.
72 Jensen, Essential part of the Volkswagen diesel repair is the owner.
73 Flitter, The price of Wells Fargo's fake account scandal grows by $3 billion.
74 Warner et al., Oceana study reveals seafood fraud nationwide.
75 Warner et al., Oceana reveals mislabeling of iconic Chesapeake Blue Crab.
76 Einstein, *Black ops advertising.*
77 Wu, Mother Nature is brought to you by . . .
78 Giddens, *Modernity and self-identity: self and society in the late modern age*, 172.
79 Bauman, *Liquid modernity.*
80 Black, A review of compulsive buying disorder.
81 Illouz, *Why love hurts: a sociological explanation*, 209.

6 Recipe for existential crisis
Step 2: weaken neighborhood ties

A community is the mental and spiritual condition of knowing that the place is shared, and that the people who share the place define and limit the possibilities of each other's lives.

Wendell Berry, *The Loss of the Future* in "The Long-Legged House"[1]

The differentiating processes

Supertrend 5: unicultural/consensual to multicultural/pluralistic

In a culture characterized by diverse belief, values, and lifestyles, and with the declining influence of community, it's more difficult to feel confident of one's point of view and easier to feel isolated. However the microculture automatically generated by prolonged discourse in egalitarian intimate relationships generates a sense of community, shores up confidence in self-identity, and serves as a protective shield against uncertain and contradictory meaning in the larger culture.

As the country has become more demographically and culturally diverse, Americans more often have to take into account the likelihood that those with whom they interact won't share their point of view or values. With diversity, it takes greater effort to generate common ground, and, thus, successful communication is likely to require increasingly sophisticated empathic skills, such as a capacity for unbiased listening and an ability to bracket off beliefs and values as relative. Diversity heightens awareness of the extent of one's own distinction, bringing the sense of self into active review, and it makes it easier to become ensnared in questions of personal value. As this happens, consciousness will tend to be directed inwardly in consideration of these issues. As this intensifies, and one is increasingly caught up in issues of self, it becomes harder to be effective in interaction with others.

As a result, one may become isolated, if not physically, at least psychologically. In the absence of supportive personal relationships where issues of self-identity can be taken for repair, this can become a downward-spiraling loop, leading to greater isolation, narcissistic focus, existential insecurity, and other psycho-emotional difficulties.

DOI: 10.4324/9781003010234-8

Recipe for existential crisis: Step 2   117

In the past, Americans more frequently lived in communities characterized by lower levels of diversity and higher levels of consensus, and, while this meant they might feel more connected to those around them, the experience of self wasn't likely to be as vivid and was, therefore, not as much a matter of concern. But increasing diversity has not only brought personal identity into doubt, it has tended to undermine faith in the idea of solid truth about anything, even about the status of the sciences, where "many now see science as a sea of social opinion, the tides of which are often governed by political and ideological forces,"[2] a point well illustrated in the recent difficulty of achieving social consensus over problems so seemingly a matter of objective data as the role of smoking in cancer, the value and safety of childhood vaccination, and the threat of climate change. Ours is an age of burgeoning diversity of opinion, rapidly shifting and contested information, sham, and pervasive uncertainty. It is ever more difficult to navigate this world without the supportive environment provided by strong social relationships, yet it is increasingly difficult to form and sustain them.

In the late nineteenth century, Emile Durkheim used the term "anomie" to describe a condition of disordered and alienated life that results as a society declines in consensual standards and values and community begins to come apart.[3] He linked anomie to the waning of tradition and religion. In their decline, and in the face of growing diversity, social mobility, and community turnover, societies become multi-valued and somewhat normless, and this engenders disorientation and alienation. To adapt, people turn from the dissensus of the larger society to the consensual haven provided by their social relationships.

Deep personal relationships – especially marriage – are the key sites for this.[4] There, routine conversation may counteract the effects of the larger culture's anomie. Discourse co-conditions the minds of conversational partners, accreting new shared symbols and reconfirming established ones. This bridges partners' minds and, in so doing, promotes psychological stability. The process establishes a local sense of community and normative order supplying otherwise alienated people with confirmation of meaning and a secure base of sensibility.

The anomic impacts of modernity have strengthened in recent decades, amplified by the isolating pressures of the mass culture and by the introduction of new electronic communication technologies that have, on the whole, tended to exacerbate feelings of personal threat (e.g., of not having sufficient followers, likes, interesting selfies, etc.) while at the same time making it increasingly challenging to sustain the deep, long term relationships that can shield against that threat. Partners who have created enough shared meaning to benefit from the nomic function of their connection now have to sustain the precepts and values that bridge their minds against a blizzard of contrary information flows and the allure of communication technologies whose unseen impacts are divisive and promote insecurity of self.

As one example, since the 1970s, television has grown from a handful of channels, all moderately voiced so as to compete for a majority audience, to

118 *The origins of uncertainty*

hundreds of channels that now compete, not for the center, but for splintered audience segments and their particular interests, values, and lifestyle choices. This compounds the sense of normlessness and uncertainty, encouraging the perception that one is surrounded by a babble of alternative values and interests, all of equal validity. Of course, the internet has accelerated this. As well, for many in America's service economy, work life often requires coordinating ideas and values with each of a wide range of well-separated groups with whom one comes in contact. These factors make it harder to sustain the particular meanings that connect intimate partners' minds.

Although it would be an overstatement to describe Colonial America as a consensual uniculture, there's no question that the country has become increasingly diverse in the 400 years since the European colonization. At the start, the colonies were populated primarily by English settlers, with small numbers of other groups, including Native Americans. By the time of the Revolutionary War, though still home to an English majority, the colonies also comprised Scots, Germans, Dutch, Irish, French, Swedes, and Africans.

The U.S. gained 80,000 Spanish American citizens after the acquisition of Texas and the New Mexico and California territories in the mid-1800s.[5] In addition, some 110,000 enslaved blacks were forcibly imported from Africa in the 1800s,[6] and 36 million people immigrated to the United States between 1820 and 1920.[7] These included, in significant numbers, Germans, Irish, Swedes, Danes, Norwegians, Italians, Greeks, Arabs, Armenians, Russians, British, Austrians, Hungarians, Poles, Romanians, Chinese, Japanese, and French Canadians. As of 2007, the number of people living in U.S. households who were born in other countries amounted to more than 12 percent across the country as a whole and more than 20 percent in California and New York State,[8] and, as of 2015, the foreign-born share of the U.S. population had increased another 2 percent to a record level of 14 percent, more than quadrupling the number of immigrants who were in the U.S. in 1965.[9]

Similarly, the proportion of U.S. households where a language other than English is spoken has increased from approximately 13 percent in 1980 to greater than 25 percent in 2010.[10] And, in some urban areas, the range of languages spoken is vast. For example, according to a recent report, more than 800 languages are spoken in New York City today.[11] Thus, in contrast with the intense diversity of America in the twenty-first century, the Colonial era was consensual and unicultural. In addition, twenty-first-century America is relatively blended such that people of diverse backgrounds are likely to encounter each other either directly or through the mass media. Against this, in the early Colonial period, colonists of differing backgrounds were more likely to be concentrated in separated geographic regions (for example, most Germans were located in the middle Atlantic colonies, and most Africans in the southern colonies). The individual colonies were fairly homogeneous, and, without technologies of rapid transportation and the mass media, ideas tended to stay put. Beliefs were more likely to be consensually and actively reinforced within the range of social encounters of daily life in stable and relatively isolated communities.

Recipe for existential crisis: Step 2   119

It's been largely the same story as regards religion. Although descriptive statistics for Colonial America's religious divisions aren't as neatly available as they are now, and there was diversity, many of the colonies were intended to operate under the authority of a single central church.[12] For a variety of reasons, this couldn't be sustained, and the remainder of America's history witnessed increasing religious diversity. Now, as we've seen, Americans divide into more than 140 religious denominations.[13] Expanding diversity is also expressed with respect to social class, race, and gender. In the U.S., truly homogeneous sites for education, work, worship, and recreation exist but are unusual. Because of this, people of varying demographic backgrounds commonly encounter each other in the United States, and where there's difference of demographic background there is increased diversity of beliefs and values, a higher probability that people will perceive the world as constituted of a smorgasbord of relative knowledge, and, as a result, a requirement of greater interpersonal skill in interacting with others of unknown moral commitments, beliefs, and sensitivities. That's a tough order. As sociologist Robert Putnam has argued, diversity undermines social solidarity and community connection, at least until enough time has passed for some degree of assimilation to occur.[14] He describes the psychological response to diversity as "hunkering down," a tendency to distrust, disconnect, and withdraw. But the larger expression of this is manifest in resurgent nationalism, the U.K.'s "Brexit," Canada's "Wexit," religious intolerance, and border walls between the U.S. and Mexico: the feeling of existential insecurity that accompanies diversity displaced, projected, and writ large.

Supertrend 6: stationary to mobile

> *With as much as 10 percent of the American population moving in any 5-year period, neighborhood turnover makes it difficult for communities to sustain themselves, to provide support, protect traditional symbols and practices, and stabilize the meanings on which members base their lives. For those with the skills to build and sustain them, symbolically interdependent interpersonal relationships can stand in.*

As discussed in Chapter 4, the population in Colonial America was stationary. Most people lived within a few miles of their paternal home, predominantly in rural areas and small communities of fewer than 2,500 people. Migration within the country was fueled by both immigration and improved longevity.[15] Both of these factors increased population density, creating pressure on living space within communities. Even so, however, until the 1800s, a majority of Americans continued to live in rural areas and rarely moved great distances. In contrast, an overwhelming majority of the population now live in urban areas, and the population isn't stationary.

The U.S. is among countries with the highest rates of internal migration.[16] With the exception of the period of the Great Depression, the proportion of Americans who have moved across state lines within their lifetime rose steadily until the end

120 *The origins of uncertainty*

of the twentieth century.[17] The rate of internal migration has declined since then, peaking at about 30 percent in 1990. Nevertheless, approximately 12 percent of Americans change residence each year, and between 5 and 6 percent of Americans move across a county boundary, in many cases a distance great enough to disrupt existing social ties.[18] In addition to these cross-county moves, each year about 2 percent of Americans move from one state to another. This may not sound like a large amount, but consider that, at this rate, during any 5-year interval, one in ten Americans has moved to a different state.

Today, many Americans have their U-Haul stories: the breakdowns, the truck wedged under the low-clearance bridge, the chaos of packing day, the misdirected GPS routing, the inadvertent separation of those in the cars from those in the truck. U-Haul's former marketing slogan, "Adventures in moving," has become part of the American narrative. These stories, often warmly recounted, are classic tales of heroism – of leaving the familiar to venture into the unknown seeking a better life. But they mask the memories of the other side, of the costs of moving: of selves left behind and friendships laid aside, of periods of loneliness, homesickness, anxiety, and the stress of disrupted routines. And of the toll taken by increased uncertainty. As sociologist Peter Berger and his colleagues wrote, "A world in which everything is in constant motion is a world in which certainties of any kind are hard to come by."[19]

On top of this, for many Americans, even if jobs don't require periodic moves, they may nevertheless involve frequent travel within the U.S. and beyond, or frequent interaction with others from other geographic locations. Today, social relationships may be spread out among people throughout the country or the world. This can occur in the context of face-to-face encounter or through the panoply of new electronic communication technologies. Email, web forums, texting, and so on, make it possible for the affairs of geographically dispersed people to intermingle, even in cases in which one is asleep while one's social partners are awake and active. As Giddens asserted, this "reordering of time and space realigns the local with the global," and, in this, "the self undergoes massive change."[20] This happens as lives become disconnected from community influence.

Population churn impedes the development of community involvement and connections with local institutions. In small towns and cities alike, the steady circulation of people in and out of neighborhoods frays cords that attach identity to community and, through that, to tradition, consensual knowledge, and common morality. The more neighbors come and go, the less a street functions collectively, and the less the neighborhood contributes to the sense of identity. Commenting on the status of life in upstate New York, one elderly respondent told a student interviewer from one of my classes, "There aren't any neighborhoods anymore. People are separate . . . leery of one another, except maybe in rural areas, but still it's not the same."

Studies of Americans' patterns of social contact document a gradual decline over the last 30 years in socializing in taverns and bars and, particularly, with neighbors, while there's been a corresponding increase in time spent

Recipe for existential crisis: Step 2 121

socializing in family relationships.[21] Why? The more we feel ourselves different from those who live around us, the more our own sense of self-identity comes into focus (as Bauman put it, "Just as community collapses, identity is invented"),[22] and the more we're forced to turn inward and to close personal relationships to nurture and support the sense of self.

Vance Packard's *Nation of Strangers* explored the impacts of growing social mobility among America's middle and upper-middle classes, on individuals as well as on the communities in which they lived.[23] As part of his project, Packard surveyed people living in then high-mobility Azusa, California, and lower-mobility Glens Falls, New York. Compared with the residents of Glens Falls, those of Azusa were more likely to "wish their life was less lonely," were less likely to have voted in a municipal election, less likely to have talked to old friends during the last year, more likely "to feel that too many people in the area are strangers," less likely to "be a member of a local club," more likely to wish that they "had more good friends," less likely to feel that there are people in the community who respect them for the way they live, and so on. Looking at the extreme, suicide rates rise strongly and significantly as a function of residential instability.[24]

Reflecting broad concern over the atomization of American society and the fraying of community, the concept of "social capital" has gained significant attention among social scientists in recent decades. Whereas financial capital refers to an individual's or organization's access to money, and human capital refers to the technical skills and knowledge assets of an individual or work group, social capital refers to the extent to which one is able to draw on the resources of interpersonal and community ties.[25] Social capital is operationalized in terms of social network density – how many different people one typically connects with during the week. This is a factor that might reasonably be expected to be negatively associated with narcissistic self-focus – the more people one is in contact with, the lower the level of narcissism – and positively associated with the advent of the digital communications revolution.

Scholars who take this view see the advent of various internet social resources, such as chat rooms and social network sites, as solutions to America's problems of eroding community.[26] There is no question that the internet makes it easy to connect with huge numbers of people. Yet, even as digital communication technologies have dramatically eased access to others, narcissistic self-focus has become all the more visible. This is because digital communication technologies provide a thin-to-inadequate degree of social connection, one that tends to disrupt empathy and is easily dismissed (nobody panhandles using texts). The intimate partnerships formed online that stay online are unlikely to have the same impact on self-definition that is associated with face-to-face relationships. In fact, some suggest that digital connectivity may actually increase the risk of mental disorders for some people.[27] The interpersonal connection is less satisfactory and meaningful without physical presence, which is why one doesn't attend weddings or funerals remotely using video conferencing, and why attending a World Series baseball game remains a

122 *The origins of uncertainty*

widely desired activity, even though the play can be seen much more clearly on television.[28] Businesses that foster face-to-face encounters among employees are more productive and profitable than those that permit employees to channel their contact through the internet and smartphones.[29] Although it may not be impossible to develop interdependent structures of meaning and shared culture through a written medium (e.g., in a frequent exchange of detailed, nuanced letters), without face-to-face encounter it's much more difficult to generate shared symbols with unique meanings that bridge the minds of partners and shore up existential security.

Greater connectedness has been associated with a number of positive outcomes including enhanced health and longevity, economic prosperity, more responsive and vibrant government, and lower crime rates.[30] And yet Putnam has documented a dramatic decline in the number of people participating in community groups during the late twentieth century.[31] By the mid-1970s, according to Putnam, nearly 60 percent of Americans attended some type of club meeting regularly. But, by the 1990s, only 30 percent did.[32]

In many small and mid-sized towns today, the Masonic halls, the buildings that housed social organizations such as the Elks, the Moose, the Veterans of Foreign Wars, and the American Legion stand vacant, as do many churches, the congregations of which have dissipated, or which have been sold and converted to private use. The internet has created new opportunity for civic influence, and many sign web petitions or donate money online. However, generally, traditional clubs such as the Kiwanis were devoted to ongoing and comprehensive improvement of the local community, whereas the typical internet-based group tends to focus more narrowly on the niche interests of its members, without any necessary relevance to the lives of the people who live next door.[33]

Arguably, club membership statistics are reflective of levels of social connectedness and, therefore, some aspects of social capital and possibly of community. But, in many clubs and in the great majority of social resources on the internet, membership does not achieve the character of true community or convey its benefits. Membership in a real community means ongoing participation in a shared symbolic environment where there's a conjoint vision of the world, shared memory and history, and commitment to a common framework of ethics and morality, even at the expense of autonomous self-identity.[34] In true community, membership shapes and even limits the self: to some degree, individualism drops away in favor of communal identity and meaningful intersubjectivity. People are more likely to share beliefs and values along a broader range of dimensions and to share methods of reasoning, agree on standards for what counts as truth or falsehood, and so on. In community, minds are connected through participation in a fabric of common sense, a largely unexamined field of foundational values and beliefs that, in their broad acceptance throughout the group, make the world seem sensible and secure. "Groupthink" may impede creativity, but shared mind is essential for mental health.

Recipe for existential crisis: Step 2   123

People can form associations or participate in groups or political or civic events, and, where there's convergence of individual interest, many Americans do participate in social and political meetups, community clean-up events, online sites for sharing baby clothes and redistributing goods that are no longer wanted, drum circles, cancer fundraisers, political protests, and so on. But this type of collective action is merely additive, not systemic: the whole is not greater than the sum of the individuals who have banded together in collective pursuit of a particular personal interest.[35] These activities are all to the good, but they don't confer the existential benefits of self-defining and meaning-stabilizing community.

When there's no shared morality or shared memory, ongoing social contact or negotiated vision of the world that binds the people in a group such that they can make claims on each other's identities, when the group's character and norms of interaction would be much the same were different people swapped in as members, the group may constitute a lesser type of social connection that sociologist Robert Bellah and his colleagues referred to as a "lifestyle enclave," a collection of individuals with overlapping interests and demographics acting in common,[36] but all still separated in their own "irredeemable loneliness."[37]

Many argue that a large number of Americans' remaining social connections do not exhibit the qualities of true community, and this has negative consequences for the vitality of American society and, especially, for the existential challenges experienced by isolated Americans who are left with fewer social resources (or within digital culture's framework of thin sociality). However, as we've seen, the trends of change that have led Americans toward greater disconnection at the level of political or community involvement have created the possibility for important personal relationships to supply a significantly deeper level of connection than in previous eras – true community on the dyadic scale. Indeed, given the fraying of connections at the community level, it's become vitally important for significant interpersonal relationships to stand in in this way. Instead of men leaving the house to commune with other men at the Odd Fellows Hall, the Moose, or the Elks, there's now the possibility for men and women with the necessary social and psychological prerequisites to obtain equal or greater satisfaction and fulfillment in deep community with the intimate partner whom they regard as their moral and intellectual equal.

Supertrend 7: rural to urban

> *Urbanization in America took off in the early nineteenth century like a space rocket. The movement of the majority of the country to dense population centers has created numerous changes in psychology and social behavior. In particular, urbanization transformed America into a nation of strangers, creating conditions that enable deception and foster distrust and fear of others. City*

124　*The origins of uncertainty*

> *life is filled with superficial interactions with people we don't know and are unlikely to encounter again. Against this, significant interpersonal relationships become more distinctive, vivid, and important for sustaining psycho-emotional balance.*

On any person who desires such queer prizes, New York will bestow the gift of loneliness and the gift of privacy . . . . the residents of Manhattan are to a large extent strangers.[38]

The roots of important psycho-social dynamics that characterize life in this era are embedded in the transition from living in small communities, where people were more likely to recognize each other and make more accurate predictions of each other's values and beliefs, to living in the midst of diverse crowds of strangers. In particular, urbanization's diversity fostered the development of distrust and protective inward withdrawal (again, Putnam's "hunkering down"). According to sociologist Robert Wuthnow, as population density goes up, "the proportion of residents who say that they trust their neighbors 'a lot' goes down – from about 60 percent in the least densely populated areas to less than 20 percent in the most densely populated areas."[39] Urbanization encourages the strategic management of social relations and self-presentation in order to regulate psychological distance and vulnerability to strangers. And it fosters reluctance to reveal the deeper parts of self outside of a cautious, slow, incremental process of disclosure that establishes trust and authenticity.

Imagine that, like me, you live in a small rural village. As you walk around town, it's likely you'll greet those you pass. Even if you haven't any desire for ongoing social contact, and you don't necessarily recognize each other, it's understood you might encounter each other again. Indeed, a time may come when you need each other's assistance. With the local volunteer fire company and ambulance team comprised of your neighbors or people a street or two away, it's vital to avoid negative relationships, lest those first responders not feel an overwhelming concern at the news that it's *your* house that's ablaze. People who live in small towns encounter each other repeatedly: at the village convenience store, at church, the post office, the park, or the walking trail. This provides a basis for enduring reputation and gossip, but also predictability and trust. So it pays to sustain cordial relations. With neighbors' cooperation, you have a better chance of influencing the circumstances of the local environment. This creates incentive to not stray far from the lifestyle standards of the town. In this way, one's stake in the web of local relationships tends to bring self-presentation and the sense of personal identity into alignment with others in the neighborhood and, in so doing, may eventually create actual community, with its many benefits, but also with its felt limitations to personal identity and autonomy.

The city affects identity and self-expression too, but in a different way. As demonstrated by Sacha Baron Cohen's *Borat* character, those who stroll through Manhattan greeting passersby risk, at the minimum, some surprised or annoyed reactions. This is an irony of urban life. The anonymity and diversity

Recipe for existential crisis: Step 2 125

of the city enable a freeform cultivation of identity, but, in packing diverse and unknown people into close proximity, the basis for trust is reduced, and so people keep to themselves, masking themselves off from others, operating more or less continually at interpersonal DEFCON 4. In this way, it's common to experience a sense of isolation even in the midst of crowded streets and towering high-rise apartments. In the city, people more often engage the defensive attitude of "civil inattention" described by Goffman.[40] This is the psychological pretense that, even in the midst of crowds, nobody's around us or, perhaps, that those around us are not so much actual human beings as some kind of lesser animated object, a trick of the mind that makes rides in packed airplanes and rush-hour subways easier to bear. Jammed together, we avoid each other's gaze, looking instead at the elevator's floor numbers, or the subway ads, placed to provide somewhere else to rest our gaze when we seek to avoid eye contact with those around us. We turn away internally too, becoming psychologically insular.

So, in the face of urban density and diversity, aside from those few who seem to regard their lives as some form of performance art, most avoid overt public displays of self, because to advertise uniqueness is to risk opening lines of contact between oneself and others whose values and sensitivities can't be predicted accurately. Part of how self-identity is established is in our assessment of the qualities others ascribe to us: we see reflections of ourselves in the way that others seem to regard us. In the city's social diversity, the quantity of and the degree of divergence in these data may be difficult to integrate, and so we avoid exposing ourselves to it. Certainly, today, some go to great lengths to bring themselves into public attention online, but most would shy from doing so in real time, in public spaces, in the presence of actual others. We're more exposed and vulnerable in close-in encounters than in the shallow, edited, and controlled exchanges that occur in digital media. So most hold back. In the city, those who fail to do this stand out as annoying and narcissistic. A prime example of the moment is the person on public transportation carrying on a loud conversation on a cell phone.

In America, the nineteenth century's massive migration from small towns to cities created fertile conditions for the appearance of con artists. Urban anonymity brings routine exposure to strangers, who may easily manipulate appearances and prey on the naïve.[41] The greater the potential for deceit we sense around us, the greater the psychological and social consequences. Recall that psychohistorian Julian Jaynes contended that the earliest human encounters with strangers gave rise to the problem of deceit, and this played a role in stimulating the emergence of self-awareness, a first step in the eventual development of modern personal identity.[42] The dawning realization that some people were not as they presented themselves, but were capable of engaging in strategic deception resulted, inevitably, in defensive contemplation of the authenticity of self and other. This type of reflective awareness would not have been characteristic of our early ancestors, who rarely encountered anyone unlike themselves. Without a sense of contrast, self-awareness fades, encounters with others are more routine, and communication is more signal-like. Over

126 *The origins of uncertainty*

the long haul of history, ever-mounting social diversity exposed humans to others they didn't know and who might be deceitful, which heightened awareness of self as distinctive and vulnerable. This dynamic, massively amplified in the modern city, changed the interpersonal world from one of unreflective coordination to an intimate world of caution, strategy, and privacy.

Con artists thrive in cities (or over the phone or on the internet), where anonymity makes it simple to present falsely. So the city encourages a self-protective suspicion of others and the deliberate regulation of interaction, characterized by a cautiously incremental process of self-disclosure. The conditions of the city discourage meaningful self-expression until a sufficient history of interaction has accumulated to establish authenticity and trust. In this way, the vast majority of interactions in the city tend to be shallow and consciously restrained. In small towns, we regulate our depth of relationship with those around us because we know about them, we know our contact may continue, and we may need their good will. In cities, we regulate our depth of relationship with those around us because we *don't* know about them, and the encounter is more likely to be transient. As we've seen, the conditions of contemporary American life tend to encourage the formation of private and particular selves, and all the more so in cities. But, in cities, where the sense of distinction is amplified to the point that it may encourage a painful sense of isolation, the public display of unique aspects of self verges between unusual and pathological. Unlike the situation in small towns, where displays of individuality are restricted out of desire to blend into a system of community standards, and relationships are comprised, at least to some degree, of mutual obligation or its potential, in the city, people hold back out of a rational sense of caution that's based in uncertainty about those around them. The net effect of this is that, whereas those in small towns may yearn for the opportunity to pursue their distinction and individuality, perhaps dreaming of the freedoms of the city, city dwellers are almost continuously reminded of their isolation: psychologically alone in the midst of many, moving among others to whom they hesitate to open up meaningfully. As a result of this, many city dwellers wistfully consider the attractions of relocating to the country or a small town in pursuit of the experience of meaningful community. So there's equivalence between the small town and the city in that both constrain self-identity, but they do so in ways that are quite different, and, in the case of the city, the psycho-emotional consequences are more severe.

Nineteenth-century urbanization gave birth to new disorders related to the pressures of atomized life in cities. These included agoraphobia, a variety of panic anxiety at being in crowded public spaces that leads people to avoid venturing out of their houses. The first mention of agoraphobia in the annals of medicine occurred in 1871, which is about the time that the rate of urbanization in America had climbed to its zenith. As well, by the onset of the twentieth century, doctors were diagnosing hysteria in women and "neurasthenia" (shattered nerves) in men with increasing frequency, particularly among the middle class. It was thought that the social and emotional complications of the city played a

Recipe for existential crisis: Step 2 127

key role in this, so much so that it was suggested at the time that neurasthenia be renamed "New Yorkitis."[43]

The deleterious effects of urban life on other areas of mental experience are now well appreciated. A recent meta-analysis of studies of psychosis attributes a 2.37-fold increase in psychotic disorders to living in cities.[44] This increased incidence of the most severe forms of madness doesn't occur because city services attract people with existing psycho-emotional disorders; rather, it's that city life is sufficiently isolating and psychologically difficult to push what may otherwise be passing episodes of low-level distress into much greater significance.[45] Social isolation poses significant problems for mental health, and, in fact, states with lower population density have much higher rates of suicide;[46] however, city life bears its own palette of stressors, among which, ironically, is also the heightened sense of isolation that results from feeling alone in the midst of massive numbers of other people.

Giddens believes that the move to cities changed the marital relationship from its status in former times as a relatively public, formal, local, and superficial connection to a new and far more intimate form: profoundly private, exclusive, unique, emotionally consequential, full of significance and mystery, and not necessarily local.[47] As Americans moved from small communities into urban spaces, in the normal case they are surrounded throughout the day by unknown people and, with them, engage in myriad impersonal transactions. It's against this backdrop of high-volume, anonymous, and superficial encounters that important relationship partners (even those across the country, at the end of an email or Skype connection) stand apart and become emotionally and psychologically vivid. Urbanization has greatly stretched the continuum of experience in personal relationships, setting the stage for our twenty-first-century expectation of them to be deeply meaningful and enriching and a vital part of the life course. This is more difficult to sustain and may well contribute to the present era's high rates of relationship dissolution. In a point that will be taken up again at the beginning of the next chapter, in former times, the family was not a private, intimate organization in the sense we understand it today, and marriage was not predicated on the generation of personal meaning, self-identity, and emotional enrichment. The spiritual and psychological experience of intimacy dramatically deepened, and the family became a haven in a world that seems increasingly anonymous, "heartless," and bereft of meaningful community ties.[48] But the family too has been dramatically weakened. As Harari notes, we live "in an increasingly lonely world of unraveling communities and families."[49]

As the mix of population in urban areas became too great to permit accurate generalization about the values and sensibilities of those living nearby, it fostered what Bauman called "mixophobia" – a tendency for people in urban spaces to retreat into enclaves populated as much as possible by those with similar lifestyle and ethnicity.[50] Industrialization, which accompanied and fueled urbanization, created "a geography of isolation" populated by "vast numbers of workers [who] knew little . . . about people unlike themselves."[51]

128 *The origins of uncertainty*

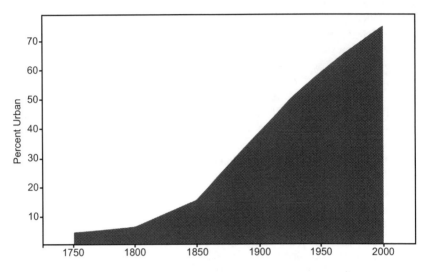

Figure 6.1 Percent of U.S. Population Living in Urban Areas, 1750–2000
Source: Data from Monkkonen (1985) and Wuthnow (2013).

Discussion of the small town – big city contrast implies the common availability of both environments, but the small town, with its stereotypically strong community ties, is nearly gone from the American experience. Americans have been migrating to urban environments since the beginning of the Industrial Revolution, dramatically so during the nineteenth century. In 1790, there were just 24 towns in the United States with populations greater than 2,500, but, only 60 years later, there were 236.[52] During the nineteenth century, 36 million immigrants entered the U.S. through its coastal cities,[53] and these newcomers intensified the strong pattern of increasing urbanization and diversity. In 1800, the city of Cincinnati had a population of 750 people,[54] but, just 60 years later, it had grown to 161,044. In the same span of time, the population of New York City increased from 60,000 to more than 800,000, nearly half of whom were foreign-born.[55] Only 5 percent of Americans lived in urban areas in 1800.[56] Today, more than 90 percent do.[57] Free of the limiting influences on meaning and self-expression of rural or small-town life, intimates dwelling in urban centers have greater opportunity to spin connective meaning that is distinctively theirs, and, because self-expression is freer in the city, they are likely to have a deeper influence on each other's sense of self. The partners serve as primary referents for each other's beliefs and values and also shape and reinforce each other's core sense of personal identity. The value of this support is felt all the more intensely in the swirl of urban diversity and anonymity.

Imagine, for example, that Korey regards himself as a careful driver, but a cop gives him a speeding ticket, which challenges that aspect of self-identity.

Recipe for existential crisis: Step 2 129

In a rural community, Korey is surrounded by people who observe his driving regularly and he may know that his neighbors have witnessed such a large sample of it that they would agree that his ticket was a fluke, unjustly issued, given their knowledge of his character and his driving habits. So this aspect of Korey's self-definition benefits by being shored up in the external community. But, if Korey lives in a Manhattan high-rise, there can be no such sense of external community-based support. Still, Korey's intimate partner and best friends have significant exposure to his character and driving habits and can credibly shore up Korey's self-perception. And so, in the city, in the absence of close community, interpersonal relationships gain importance in creating and sustaining the sense of personal identity and worth.

Notes

1 Berry, The loss of the future, 71.
2 Gergen, *The saturated self: dilemmas of identity in contemporary life*, 16.
3 Durkheim, *The division of labor in society*.
4 Berger and Kellner, Marriage and the construction of reality: an exercise in the microsociology of knowledge.
5 Parrillo, *Diversity in America* (3rd ed.).
6 Trans-Atlantic Slave Trade Database, Trans-Atlantic slave trade – estimates.
7 Daniels, *Coming to America: a history of immigration and ethnicity in American life* (2nd ed.).
8 United States Census Bureau, Statistical abstract of the United States: 2008.
9 Pew Forum on Hispanic Trends, Modern immigration wave brings 59 million to U.S., driving population growth and change through 2065. Views on immigration's impact on U.S. society mixed.
10 Ryan, Language use in the United States: 2011.
11 Roberts, Listening to (and saving) the world's languages.
12 Bonomi, *Under the cope of heaven: religion, society, and politics in colonial America* (updated ed.).
13 Pew Forum on Religion and Public Life, U.S. religious landscape survey: religious affiliation: diverse and dynamic.
14 Putnam, *E pluribus unum*: diversity and community in the twenty-first century.
15 Bender, *Community and social change in America*.
16 Molloy et al., Internal migration in the United States.
17 Comprehensive data from earlier periods aren't available; however, see Ferrie, The end of American exceptionalism? Mobility in the U.S. since 1850.
18 Pew Center for Research on Social and Demographic Trends, American mobility: Who moves? Who stays put? Where's home?
19 Berger, et al. *The homeless mind: modernization and consciousness*, 184.
20 Giddens, *Modernity and self-identity: self and society in the late modern age*, 80.
21 Dunkelman, *The vanishing neighbor: the transformation of American community*; Marsden et al., Trends in informal social participation, 1974–2008
22 Bauman, *Liquid modernity*, 171.
23 Packard, *A nation of strangers*.
24 Barkan et al., State and regional suicide rates: a new look at an old puzzle.
25 Halpern, *Social capital*.
26 For example, see Baym, *Personal connections in the digital age*.
27 For example, Gold and Gold, *Suspicious minds: how culture shapes madness*.
28 See Collins, *Interaction ritual chains*.

130   *The origins of uncertainty*

29 Turkle, *Reclaiming conversation: the power of talk in a digital age.*
30 Halpern, *Social capital.*
31 Putnam, *Bowling alone: the collapse and revival of American community.*
32 *Ibid.*
33 Dunkelman, *The vanishing neighbor: the transformation of American community.*
34 Bellah et al., *Habits of the heart: individualism and commitment in American life.*
35 Bauman, *Liquid modernity.*
36 Bellah et al., *Habits of the heart: individualism and commitment in American life.*
37 Bauman, *Liquid modernity*, 35.
38 White, *Here is New York*, 19.
39 Wuthnow, *Small-town America: finding community, shaping the future*, 113.
40 Goffman, *Behavior in public places: notes on the social organization of gatherings.*
41 Kasson, *Rudeness & civility: manners in nineteenth-century urban America.*
42 Jaynes, *The origin of consciousness in the breakdown of the bicameral mind.*
43 Blom, *The vertigo years: Europe, 1900–1914.*
44 Vassos et al., Meta-analysis of the association of urbanicity with schizophrenia.
45 Gold and Gold, *Suspicious minds: how culture shapes madness.*
46 Barkan et al., State and regional suicide rates: a new look at an old puzzle.
47 Giddens, *The consequences of modernity*; Giddens, *Runaway world.*
48 Lasch, *Haven in a heartless world: the family besieged.*
49 Harari, *Sapiens: a brief history of humankind*, 382.
50 Bauman, *Liquid times: living in an age of uncertainty.*
51 Sennett, *Together: the rituals, pleasures and politics of cooperation*, 37.
52 Bushman, Family security in the transition from farm to city, 1750–1850.
53 Daniels, *Coming to America: a history of immigration and ethnicity in American life* (2nd ed.).
54 Coontz, *The social origins of private life: a history of American families 1600–1900.*
55 New York City Department of City Planning, NYC total and foreign-born population 1790–2000.
56 Monkkonen, *America becomes urban: The development of U.S. cities & towns 1780–1980.*
57 Wuthnow, *Small-town America: finding community, shaping the future.*

7 Recipe for existential crisis

Step 3: foster isolation

When asked how often they felt like no one knows them well, more than half of the respondents surveyed said they feel that way always or sometimes. Just under half of all those surveyed report sometimes or always feeling alone and or left out. At least two in five surveyed sometimes or always feel as though they lack companionship, that their relationships are not meaningful, that they are isolated from others and/or that they are no longer close to anyone.

Cigna Corporation, Cigna U.S. Loneliness Index:
Survey of 20,000 Americans[1]

The atomization of experience

Supertrend 8: lives intensely public to lives intensely private

Privacy catalyzes self-awareness but was virtually unknown in America's deep Colonial past, unusual in the social and material circumstances of the times. Even the family wasn't a private social unit as we think of it today. Between then and now, opportunities for privacy have greatly expanded. As a result, the inner life of most Americans has become more complex, distinctive, and individuated, and there is now an ever-present risk of isolation. In the past, when people were always in the public gaze, social differentiation was difficult, but today the problem is connection.

In 1929, author and critic Virginia Woolf famously asserted that, in order for a woman to contribute significantly in literature, she must have an independent income and, figuratively, "a room of one's own." In other words, a woman cannot find her stance in the world without independent means and the opportunity that this affords to withdraw from the confining web of self-definitions and expectations of the broader culture and emerge as someone with distinctive perspective and voice. Woolf was writing about the history of women in literature, attempting to explain why so few had made notable contributions up to that time.[2] As we've seen, the beginnings of the decline of patriarchy and the possibility of economic independence were stirring by 1929. So too was the possibility of personal privacy – a room of one's own – the availability of

DOI: 10.4324/9781003010234-9

132 *The origins of uncertainty*

places to withdraw from contact with others. And urbanization, by then in full force, was working its irony, promoting awareness of personal differentiation and isolation in the midst of the immense diversity and anonymity of the city. Privacy enhances the opportunity to develop a sense of self as distinct, constituted of a particular history and unique ideas, preferences, values, and virtues. The flowering of identity, which tends to occur in late adolescence or early adulthood, is catalyzed by privacy.

As a negative illustration, the relationship between privacy and the development of an awareness of self as unique is manipulated in military boot camp, where recruits are denied privacy in order to suppress their sense of their own individuality and promote group identification, where, as in Stanley Kubrick's film *Full Metal Jacket*, marines in their training platoon jog together singing the cadence, "I love working for Uncle Sam. Let's me know just who I am." Recruits are required to give up symbols of individuality (personalized clothing and hairstyles) and to work, move about, sleep, shower, and eat in common – even to defecate publicly in toilets without stalls or doors. The recruit's sense of personal distinction is deliberately broken down because the military doesn't want its platoons comprised of independent thinkers, but of cohesive, like-minded teams. So it forces recruits to suppress individualism and merge self with the group. (This may have been easier to accomplish in pre-modern times when there was less individual distinction to suppress.)

Privacy refers to the state of being alone and undisturbed, but also to secrecy, concealment, and protection from public knowledge. These separate aspects of privacy – physical and psychological – interact. The privacy of physical seclusion gives rise to our sense of ourselves as clearly distinguished from others in our inner experience: the secret feelings, meanings, tendencies of thought, emotions, and so on that we conceal from those we work with, from our neighbors, our children, our parents, and so on. Today, we know little of the interior lives of each other, unless we've become intimates, which means that, through the normal process of incrementally deeper disclosure, we've gradually made each other aware of our private universe of internal experience (and, in a deep enough relationship, have mutually shaped it). Because privacy, as physical retreat, seeds the emergence of the rich, differentiated subjectivity typical of modern American life, and because, by any modern standard, physical privacy didn't exist in America's Colonial past, intimacy, as a condition of two individuals entrusting each other with their interior secrets, couldn't have then existed to the degree that it does now. Our experience of intimacy is historically and culturally unique and accompanied by its particular rewards (community and deep friendship) and its trademark difficulties (fragility and the risk of psychic disorientation in the termination of a relationship – see Chapter 13).

Physical privacy is a prerequisite condition for our sense of who we are to emerge as distinctive, but physical privacy was virtually nonexistent in the past. The modern understanding of the concepts "public" and "private" dates only to the late seventeenth century when these words began to be used to differentiate events open to scrutiny by anyone from those witnessed only by family and friends.[3] This marks the initial point of separation between public community

Recipe for existential crisis: Step 3   133

life and an increasingly vivid and psychologically important intimate life. Gradually, the family became an intimate group with its own sequestered culture, and this created a site where we cultivate a sense of ourselves as members of a family independent of our status in the external public order.

But, in the deep past, this wasn't so: the family wasn't as we assume it to be today. It was neither private nor intimate. In other eras, the family lacked firm boundaries and has been described as "an open-ended, low keyed, unemotional, authoritarian institution" that was "short-lived, being frequently dissolved by the death of the husband or wife or the death or early departure from the home of the children,"[4] which may have been as soon as at 10 years old.[5] In historian Lawrence Stone's terms, the family of the seventeenth century and earlier was more like a bird's nest than any model we might relate to the family today. It was characterized by an atmosphere of distance, deference, and manipulation.[6] Colonial Americans, "had little sense that interactions among people were qualitatively different within the family than outside it."[7] (There were none of Betsy Rath's secrets there.)

And the seventeenth century was just the beginning of the distinction between public life and family life. Privacy *within* the family – personal privacy – didn't evolve until later. Even while the concept of privacy was beginning to take root, up to 1800, "the realm close to the self was not thought to be a realm for the expression of unique or distinctive personality"[8] – privacy was not yet personal. Indeed, the word "personality" didn't come into wide use or acquire its modern psychological connotations – its association with the nature and structure of inner experience – until the nineteenth century. It took time for modernity to socioform American society into its present atomized condition of people with highly distinctive interior experiences.

Today, our experience of the world is private, individuated, and deeply subjective, and communication in the interpersonal realm often focuses on the regulation of who shares what with whom and how far we allow our relationships to become mutually transformational. As we've seen, Sennett believes that communication may have been more signal-like in earlier times, more a matter of delivering information, and less like today's process of coordinating personal perspectives. Self-disclosure of privately held beliefs and values has become the key dynamic in building intimate bonds, but, in a society of relatively like-minded people, living in the public eye in smaller, tighter communities, communication may be more like a system of signal exchange. There, the function of self-disclosure is reduced, as there's much less unique personal experience to impart. Language doesn't convey as much private meaning because there's less private meaning to convey.

On the other hand, as the processes of modernity ramped up, and Americans began to experience the world in increasingly private terms, the fact that we do communicate using symbols added fuel to the movement of America from a mostly public and communal society to one ever more finely segmented and experienced differently from person to person. Without the constraining influences of tradition, community, hierarchical authority, and so on, symbols so easily acquire private spin. And, as they do, language functions both to connect

134　*The origins of uncertainty*

but also to separate, and we become ever more aware of our own differentiation and isolation, of the difficulties of bridging our private worlds, and are compelled to seek validation of our uniquely nuanced meanings through disclosive talk with confidants. Without constraint of strong external authority, communication-as-symbol changes the world into one full of private points of view, and interpersonal life then begins to center on the assessment of credibility and trust, the coordination of meaning, and on problems of connection and communion versus loneliness and isolation, and support versus insecurity. The emblematic illustration of this transformation in the early twentieth century is T. S. Eliot's masterful statement on the existential condition of modern life, *The Love Song of J. Alfred Prufrock*, in which Prufrock agonizes over the difficulty of articulating his inner experience in the context of intimate conversation ("It is impossible to say just what I mean!"). In the modern world, where there are no longer strong external anchors of meaning, all is sufficiently subjective that the achievement of common understanding between intimates can at times feel complicated to the point of hopelessness. Overwhelmed by the difficulty of making himself understood, Prufrock retreats into his brooding subjectivity.[9]

As well, in pre-modern times, the link between the role positions that people occupied and their understanding of the world and themselves was much stronger than now. In a time when perspective was linked to one's place in a relatively fixed and consensual social order, more than now, the person *was* the public role, not a private being *playing* the role. Today, however, for most of us, there's considerable distance between our private views and priorities and those we represent on the job or in our other public role performances. This is where modern concerns about the management of public reputation and image, social facades, professional confidentiality, deception, and "face-work" come into play, as we'll explore further in chapters ahead.

Distinctive experience is associated with the partitioning of physical space, changing publicly shared locations into private, intimate spaces, and, as historians have described, the architecture of the American house didn't evolve structurally to permit much privacy until the nineteenth century. In Europe, prior to the 1800s, home dwellings often housed 20 or more people, and in some cases included livestock. Up to three generations of a family might share the same bed each night. As late as 1880, 49 percent of the population of Berlin lived in one-room households.[10] A typical house in the Tidewater area of Virginia and Maryland in the seventeenth century had only two rooms,[11] while a typical New England dwelling in the same period had only four rooms (living room, kitchen, and two bedrooms), and this served an average family of six individuals.[12]

Often, the bedrooms didn't have walls that extended completely to the ceiling, allowing sound to carry and people to look over the wall into the next room. An absence of hallways in houses meant that people had to pass through adjacent rooms as they moved from one part of the house to another. In this way, family members were in more or less continuous contact with each other

Recipe for existential crisis: Step 3 135

while at home, and so physical privacy, by any modern standard, was impossible. Adding to this, as Colonial America was primarily agrarian, there was often no separate work site that might supply an alternative social context, apart from the home, to which family members might retreat for at least some relief from continual contact with each other. For the most part, one worked throughout the day alongside those with whom one slept throughout the night.

Now, for many middle-class American teens, their own bedroom is sacrosanct turf. Parents may not be allowed entrance without permission. The private bedroom is a special theater-of-the-self decorated with artifacts that represent the values and interests of the emerging person. The self is projected onto these objects, the room functioning as a kind of testing ground for personal identity. Such would not be possible to the same extent in an environment in which the bedroom was shared with siblings, and certainly not at all if a single bedroom was shared by the entire family in common, as was the case in many early American dwellings.

Self-differentiation is a matter of privacy, and privacy is a matter of boundaries, of spaces that allow people to live distinctively from others and to experience autonomy of action and independence of thought. Apparently, this relationship has been apprehended and is valued by many adult Americans today, who are now opting for solo living at the highest rate in history. Today, single-occupant households are tied with the households of childless couples as the most prominent residential type in the United States.[13] According to recent census data, 27 percent of adult Americans now live alone, with the rate at more than 50 percent in some large cities.[14] From our vantage in the twenty-first century, it may be hard to imagine the extent to which privacy was not always part of life, but consider the depiction in Figure 7.1 of travelers arriving and booking in at a fifteenth-century European inn.[15] Men traveling together share a large dormitory-type room at the inn, remove all their clothes, and sleep together in bed. Similarly, in early Colonial America, "unrelated persons of the opposite sex often shared bedrooms and even beds."[16] But the boundaries of privacy were evolving. By the early nineteenth century, in Melville's *Moby Dick*, Ishmael is agitated by the thought that circumstances might require him to sleep naked in the same bed with Queequeg, the South Seas harpooner and cannibal. But, if not in the same bed, and if not with people who might snack on your feet, Ishmael did think shipmates sharing a room at an inn was acceptable, as people today might share an expensive hotel room at a professional conference.

Sleeping in the same room with complete strangers is another matter. The remarkable diary of the Marquise de La Tour du Pin (1770–1853), a French aristocrat in exile to America following the French Revolution, describes her trip from Boston to Albany, New York, with Monsieur de Chambeau. They stopped for the night at an isolated inn in the woods (likely near modern Stephentown, New York), which was inhabited by a man and wife who were 40–45 years old, as well as eight or ten children and a grandfather (perhaps 13 people, one of whom was likely pregnant every 2–2.5 years of her adult life):

136 *The origins of uncertainty*

Figure 7.1 Travelers at an Inn
Source: Wright, 1871, p. 345.

>This is what happened to Monsieur de Chambeau that very evening [...] Some French oaths, which he alone knew how to pronounce, were heard suddenly, in the middle of the night. In the morning he told us that toward midnight, he had been awakened by a gentleman who was sliding into the vacant part of the double bed where he was resting. Furious at this invasion, he had hastened to jump out of his wooden bedstead from the opposite side, then he spent the night on a chair.[17]

Disconnected from community, withdrawn into our own spaces, values, media encounters, and beliefs, the sounds of the outside world blotted out by the personal playlist pumped though our earbuds, much of our experienced world is now uniquely ours. With communal experience on the decline,

Recipe for existential crisis: Step 3 137

consciousness has become sequestered to a degree unknown to previous generations of Americans.[18] The freedom to craft self-identity as we wish and think what we will can be intensely liberating, but it can also trigger forms of disquiet that accompany physical or psychological isolation: anxiety, loneliness, distrust, and a vulnerability to thinking in extremes. Consider how common it is to churn over some slight experienced during the day, perhaps from a relationship partner or a colleague at work, rehearsing what we'll say when the injustice is finally brought to dramatic confrontation. But the whole business immediately dissipates from consciousness the instant we actually come into contact and begin talking. In isolation, the mind is a composter of extreme thought.

As argued throughout this book, although privacy catalyzes the emergence of a vivid sense of self, self-identity is nevertheless a social production requiring some degree of communal validation. Privacy stimulates recognition of ourselves as distinct, but doesn't in itself solve the problem of personal definition. And so we don't have to look far to observe people struggling to establish themselves as highly distinctive and differentiated from those around them – but in front of an audience, which is required for the display of distinction to have meaning (e.g., selfies taken from the rim of an active volcano and shared on Facebook; marriage proposals staged in a busy urban park and accomplished with the assistance of a flash-mob marching band, the video uploaded to YouTube; arriving at the prom in a surrealistically stretched limo; becoming an internet icon by performing awkward dances in public locations – in general, in many kinds of strategically conspicuous *public* performances).

So this dynamic cuts both ways: the high levels of privacy in modern life allow us to establish ourselves as differentiated, but this feeds our sense of isolation and propels us to seek confirmation in social communion with others. With opportunities for meaningful communion now in shorter supply, we may run into difficulty. This wasn't the case in America's past. In the stronger communities of former times, self-identity was submerged in group identification, never emerging as distinctive to the extent we moderns experience it. Sociologist Rose Coser was not a fan of this, writing of the "greedy" nature of communal life: the problem of tight community making self-differentiation, flexibility of perspective, and cosmopolitan appreciation of the modern world difficult.[19]

Some of the boundaries that separate us from others are physical, as in having one's own bed, bedroom, car, apartment, studio, or office. The more of these spaces that are ours, and the more control we're able to exercise over them (especially who else gets access), the more vivid our sense of ourselves. As modernity has advanced, it's brought increasing opportunity to differentiate physically in this way. But the circumstances of modernity also allow us to differentiate ourselves in new linguistic and sociological terrain. Opportunities to see ourselves as psychologically distinctive increased with the virulent spread of vocabulary related to mental dispositions, mostly cooked up by psychologists and psychiatrists as America became increasingly preoccupied with issues of interior experience in the twentieth century.

138 *The origins of uncertainty*

Only a generation and a half back, no one would have known what you were talking about if you spoke of being OCD, an alpha male, a low or high self-monitor, having ADHD, attachment issues, superego conflicts, alexithymia, separation anxiety, a death wish, being an introvert, a satisficer or a maximizer, suffering from afluenza, having borderline personality, low self-esteem, PTSD, an inferiority complex, ego problems, and so on. However, each mention of one of these hypothetical and often controversial dispositions, now common in talk and writing, calls forth reflection about our own qualities of self. Thus, psych-speak comprises another new conceptual system in which we distinguish ourselves from those around us. And, here again, we exercise discretion over what of this we reveal and what we retain in the privacy of our minds. We control access to this information to regulate intimacy and we present different versions of our self to others for strategic social purposes, such as getting a job, charming someone on a dating site, or speaking to our children. Pushing the consequences of the new privacy of language to its extreme, in his analysis of the relationship between modernism in art and literature and the particular forms of psychopathology found in our era, psychologist Louis Sass notes that, in some cases, the assignment of private meaning may result in such extreme interiorization that language becomes overly private, and communication becomes impossible: the speaker stands in relationship to language alone, "a language that, in its emphatic self-sufficiency, has itself come to stand as an epitome of isolation and self-involvement."[20]

As regards the sociological terrain, in addition to modernity's increasing opportunities for physical and psychological distinction, American society has also become more diverse and segmented (the topic of the last section of this chapter). The sense of self arises in the perception of our membership of different sociological categories, not only in the qualities we associate with those who occupy a particular social category, but also in differentiation from the alternatives:[21] I'm Catholic, not Protestant. I'm middle-aged, not old. Male, not female. Live in New York, not Missouri. A vegetarian, not a vegan. And so on. As Sartre argued, the self is defined not only in who you are, but also in who you aren't, who you make yourself not be.[22] And the range of possibilities has greatly increased. The net result of all this is our sense of ourselves as distinctive and our lives as well separated from others and private. The anonymity of urban life has greatly fueled this, allowing personal identity to become more private and complicated and presented in multiple ways in pursuit of complex social objectives.

In summary, I want to bring attention to four considerations about privacy as an historically variable condition related to the development of a visible self-focus in contemporary America, a focus now often referred to in modern psych-speak as narcissism, as if the root of this was a recent epidemic flaw in personality, rather than a sensible, conditioned response to the circumstances of modern life. Physical privacy, the privacy made possible by our participation in a language of symbols whose meanings we can spin in our own ways, psychological differentiation, and sociological segmentation boost our sense of self as unique and hidden. Seeing oneself as vividly distinctive can

Recipe for existential crisis: Step 3   139

be thrilling at times, but, overall, the heightened experience of self as private and distinctive encourages inward focus. Some degree of stress may result from the need to juggle conflicting impulses about autonomy and connection, leading sometimes, perhaps, to a wistful longing for a kind of communal connection that was more common in America's past (likely, one whose limitations would probably leave most of us yearning for greater personal freedom). We may obtain this type of connection in our intimate relationships where the process of differentiation and privacy reverses: physical boundaries are broken down so that our partner is incorporated into our private spaces – our private physical spaces as well as our private inner subjectivity (in a sexual relationship, these factors combine and may achieve their deepest expression in the act of making love). But the physical sharing isn't essential (many people have sex without being intimate, and many are intimate without having sex). Deep intimacy is a psychological experience that occurs as we construct the world together. To a degree, we may feel ourself and our partner to be more than just a team, actually a kind of corporate entity. In a friendship or a marriage that has achieved deep intimacy, distinctions between self and intimate other blur. In an intimate marriage, a threat to the spouse's reputation may be experienced as a personal threat, because the sense of self has expanded to include the partner. Stereotypically, one thinks of marriage as involving partners living in the same dwelling, sleeping in the same bed, intimately familiar with each other's bodies. However, whether we marry each other or not, or live in the same house or not, or sleep together or not, a deeper intimacy connects us when we open the private contents of our mind and emotions to our partner and, in our interaction, engage in a process of mutual influence. In this, our minds bridge, and we become symbolically interdependent.

In our deepest relationships, whether or not we cohabit, we shape each other's mental experience, coordinating private ideas about the world, coming to agree about what morality requires of us, constructing a story of the relationship's past, developing a shared language, and, importantly, participating together in formulating and then supporting each other's self-story: coming to agree about who we are, where we've come from, what we stand for, and where we're heading. We develop a shared *internal* privacy. Happy and affectionate partnerships are certainly possible without this, and, no doubt, are common. Indeed, as we saw in Chapter 3, some may recoil from deep psychological intimacy, perhaps out of fear for a fragile sense of self (maybe badly wounded in prior intimate experience, or never established securely in childhood, and so on), skittish about the risks that inhere in reformulating the self-story with significant dependence on another person. My point is only that the unique conditions of life in twenty-first-century America provide the possibility for this transformational depth of connection in which those in a significant relationship can become mutually influential partners in a joint consciousness, co-authors of a framework for interpreting the world and appreciating each other, a shared history and morality, and emotional coordination: true community on a micro scale – a marriage of minds.

140   *The origins of uncertainty*

Supertrend 9: linear information flows to self-reflexive loops

The warp-speed acceleration of information flows has contributed to a sense that knowledge is ephemeral, sometimes irrelevant before it can be fully understood, that it is difficult to find solid ground in which to sink foundations for self-identity and ideas about the larger world. The often self-referential nature of fast-changing information contributes to a sense of irreality. This amplifies the importance of deep relationships, which stand out for their ability to function as sites where one can experience stability of support for premises about self-identity, morality, and the external world.

The information dam had broken in the hills,
the town was flooded with information.
All autumn the data rains had fallen heavy,
Making a violent rattle on roofs and windowpanes.

It had been a very heavy information season.
Then in winter information continued to swell the streams;
the memory reservoirs were full.

(Hoagland, 2018, "Data Rain")

Beginning in the early 1800s, a stream of inventions accelerated the distribution of people and information throughout the United States, and this increased the likelihood that Americans would encounter varied and unfamiliar points of view. This had a variety of effects including (1) destabilizing self-identity and bringing it into sharper focus, (2) promoting a sense of separation from others, a feeling of uniqueness (and sometimes isolation), and (3) making personal relationships seem more vivid, deeper, and of greater importance (and, hence, riskier). These outcomes result from routine exposure to the ever widening range of beliefs, value systems, and epistemologies of American society. Diversity calls values and beliefs into question and, where diversity is sufficiently intense, causes us to turn more often to our intimate partners for support and the psychological benefits of community. Beyond this, as information flows increase in speed and intensity, and information sources increasingly engage in deceit in order to garner attention and advertising revenue (sensationalism in commercial advertising, political deceit, fake news, etc.), it tends to foster the perception that the world is made of a great deal of hype and spin. With this comes cynicism, personal insecurity, and reduced faith in social institutions, especially those more obviously connected with the manufacture of information for economic purposes such as journalism, politics, public relations, and marketing/advertising. Added to this, the sheer volume of information pumped through the culture everyday can generate stress.

Kenneth Gergen identified six "technologies of social saturation," inventions that sped up information flows in the United States: rail, post, automobile, telephone, motion pictures, and commercial publishing.[23] These are relatively

Recipe for existential crisis: Step 3 141

low-tech inventions, and the list is missing canal travel, the telegraph, and photography, all introduced in the nineteenth century. Augmenting this are the high-tech innovations of the twentieth century in communications and transportation, especially the advent of air travel, and radio, television, and video, followed by the computer-based digital innovations that have come along since the 1980s, including the internet and smartphones. No transoceanic voice communications cables were in place before the 1950s, and there were no information satellites in orbit prior to 1969, though there are now hundreds.[24] The rate of introduction of technologies of consequence in this process was gradual but increased to a high level by the late twentieth century. Table 7.1 lists approximate dates of introduction for some of them.

In addition to these inventions, improvements in transportation systems also increased the speed and reach of information flows in the United States. Before the development of canals and railroads in the 1800s, news traveled by horse or coastal ship, spreading very slowly. For example, it took fully 6 days for the news of the signing of the Declaration of Independence in Philadelphia to be published in the newspapers of New York City, 12 days before the news appeared in Boston's papers, and 15 days before it appeared in Williamsburg, Virginia.[25] Wars have broken out and been fought to conclusion in less time (indeed, in the War of 1812, the Battle of New Orleans was fought *after* the signing of the treaty ending the conflict, but communications were then so slow that no one on the battlefield knew the war was over). A society in which information moves so slowly can be said to be characterized by linear information flows. This means that feedback is so delayed that it becomes irrelevant.

On the other hand, distribution of information is now virtually instantaneous via the internet and television. The U.S. television news networks supplied live coverage of the Marines landing on the beaches in Somalia in 1992. In other words, the journalists invaded Somalia in advance of the military

Table 7.1 Approximate Year of Introduction of Communication Technologies

Telegraph	1830s
Still photography	1830s
Rotary power printing	1840s
Typewriter	1860s
Facsimile	1865
Transatlantic cable	1866
Telephone	1876
Phonograph	1880s
Motion pictures	1894
Radio	1900s
Television	1928
VCR	1980
Personal computers	1985
World Wide Web	1994
Cell phones and texting	(about 2000)
Facebook, Twitter, and digital social networking	(mid-2000s)

142 *The origins of uncertainty*

whose invasion they were there to cover, and, because of the presence of the news media, it was possible for feedback and commentary on the invasion to occur in real time. In recent years. the military has recognized that unmanaged live media coverage of operations can be disruptive of military policy and goals. Not only does the broadcast media's instant feedback create the possibility of public censorship before an operation can show benefit, it may even allow opposing forces to learn campaign plans and troop dispositions, as happened in the Falklands War of 1982, where BBC news broadcasts explaining why Argentine bombs were failing to explode led the Argentine military to recalibrate their weapons for greater effectiveness. The military now keeps a managing hand on the feedback circuit: embedded journalists are managed journalists.

The speed of feedback is now so highly accelerated that it tends to coat our experience with a patina of doubt and insubstantiality, undermining faith in the integrity of information. To some degree, this is so every day, but the days following the 2013 bombing at the Boston Marathon provided a particularly vivid example. Immediately after the bombing, Twitter and other online instant news forums became a chaos of information, which James Gleick characterized as a "fog of news."[26] Flows of mostly inaccurate information tweeted and microblogged were so heavy that they left constantly on television news reporters inarticulate, staring at their smartphone screens and struggling to keep up with the general public's more quickly evolving assessment of the story the journalists were supposed to be on top of so that they could interpret it, vet the facts, and report the story to the general public. But the public had left them behind. The Cambridge, Massachusetts, police department had to use Twitter to beg the public not to rebroadcast tactical police information picked up from police scanners for fear that suspects the police were pursuing would learn their intentions. In its struggle to compete for relevance in the torrent of information, the *New York Post* ran 3 days of inaccurate headlines about the event, at first grossly overstating the number of dead and then misidentifying suspects. On Reddit, the user-generated information sharing service, users assembled their own analysis of suspicious characters based on user-supplied cell phone pictures of the marathon. According to Gleick, virtually all of the crowd-sourced analyses on Reddit and other internet sites turned out to be inaccurate. In a coda to this display of runaway information, 1 week later, on April 23, hackers took over an Associated Press Twitter feed, falsely asserting that the White House had been bombed and the president injured. The Dow Jones index instantly lost more than 140 points.

In addition to problems created by the viral spread of unverified information, there are two additional consequences of the presence of highly accelerated information flows and feedback loops. First, a source who yields to the temptation to take advantage of instant feedback to modify a message on the fly undermines faith in the authenticity of public communication. Consider, for example, the impact on public trust in political communication now that it's become routine for candidates for national office to quickly reverse

Recipe for existential crisis: Step 3 143

their positions on issues in response to unanticipated negative public reaction. The easy example is 2012 Republican presidential candidate Mitt Romney's instant retraction following broad negative reaction to his video-captured remarks arguing to his followers that the Republican party should write off the 47 percent of the American population who would never vote for a Republican under any circumstance. Or, as the 2016 campaign got under way, candidate Jeb Bush's immediate reversal following public outrage over his statement of support of his brother's decision to go to war in Iraq following the 2001 terrorist attack. It's not just that political candidates appear to be made of mirrors, willing to voice any opinion likely to gain them advantage; the effect spills over, calling doubt on all public discourse. We live in a world in which the manipulation of perception has become more visible than in the past. And not just in politics. Consider the stock market, where rumor of a stock's possible increased trading price may lead to immediate increases in the trading price of the stock. A substantial proportion of the estimated 8 billion spam emails released into the internet each hour attempt to produce exactly this effect.

Both the stock market and the political process are driven by perception, but so is much of the rest of our unanchored, disembedded experience of the world, and, in the context of the ultra high-speed communication flows of modern societies, many aspects of life take on this quality of looping self-reflexivity in which information has a tendency to contaminate its own factual basis. For example, when social scientists report data about the precarious nature of modern marriage, this information tends to be quickly and generally disseminated and then becomes part of the background of information that influences couples' decisions about whether to sustain or end their relationships.[27] When you've been informed by expert sources that nearly half today's marriages end in divorce, and serial monogamy is the dominant pattern, it's considerably easier to contemplate giving up on your marriage and moving on in search of your next partner.

Christopher Lasch wrote of the self-referential nature of modern mass media, which "conjure up a world in which it is hard to tell the difference between fantasy and actual events,"[28] and Lasch, who died in 1994, didn't live long enough to witness the extent to which this has been amplified by the chaos of unfiltered information on the internet that feeds upon itself.[29] The sense that there's no steady independent external reality, that, ultimately, all is perception, is disquieting. Layering on top of this the knowledge that perception is often actively and effectively manipulated by the media and others for political and financial gain contributes to a generalized sense of distrust in the veracity of what we hear and read. The condition of public information flows in contemporary America's society of spin fosters a psychological response that effectively encloses all knowledge in quotation marks.

A second consequence of highly accelerated feedback is confusion of the relationship between two of the traditional components of communication systems: between the originator of a message and the audience. To a significant extent, self-knowledge arises in our assessment of how others see us, which

144   *The origins of uncertainty*

can promote this kind of confusion about self-identity (who am I aside from your vision of me?). This really isn't a great problem when lives are embedded in strong and stable structures of community and family, and linked to ongoing participation in creditable social institutions. But insecurity may result for those whose self-concept is not firmly grounded in these circumstances, but rather is blown about in the bounce-back from interaction in diverse and well separated social contexts and short-term role commitments.

Like holding a mirror in front of a mirror and seeing the infinite regress of images, we see who we are in the eyes of others seeing us seeing them seeing us and so on. The house of mirrors in a carnival is fascinating in this way, and a lot of fun because we lose the ability to distinguish the real from the mirrored image. However, if each mirror reveals a bit of a different image of ourselves and we can never straighten out which is the right one, if we don't have a secure basis of support for our self-story because the audience of that story (who are also co-authors) turns over too frequently, it can be unsettling. There's a lot of this in the frenzied, self-referential information flows of the internet and the mass culture generally, but, as well, there's more of this now than in the past in the personal circumstances of many people's lives. As a result, in the absence of strong and consistent external support, self-identity loses consistency, and we may feel somewhat estranged or insubstantial at times. This is what is being referred to in so much writing these days about "ontological insecurity" as a part of the character of modern times.

Supertrend 10: unified world and self-concept to segmented world and fragmented self-concept

> *In our time, for many, the experienced world is parsed into a range of relatively distinct social contexts, which are distinguished to some degree by variation in the nature of the self and moral profile we project into those contexts. As we express ourselves in different ways to different people in different places, it complicates our relationships, raises questions about who we really are, and fosters undercurrents of stress and anxiety.*

The freer and more technically developed a society is, the easier it is for its members to isolate themselves from each other and from society as a whole; and the greater the desire to do so in the interest of nurturing an integral sense of self. A heterogeneous sociocultural whole becomes, in the course of time, fragmented. Objects, people, and activities are compartmentalized, taking on individually a distinctiveness they did not formerly possess, but also, in the case of people, acquiring a wistful air of self-conscious isolation.

(Tuan, 1982, p. 32)

Panning across the course of America's history from the Colonial period forward, a relatively homogeneous and undifferentiated society becomes

Recipe for existential crisis: Step 3   145

increasingly segmented along the pathway to the present. "Segmentation" refers to the process in which activities and experiences become compartmentalized: what was once whole becomes ever more finely dissected and differentiated. There are many examples of this process in America's history (and likely in one's own life), but, perhaps in the most basic expression of segmentation, modern Americans think of religion, government, family, and work as well-differentiated contexts. Yet, for the Puritans, this wasn't the case: religion infused work and government, and church and government were integrally invested in the management of families. As well, in Colonial America, daily life wasn't separated from the natural world as it is now for most people. Then, America was predominantly agrarian, and so, for many, life was more strongly coordinated with nature's rhythms than with the arbitrary divisions of the clock adopted to accommodate the needs of industrial economy during the nineteenth century.[30] Before the introduction of time zones in the 1880s, noon was defined as the time when the sun was located directly overhead – when the shadow cast by the sun was the shortest length. This way of defining time, which connects the experience of time directly to nature, couldn't be sustained during an age trying to link a national system of railroad timetables. Now, regardless of how the sun appears locally, "noon" occurs at the same moment on a clock in Boston as it does 800 miles west in Cincinnati (the extent of the sun's shadow at the same moment in these two locations is quite different). This supplies one example of the way in which the natural world was partitioned from immediate experience and became remote and abstract. Others include the movement of people's labor from agrarian settings, where there was direct contact with the land, to industries in concentrated urban centers, where even the sky may be obscured from vision and contact with nature may be reduced to moments on vacation, visits to urban parks or zoos, wildlife web cams, or to other media experiences.

On the social/professional side, nineteenth-century industrialization sharply divided the roles and life experiences of husband and wife by removing economic production from the home (making clothing, growing food, etc.). As economic production was taken over by factories outside the home, so was a majority of the lives of husbands. And, according to Ehrenreich and English, "When production entered the factory, the household was left with only the most personal biological activities – eating, sex, sleeping, the care of small children, and . . . birth and dying and the care of the sick and aged." Life would now be experienced as divided into two distinct spheres: a "public" sphere of endeavor governed ultimately by the market, and a "private" sphere of intimate relationships and individual biological existence.[31] In that move, the experiential worlds of men and women were separated and sharply gendered: domestic – particular – intimate – feminine versus public – anonymous – formal – masculine.

This division was reflected in the differentiation of styles of clothing. Beginning in the industrial age, women's dress became particular and expressive, while men's dress became functional and anonymous. Men's dress in the

146 *The origins of uncertainty*

fashion of George Washington (capri pants, ornate shoes, powdered wigs, silk stockings, fluffy ruffled shirt sleeves, etc.) would be seen as feminine in style today. Only 60 years after Washington's time, men were dressing anonymously for work in factories and the professions. Although men and women now both dress with similar variety of style at work, the gendered pattern is still familiar today. Oscar night attracts a sea of men in relatively anonymous black tuxedos and women dressed as particularly as possible. Childhood dress also became gendered where it had not been prior to the early twentieth century.[32] Young children of both sexes wore white dresses in Colonial times. Blue and pink for boys and girls was a twentieth-century invention. Industrialization created and differentiated blue- and white-collar labor, segmenting society into social classes. It divided the week into periods of work and leisure and segmented the work environment by promoting occupational specialization and, especially, bureaucracy.

An ultimate hallmark of modern life, bureaucracy both reflects and accelerates segmentation. Flying red tape as their battle flag, bureaucratic practices are created in organizations as a means of establishing control in the face of growing complexity.[33] As the small business you run out of your house gains market and grows, you need eventually to hire someone to process orders, someone else to do accounting, someone else to deal with packaging and shipping. A little business starts this way and, perhaps in 30 years, occupies a building or two, employs 100 people or more, and has hired managerial staff to develop rules of governance and procedure. By this time, everyone is a specialist, and workers no longer see the totality of the organization, experiencing just the activities of their own office.

It may seem miraculous when information flows smoothly between all the offices and agencies of complex modern organizations, which is to say that bureaucracy strongly conditions communication practices. In complex organizations, responses must be routinized. As people and situations can't be treated as unique, bureaucratic encounters have an ever-present potential for alienation. Digital technologies play a significant role in this, even at the interpersonal level, where texting, email, social network sites, and other digital tools have restructured modes of human contact. Contact has become more efficient, but also more constrained and segmented, and less particular. The ultimate expression of this are the interactive voice response systems increasingly deployed as a way for a consumer to interact with a company.

The word bureaucracy didn't enter the English language until 1815, by which time the Industrial Revolution was well under way. In 1831, the U.S. federal government was run by just 666 employees, which included the president.[34] Only 50 years later, it employed more than 13,000 to operate its ever more complicated structure of agencies. Bureaucracy took areas of experience once as simple as seeing a local physician or attending the University of Paris, where originally there were just four academic departments and grew from them the complicated bureaucratic structure of the modern hospital and the university. Medicine currently recognizes more than 130 distinct specialties and is attended by a vast, compartmentalized infrastructure to handle insurance, billing, and logistics.

In a similar way, the university now slices up study of the world into myriad isolated academic departments and subspecialties. The U.S. National Center for Education Statistics currently lists more than 2,000 distinct majors at American universities. A large university might offer more than 100 different majors. These are supported within systems of institutional offices and agencies that include, among many others, institutional research, environmental sustainability, international development, career services, campus security, parking enforcement, public relations and communications, university attorney, library and computer services, student housing and dining, maintenance and groundskeeping, alumni outreach, billing, sports and athletics, health services, human resources, and a sufficient number of separated administrative offices to provide hiding places from the classroom for legions of deans, associate and assistant deans, provosts, vice-provosts, presidents and vice-presidents, and their schedulers, assistants, secretaries, technology support people, and other staff. Every office has its own turf, its unique domain of authority and responsibility, and operates in terms of ever more complicated protocols and rules. Between 2010 and 2012, the Ohio State University hired 45 full-time faculty members to teach its students and 670 administrators and staff to operate its bureaucracy.[35]

In the last 40 years, the shrinking wealth of most American households propelled wives from the home into additional paid labor and contributed to the now not uncommon situation of people dividing their working time between multiple jobs, each of which may have distinct psychological and moral demands. The lives of family members have, thus, become increasingly compartmentalized and obscure to each other, as have the professional lives of doctors in different medical specialties and philosophers, humanists, and scientists isolated from each other across the spectrum of the university's academic departments.

To be sure, the family has long been regarded as comprised of members with differentiated role functions and moral perspectives. Stereotypically, during the era of separate spheres, wives had greater responsibility for home management and were more likely to give priority to values promoting interpersonal relationships and emotional support. Husbands worked outside the home, were more likely to give value to careers and instrumental accomplishment, and were notoriously less involved with the emotional dimensions of interpersonal experience. But, in its simplicity, this level of role differentiation is easily managed and to some degree protective from stress because this type of elementary compartmentalization streamlines and clarifies responsibilities. However, the post-millennial American family, not infrequently with children shared back and forth between exes in different houses, has a much more complicated and individualized internal structure and patterns of transaction with the outside world. For many, the boundaries between work and family life have become exceptionally complex and fluid, if not chaotic, creating stressful difficulties of boundary management and integration.[36]

148   *The origins of uncertainty*

On the domestic side, for those who could afford it, architectural changes in houses built in the nineteenth century reflected the broad processes of segmentation occurring in American society. Formal parlors were added for receiving outsiders, private rooms were added for the family, and additional rooms were added for service activities. The house was transformed into a more complicated structure that permitted nuanced management of self-presentation and social relations.[37] This was coincident with urbanization and the growing need to protect self during interaction with strangers of unknown character or established authenticity. Outsiders were brought into the parlor, but not into more intimate spaces. Household inventories attest that, prior to the nineteenth century, most houses had just one mirror, but in time mirrors became increasingly common and were placed in virtually every room of the house. This may echo a preoccupation with the management of self-presentation and the need, as Eliot's Prufrock put it around that time, "to prepare a face to meet the faces that you meet." Houses were becoming more complicated in structure to assist with the increasingly complicated demands of interpersonal life and their influences on interior being.

These changes signal the development of a sense of self as private, revealed to intimates but not to others, a self increasingly managed strategically in self-conscious performance.[38] The birth of psychoanalysis and the formal study of the unconscious mind occurred during this period too, suggesting that people's interior lives were undergoing a somewhat parallel process of segmentation, resulting in such a radical apportionment that people today might, in some cases, have a repressed mental life influencing their behavior but dissociated from conscious awareness. This is a thoroughly modern idea. Though widely accepted today, its origins extend only to the mid-nineteenth century.

In recent years the process of segmentation has continued. As regards architecture, the house in the Colonial period, with a single bedroom used simultaneously by an entire family, became, by the mid-twentieth century, a house with multiple bedrooms for adults and children, at least for many middle-class families. In recent years, this trend of the partitioning of housing into segmented, private spaces has evolved to such an extent that, according to a 2007 report in the *New York Times*, the National Association of Home Builders then projected that 60 percent of custom-built houses in the United States would soon sport dual master bedrooms – a private bedroom for each marital partner.[39] Ten years later, *Bloomberg News* reported that the idea of a spacious master bedroom was obsolete: the current trend is for sleeping areas subdivided into "a complex of private chambers, jigsawed together around a smaller, cozy space that's home solely to a bed."[40]

And, importantly, consider segmentation as it occurred in the area of information and entertainment media. Americans born in 1950 grew up in a country in which everyone who watched television selected programming from only four sources (ABC, NBC, CBS, and PBS), which meant that Americans often had media experiences in common and could talk about these shared experiences at home, on the job, or in the classroom. But the arrival of cable television in the

Recipe for existential crisis: Step 3   149

1970s eventually distributed viewership over some 200 channels of simultaneous programming content, slicing the audience into small segments comprised of viewers with particular values, demographics, and lifestyles. Information and entertainment media that had once catered to a seemingly more unified America abandoned the attempt to speak to everyone and went after one niche group or another, which many feel has had disastrous consequences for civic and political life. The internet pushes this even further by providing the possibility of streaming current and historical content from countless sources.

In the time-shifting capabilities provided by modern communication technologies, including telephone answering systems, websites, automated computer response systems, and video recorders, social life and economic life have continued their odd evolution in which, outwardly, there is growing uniformity across the globe (e.g., similar pastimes, shops, styles of dress, and architecture). However, on the personal level, psychological experience has become ever more isolated from one person to the next and so compartmentalized as to threaten common sense – that is, to undermine the binding framework of foundational presumptions that constitutes the unassailable, taken-for-granted world. In the modern world, one cannot take for granted that each context one enters operates within quite the same terms of rationality. Even social interaction itself is often segmented in time, as ongoing conversations occur asynchronously between people who may never actually meet, or even be awake at the same time, and certainly not likely to have the same sensibilities. Or simultaneously between people who may not know that the person they're interacting with is multitasking several other conversations in addition to theirs. The segmentation process in housing is now so far along that it's no longer a matter of adding more rooms for increased privacy within the house now that more people than ever before in history are opting to live alone, a trend echoed in other modern nations.[41]

Life in the relatively traditional and religious world of seventeenth-century Colonial America was more cohesive. The experiences, values, and beliefs of a majority of Americans were sufficiently similar to support a unifying common sense, greatly facilitating common action and a sense of common purpose. And, with the external world more homogeneous and self-consistent, Americans' internal world was more likely to have been experienced as more integrated, coherent, and less troubled. However, in our time, we often find ourselves interacting throughout the week in relatively separated contexts, each potentially sporting its own particular slant on worldview and moral values. Navigating this type of segmented social landscape requires relativizing self-presentation – the personal qualities, information, and values we represent to the different categories of people we encounter. In this, if one has a strong, stable, and well-supported sense of self, one may simply exercise an admirably cosmopolitan manner. But, without those qualities, this process can foster a stressful sense of interior fragmentation as a result of the continual small adjustments of outlook and values that one represents to others in order to connect with them. There's more and more that you can't tell your spouse,

150 *The origins of uncertainty*

because, small matters that each may be, they would conflict with the value positions that the two of you share.

Most of us effortlessly alter important aspects of self-presentation (the language we use, the values we represent, the type of jokes we make, media experiences we admit to liking, the demands we permit others to make of us) when we're at home with our families versus out with our friends. But, in the face of America's multiculturalism, the advent of global commerce and communication, and mid-twentieth-century America's shift from work on the production line to work in jobs that place us in contact with diverse teams and clients, the likelihood that our day will require that we navigate such segmented contexts is much greater. The resulting possibility of psychological fragmentation is a signature difficulty of modern experience. Its impacts are exacerbated in the decline of community and the instability of primary ties in marriage and family. Even the strongest intimate relationships, bound together in shared meaning and mutual self-definition, are likely to be destabilized to the extent that partners' beliefs and experiences are continually pulled in new directions that can't be shared or integrated.

Conclusion

It's difficult to imagine how a twenty-first-century American could feel at ease in former times. As we've seen, modernity shapes our sensitivities and consciousness, affecting what we see and the way we think and feel. It conditions who we become and how we behave and has created common difficulties for intimacy, personal identity, and psycho-emotional balance. With every modern American's life experience comparatively unique, personal, and private, and rarely situated in meaningful community, the problems of our times are often of establishing and sustaining connection, of finding satisfactory points of balance amidst the small but continuous stresses of the era that tend to render meaning ambiguous and unstable and undermine security of self.

As we'll see, philosophical and scientific discussion of the self didn't begin until the end of the nineteenth century and accelerated, at first slowly, but then galloped off with breathtaking speed during the second half of the twentieth century. This happened as the large trends we've explored in this and the previous two chapters became more apparent and better understood, and many began to realize that problems of identity and self, autonomy and security, and community and isolation are the handmaidens of modernity, together constituting some of the greatest challenges of life in this era.

The chapters ahead zoom in on the nature of personal identity. Having described in Chapter 2 how, in early human history, the co-evolving circumstances of language and social being gave rise to mind, we'll now see how the sense of self is built in language and show how modernity transformed understanding of unconscious motivation and greatly intensified awareness of it, making accurate perception of self and other particularly tricky. We'll then explore the relationship of personal identity to social roles, institutions, and

Recipe for existential crisis: Step 3 151

technologies, and briefly review landmark theories of the self-concept that are particularly helpful for understanding the way that communication in interpersonal life works today.

Notes

1 Cigna Corporation, Cigna U.S. Loneliness Index: survey of 20,000 Americans examining behaviors driving loneliness in the United States, n.p.
2 Woolf, *A room of one's own.*
3 Sennett, *The fall of public man: on the social psychology of capitalism.*
4 Stone, *The family, sex and marriage in England 1500–1800,* 8.
5 Degler, *At odds: women and the family in America from the revolution to the present.*
6 Stone, *The family, sex and marriage in England 1500–1800.*
7 Coontz, *The social origins of private life: a history of American families 1600–1900,* 87.
8 Sennett, *The fall of public man: on the social psychology of capitalism,* 89.
9 Eliot, *The love song of J. Alfred Prufrock.*
10 Tuan, *Segmented worlds and self: group life and individual consciousness.*
11 Kasson, *Rudeness & civility: manners in nineteenth-century urban America.*
12 Flaherty, *Privacy in colonial New England.*
13 Klinenberg, *Going solo: the extraordinary rise and surprising appeal of living alone.*
14 United States Census Bureau, *America's families and living arrangements: 2013: Households (H table series).*
15 Wright, *The homes of other days: A history of domestic manners and sentiments in England.*
16 Coontz, *The social origins of private life: a history of American families 1600–1900,* 89.
17 Harcourt, *Memoirs of Madame de La Tour de Pin,* 236.
18 Giddens, *Modernity and self-identity: self and society in the late modern age.*
19 Coser, *In defense of modernity: role complexity and individual autonomy.*
20 Sass, *Madness and modernism: insanity in the light of modern art, literature, and thought,* 169.
21 Zerubavel, *The fine line: Making distinctions in everyday life.*
22 Sartre, *Being and nothingness: a phenomenological essay on ontology.*
23 Gergen, *The saturated self: dilemmas of identity in contemporary life.*
24 Giddens, *Runaway world.*
25 National Geographic Society, *Historical atlas of the United States.*
26 Gleick, "Total noise, only louder."
27 Giddens, *The consequences of modernity.*
28 Lasch, The culture of consumption.
29 See Seife, *Virtual unreality: Just because the Internet told you, how do you know it's true?*
30 O'Malley, *Keeping watch: a history of American time.*
31 Ehrenreich and English, *For her own good: two centuries of the experts' advice to women,* 13.
32 Paoletti, The gendering of infants' and toddlers' clothing in America.
33 Beniger, *The control revolution: Technological and economic origins of the information society.*
34 *Ibid.*
35 Wiener, What makes Ohio State the most unequal public university in America?
36 Conley, *Elsewhere, U.S.A.*

152 *The origins of uncertainty*

37 Kasson, *Rudeness & civility: manners in nineteenth-century urban America.*
38 As vividly described by Goffman, *The presentation of self in everyday life.*
39 Rozhon, *To have, hold and cherish, until bedtime.*
40 Ellwood, These luxury home mainstays may be gone in 20 years.
41 Klinenberg, *Going solo: the extraordinary rise and surprising appeal of living alone.*

Part 3

The shape of the modern self

8 Selfie nation

> foremost among the complexities of human life is communication . . . where each ego tests all the information received sensorily and sensually, linguistically and subliminally for the confirmation or negation of its identity.
>
> Erik H. Erikson, *Identity: Youth and crisis*[1]

> By leaving her difficult marriages and telling me why she'd left, my mother gave me, by both example and advice, the ability to do whatever it takes – to make any sacrifice and give up any and all security – in order to be true to myself . . . . No one should ever have to get divorced. But I survived.
>
> Kate Christensen, *Second Time Around* in "The Bitch is Back: Older, Wiser, and (Getting) Happier"[2]

Everyday, uncountable numbers of people shoot selfies with their smartphone cameras and upload them or send them off to others. Suddenly, selfies are everywhere. But what exactly is one? Selfie isn't merely a synonym for a snapshot. People understand the selfie to be, at some level, a visual declaration of personal identity. And so, sharing a selfie represents an unusual new form of self-disclosure. It's unusual in that in the normal case self-disclosure tends to be reciprocal, incremental, private, and intimate. But the selfie, ubiquitously on display on social network sites, is more likely to be broadcast indiscriminately and outside of any framework of reciprocity, and this aspect of the selfie phenomenon probably contributes to the aura of narcissism that's now often associated with digital culture. Indeed, the taking of selfies is sometimes facilitated by a kind of pole to which a smartphone can be attached and held out. This device is known as a "selfie stick," but also as the "narcissistick" and "the wand of narcissism." At any rate, although a selfie may very well represent a bid to be seen as a certain type of self, it certainly isn't the whole thing. The self isn't just the physical body, or the setting, or the depicted activity. The self is something more.

One must come to terms with this because, here in the early twenty-first century, self-identity has become a compelling concern for many people, and the fallout from this spills over into many areas of life including intimate interaction, political life, and, especially, personal well-being and mental stability. As per Erik Erikson, quoted at the opening of this chapter, because self-identity is

DOI: 10.4324/9781003010234-11

156 *The shape of the modern self*

socially negotiated, potentially *all* communication is implicated in this negotiation. Issues of self are fundamental to our sense of desire for each other, keeping us in each other's orbit, but they are also a prime source of relationship conflict and disruption, and, now, as a stable and fulfilling sense of self has become difficult for many people, with epidemic frequency, issues of self generate significant levels of despair, manifest as anxiety, depression, and other forms of psycho-emotional distress.

So, again, what's a self? It's what is referred to when we use the words "I" and "me." But what does it mean to say "I think," or "I can't," or "I feel," or "I want"? What exactly is the "I" to which we so often refer? And what does it mean to "know yourself" or to say, as we do, "you should be true to yourself"? Is there a *true* self that you should find and honor? Is life a journey of self-discovery and the self a sort of Jungian geocache: an intriguing hidden aspect of the psyche that one can locate by following mystical clues and spiritual waypoints? To say "I know myself" is to have had a transcendent insight through which you've come to understand yourself as an entity in the world in the same manner that you understand some other person (e.g., "I know Fred" – meaning you are familiar with his history and his capabilities, biases, tendencies of perception, likely ways of responding, and so on) or phenomenon (e.g., "I know loneliness"), and that's different from saying "I want you" or "I love you," which are descriptions of your immediate desires and feelings in the present. So here, then, are two different senses of the self: on the one hand, the flow of consciousness, and, on the other, a kind of story told about who we are and what we're all about. As we'll see, this is a basic, useful, and important distinction.

Where does the sense of self come from? Is it, as suggested by some, an illusion generated by neural activity in the brain? Is it, as suggested utterly incoherently by the Disney movie *Inside Out*, the product of a team of bickering emotional agents that run around in your skull? Is it imprinted by society? Or does everyone have to create it on their own? If it is influenced by culture, would the sense of self change if you learned to speak Pirahãs and went to live in the Amazon? Is it influenced by your friends? If that's so, would there be any consequence to your sense of self if you lost an important friend? And what happens to the self during sleep? Does it go away and come back in the morning? Or is it still there, visible in the content of dreams? Is the self stable over time? Look at a picture of yourself as a child: how is it sensible to claim that you are the same person today that you were then? Can you leave a self behind? For example, is it possible to have a former self in the same way one might have a former spouse? What about the boundaries of the self? Does it include your possessions? Your artistic creations? Your body? Your name? Your family? Your shadow? Can there be aspects of your self that you aren't aware of but are visible to others? What's the relationship of the self to the soul?

And what about pets? Do they have selves? Or souls? Does each of us comprise just one self, or might there be several? It was reported after *Titanic* sank in 1912 that 1,800 "souls were lost." Is it possible that a greater number of

Selfie nation 157

selves were lost? And, if *Titanic* had gone down with the same number of people aboard in 2012, might the loss of selves have been even greater? Why has the self-concept become so central in the expressive lives of those in modern societies who now exchange selfies and posture in painstakingly fussed-over accounts of self posted on social network and dating sites?

And, finally, why have questions like these been so much discussed by philosophers and scientists in the last 200 years, whereas they were rarely mentioned before then? The answers to these questions are of practical value because, aside from their being interesting for the light they shine on our era's presumptions about being human, in these issues reside important insights into common difficulties in intimacy, inner experience, and psychological well-being.

The awareness of self in America

As we've seen, in America, as in other Western nations, evolving conditions of the past 400 years have made the quest for self-definition, life purpose, and personal meaning much more difficult. In previous centuries, Americans lived in small communities, with little privacy, more or less in full view of each other. Opportunities to be one kind of person or another were relatively limited, if not fixed at birth. Self-identity was formed from meanings that tended to be more stable and consensual, associated with a restricted set of role options and limiting conceptions of masculine and feminine identity. In previous eras, there was greater agreement about the ethical and moral requirements of life. These derived to a larger extent from religion, which played a more influential part in Western societies than it does now. There was also greater consensus about the duties associated with social roles (teacher, military officer, priest, etc.), and, for most people, occupational roles tended to play a larger part in self-definition than they do now. By and large, people lived within families that were more likely to lose membership through death than, as they are today, through loss of sentiment.

Marriage, today a primary site for the creation and maintenance of ideas about who we are (but a precarious one), was in the past more likely to be a bond for life, held together by external forces including law, religious restriction, and economic necessity. As with other roles, the roles of husband and wife were more static and consensually understood compared with our era in which the institution of the family has been rapidly reconfiguring and in which there's been ongoing public struggle over what forms it should be allowed to take and what expectations we have for the behavior of mothers, fathers, and children. And, of particular importance, until recently, spouses were not necessarily equal in society or even in each other's estimation and so couldn't provide each other the same service in helping to form and support personal identity.

A part of the story of the progression of thought about the self-concept has to do with the interplay of the concepts soul and self. It's often said that the idea of the self evolved from the idea of the soul and, to a noticeable degree, has

158   *The shape of the modern self*

displaced it. Soul is a spiritual idea that belongs to religion and the humanities, while the self is a predominantly secular idea that belongs to philosophy and the sciences. Soul is deeply historical. Self is a newcomer. To speak of soul is to speak of the animating spark of life, and of human dignity, of morality and enduring (or immortal) qualities of character. Problems of soul include matters of guilt and redemption, of living ethically, of interacting with others in good faith. According to philosopher Ian Hacking, "The Delphic injunction 'Know thyself' did not refer to memory [and certainly not to our modern idea of self-identity]. It required that we know our character . . . It required that we know our *souls*" (my emphasis).[3]

On the other hand, the secular/scientific discussion of the self-concept tends to go in either of two directions (sometimes both): one stressing biology and the other culture. Today a hot topic in neuroscience, the discussion of self-identity centers on the mechanisms of memory, emotion, perception, and other types of brain events. Neuroscientists characteristically concern themselves with investigating *where* various mental phenomena occur (in which locations in the brain). But the cultural discussion of identity tends more to center on *when* mental events occurred, which is to say on narrative history. The self is a story we tell of our personal history, our fantasized futures, relationships that have been important to us or that we hope to form. These stories are related in internal talk as we think about our lives, and we often share them in conversation with others, following which it's not uncommon for there to be some editing and revision.

On the biological/neuroscience side, problems of self are often posed as problems of the body (e.g., endocrinological or nervous system disorders that affect mood, focus, energy, and memory) or, on the culture side, of the difficulty of forging or sustaining a coherent personal narrative in an historical period with dramatically less consistency, stability, and coherence than there has been in the past. Neuroscience treats the idea of self independent of questions of character and morality. But this reflects a failure to appreciate the vital relationship between them. To know who you are is know how to choose and how to act, and this allows you to operate your life deliberately with respect to a program of selected values. And that, exactly, is the essence of morality, character, and soul. When people struggle with self-definition, when identity is weakly established and easily blown about – as it more frequently tends to be in modern societies – there is then no clear core template of being around which values can be organized and given priority. In this state, one can never be confident that one has chosen correctly, which generates anxiety, depression, and moral anguish.

The soul-to-self shift forms a part of the story of the declining influence of religion and the ascent of the influence of rational thought and secular science. But this is only one of multiple factors that have contributed to the character of our times and, particularly, to problems in the areas of self-identity and interpersonal relationships that became visible as the twentieth century progressed, and now, in the twenty-first, seem to have achieved critical mass. The advent

Selfie nation 159

of Freudian psychology and its massive influence on modern culture is clearly prominent in this story. Freudian psychoanalysis and its derivative schools of thought ushered modernity into the family, the bedroom, and the common conception of how we get to be who we are. Sitting in a position that bridged the late nineteenth and early twentieth centuries, and virtually all areas of human enterprise, psychoanalytic theory stimulated a sweeping new awareness of self and how it is influenced by our relationships with others.[4] Accompanying this has been the creation of a cultural fascination with self-exploration, autonomy, authenticity, and self-actualization that's been amplified by the psychotherapy industry, humanistic psychology, and numerous popular literatures treating topics in self-discovery, intimate relationships, unconscious motivation, conflict management, emotional health, and personal potential.

Freud's ideas also influenced the early twentieth century's burgeoning marketing and advertising industries, which sought to profit in one way by aiming persuasive messages about products at presumably unconscious layers of motivation. This was reflected at its peak in America's mid-twentieth-century preoccupation with the possibility of brainwashing and subliminal persuasion,[5] exemplified in influential films such as *The Manchurian Candidate* and books such as Vance Packard's *The Hidden Persuaders*[6] and Wilson Key's (1974) *Subliminal Seduction*.[7] Another insidious strategy was to sow doubts about self-identity (not masculine enough, not feminine enough, not energetic enough, not rich enough, not a good enough parent, not sexy enough, not athletic enough, not well enough liked by others, not sufficiently sophisticated, not hip enough, not devout enough, no longer youthful, not happy enough, not smart enough, etc.), seeking to profit from the surging tide of insecurity of self that accompanies life in modernity.

Social insecurity

Early advertising was quaint by today's standards: a breeze of tame rational appeals, as against the twenty-first century's scientifically crafted whirlwind, pressing down at the center of confidence in who we are and how we live, suggesting our physical, spiritual, and material deficiencies (if only by surrounding us with endless images of perfect people to compare ourselves with) and providing information about various commercial products that supposedly can solve these problems, increasing our sense of security and happiness with our vision of self. The typical advertisement of the nineteenth century and early twentieth century was a printed announcement containing reasonably objective information about a product, and sometimes a lengthy rational analysis of the product's benefits. However, as the twentieth century got underway, many advertisers changed strategy, inaugurating campaigns that pitched the benefit of the product to the consumer's fantasies of self rather than objective qualities of the product, pitching "prestige instead of automobiles, sex appeal instead of mere soap."[8] The shift was from analysis of the qualities of the product to suggestions about the personal qualities of the consumer that the product might

160 *The shape of the modern self*

correct or enhance, playing to insecurity in the targeted consumer's sense of self, or creating that insecurity if necessary.

Advertisements proposed that inhaling toxic tobacco vapors could amplify masculine or feminine appeal; rubbing chemical products into the skin could restore youth or arrest aging; consuming unregulated substances called "food supplements" could protect against disease where medical science cannot; buying "Baby Einstein"-type products could save a child from a life as a dull wit; buying an Apple computer could identify one as either a social radical or a genius; buying King Arthur flour could allow one not merely to make something to eat, but to create "lasting family memories"; taking the amphetamine Vyvanse for your vague symptoms of ADHD could make you a better parent;[9] spreading Grey Poupon mustard on your hot dog could suggest to others that you have refined and aristocratic sensibilities.

Even when not making overt reference to self-identity, advertisers often link products to self-definition by placing ads in magazines, films, YouTube videos, or television shows designed to appeal to those pursuing particular identities and associated lifestyles. Feeling ordinary and indistinct, I'm interested in the lives of celebrities, read *People* magazine, and inside it find ads for cosmetic products that propose that I too can become glamorous and vivid. Or there's the women's magazine *Self,* where readers encounter ads for prescription antidepressant medications, Botox, and plastic surgery among its tips on beauty, health, and workplace success.

The average person in the twenty-first century now moves through a world so densely saturated with advertising designed to play upon personal insecurity over self-definition, or create it, that it's one of the remarkable features of modern life (and among the most alarming) that this can actually fade from conscious awareness. Moreover, with automobile manufacturers and large internet companies leveraging massive amounts of stored personal information (e.g., the contents of all your emails, continuously recorded GPS tracks of every trip you take in your car, all your web click-thru data, your affiliations on social network sites, everything you've ever selected to read from online newspapers) to micro-target commercial and political advertising, and with technologies of location-sensitive advertising arriving, the sense of self is now on the brink of unprecedented exposure to personally targeted commercial exploitation. Firms such as Cambridge Analytica and TargetPoint, for example, claim to be able to provide relatively precise psychological profiles of most U.S. citizens based on analysis of their online behavior. These data are sold to political campaigns to develop ads that target the psychological vulnerabilities of particular people. A person whose online profile suggests they're prone to be fearful might be shown ads that stress that a candidate is tough on crime and terrorism.

As America changed from a society in which life frequently played out in families in small communities to one in which life is now more frequently lived as singles amidst strangers in large urban centers, as the force of tradition decreased, as immigration and population mobility transformed America from a relatively consensual culture into an super-diverse multiculture in which one is witness to many different value systems and ways of being, and as America's mass communication systems began transmitting information so quickly and in such volume that it undermines confidence that the world consists of stable facts (including facts relevant to one's personal narrative), it's difficult not to have moments of doubt about self-identity. No longer as able to look outside ourselves for consensual definition, Americans increasingly turn the search for self inward, in a more or less perpetual subjective quest for answers to the questions, "Who am I?", "Am I good enough?", "Who should I try to be?", "What can I believe in?", and "What are reasonable benchmarks for judging if my life's been a success?" This questioning has been forced on everyone by the historically unique conditions of this era.

Americans now enjoy greater privacy, individuality, and independence from community expectation than at any point in history, and these conditions convey unprecedented freedom. But this cuts both ways. In the circumstances of anomic culture, heightened freedom and choice easily generate doubt about the viability of options pursued, and anguish over those passed by. In modernity, everybody's free to inch out onto whatever limb they like and there, in their uniqueness and isolation, lie awake at night wondering if that was the right thing to do and whether the branch they're sitting on will crack in the next strong wind. Children's films such as Disney's *Zootopia* (2016) and books such as Peter Reynolds' (2009) popular *The North Star*[10] (this one not just sold to the public but actually taught in schools) directly admonish children to avoid traditional pathways through life. In *Zootopia*, a city dedicated to the idea that "anyone can be anything," all the animals can break free of their traditional roles: a lamb can be an astronaut, a lion can be an actuary, and a bunny can be a police officer. The movie teaches that all this requires is freedom of thought, determination, and grit. Reynolds's book advises kids that the common path, the signposts that other people follow, only lead to swampy, dismal places where frogs live under dark skies. The child should instead look inside to locate and follow his or her own star. But how practical is this? What would it be like if a majority of the population of the United States lived free of the constraints of tradition and the common pathway, all pursuing their own individuality, most regarding the success or failure of their project of self as the signal test of their moral worth? Of course, that is what predominates today.

Emancipation from the constraints of tradition and community hasn't resulted in a society notable for happiness or peaceful inner contentment. Rather, self-identity has become ever more precarious, and the result has been reduced empathy, heightened social disconnection, and weakened community, accompanied by surging levels of anxiety, depression, and other psycho-emotional difficulties. *Zootopia* and *The North Star* tell America's children what most of us would not hesitate to tell our own children: Chart the course of your heart. Don't let convention suppress your potential. Follow your ideals. But, if people are to successfully pursue creative and autonomous self-expression, they need exceptionally strong social support. They need meaningfully

162　*The shape of the modern self*

deep and stable interpersonal relationships, which, there's no avoiding it, require limiting choice and giving back some measure of freedom.

Other times and places

> The Western conception of the person as a bounded, unique, more or less integrated motivational and cognitive universe, a dynamic center of awareness, emotion, judgment, and action organized into a distinctive whole and set contrastively both against other such wholes and against a social and natural background is, however incorrigible it may seem to us, a rather peculiar idea within the context of the world's cultures.[11]

No significant literature about the self was produced before the modern era, but there's been a great deal of study of the nature of the self-concept among non-modern people, and this is useful for the contrast it provides to the way in which the self is experienced today among those in modern societies. By far, the modern experience of being a person is not the only way. The fact that the conception of self is clearly variable across cultures removes any doubt that self is a deeply cultural production, and that the experience of self changed along with changes in American culture. For modern Americans, the self belongs to a single individual – that is, it's one person's story uniquely, each of us experiences our self as a detached, self-contained, and private center of consciousness. We locate our personhood within our own body and we construct our self-story out of the episodes of our personal history. We assume ourselves to be autonomous centers of conscious, private experience and, unless we're in crisis, we control the revelation of deeper aspects of our self-story to others cautiously and selectively, in an incremental process of self-disclosure. In our most important social relationships, there may be some degree of transformation of our sense of ourselves as individuals to a joint or corporate self, a "transcendental ego,"[12] but, even so, we sustain a distinct sense of our individuality.

There are numerous examples of how historically and culturally specific this is. For example, in some cultures, the self is not limited to the physical body, but extends beyond it to include the shadow.[13] There, to step on another person's shadow is viewed as an offensive insult, as if there had been a physical attack on the body. There have also been cultures in which the self was not autonomous, not constructed only of the experience of the living individual; rather, the self was understood to be composited of dead ancestors and their histories. A literal belief in reincarnation is one form that this may take.[14] (Recall that recent surveys show that 24 percent of Americans believe in some form of reincarnation.) The self may also be experienced as extending to include the larger group of relatives and kin, and sometimes of spirits presumed to have the ability to metamorphose between animal and human form. Further, in some cultural situations, the self isn't assumed to be created of the individual's conscious experience but is bestowed in ritual ceremony, with the corollary that those who don't pass through the ceremony have no valid sense of being (there are traces of this in some people's feelings of not being *really* married unless there was a church ceremony). As for relationships between selves in intimacy, even in our time there are accounts of the practice of "ghost marriage" in some areas of China and Sudan, in which a woman may marry a deceased male who was single when he died in order to obtain the social affordances and self-definitions that accompany the status of widow.[15]

The modern self, experienced as solely our own property and embodied within our physical/mental being and personal history, likely didn't exist prior to the advent of industrial society in the late eighteenth century.[16] It was forged in the massive changes to social relationships and consciousness wrought in the Industrial Revolution. Self-construction is a malleable process linked to changing cultural circumstances, which has meant that America has passed through historical periods in which the basis of the self is almost completely untranslatable to our time. So it's important to understand that the reason so many people are concerned about the sense of self today is not that science has recently stumbled on the fixed reality of the self and is now exploiting that knowledge. Rather, it's that the self, which is properly understood as a dimension of individual experience, inexorably caught up in changing social practices, cultural values, and beliefs, is now receiving a lot of attention because of the problems and complexities that modern life poses for the construction of a stable and satisfying account of who we are. In our time, the self is "fractured, fragmented . . . brittle" and "decentered."[17] The self-narrative now is crafted in social relationships, but this is an era of heightened instability in those relationships. As the problem of self-definition has come to the foreground in American life, it's become a major focus of public and scholarly discussion.

Snowballing interest

Unlike the unconscious mind, which was never written about until the late eighteenth century, the self was occasionally in focus in writing prior to the Enlightenment, but, as literary historian John Lyons commented, those incidents where the self seems to have been discovered by one writer or another were like the Viking discovery of America: each an isolated historical moment without notable influence on the ongoing record.[18] Scientific interest in the self-concept began in the late nineteenth century, stalled in the early twentieth century, started again about 1950, and then rapidly picked up speed. If you anchor the timeline of scientific and philosophical thought about the self, with Aristotle at one end and this day at the other, the span of time is roughly 2,400 years. That's about 100 years for each hour of the day. On such a scale, with Aristotle's work occurring in the first minute of today and this moment being midnight, the Enlightenment occurred during the evening hours, between 8 and 9 p.m., the Industrial Revolution happened just 2 hours ago at 10 p.m., and, consistent with the homework habits of so many university students, more than 90 percent of all the scholarship about the self-concept ever written was penned just 30 minutes before midnight.

164 *The shape of the modern self*

The nature of the self became a focus of discussion among scholars near the beginning of the twentieth century, and this discourse intensified as the century unfolded. The first research publication on the self-concept in the sociology literature didn't appear until 1954.[19] References to the self-concept in the psychological literature were scarce before 1950, but increased 300 percent between 1950 and the end of the 1960s,[20] and there was a 70-year period between 1870 and 1940 during which mainstream psychology "ignored the self as a useful concept."[21] In fact, although off to a slow start, the scholarly literature on the self-concept built throughout the twentieth century like an accumulating snowball, eventually achieving massive size and momentum.

Academic journal articles classified as a having a "self-concept" focus increased from a trickle to a torrent from the early twentieth century to the beginning of the twenty-first. According to the PsycINFO database, an accumulated total of 88 academic journal articles treating the self-concept were published during the 60 years between 1890 and 1950 (slightly more than 1 article each year), 82 more appeared in the next 10 years (8 articles each year), and then all hell broke loose. By the first decade of the twenty-first century, an average of 645 academic publications with relevance to the self-concept were published *per year*, or about 2 per day, every day, during that 10-year period. Considering that the publication of an academic journal article generally involves 2–3 years of research work, peer review, and revision prior to publication, this rate of output represents a staggering volume of activity.

These data provide one way of illustrating the observation that the self has come into focus since the second half of the twentieth century. A full account of this rapidly accumulating and immense body of work is beyond the scope of this book.[22] Instead, in the four chapters ahead, we'll selectively examine certain ideas central in conceptualizing the self, placing them in historical perspective as waypoints in the evolving landscape of interpersonal experience in the United States. A variety of positions have been in play, ranging from Descartes's notion that the self is a special immaterial entity, pure mind distinct from the body (*"cogito ergo sum"*), to the similarly radical neuroscientific position that the self is an accidental but immensely consequential byproduct of the neurobiological processes of the material brain, to the postmodern idea that, in response to the world becoming saturated with media images without any particular link to external reality, the self has become so fragmented that it no longer exists as a coherent and sustaining center of existential experience.

Tongue just slightly in cheek, these positions could be summarized as "your body doesn't matter," "your consciousness is irrelevant," and "you're really just a fiction of your media-stoked imagination." However, the position argued in this book is that a vivid sense of self-identity is an adaptive byproduct of the use of language in the context of the fluid and psychologically demanding conditions of modernity, and, like all other meaning, the sense of self is created, revised, and sustained in our communication with others. Looking at our world through this lens will reveal the threads connecting many of the prominent concerns of interpersonal experience today, including elevated rates of

Selfie nation 165

relationship disruption, narcissism, solo living, decreasing happiness, declining trust and empathy, disconnection from community and neighbors, and so on. Yet, the nature of the self is a matter of active debate, and it's useful to take a look at alternative views, because, again, as Jean-Paul Sartre maintained, we know something not only by studying what it is, but also what it isn't.

Notes

1 Erikson, *Identity: youth and crisis*, 220.
2 Kate Christensen, Second time around, 251.
3 Hacking, *Rewriting the soul: multiple personality and the sciences of memory*, 260.
4 Illouz, *Cold intimacies: the making of emotional capitalism*.
5 Carruthers, When Americans were afraid of being brainwashed.
6 Packard, *The hidden persuaders*.
7 Key, *Subliminal seduction*.
8 Marchand, *Advertising the American dream: making way for modernity 1920–1940*, 10.
9 Schwarz, *ADHD nation: children, doctors, big pharma, and the making of an American epidemic*.
10 Reynolds, *The north star*
11 Geertz, On the nature of anthropological understanding, 48.
12 Bessant, Authenticity, community, and modernity.
13 Todd, Primitive notions of the "self."
14 See, for example, Baggini, *The ego trick: what does it mean to be you?*
15 Coontz, *Marriage, a history: how love conquered marriage*.
16 Todd, Primitive notions of the "self."
17 Elliot, *Concepts of the self*, 8.
18 Lyons, *The invention of the self: the hinge of consciousness in the eighteenth century*.
19 Rosenberg, Self-concept research: a historical overview.
20 Viney, Self: the history of a concept.
21 Johnson, The Western concept of self, 99.
22 For excellent summary treatments, see Elliot, *Concepts of the self*; Mansfield, *Subjectivity: theories of the self from Freud to Haraway*.

9 Self from the inside out

Language, mind, and the sense of self

> Each of us lives intensely within himself or herself, continuously assimilating past and present experience to a narrative and vision that are unique in every case yet profoundly communicable.
>
> Marilynne Robinson, *Absence of Mind*[1]

> "I" consists of words, images, implicit understandings – symbols; and emotions, feelings, sensations, provided by or associated with symbols.
>
> Liah Greenfeld, *Mind, Modernity, Madness:*
> *The Impact of Culture on Human Experience*[2]

What's a self made of?

Seventeenth-century philosopher René Descartes argued that conscious experience – mind – originates independently of others and, especially, independently of the material body. As he saw it, if you accept that there's an "impassible boundary"[3] between mind and body, then you have to accept that the death of the body may not necessarily mark the end of conscious existence. This is the essence of the famous "Cartesian split" that continues to animate philosophical and scientific debate about the relationship of the physical brain and body to consciousness and mind. In a time of growing skepticism about religion, Descartes provided a rational defense for the belief in God and an afterlife. In his view, conscious experience is incorporeal and mysterious, constituting the potentially transmigrating core of being – the soul. And, in connection with religion's ideas about souls being posted to either paradise or perdition depending on the tally sheet of conduct in the present, the salvation of the soul is a matter of moral conduct and character (your will and tendencies of choice). This view remains common today. Although the rate has been declining, a 2013 Harris poll found that still more than 60 percent of Americans believe in an immortal soul.[4] Of course, not many people push the implications of their beliefs very far, but, presumably, this religious majority would endorse Descartes's view that consciousness and the sense of self (or soul) are an expression of God.

Be that as it may, according to Ernest Becker, by the late nineteenth century the concept of the soul was being rejected by scientists and philosophers who

DOI: 10.4324/9781003010234-12

had begun to speak instead of the self-concept.[5] Most likely Becker had in mind the seminal writing of William James who emphatically denied any useful role for the concept of soul in the science or the philosophy of conscious life. James focused instead on the self, and, like many of today's cognitive scientists and neuroscientists, more than 100 years ago, he argued that the sense of self is something that comes into being from moment to moment in the mind's stream of consciousness.[6] This position is sometimes traced further back to 400–500 BCE and the Buddhist concept of *anatta*, which proposes that the feeling of having a coherent and continuing self is an illusion of the senses.[7]

Consider this description of consciousness of self penned by the Eastern-oriented theologian Alan Watts: "The notion of a separate thinker, of an 'I' . . . comes from the rapidity with which thought changes. It is like whirling a burning stick to give the illusion of a continuous circle of fire."[8] Compare that with the following remark from neuroscientist Antonio Damasio: "the self is a repeatedly reconstructed biological state; it is not a little person . . . inside your brain contemplating what is going on."[9] Or, as neuro-philosopher Thomas Metzinger puts it, the self is a continuously active internal model of the external world created by the brain out of the limited information of the external world that human sensory systems are able to apprehend. For Metzinger, the perception of time, vital to our narrative sense of who we are, is, like our sense of color, an illusion, a mental construction with no independent validity in the external physical world (hang on to this – we'll visit this again below): "The sense of presence is an internal phenomenon, created by the human brain. Not only are there no colors out there, but there is also no present moment."[10] This is the voice of the body half of the Cartesian mind – body dualism.

"It's the social, stupid"

In the face of several hundred years of active debate over the nature and origins of the self, it might be tempting to discard it as a useful idea or try to work around it, as science has done with regard to the soul. However, as we've seen, the idea of self-identity is now critical to our understanding of contemporary interpersonal and psychological life, and we need to take a close look at what we mean when we speak of a self – what it is and how it is constituted. The view currently in play in some corners of cognitive science/neuroscience – a sort of Cartesian whiplash that posits that the sense of self is wholly a byproduct of the operations of the material brain and an illusion – is unhelpful and incorrect (and, as will be argued in Chapter 14, it is an idea that represents a truly dangerous affront to the dignity of human experience). Indeed, the idea of the self is indispensable for understanding how we develop as human beings, the character of modern cultures (including emerging political difficulties), the organization of interpersonal interaction (how and why we interact with each other as we do), and historical changes in interpersonal life (e.g., why we're living alone more frequently, marrying less often and later, have a greater tendency to distrust each other, have dramatically higher rates of anxiety,

168   *The shape of the modern self*

depression, and mental disorders, and spend so much energy posturing online). No surgeon can open your skull and point to your self-concept (and that's not because it dissolved in a mist of postmodern fragmentation – an idea we'll take up again later); but the self-concept *is* an empirically verifiable phenomenon, "an undeniable feature of *contemporary* [my emphasis] social life,"[11] instantiated in our endless narrative accounts of our lived experience, not to mention all those selfies.

This period of American history is characterized by exhilarating new freedom to construct personal identity as we want, regardless of the practicality of our unfettered fantasies. But this brings with it the necessity of choice, often among options that aren't clearly understood or whose implications for the future can't be reliably forecast, if only because the future has become so unstable. With this comes anguish and insecurity as we fret about the choices we have to make and whether the ones we have made were the right ones. In the disconnected and fluid conditions of this era, the greater instability of economic and family life, free-formed self-identity is more often challenged and disrupted, and more frequently needs to be revised, or even rebuilt. This turmoil has rendered the interpersonal processes of mutual self-definition, support, and repair increasingly central in our personal relationships. So, rather obviously, what we make of ourselves is no accidental byproduct of the brain. The creation of personal identity is an historically variable process, managed socially in language, and highly responsive to changing conditions of society and culture.

The Cartesian mind – body division was always a false dichotomy, one that was formulated, understandably, in an age in which lives were embedded in relatively fixed external structures of meaning, so that the social and cultural influences on the self weren't as visible as they've come to be. So, in our modern era, it's certainly no longer a matter of mind *or* body: today, personal identity is created and sustained in our talk with each other. Language enables mind and connects us to each other, extending our powers of intellect by weaving our experience into that of all other human beings who have written, talked, signed, or gestured and, thereby, contributed in large and small ways to the cultural circumstances in which we find ourselves. Culture is the collective expression of mind,[12] and so, as America has become ever more diverse and complex, American culture has increasingly become constituted of diverse and contradictory ideas. Given this diversity and inconsistency, if culture now entered the mind unfiltered, thought would be constituted of the same contradictions, fabrications, disparate images, and ideas that populate the super-diversity that surrounds us. As a thought experiment, imagine that, as you walked through a densely populated urban area, the points of view, preferences, odd ideas, and values of everyone around you entered your thought process uninhibited and with equal validity and priority. And, on top of this, imagine that all the facts, fictions, pitches, fake news, and other distortions of commercial and political culture and the mass media that you're exposed to daily entered your thought with equal force and influence. What would this be like? You would experience wildly conflicting commitments and religious perspectives, irreconcilable loyalties, contradictory ideas, tastes, and prejudices,

Self from the inside out 169

impossible fantasies of self. Your mind would be a chaotically structured slurry of perspective and beliefs. Normal life would quickly become impossible in the face of extensive confusion and crippling levels of anxiety. In short, your mental process would begin to take on the distortions characteristic of psychotic consciousness.

So, as modernity has come on, we've learned to keep culture from entering our minds directly. We protect ourselves from the chaos and contradiction of modern diversity by blocking out a great deal of it, and, for the rest, sifting it and prioritizing it in terms of a foundational structure of ideas about what we believe and value, and the nature of our being, our powers, and predispositions. This organizing system is constituted in the constructed narrative that we call personal identity, or the self. It's our internal strategic template for coping with the churning, buzzing world around us. It provides a sense of personal being and a basis for the expression of our agency and will. It is the foundation on which decisions are made. But, although this identity is uniquely ours, we don't create it by ourselves. In the challenging diversity of modern culture, it's too difficult to hold on to belief without the support of others we regard as trustworthy and credible, and so our sense of who we are is formed and reformed, modified and reinforced, with the participation of our closest conversational partners. And this always goes two ways. We define each other and the world around us in our discourse and so become immensely important in each other's consciousness and each other's lives. Absent deep relationships in which we obtain this type of mind-bridging connection, the sense of personal identity inevitably frays and becomes nonviable, leaving the mind unprotected from the confusion of unfiltered culture. Thus, ultimately, answers to the question "Who am I?" are enacted continually in everyday interpersonal discourse as we review our lives and reconstruct our sense of personal being together. This process calms, strengthens, and reinvigorates. Yet, in response to the increasing pressures of modernity, defensive behavior, anxiety, depression, and mental disorders have become the fate of growing numbers of unfortunate people who are isolated (even in the midst of technological/urban American culture) and otherwise have difficulty creating and sustaining a viable idea of self.

Although, at our best, our powers of thought and will allow us to orient our lives in accordance with transcendent ideas and values, the self is not a being divinely breathed into the body, nor is it an artifact created in the neurological processes of the brain. As argued by psycho-historian Julian Jaynes (see Chapter 2), the self is an historically emergent structure of language-enabled mind that came into being perhaps 3,000 years ago in the opening moments of human social diversity, one that has become particularly prominent in the growing complexity of modern societies in the last 500 years. Although it's ever more difficult to sustain personal identity in the challenging conditions of America's hyper-modernity, the self is a socio-cultural construction, no less real than other socio-cultural constructions, such as IBM, China, the Smithsonian Institution, or Major League Baseball.

This is not to undersell the role of the body and certainly not to deny it. As those can attest who've lost a limb or suffered an endocrinological disorder

170 *The shape of the modern self*

that affects perception and emotion, or who've known someone with global aphasia or experienced the memory loss of the elderly victim of advanced dementia, self-identity is profoundly influenced by the condition of the body in which it's physically situated, and in important and non-obvious ways by the brain's mechanisms of perception and cognitive processing.[13] More generally, the body isn't just the material site of the self; it's also a "tool kit" for exercising its constituent dispositions, and the types of tools in that kit may be a little different from one person to another.[14] But the body isn't the whole story. Rather obviously, the self is influenced by the social, intellectual, emotional, and moral interior of the family during childhood and adolescence. In other words, the self-narrative is not just any story and is neither an illusion nor an arbitrary epiphenomenal construction of our biology. Our self, our humanity, is certainly not, as the linguist George Lakoff would have it, "wholly a product of our physical bodies and brains."[15] If it were, we would find it manifest in a consistent fashion across cultures and throughout history. But the historical and cultural evidence strongly supports the socio-cultural view and contradicts the biological. In the West, mental illness has intensified with modernity,[16] yet, at the same time, the mental disorders that are so prevalent in America today are nearly unknown in those non-modern cultures that exist in other parts of the world. The body is a constant, but the self is a product of socio-cultural circumstances that are historically variable.

Like the nature/nurture debate, the Cartesian split sets up a misleading and confused dualism, "one of the great spurious quandaries of modern psychology."[17] The self isn't a matter of mind *versus* body, it's both. The mind is embodied, but, moreover, it was always a mistake to regard the self as influenced by just these two sources. A third, and primary, source of our consciousness and sense of self is social interaction. We grow our mind and construct our self-story in communication with others, and that story is responsive to the visions those others have of us as well as to our personal history of emotionally important experience – you cannot simply hit the delete key and rewrite your self-narrative as though your past didn't exist, or edit your self-story at will as though your friend's ideas of you are of no consequence.

Currently, neuroscience enthusiasts speculate that science will one day develop techniques that could permit specific memories to be erased by disrupting the particular neural pathways in which a troubling memory is encoded.[18] Thankfully, this idea is highly unlikely. Memories, so important as moral guides and vital to our sense of who we are, are not made of isolated neurons, but of symbols whose meanings co-mingle and contextualize each other. You can't cleanly snip memories out without consequences for the entire self-structure. Companies such as thebreakupshop.com propose that you can escape the pain of a terminated relationship by employing their services to hide all references to your ex that appear in your photos, old emails, Facebook, and so on. This could be possible if the mind was a sort of signal-processing computer, but it isn't. It's a symbol processor, and symbolic meaning is holistic. Our sense of self is constituted of the totality of our experience,

Self from the inside out   171

painful and otherwise. The idea of neurologically snipping out a memory is something like the idea of excising all the B-flats from Beethoven's *Ninth Symphony*. You don't end up with a person absent a memory: you end up with an incoherent mess.

Consciousness of self and world inheres in language and the mind's capacity for metaphor. We understand things (ourselves) not on their own, but in terms of their resemblance or opposition to something else. As an example, Lakoff and Johnson, in the lead to their influential book *Metaphors We Live By*, contend that we understand arguing in reference to the activity of war. We try to "win" arguments, to "defeat" our opponent, to "attack," "demolish," or "shoot down" opposing ideas.[19] One might not recognize one's own orientation to argument here, but let's grant Lakoff and Johnson's example for the sake of illustration. And then, imagine, if you can, what would remain if you could somehow erase your understanding of the meaning of war. What then would argument be? And what would become of your meaning for "peace," a concept substantially meaningful in its oppositional relationship to war? If, as a result of losing your concept of war, you simultaneously lost the concept of peace and, with that, much of the meaning of the concepts of contentment, tranquility, heaven, and so on, then, at that moment, the content of the normal human mind would become a sort of semantic Swiss cheese. Chunks of experience would evaporate as the meaningful anchors of the interdependent metaphors that describe essential parts of our experienced world would flicker out of comprehensibility. This was the flaw of the film *Eternal Sunshine of the Spotless Mind*, in which a couple erases memories of each other. Following the procedure, you wouldn't wake up the same person, just without memory of your former partner; you'd wake up with holes in your sense of reality, significant disorientation and anxiety, and an intermittent but recurring inability to make sense of your own perceptions. Perhaps something like this underlines the apparent hallucinations and cognitive and behavioral abnormalities that sometimes occur among those with advanced dementia or Alzheimer's disease.

In the words of poet Wendell Berry: "The mind is the continuity of its objects . . . the understanding of each one thing by the intelligence of an assemblage,"[20] an idea known as "content holism" in the philosophy of mind.[21] The meaning of a symbol is not fixed, but influenced by its associations with other symbols that contextualize it. Extended, all meanings are intensely interactive, so that the impact of the loss of one symbol may reverberate through all the fields of meaning that constitute your mind. This interconnection is in evidence in Freud, who drew attention to this in his analysis of slips of the tongue and the pen, which, if nothing else, demonstrate the densely associational nature of thought.[22] For example, a young woman I know was convicted of arson in high school. Out with friends one night, they started a bonfire in a town park and sat around it talking and drinking beer. They thought they'd put the fire out when they left the park, but it rekindled, got out of control, and burned down the park gazebo. All involved were arrested and incarcerated. Several years later, in her written petition to

172 *The shape of the modern self*

be allowed to sit for her medical exams in spite of her juvenile felony arrest record, she wrote that she and her friends had started a small "bomb fire." Aptly put. The incident had dynamited both her future and her sense of self. Memories aren't isolated. They exist in language and they're heavily linked in semantic associations. But, more than this, many of our memories are as much stored in others – in our community of significant relationships – as they are in our own brains. How sweet it is to sit with old friends recalling bits and pieces of shared history, and how awful it is when some circumstance requires that we renew interaction with someone from our past who knows things about us we'd prefer hadn't happened.

Episode 5 of the 2008 season of the Showtime series *This American Life* opened with a short story of a man who adopted his wife's memory of an embarrassing moment when she found herself vigorously waving, by mistake, to Jackie Onassis in midtown Manhattan. The wife was really there, and the husband really wasn't, but he acquired her memory of the incident, and maintains with certainty that he was there too. Of course, in a sense, he *was* there. Likely, his wife's mind is a corporate construction that includes his intelligence and sensibilities. In a symbolically interdependent husband's exquisite empathy for his wife's experience, to a significant extent, he too acquires the experiences his wife recounts to him, especially those of emotional intensity, as might well be exemplified in the excruciating embarrassment of waving vigorously in public to an international celebrity you think is waving to you as though you were a friend, but who is, as is obvious to everyone around you on the street, just waving in an attempt to hail a taxi.

Language, which is the vehicle of memory, is a social instrument built of symbols whose meanings are created and sustained in our interaction with others. Constructed in language, our personal history is a *social* production. Therefore, the solution to painful memory is interpersonal – rich communion and the integration of experience through insight, interpretation, and persuasion – not some future version of targeted lobotomy.

Hopefully self-evident, the influences of the body, personal history, and the family need to be kept in mind. But self-identity is also situated within an unfolding cultural-historical process. As we've seen, within our own period, personal identity has become disembedded and more free-form, less determined by social position and gender, and more an interpersonal production. It's now best conceptualized as a narrative biography that's more or less continually in revision and constructed and performed in our ordinary interactions *with others*, with the particular influence of those with whom we communicate regularly and with whom we form ongoing relationships: our community of significantly intimate partners. This process has come to be deeply influential in our interpersonal relations at home and at work, to the point that disruption of these relationships can trigger a serious crisis of existential being. Speaking with someone who lost a partner in a happy long-term relationship, it's common to hear that they feel they've not only lost an important source of companionship, but have actually lost a stable vision of their own identity ("I don't

Self from the inside out 173

know who I am anymore"). The impact of interpersonal loss on the mind is explored further in Chapter 13.

In this way, the interpersonal process is now virtually unsurpassed in its ability to infuse life with meaning and purpose or, when things aren't going well, isolation and anguish. This is the first period in history in which there's nothing other than the quality of this process that keeps marriages and other vital relationships together, relationships that increasingly represent the primary source of self-sustaining community in our lives. And it now has unprecedented consequence in shaping the sense of identity. At the center of intimate discourse is an ongoing biographical dialogue, visible when a sensitive observer knows where to look, a dialogue about who we are, where we've come from and where our lives are heading, and how we wish and expect others to regard us – our self-concept. This dialogue may at times be overt ("You can't talk to me that way, I'm your wife!") or deeply coded, visible only in the subtext of conversation (who speaks longest, who asks for information more and who gives information more, who avoids and who initiates, who interrupts or shifts topics, etc.), but most often it's inherent in the unremarkable, untroubled verbal and nonverbal discourse that occurs between people in ongoing relationships who, in their talk about teapots and politics, neighbors and job problems, romance and TV shows, dog training and bicycle repair, unavoidably reveal to each other their understanding of their own position in the world, their history, and their vision of themselves in the future, often to be reinforced or subtly edited, corrected, and edged in new directions by those who care for them the most.

This function of cooperative self construction is almost constantly operating, though not always at the level of conscious awareness. However, sometimes the process *is* vividly direct and in the foreground. Herman, in her seminal work on the psychological impact of trauma, quotes a childhood rape survivor disclosing to her friend:

> I said, "I'm fourteen years old and I'm not a virgin any more." He said, "This doesn't have anything to do with being a virgin. Some day you'll fall in love and you'll make love and *that* will be losing your virginity. Not the act of what happened . . . . That doesn't have anything to do with it."[23]

And so, on many occasions, the process of the cooperative construction of personal identity occurs in the clear. Friends and intimates function like white blood cells helping to repair the tatters of our biographical understanding of self, nudging our perspective on our life into a new frame, one that permits us to mend, and to pick up and go on. The brain exerts its influences, but the self is created and sustained in talk in social relationships. Absent those relationships, self-identity and, indeed, one's very sense of reality may unravel, as Guenther has described with regard to the experience of prisoners in solitary confinement.[24]

Part 2 of this book took a broad focus in reviewing changing circumstances of modernity that gradually reconfigured the context of self, intimacy, and

174   *The shape of the modern self*

other aspects of interpersonal life. Now, we turn the focus ring in the other direction, putting language, consciousness, and interaction under the lens. Here, again, evidence of historical change is extremely important because it allows us not only to understand how our world got to be the way it is, but also to project the directions of the future. Central in this story is the changing conceptualization of unconscious motivation, its relationship to historical conditions of Western life, to self-identity, and the ways in which we've come to regard the possibility of nonrational and extra-conscious influences on our own and others' behavior.

As for projecting the future, the evidence suggests that British neuroscientist Susan Greenfield could be proven correct in her prediction that, "identity is likely to become an increasingly . . . fragile and questionable entity as this century unfolds."[25] This is no small matter. As noted, the National Institute of Mental Health currently estimates that 1 in 5 Americans now exhibits a diagnosable mental disorder. As this rate stood at about 1 in 1,000 at the beginning of the twentieth century, this suggests that the prevalence of significant psychological distress in the United States increased at a phenomenal rate over the course of the last 100 years. If this trend were to continue, even at a reduced rate, we'd be looking at a level of social disruption and psycho-emotional distress on a scale similar to the level of social and economic disruption that could become manifest in the world's coastal regions if sea level were to rise by several feet by the end of this century, as some suggest is likely. So, it's really no wonder that, as the modern era has come roaring up, there's been a visible scramble to better understand modernity's effects on core processes of social experience: identity, personal being, and interpersonal support. This discussion will span the remainder of this book. The rest of this chapter examines foundational ideas about how the self is constituted in linguistic consciousness, and how it arises as an emergent product of the communicating mind, linking us to others and establishing our moral priorities.

The I and the Me

The self is a product of many things, but the foundation of all of them is conscious awareness, which is usually conceptualized as having two aspects. First, there's the consciousness of the active mind in the present moment. Likely at this moment, at least partly, you're experiencing this as an internal voice, the one articulating these words as you read or hear them (or, at least, that was so until your attention was called to this and you stopped to notice it, flipping out of primary consciousness into a second mode of awareness that we'll talk about in due course). This mode, which consists of mental images that flow without reference to the past, has been referred to as "primary consciousness."[26] This process can be experienced in language, but also in immediate sensation, visual images, music, and emotion. Either way, it's rarely at rest (as poet Mary Oliver lamented: "Here in my head, language keeps making its tiny noises," concluding that the mind is only silent in death).[27] In his classic work

The Principles of Psychology, William James referred to this as the "stream of thought, of consciousness, or of subjective life."[28]

When the mind isn't occupied with one thing, it often seems to abruptly shift to consider something else. As James pointed out, consciousness is continuous. It may change direction, but it never stops. We may get fatigued with reading, but, when we stop, the mind doesn't shut off; it just goes somewhere else. It's the unceasing nature of this that we sometimes seek to minimize through distractive, meditative, or ecstatic practices such as music, prayer, sports, artistic creation, absorbing work, or media experiences, or, sometimes, alcohol and drugs (note here that the word "ecstasy" means to be beside yourself, to locate consciousness outside of self, neatly making sensible what use of the drug ecstasy accomplishes for those using it to escape the psychological impacts that inhere in insecurity of self). This is the unfocused awareness of the unfolding present, like images streamed from a video camera that's constantly on and moving about, seemingly aimed according to its own volition, and interwoven with feelings, emotions, and a verbal accompaniment that's not necessarily in sync. Primary consciousness is the site of basic energies, impulses, feeling, appetites, and desire. It's referred to as the "I" by William James and others.

At times, we become analytically aware of this process, perhaps collating and analyzing what we're experiencing, comparing it with previous experiences, maybe noting that our awareness tends to be drawn to particular types of images or stuck in recurrent patterns of emotion or thought. This kind of awareness is *meta* to the first: it's an appreciation of the data of immediate experience and, possibly, an awareness of our patterns of awareness. In this type of second-order consciousness, we reflect on ourselves as if in the mode of an outside observer, in the same way that we might reflect on the behavior or motivation of a friend or someone we work with.

This type of self-awareness (becoming analytically conscious of self) is a consequence of routine problem solving.[29] Philosopher Isaiah Berlin sees it this way: awareness of self arises when our impulses meet resistance in the outside world.[30] If there's no resistance, and if the mind doesn't perceive problems that need to be solved, awareness tends to settle, and the self isn't in focus. We're just lost in the stream of images and feelings of the moment, absorbed in what has been described as "optimal flow," where "there is no disorder to straighten out, no threat for the self to defend against," and "the information that keeps coming into awareness is congruent with goals [so that] psychic energy flows effortlessly."[31] Self-awareness awakes to disturbances of energy, feeling, perception, emotion, and so on (literally, one becomes "self-conscious"). In consequence of this, we tend to be more aware of the negative aspects of our experience, more likely to focus on episodes of conflict, remorse, unfulfilled desire, threat, and so on, as the perception of problems, loss, or need always calls the mind to awareness of self. As the Buddhists teach, an individual at peace has a quieter, more accepting, less analytic mind, a state possibly obtained through acceptance that trauma, disappointment, and difficulty are universal conditions of modernity and so not worth as much

176   *The shape of the modern self*

conscious attention. This second dimension of awareness has been referred to by William James and others as the "Me."

Primary consciousness, the I, can be regarded as historically stable because the body structures that influence it evolve very, very slowly. Although we might wonder about the eventual neurological impacts of life in a culture in which sustained digital multitasking is a common experience, there's no reason to think primary consciousness operates for us today in any dramatically different way than it did at the time of Homer. Jaynes argued that the anthropological record suggests that there was a dramatic change in human mental process at some point just before the dawn of Classical Greek civilization (that is, before approximately the eighth century BCE and the authorship of the Homeric epics), and that momentous change – possibly due to a change in human brain structure encouraged by social upheavals produced by the collapse of Bronze Age civilization and followed by the rapidly increasing sociological complexity of the Greco-Roman world – encouraged the first appearance of modern consciousness.[32] Whether or not there was such a change in brain structure, Jayne's theory is consistent with the view of this book that communication was once more signal-like (and, for Jaynes, radically so in early human history), but eventually became a fully symbolic process, perhaps, as Jaynes has suggested, in response to the rapidly changing cultural conditions that accompanied the Bronze Age collapse, about 1250–1000 BCE.

Irrespective of where one stands with regard to Jaynes's theory, once past the Homeric period, changes in the self-narrative, the Me, are not so much a matter of changing body structures as they are dependent on socio-cultural circumstances. As we've seen, there's no question that the narrative self has been subject to dramatic historical change, especially since the Industrial Revolution. And, because the scope of this change has been so extensive as to greatly increase the degree of differentiation within the Me with respect to conscious and unconscious aspects, although the idea of the Me has now been introduced, I will delay our main discussion of this aspect of self-consciousness for the next chapter, which deals with nonconscious influences on self-conception. My purpose in the remainder of this chapter is to explore contemporary views on communication, thought, and self-conception, and to make clear some limitations of the radical views promoted actively in some corners of cognitive science/neuroscience.

Contrasting views on symbolization, thought, and language

> Unlike most other animals, we're not locked inside a . . . limited world of immediate sensory experiences . . . . . We imagine the possible through words. We use words to help us remember who and what we are . . . . . The more complex our words, the more layered our story, the more refined our understanding.[33]

Naturally, all animals have an internal flow of mental energy – primary consciousness – but only we have the ability to represent it symbolically in

Self from the inside out 177

language. Every pet owner knows that animals possess a rich life of sensation, emotion, and visual imagery, but the ability to communicate with symbols adds a capability that's necessary for the formation of a sense of self. Some animals do communicate with signals. For example, African vervet monkeys use one kind of vocalization to alert others in their band to a threat of eagles and a different vocalization if there is a leopard in the area, but these signals are not arbitrarily chosen like human words. They are genetically built in. Vervets are born with this capability. Some chimps and parrots reared with humans do have a primitive and limited capacity for symbol recognition, but, without the full apparatus of language, animals aren't capable of modeling, analytically manipulating, and channeling their impulses and emotions in the manner of humans. Animals process sensation as a stream of signals, emotions, or other sensory data, not as linguistic symbols or other conventional abstract representational images.

My cat Brandenburg responds to "bowl?" without hesitation, usually stretching for a moment and then smartly trotting across our apartment to her wet food feeding station, fixing my gaze and uttering a single meow. But, for her, "bowl?" isn't an abstraction, a broad category of meaning, a means of poetic or mythic expression, a proposition, part of a story, or a vehicle of relational definition: the utterance "bowl?" is a certain sign that tasty food is forthcoming. (And, as every pet owner knows, to keep being able to use it as such you'd be wise never to utter "bowl?" without producing the goods.) Thus, "bowl?" is a *signal* with a single, fixed meaning established through operant conditioning. On the other hand, when an acquaintance you imagine (or hope) might conceivably be seeking a more intimate relationship looks coyly at you over her glasses, raises her eyebrows a little, smiles, and says "dinner?", she's thrown you a *symbol*, not a signal, so there's no one-to-one translation of meaning. Her intent may be exquisitely complex and purposefully masked within a universe of possibility and contingency, and likely will require delicate follow-up and clarification. Because of the slippery, open-ended, highly symbolic nature of communication in modernity, we all operate in a world of plausible deniability ("Oh, I just wondered if you were getting hungry too"), a state of perpetual uncertainty, which, as Oscar Wilde pointed out, constitutes the essential foundation and vehicle of romance. However, unfortunately, in modernity's super-diversity of meaning, uncertainty reigns, and the freedom afforded by communication with symbols may often constitute the essential foundation and vehicle of isolation, anxiety, and depression.

It's not just that symbolization is the essential act of thought: it's a prerequisite condition of thought.[34] And language is the prerequisite of symbolic communication. British psychiatrist Peter Hobson has argued that interpersonal transactions between preverbal babies and their caregivers establish the basis for the child's eventual mastery of symbolic language and the capacity for thought and self-reflection.[35] The infant (we should note here that the original meaning of "infant" is "one who is incapable of speech") observes and imitates the expression and actions of his or her caregiver, and these observations

178 *The shape of the modern self*

provide the basis for perspective taking – that is, for understanding how the world is seen and experienced by others. Initially, the baby makes emotional sense of his or her world through the cuing of his or her caregiver (for example, in associating love and warmth with food, or, if the caregiver has neurotic tendencies, perhaps in associating food with fear and insecurity). Particularly in the circumstances of highly diverse modernity, as the baby encounters a range of others, he or she develops the sense of multiple perspectives, because not all people communicate the same orientations to things (mommy likes tofu, but daddy says it's yukky goop). This encourages her to understand that things (activities, events, beings, and objects) may have different meanings for different people. Later, she grasps that one object (e.g., a sheet of paper) may stand for something else (e.g., in being used as a blanket for a toy figure).

Hobson believes that these two mental operations – the use of one thing to represent something else – combined with the acquired understanding that meanings for things vary to some degree from one person to the next, are the direct precursors to the acquisition of symbolic language. Language is a vast system of conventional symbols ("love," "mother," "commitment," etc.) that evoke some degree of common ideation but, especially in circumstances of modernity, are never understood in exactly the same way by all people. The leap to language and the capacity for analytical thought that it makes possible generally occurs in the latter part of the second year of life and inaugurates the process of self-reflection and the emergence of the self-concept. Hobson's theory is grounded in the idea that symbols become meaningful in interaction with other important figures in our lives and is consistent with the earlier work of psychologist Lev Vygotsky and, especially, sociologist George Herbert Mead (whose ideas we will take up in more detail in Chapter 12).

In contrast, although cognitive scientists/neuroscientists also speak of symbolization as a vital part of thought, their ideas about symbols often miss that symbols are *socially* constituted. In this view, raw perception consists of processing vast numbers of received sensory signals, some patterns of which may trigger awareness of abstract symbols, which in this case are regarded as stored neurological templates (patterns of neuronal interconnection located in the huge network of neurons of the brain) that are coded in such a way as to represent and convey meaning. Thus, it's proposed that within our brains are located an extremely large number of symbol templates (neuro-theorists such as Antonio Damasio[36] and Gerald Edelman[37] call them "maps"), capable of activation on perception of particular patterns of internal or external stimuli and, as well, capable of stimulating each other so that, in principle, they're self-generative: the set of templates are capable of extending themselves. Here, the idea is that higher-order cognition can operate independent of language, that the brain works at a foundational level using a kind of private code, a "mentalese" as it's sometimes called, and, thus, a sense of self can arise independent of social communication.

My nose detects a pattern of odor molecules that stimulates a particular structure of interconnected neurons which comprise the composite symbol

Self from the inside out   179

template "English lilacs in summer along the Thames Path." The activation of this triggers a flood of associated symbols from my childhood home along the Thames in London and a host of additional elements of remembered experience. In conscious contemplation of this combination of immediate and distant experience, perhaps through a process of metaphoric thought, I arrive at a new conclusion about my personal development at that time that nudges my sense of myself in a new direction. The metaphoric aspect of this is that I understand something now in terms of distant experience (I see the "thisness of a that or the thatness of a this," as Burke put it).[38] This new understanding may add to my repertoire of symbol templates (a new group of neurons knit together) and to the biographical/narrative account of my life.

What's different in this cognitive science/neuroscience notion of "symbol" is that the symbol's meanings have somehow been established independent of others, not negotiated within particular social relationships. For cognitive science/neuroscience, "symbol" is a shorthand for a pattern of neuronal interconnections, and there's no social requirement in this. However, consciousness is wholly social. This is memorialized in its Latin root *conscius*, which carries the meanings "confidant" and "privy," concepts that assume a social relationship (you can't be privy to anything, much less anyone's confidant, if you live alone on a desert island). Consciousness derives from our experience in communication with others. It means having access to the private perspectives of others and regulating social access to one's own thoughts. Thus, "meanings," in the normal sense, are more than neuronal associations. The symbols (meanings) that reside at the center of our vision of the world and our sense of who we are are the building blocks of our sense of reality and are established in language, in terms that are formulated in historical/cultural context in interpersonal interaction with others, and this connects us to our social partners at varying levels of shared mind. Our consciousness is never our own alone. Indeed, meanings that we construct on our own tend to fade quickly unless they're kept alive in active social expression. On the whole, the cognitive science/neuroscience vision of the world is a starkly lonely one.

And the cognitive science/neuroscience conception of mind stands in contrast to Hobson's view, which is worth quoting at length:

> Symbols play their part by anchoring meanings, so that meanings can be kept separate from and combined with each other. They become the coinage of thought. But they arise in the context of communication between people. They come into existence, not privately and mysteriously inside the head, but out there in the world through movements in psychological stance that have their origins in the to and fro of interpersonal relations.[39]

In other words, the meaning of "London" or "Thames Path" or "English lilacs" or "summer," much less our childhood memories, don't spring native from the brain. They are all based in social experience, expressed in language, and saturated with socially negotiated meanings that connect us to others. Memory

180 *The shape of the modern self*

may occur in the brain, and the memory of meanings we've created together may be stored there, but, at least in humans, meaning (and memory) doesn't occur independent of language. According to Wittgenstein, "I don't have 'meanings' in my mind in addition to the verbal expressions; rather, language is the vehicle of thought,"[40] and, further, "The words with which I express my memory are my memory."[41] Without the system of abstract symbolic representation that's language, there can be visualization, associational learning, reactivity, or reflex (as in Pavlov's dogs), but not reflection, abstract analysis, the generation of new meaning, or a sense of oneself as a coherent and distinctive entity situated in the flow of time, carrying along a personal history and some range of possible futures. Without language, there may be a sense of embodiment, a boundedness to being, rich emotional association, and ongoing awareness of the environment; but, rather obviously, language takes the normal human experience far beyond this, just as the loss of language (possibly through disease processes such as dementia or global aphasia) reduces the human experience disastrously.

Our conscious and unconscious awareness of the meaningful world occurs through the apparatus of the brain and the central nervous system, which so profoundly filter, parse, and channel the "real" world as to create the range of illusions that become the taken-for-granted experienced world. Neuroscientists remind us that the actual world is not colorful in the way we experience it – roses are not red, nor violets blue – but more like a storm of various kinds of radiant energy from which the brain selects and constructs its own images, painting them internally. The red we see in a rose is not an inherent property of the rose, but rather an outcome of the way our brain functions. The proof of this lies in the fact that the brain sustains a constant sense of the rose's hue even as light waves bouncing from it to the eye are altered. Because felines don't have color vision, when my dear old cat Magnolia looks out our window at the garden, she doesn't see the red color of the rose, but that isn't because she fails to see something that's out there in the rose. Rather, it's that, unlike our brains, her brain doesn't color the rose red. Similarly, as we've seen, modern neuroscience asserts that the self is also not a real thing, but rather is created in the brain process. The neuroscience view holds that the perception of self is a fiction that functions in the service of the brain.[42] Novel and fascinating as neuroscience insights tend to be, the story of self emerging from this corner skids off course and crashes through the guard rail in imagining the person to be a monad, like a robot, an isolated being without social partners, or at least whose meanings are never significantly affected by them.[43] There are exceptions; as a particularly vivid example, cognitive scientist Douglas Hofstadter's deep grief over the loss of his wife forms a significant theme in his theory of selves formed of looping interdependencies of meaning between the minds of intimate partners. There's no question that Hofstadter felt that *his* mind is comprised to a great extent of meaning generated interdependently in discourse with his wife.[44] However, in many more accounts from the burgeoning cognitive science and neuroscience literature, it's as if any individual with a normally functioning brain and body

Self from the inside out   181

would naturally construct a self. Emphatically, this isn't so. The acquisition of language requires interaction with other people. And, without language, there can be no self, because a self is a narrative construction, built from the shifting, historically specific stock of meanings available within the language and culture in which a life is situated.

According to philosopher Daniel Dennett, who is a proponent of the cognitive science/neuroscience view of self as an accidental artifact of the material brain,

> the strangest and most wonderful constructions in the whole animal world are the amazing, intricate constructions made by the primate, Homo sapiens. Each normal individual of this species makes a self. Out of its brain it spins a web of words and deeds, and, like the other creatures, it doesn't have to know what it's doing; it just does it.[45]

But this could only be so if we reduce our understanding of "self" so significantly as to render it unrecognizable in its normal sense as the story of a human life. Because cats, dogs, monkeys, and fish don't have language, they don't have selves as we do. Sartre wrote, "I *am* language" (his emphasis).[46] In other words: no language, no Jean-Paul Sartre. Daniel Dennett to the contrary, brains don't spin out language on their own, and selves don't emerge independently of language. Language is a cooperative system of meaning acquired when young brains are acted upon and shaped within the densely interpersonal environment of a communicating human collective (of course, normally a family).

Michael Graziano, who is another leading figure in the neuroscience camp, believes that all social experience is actually monadic in that humans can only know each other by building internal hypothetical models of each other's consciousness. According to him, a husband and wife can't actually share minds. He writes,

> If consciousness is an emergent state of the brain, if it is a feeling that is generated by the information in your brain, then how can two people share it? How can the consciousness from your brain merge with the consciousness from John's brain? . . . There is no way for people to experience consciousness in that way.[47]

Again, to the contrary, as Wittgenstein asserted, all thought occurs in language, and language is a system of *shared* meaning.

When you and your spouse characterize each other and the world in the same terms and come to choose and spin those terms interdependently, your consciousness and your emotional life are increasingly coordinated and shared. Philosopher Maurice Merleau-Ponty asserted that, "There is . . . a taking up of others' thought through speech . . . an ability to think *according to others* [his emphasis], which enriches our own thoughts."[48] Because of the scope, practical relevance, and emotional intensity of the whole of your communication,

182 *The shape of the modern self*

you do indeed begin to experience the world as your spouse does. You become, as Kenneth Burke put it, *consubstantial*, by which he meant that your consciousness is constituted of common symbolic meaning.[49] You aren't clones (and, of course, spouses may often marvel (and grumble) at the extent of their differences, as we would predict – remember that we're more likely to be conscious of conflict and difference than harmony and similarity), but, assuming you regard each other as equals, you and your spouse increasingly share perspective. This is the essence of intimacy.

The extraordinary character of this is vividly apparent in the circumstance of global aphasia following stroke, where, in a relationship with high symbolic interdependence, one spouse can actually function as a spare mind for the other. The aphasic stroke victim may temporarily lose all understanding of language, not only unable to communicate with others, but internally too: the voice in the head may go silent. Yet, in the case of a symbolically interdependent relationship, the spouse may have a keen appreciation of the physical and psychological experience of the stroke victim and may be able to communicate for them with fair accuracy.

Poet and author Diane Ackerman described her marriage to novelist Paul West, who suffered a stroke and aphasia. She states that, over their years of marriage, their consciousness had mingled to such an extent that it was no longer clear which thoughts had originated from which person. As she put it, "a merry confabulation of ideas and phrases can arise in a twosome."[50] She recounts that, during her husband's rehabilitation, speech therapists often missed signs of his progress that were apparent to her because of her intimate familiarity with his unusual breadth of vocabulary, the extent of private language they had developed as a couple, and their idiosyncratic patterns of speech and thought. When the speech therapist pointed to a telephone and asked her husband what it was called, the therapist thought he was uttering nonsense sounds when he responded with "tesseract." But Ackerman knew that, obscure though the word may be, a tesseract is a three-dimensional object that extends into a hidden fourth dimension, which, in a way, is what a telephone is.

Burke asserted that we see the world through "terministic screens," by which he meant distinctive systems of understanding, meaning, and epistemology: in other words, language spun in idiosyncratic ways.[51] These fields of meaning constitute the fabric of our unique consciousness and connect us socially. They're formed as we talk in our important relationships. The deeper those relationships, the more vivid, distinctive, and screen-like these shared fields of meaning become – and, assuming we are speaking of relationships between equals, they're *always* co-authored. If there's no consciousness independent of language, and we share language whose meanings we've formed cooperatively, then we share mind. Mind isn't reducible to the patterned activation of neurons; it inheres in language.

Tellingly, books by cognitive scientists and neuroscientists are *never* dedicated to the author's brain structures, to their neocortex or to their limbic system. Like the rest of us, these scientists dedicate their great creative

Self from the inside out   183

accomplishments to their primary interpersonal partners: usually husbands, wives, family, and friends, who, presumably, talked to them, encouraged them, inspired them, and helped them find meaning in their work and the resources of self required to imagine the possibilities of their lives and complete their labors. It's an easy bet that eminent neuroscientists and marital partners Antonio and Hanna Damasio have had a great deal of influence on each other's minds, and, that Daniel Dennett's and Michael Graziano's partners have heard quite a bit of detail about their theories, and, assuming that these are happy, egalitarian relationships, through their talk they've come to see the world through the fields of meaning they've built together of commonly understood symbols.

So, to sum up, the primary reason animals can't have selves in the same sense as humans is that they don't have language and the distinctions that language affords, which is the prerequisite for the articulation of a self in the sense relevant to our focus on communication and intimate connection. I want to reiterate, so as to be perfectly clear and not alienate my fellow animal lovers, that this is not to say that our pets don't have rich emotional lives or intelligence, or awareness, sensation, desire, all of which we may be keenly in tune with and which make our pets so dear to us, so much a part of our own emotional lives. Recall that, like humans, higher animals have limbic systems, and this makes possible the profound emotional connections that so often grow between ourselves and our pets. However, without language, pets can't have self-concepts. Further, if your personal philosophy admits of the existence of souls, I'm afraid our pets can't have souls either, because, without language, animals don't have the means of making the distinctions and choices that constitute moral activity.

The ability to choose consciously and actively – to deliberately say "yes" to one impulse and "no" to another – is the essence of moral behavior and this facility originates in language. Choice is the basis of moral character (and, as emphasized in the closing chapter, a defining aspect of what it means to be human). We think of our pets as good or bad dogs and cats, but their behavior is primarily innate, and that which isn't has been shaped by operant conditioning. We praise and pet them when they behave in the ways we like, and so they do more of it. Thus, with behavior determined by extralinguistic factors, our pets are without agency of conscious action and, therefore, don't have the capacity to exercise choice. (And, on that note, if there's a heaven, surely our pets won't be excluded, as some maintain, because, without the possibility of conscious moral choice, they exist in a perfect state of grace, incapable of sin.) This relationship between morality and the agency of action bestowed upon us by language will be important to keep in mind when, in the final chapter, we'll turn to a discussion of the extent to which our understanding of the range of our human agency has been undergoing an aggressive assault by cognitive science and neuroscience, evolutionary psychology, meme theorists, and medical psychiatry, primarily because of their inadequate conceptualization of the symbiotic relationship between mind, language, and social interaction.

184 *The shape of the modern self*

How communication defines us socially, and morally

Philosopher Charles Taylor argued that the construction of self-identity is an inherently social process and, at the same time, an inherently moral one.[52] As we've seen, the story of self is always a social production because the language you use to describe yourself has no meaning except in reference to other people who understand your meanings as you do (or from whom you differentiate yourself because you perceive that they don't have the same meanings for things that you do). A definition of self is also situated within the meaningful framework of an historical/cultural period. Imagine, for example, that an important plank in your neighbor's self-concept is that he's a "patriot." The general sense of "patriot" in 1776 in Connecticut was distinct from "patriot" in Georgia in 1861, and today the label has been appropriated by conservative Americans and anti-government activists who passionately oppose gun control legislation. But, more significant than these historically and culturally varying contextual frames, we establish particular meaning for things in interaction with important others.

As Taylor says,

> in talking about something, you and I make it an object for us together, that is, not just an object for me which happens also to be one for you, even if I add that I know it's an object for you, and you know, etc. The object is *for us* [my emphasis] in a strong sense.[53]

And, of course, in our modern world, much of our talk with our important relationship partners is, directly or indirectly, about who we are, about self-definition. "Self," therefore, only becomes meaningful within the shared frame of reference generated within particular social relationships (and, as we'll see later, we'd expect a truly isolated person to confront important difficulties in sustaining a sense of personal coherence – loneliness is a warning sign that self-identity is in danger of fraying and becoming indistinct, resting on structures of meaning that require periodic reconfirmation but for which there is, now, inadequate opportunity). As mentioned, although a range of factors influence suicide rates, living in sparsely populated regions of the U.S. is one of the strongest.[54] In previous historical eras, the definition of self was to a greater extent constrained externally, but now, more of it is free to be created by each of us in conversation with others.

Taylor writes,"one cannot be a self on one's own."[55] This is the reason the loss of a long-term relationship partner may lead to a severe and ongoing crisis of identity. It's not, as some in psychology would have it, just that trauma springs from the severing of some mysterious DNA-based "bond of attachment," a view now as popular as it is incoherent. Lehrer summarizes that position: "there is an underlying attachment system which coordinates proximity seeking and that . . . shares common biological substrates for pair bonds and parent – infant bonds. All lasting love is made of the same nerves and wires."[56]

Self from the inside out 185

This is malarkey. It's true enough that people without functioning brains and central nervous systems – dead people in other words – don't fall in love. But even though love may be experienced viscerally, it is not a product of biology. As so many scholars have documented, love is an historically variable product of mind and culture, an experience that didn't exist in anything like its current form prior to the advent of modernity and the emergence of the modern sense of self. To say that people are "attached" is no more than to say that they feel trust and comfort in each other's presence and prefer it, perhaps long for it. This may easily be true, but it's just descriptive. It doesn't explain anything. The attachment concept is to social bonds as the now largely obsolete instinct concept is to social behavior, just a way of saying we see a pattern of regular behavior, without saying anything about how it has come to be, what caused it, and what constitutes it. With both attachment and instinct, we overreach the concept when we use it as explanation. Saying that Alex and Janine are attached is like saying that David is a naughty boy – description, not explanation.

Happily, we are now in a position to do much better. We have seen that there are two ways that the sense of attachment can form. First, there is the growing interdependence of emotional experience that occurs as individuals (either humans, or animals, or humans and animals) become mutually conditioned to experience positive or negative feeling in reaction to each other. This is an outcome of the limbic system and may often occur outside of conscious control, through mutual operant shaping (which, in the case of humans, may to some degree be self-generated because our relationships, especially human – pet relationships, so often involve considerable fantasy and projection). And now, with Taylor, we can see that the trauma of the ending of a symbolically interdependent relationship stems from the loss of a primary source of validation for the fields of meaning that partners had jointly established that made sense of themselves and the broader world. In the modern world, this loss leaves one isolated, not only in social space, but in semantic space: lonely, disoriented, possibly terrified, unable to find confirmation for core meanings that provide order and make sense of the world. It undermines confidence in the continuity of truth. It upends the taken-for-granted and threatens a reordering of phenomenal experience. In other words, those who suffer a major interpersonal loss may need to reestablish a significant portion of the system they rely on for making sense of who they are and the other elements of the world of meanings in which their life was formerly situated and in which their minds were sustained. Loss may require a substantial reorganization of values and a reconstruction of self-identity. In time, important domains of memory may fade. Indeed, recent research has established that dementia is significantly more likely to be diagnosed in the immediate few months after the death of a spouse, but this elevated level of risk fades with time.[57] Loss is a potentially tortuous process, and, for this reason, it's not uncommon for people to tenaciously cling to their past, continuing to order their lives in terms of a fantasy of continuing relationship with a lost partner, even to the extent of hallucinating their presence (more on this in Chapter 13). For Taylor, the construction of

186 *The shape of the modern self*

self-identity is, inevitably, an articulation of one's morality, because inherent in the process of choosing to define yourself in a particular way is embedded an understanding of what constitutes good and bad. Obviously, if part of your self-definition is that you're Catholic, that brings with it a tendency toward a set of positions on matters of morality. Equally, though perhaps less obviously, if part of your self-definition is that you're a classical musician or a farmer or a patriot or British or a girl scout leader or a student, then in each of these too you position yourself with regard to issues of right and wrong. Again from Taylor:

> To know who you are is to be oriented in moral space, a space in which questions arise about what is good or bad, what is worth doing and what isn't, what has meaning and importance for you and what is trivial and secondary.[58]

Thus, just as the definition of self is an inevitable consequence of language, and the meanings that language represents to us are produced in particular social encounters that connect us with our ongoing relationship partners, so too these relationships define and bind us morally. As we'll see in chapters ahead, this can be particularly difficult to the extent that our significant social partners represent moral positions that don't line up well, a condition increasingly possible in the kind of super-diverse and segmented society characteristic of this era.

Notes

1 Robinson, *Absence of mind: the dispelling of inwardness from the modern myth of the self*, 132.
2 Greenfeld, *Mind, modernity, madness: the impact of culture on human experience*, 42.
3 Makari, *Soul machine: the invention of the modern mind*.
4 The Harris Poll, Americans' belief in God, miracles and heaven declines: belief in Darwin's theory of evolution rises.
5 Becker, *The denial of death*.
6 James, *The principles of psychology, Volume 1*.
7 Rahula, *What the Buddha taught* (2nd ed.).
8 Watts, *The wisdom of insecurity: a message for an age of anxiety*, 85.
9 Damasio, *Descartes' error: emotion, reason, and the human brain*, 226–227.
10 Metzinger, *The ego tunnel: the science of the mind and the myth of the self*, 38.
11 Holstein and Gubrium, *The self we live by: narrative identity in a postmodern world*, 4.
12 Greenfeld, *Mind, modernity, madness: the impact of culture on human experience*.
13 For example, Bergen, *Louder than words: the new science of how the mind makes meaning*.
14 Harré, *The singular self*.
15 Lakoff, Foreword, x.
16 Greenfeld, *Mind, modernity, madness: the impact of culture on human experience*.
17 Jaynes, *The origin of consciousness in the breakdown of the bicameral mind*, 291.
18 For example, Seung, *Connectome: how the brain's wiring makes us who we are*.
19 Lakoff and Johnson, *Metaphors we live by*.

Self from the inside out   187

20 Berry, The handing down, 35.
21 Carruthers, *Language, thought, and consciousness: an essay in philosophical psychology.*
22 Freud, *Psychopathology of everyday life.*
23 Herman, *Trauma and recovery*, 68.
24 Guenther, *Solitary confinement: social death and its afterlives.*
25 Greenfield, *ID: the quest for meaning in the 21st century*, 131.
26 Edelman, *The remembered present: a biological theory of consciousness.*
27 Oliver, Stars.
28 James, *The principles of psychology Volume 1*, 233.
29 Whyte, *The unconscious before Freud: a history of the evolution of human awareness.*
30 Berlin, *The roots of romanticism* (2nd ed.).
31 Csikszentmihali, *Flow: the psychology of optimal experience*, 39–40.
32 Jaynes, *The origin of consciousness in the breakdown of the bicameral mind.*
33 Ackerman, *One hundred names for love: a memoir*, 138–139.
34 Langer, *Philosophy in a new key: a study in the symbolism of religion, rite, and art.*
35 Hobson, *The cradle of thought: exploring the origins of thinking.*
36 Damasio, *Self comes to mind: constructing the conscious brain*; Damasio, *The strange order of things: life, feeling, and the making of cultures.*
37 Edelman, *The remembered present: a biological theory of consciousness.*
38 Burke, *A grammar of motives*, 503.
39 Hobson, *The cradle of thought: exploring the origins of thinking*, 120.
40 Wittgenstein, *Philosophical investigations*, 113.
41 *Ibid.*, 117.
42 See, for example: Frith, *Making up the mind: how the brain creates our mental world*; Metzinger, *The ego tunnel: the science of the mind and the myth of the self.*
43 See Rose and Abi-Rached, *Neuro: the new brain sciences and the management of the mind.*
44 Hofstadter, *I am a strange loop.*
45 Dennett, *Consciousness explained*, 416.
46 Sartre, *Being and nothingness: a phenomenological essay on ontology*, 485.
47 Graziano, *Consciousness and the social brain*, 104–105.
48 Merleau-Ponty, *Phenomenology of perception*, 179.
49 Burke, *A rhetoric of motives.*
50 Ackerman, *One hundred names for love: a memoir*, 121.
51 Burke, *Language as symbolic action: essays on life, literature, and method.*
52 Taylor, *Sources of the self: the making of modern identity.*
53 *Ibid.*, 35.
54 Barkan et al., State and regional suicide rates: a new look at an old puzzle.
55 Taylor, *Sources of the self: the making of modern identity*, 36.
56 Lehrer, *A book about love*, 106.
57 Forbes et al., Partner bereavement and detection of dementia: a UK-based cohort study using routine health data.
58 Taylor, *Sources of the self: the making of modern identity*, 18.

10 From the basement up
Modernity, the self, and the unconscious mind

The unconscious is not so much a thing as it is an idea.
Robert C. Fuller, *Americans and the Unconscious*[1]

Modernity and the unconscious mind

We turn now to consider the question of nonrational influences on personal identity. These can originate in a range of sources, including, on the one hand, the biases of the material brain and the physical body, and, on the other, what some sociologists have termed "habitus," or what I have been calling the common sense: the totality of the traditions, sensibilities, scripts, and deep cultural presumptions in which a life is embedded (e.g., ideas of the powers and proclivities of your gender). As well, some believe in spiritual influence (e.g., demonic possession). We'll take up all of these to some degree in this chapter and the next, but our primary focus will be the question of the historical situation of the modern sense of the unconscious mind and the many ways it is manifest in ordinary interpersonal affairs.

In our time, almost any discussion of interpersonal motivation assumes that there are unconscious influences to behavior and self-identity. We draw from an extensive vocabulary to describe the operations of the unconscious, especially in the defense of the self: denial, repression, sublimation, dissociation, projection, and others. Some terms, such as transference and splitting, are mainly used by specialists, but others, such as projection, identification, and denial, have become so broadly understood that they have dropped into common discourse. As we'll see, the roots of the modern idea of unconscious motivation are not very deep. There was no general notion of systematic unconscious mental operations much before the beginning of the Freudian era in the mid-to-late nineteenth century. But thereafter, talk of unconscious motivation quickly became common, infusing everyday discussion of social and psychological life. Is it possible that, though many take the dynamic operations of the unconscious mind for granted today, no one was as much motivated by unconscious factors prior to the nineteenth century? The answer to this question is complicated, but, in general, that's the way it appears to be. In fact, by extension, today, in other parts of the world where modernity's

DOI: 10.4324/9781003010234-13

From the basement up   189

influences aren't as prominent, it's likely that there's less of the unconscious at play in everyday interpersonal and psychological experience. The argument I will pursue in this chapter is that, whether or not some manner of unconscious influence has always been part of human experience, the role of the unconscious expanded dramatically as a consequence of the social and psychological demands of modernity. This happened for two reasons: first, that the mounting civic requirements of modernity promote repression of impulse, and, second, that, in modernity, the narrative self becomes much more prone to moral conflict and incoherence.

The early psychoanalytic theorists didn't invent the unconscious out of their imaginations. Modernity transforms mental life along with everything else, and the problems modernity creates for the coherence of the sense of self-identity result naturally in what we understand as unconscious operations of mind. Thus, the unconscious came into prominence as a result of the hallmark social psychological circumstances of modernity – isolation, rapid change, social diversity, failing community, segmentation, heightened stress and anxiety, and other factors described in Part 2, which were reaching a state of critical mass during the last half of the nineteenth century.

The unconscious isn't a material substance or a physical structure of the body. It's a descriptive term that refers to psychic phenomena defined in characteristic mental operations and accompanying social practices that are important in maintaining a sense of personal coherence in the face of the contradictory pressures of modern life. As per Fuller in the quotation that opens this chapter, the psychodynamic unconscious is not a thing, but a description of the way the mind operates. It is not that there is no reference to unconscious phenomena before the nineteenth century, but, as we'll see, observations about the unconscious were less common, more likely to be understood in religious terms (e.g., demonic possession) or in the terms of traditional ethnic folkways and superstitions, and much less likely to be recognized as a part of everyday experience.

That those in modern societies have come to believe in an unconscious layer of motivation in interpersonal affairs – and there's no doubt that this belief is widespread – is of great consequence, because at the moment this belief becomes common, we no longer take each other at face value. All behavior becomes symbolically communicative, even to the point of physical illness being understood as, potentially, a kind of language for the expression of self (for example, in psychosomatic phenomena such as hysterical blindness or seizures, or a tendency to develop headaches that keep you off the job or rule out sex with your spouse, eating (or not eating) as a method of managing anxiety, or, perhaps, in the retreat to texting and other digital media in place of the risks of rich face-to-face encounters with others). Obviously, people have always had to consider the question of the degree to which they are being purposefully deceived or manipulated by others (and, as has been noted, much more so in the decline of close community and the advent of urbanization), but, with the modern idea of the unconscious came a radical new twist to this difficulty: the possibility that we also routinely deceive ourselves. And so, we

190　*The shape of the modern self*

must now examine how it came to pass that the conceptualization of the self and the explanation for why we interact with others as we do so recently started to include an idea of unconscious motivation. We've seen some of this story already. Now, we'll drill deeper in a brief look at the history of manners, and how the control of impulse leads to unconscious layers of self and distortions in self-perception. As usual, it began with language.

Manners: suppressing impulse in the service of civility

> it is not a refined habit, when coming across something disgusting in the street ... to turn at once to one's companion and point it out to him. It is far less proper to hold out the thing for the other to smell, as some are wont, who even urge the other to do so, lifting the thing to his nostrils and saying, "I should like to know how much that stinks."[2]

Language abstracts from direct experience similarly to the way that a map is an abstract representation of the physical world. With the world represented on a computer screen or on paper, or described in spoken language, we can plot and compare routes for a trip independent of taking the trip itself. Similarly, experiencing the hunger impulse linguistically as the thought, spoken internally, "Hmm. I'm getting hungry," places the mind's awareness of the experience of hunger at a remove, allowing reflection on various avenues of response ("stick with the diet," "chew gum," "order a cheeseburger," "send food aid donation to Americares," etc.). A characteristically nervous kitten acts directly on each unmediated anxious impulse and may hide or become aggressive, but a nervous man has the potential to anticipate his anxiety and represent it symbolically in language, turn over options for expressing it, project it onto others (perhaps taking his perfectly calm girlfriend's hand and, in a deeply concerned voice, admonishing her to be brave, etc.), or to otherwise sublimate it in a thousand activities.

Clearly, there's always been some type of lower-level, sign-like, nonlinguistic mental flow: direct awareness of sensation, desire, emotion, and impulse. This is primary consciousness, or the I, the consciousness of human infants and nonhuman animals, as described in the previous chapter. But, in the distant history of human evolution, when primitive social communication eventually spawned symbolic language, consciousness, now linguistically encoded, became uniquely capable. Language bestows the possibility of awareness of a potentially limitless universe of concepts (things real as well as things imagined) and analytic distinctions, including the idea of self as unique and the distinction between concepts of time, such as the idea of before, now, and later. With direct lower-level stimuli (pain, pleasure, body appetites, the data of external experience, etc.) feeding into the system of distinctions afforded by language, the experience of being a unique person takes shape: self is described in a personal narrative involving some sense of our own history and a range of imagined futures. With the transformation to symbolic language, humans

From the basement up 191

acquired the option to relate to each other, not just through reaction to impulse in the present (i.e., signals), but through abstractly encoded symbols. In this, civilization began to evolve in earnest.

You may recall from Chapter 2 that psychohistorian Julian Jaynes believed that there was likely a lengthy transitional period in which early humans, though enabled of language, still engaged it predominantly as a set of signals, as though the commands of gods. As a method of communication, the signal is an impulse, not a considered choice. Social coordination via signal was adequate within small groups living in isolated agrarian circumstances, but such a system will break down as the world becomes more sociologically complex and variable. Signals that worked to coordinate activity in one group will not be comprehensible within other groups, or as the group grows and diversifies. At a point that Jaynes placed somewhere between the period of authorship of the *Iliad* and the authorship of the *Odyssey*, humans began to acquire a sense of individuality and personal distinction, and with that came an awareness of each person as an individual with distinctive points of view and varying motivation. As this revolution in the awareness of self and other took root, impulsive, signal-like responses to stimuli not only became less functional, they also became potentially troublesome and, indeed, even dangerous.

As Western society became more densely populated and intricately structured, it became increasingly important to develop the capacity to interrupt impulse – to repress reflex-like response – as impulsive behavior represents a continuous potential threat to civil life, as well as to our vision of self. The idea of society is virtually synonymous with social control and the suppression of impulse,[3] and these controls are not only external (e.g., through legal, religious, or economic pressure, or through bureaucratic regulation) but internal too. On the neurological level, the brain has a built-in capacity for repressing self-threatening information,[4] and, on the psychological level, irrational impulses, such as sexual lust or hostile fury, are repressed because they challenge the story we tell ourselves that we are rational, moral agents. And so, to a greater or lesser extent, in the service of civility, every child must learn to repress, sublimate, and delay gratification : in general, to tame impulse.

Indeed, impulse control became ever more important in the movement from dwelling in public in small communities to the intense privacy afforded in urban environments, where, as one is increasingly aware, the mixture of easily accessible deadly weapons amidst multitudes of disconnected people of uncertain sensibilities and diverse values can have disastrous consequences. Recently, there's been much discussion of failing impulse control, particularly with regard to such problems as obesity, premarital pregnancy, domestic violence, sexual harassment, gun violence, and road rage. But historians of social forms and manners have documented that impulse control has actually become ever tighter, at least within upwardly aspiring social strata.[5]

How far have we come? As recently as the seventeenth century, the etiquette books of the times advised people seeking to advance themselves socially to adopt restraints on impulse that would probably strike a modern reader as

192 *The shape of the modern self*

remarkably basic. Readers of this literature were advised to refrain from urinating or defecating directly in front of others or in front of someone's door; not to blow one's nose on the hand and then pick up food from the public table; not, upon spotting a turd lying in the street, to yield to the impulse to hold it up to their friends for inspection; and not to fart loudly and openly in holy places, but to cover the noise with a cough.[6]

This is quite a distance from today's "Dear Abby" and "Miss Manners" columns and their advice about modern concerns, like how to repair relationships after accidentally sending invitations to join you on AshleyMadison.com to everyone in your email contacts list, what form of address to use when referring to your father's new transgendered girlfriend, or what obligations you have toward the genetic parents of your child after learning that the baby you carried to term was implanted by mistake in a mix-up during the in vitro procedure.

During the Middle Ages, it was much more likely that emotion might be expressed immediately and without civil restraint, and so the potential for physical violence in public was much higher than today. The murder rate in certain areas of France in the mid-1500s was as much as 40 times what it is in European countries now.[7] Most of this was accounted for by young males in their 20s who were virtually all armed and commonly engaged in competitions of violence. The rate of violent death in Colonial America was also high,[8] but it varied systematically with other historical and cultural factors specific to the country's development.

As Western societies moved ever deeper into modernity, the adoption of codes of conduct that differentiated people in varying social strata gradually brought impulsive behavior under control. Eventually, prohibitions on expressiveness (ideas about proper and refined behavior, accepted ways of comporting oneself in public, appropriate modes of speech, etc.) become internalized as habitual self-limiting controls, dropping from awareness and becoming part of the common sense. So effective is this internalization that we don't resist or even recognize these strictures, even when alone. They are the floorboards of perception, constituting a tacit field of unexamined foundational truths that subtly prefigure all other beliefs overlaid on top of them, including, especially, the beliefs that become pivotal in our sense of who we are. As modernity intensified, packing more people together in close contact, the requirements of urban/civil life and of the bureaucratized workplace ever more finely conditioned the perceived world by adding layers to this foundation. Twenty-first-century Americans, no less than their famously repressed Victorian counterparts, are defined by what they can't imagine themselves doing, and, indeed, by what's all around them that they don't see.

To some extent, the ability to control impulse still permits us to place ourselves socially (for example, in my recognizing my social superiority in the difference between my kind and my neighbors across the street with their muffler-less cars and accumulating glacier of lawn junk). We differentiate ourselves on the basis of the degree of constraint and sophistication of our

From the basement up   193

expressive behavior, including speech, as exemplified in today's evolving strictures regarding hate speech and modes of gender address (as one of my undergraduates wrote in a class paper, "Today there are no truly defined gender roles, or, at least, we are not allowed to say so"). Yet the concerns addressed in today's advice columns are less often about how to comport self so that one might move up the social ladder in a hierarchical society. Modern America isn't constituted of the kind of widely recognized structures of social hierarchy that made that sensible in other times and places. In America's egalitarianism and segmentation, and in the diversity of today's interpersonal landscape, advice columns now more often treat questions about interpersonal interaction and social ethics. The great changes of modernity have so limited the extent to which one can assume values and moral assumptions are generalizable – that there is still a binding common sense to the world – that there are now many ways to inadvertently disappoint or offend, and this encourages, if not withdrawal and isolation, then careful and cautious response, even repression.

This distancing from unmediated expression of base impulses is a type of socialized repression, a factor that has heightened the influence of unconscious processes in shaping social behavior and the sense of self. Base impulses are still there, but recognition of them is blocked from consciousness. Underneath the veneer of civilized behavior lie impulses, particularly aggressive or sexual, that have to be kept in check. It may be that we see the unconscious in action (of course, in others, not in ourselves, while others see it in us, but not in themselves) more often in our era than was the case in the past because, in this time of diversity, urbanization, and increasing accountability for uncivil behavior, more of immediate impulse requires restraint, and so the residuals of impulse and raw inclination, which can only be satisfied so far in normal civil life, rattle around beneath awareness, coloring what is seen and shaping the ways in which people act toward each other. Naturally, the suppression of impulse is stressful, and many seek vicarious outlets in the unrestrained violence and sexuality of pop culture media, violent sports, and the like.

How impulse management influences self-identity

As a byproduct of the invention of language and the shift from direct, reflex-like reaction to stimuli to abstract reaction-at-a-remove (movement from the world of signal to the world of symbol), we accumulate a record of our experienced impulses and feelings and impressions of how we typically respond to them (e.g., "I'm often hungry but usually manage my appetite with disciplined exercise," "I sometimes feel depressed even though I have pride in my accomplishments," "I'm a sucker for a pretty face"). Sometimes, this happens in the clear. We recognize our base feelings for what they are (e.g., intense hostility after an injustice from a supervisor at work: "I felt like leaping over the conference table and wringing his neck!") and, knowing that we can't indulge them directly, we come up with an acceptable if somewhat diluted substitute (e.g., "He'll be under review for promotion next year and then we'll see what's what").

194   *The shape of the modern self*

More commonly, these processes are murky or altogether invisible because the raw desire is experienced as morally unacceptable to our vision of self or places the coherence of our self-narrative too much at risk ("I'm not *that* kind of person"). But the impulse must be dealt with. In such cases, the crafty symbolic repackaging of base impulses (through sublimation, projection, etc.) may go unnoticed or is misunderstood, resulting sometimes in unusual patterns of behavior (compulsion, irrational avoidance or fear, emotional reactivity, etc.) and a vision of self that may seem to others to be oddly out of sync with reality. This is the perpetual conflict between, on the one side, impulse and animal desire (in psychoanalytic terminology, the id) and, on the other, the moral requirements of civil life (the superego). This conflict is the source of the normal neurosis, the irrational aspects of motivation and cognition that virtually no one escapes. The well of irrationality is fed by the dual streams of repression and moral inconsistency that flow strongly through modern societies.

This process can also loop interpersonally: (a) The anxiety I feel about expressing my actual raw sexual desire for you results in my reluctance to allow that passion to be expressed, or even noticed by me ("I'm not *that* kind of person"). But my controlled demeanor doesn't go unnoticed by you, and so you act cautiously toward me, which I rationalize as evidence that my anxieties are well founded, which leads me to keep my passion in check, which doesn't go unnoticed by you, etc. (b) You were insensitive to me last week but you didn't see it. It actually made me intensely angry at you but I repressed that so well that I can't see any evidence of that anger in me. I maintain, in inaccurate honesty, that I'm not angry and never was. Because of your insensitive manner you seem comfortable with my unlikely denial, an insensitivity that would make anyone angry, but not me, of course.

The confluence of these accurate and inaccurate self-observations forms the basis for the second dimension of self-awareness, the "Me" introduced in the previous chapter. This is a higher-order consciousness, a sort of clinical, third-person view of oneself as though a character in a play, with a biography (heavily edited) and an unfolding story line, a past and a future. As we've seen, some theorists believe that awareness of self arises as a result of disturbances in energy, perception, or emotion that interrupt psychological "flow," placing the mind in a state of reflective arousal.[9] This is precisely what happens when the restrictions of civil life dictate that impulse must be suppressed and is one part of the reason why, with growing intensity, issues of self have become a visible preoccupation for many in modern societies.

Perception, memory, and the Me

When we reflect on the remembered data of the experience of our lives – perhaps picking over our past behavior and feeling states, looking at the choices we've made, musing about what we stand for, what enduring attributes, ambitions, talents, liabilities, and quirks our friends and associates might attribute to us based on what we think they've seen of this data – we're considering

From the basement up   195

ourselves then as a character at arms' length, as though in the third person. As we saw in the previous chapter, self-awareness in the first sense, as we experience it in the flow of the present in linguistically encoded sensation and emotion – the "I" – has been around from the first moments that humans acquired speech, and a more primitive nonlinguistic process underlies it and preceded it. But self-awareness in this second sense, as a sort of third-person-narrative biography, could only have developed following the advent of language and is its natural outcome. The facility of language compels us to observe and classify our own experience, to synthesize these observations and reflect upon them, and, inevitably, to distinguish between ourselves and others, and between what happened in the past, what's happening now, and what might lie ahead. Without language, you can't do any of these things. Once you have language, you can't avoid doing them.

As Douglas Hofstadter pointed out, the very reflections and conclusions this produces become part of the accreted data that we reflect upon, resulting in what he referred to as "strange loops" – self-amplifying feedback circuits.[10] Thus, a woman thinks about her past and, noticing herself doing this, concludes that she's a rather self-analytic person who engages in frequent self-reflection. Like an audio feedback loop between a microphone and a speaker that quickly gets very loud, that she engaged in the process of making that analysis reinforces her conclusion that she's a self-analytic person. Her conclusion has become part of the data that support it, and so it amplifies itself. This type of feedback-driven system is uniquely human. When a kitten becomes fearful over some perception or sensation, it engages in sensible behavior with regard to the stimulus – perhaps hiding or attacking. But, on feeling fear, only a human can crank up the meta-panic that results from the perception of being anxious and unable to control it: only a human becomes anxious about being anxious. The basis of this anxiety is the perception we're losing control of our self-narrative.

This is the soldier's fear of freezing in the face of enemy fire, or the common fear of coming apart as we approach a moment of personal significance: an intense conflict, burying a loved one, telling your partner you're leaving, giving a public speech. The self-narrative is built in this circular interplay between conscious awareness (the I) and the self-concept (the Me), wherein information that comes to attention may have implications for the self, and so for how one directs oneself in the future.[11] This second-order awareness can't exist without language and is its natural offspring: it's only humans who marvel or despair about the condition of their lives.

As for despair, because self-identity is no longer something one is born into, but is now more of an abstract vision created in language, people are more likely now to experience anguish, which is a condition of apprehension about the ability to sustain a stable and certain sense of self in light of all the possibilities ahead of us.[12] Anguish comes from the impossibility of being true to all the futures we imagine but can't actualize, or the visions of ourselves that we had formed last month but were unable to sustain (perhaps that was New

196 *The shape of the modern self*

Years when you said you'd go on a diet, or that you'd never drive over the speed limit again, or you wouldn't spend more than another month in your lousy job, but here you are speeding off to that same job, drowning your despair in cheeseburgers). This type of anguish is more a property of life in modern societies than it was in the past because, as Sartre argued, anguish is a byproduct of the enhanced possibility and freedom that have come along in the decline of the force of traditional, religious, and hierarchical life. This freedom from constraint in who one may become is another part of the reason the self has become such an issue, so fraught with possibility.

Some scholars believe that self-identity exists in a perpetual state of revision, based on more or less continuous reassessment and reappropriation of the past, the facts of which may be repressed or revised if it serves some advantage for our vision of self. This may serve the purpose of reducing anguish or smoothing over perceived moral failures or inconsistencies, or of helping to promote some new vision of self-identity, as in the common case of presidential candidates who promote stories of their childhood that they hope voters will take as evidence of their character and qualifications. (Sartre quipped that Decartes's famous dictum ought to be revised to be "I think; therefore I *was*.")[13] This process is visible at the group level in some places where textbooks are required to teach differing versions of history as the educational system comes under the sway of one ideological group or another.

Our concern, however, lies with the individual level, where this dynamic is visible in cases of trauma linked to acquired (rather than actual) memories in post-traumatic stress disorder (PTSD),[14] cases in which a person may adopt memories of traumatic events in their history that never actually occurred (recall NBC anchor Brian Williams's acquired memory about being under fire in a military helicopter during the 2003 Iraq war, or Hillary Clinton's false memory of being under sniper fire in Bosnia). Similarly, self-revision may result from cultural redefinition of the meaning of behavior that occurred in our personal history that results in a conclusion, long after the fact, that one is actually a victim of trauma (e.g., when rapid cultural change in what counts as child abuse leads one to reclassify oneself as having been an abused child, and this creates some new degree of anxiety and suffering).[15]

The continually evolving product of this type of internal review – whether circular and self-amplifying or not, or based on factual versus appropriated memory, or on transparent insight versus a view of self clouded by the neurotic distortions of difficult memories or morally disturbing impulses – is what we usually think of as the self-concept. It is this second sense of self-awareness: self as an object reflected upon as if in the third person, the narrative self, or the "Me." Of the two aspects of self-awareness, the I and the Me, the Me is the one that's become complicated in the stresses that result when freedom of self-definition seeks expression in the bureaucratized, disconnected, and chaotic context of disembedded modern society. Hence, it's the Me, the narrative self, not the I, that's at the center of our effort to understand the unique situation of interpersonal life in this age. The Me reacts to changing historical

From the basement up   197

circumstances. Generally, the I does not. And, along with the rising existential difficulty created by modernity's expanded freedoms, the necessity of repressing impulse has been on the rise in the modern world's more intricate civil requirements. These two factors – repression of impulse in the service of civility and the stress that results in modern societies from the difficulty of maintaining an internally consistent and morally defensible self-story – have amplified subterranean mental influences. Thus, as the forces of modernity strengthened, the role of the unconscious became more prominent.

Western history and the unconscious mind

There has been much variation in the way that unconscious influences have been regarded in different historical periods, with fascinating consequences for how people in modern societies now understand and relate to each other. Overall, the trend has been toward a view of mind and motivation, and their relationship to social experience, as ever more intricate, ever more the subject of buried influences. Like a trail of lights in the forest, the varying status of phenomena such as demonic possession, shamanic healing, animal magnetism, hypnosis, dreams, and the defense mechanisms of the self demarcates the transition to modernity.

It seems clear that Colonial Americans weren't as influenced by unconscious process – not as likely to be constituted of both conscious and hidden aspects of self – as we assume to be the case for ourselves and those with whom we interact and whose self stories we struggle to understand and sync with. Today, it is commonplace to speculate about the unconscious motivations of politicians, colleagues, family members, and friends, but this was unlikely to have been as much the case in the past. There was little mention of any unconscious aspect of self prior to the seventeenth century, and it wasn't until the middle of the eighteenth century that the term unconscious began to appear in the modern sense in English and German usage.[16] The term didn't surface in French writing until the 1850s, nearly 100 years later. In the years prior to Freud, in the limited instances where phenomena relevant to the modern unconscious were visible, they were described in other systems of conceptualization and not in the modern sense.[17] A vivid illustration of this, one that neatly captures the change in key from religious to secular conceptualization, which, as we've seen, is a hallmark of the modernizing world, is given in the account of the healing practices of two Europeans of the late eighteenth century: Johann Joseph Gassner and Franz Anton Mesmer.

Exorcism, animal magnetism, and hypnosis

Gassner (1727–1779) and Mesmer (1734–1815) were contemporary healers who used similar procedures but maintained radically different conceptualizations of how and why their methods worked.[18] These two practiced in the cultural frame and time period dramatized in the 1994 film *The Madness of*

198 *The shape of the modern self*

King George, which depicts the primitive state of medicine and the psychiatric arts in Europe during that period. Ideas about the reality of mind and soul and their relationship to spirit and body were then in turmoil. Medicine was largely quackery, but empirical science was well along in gaining authority, and long-standing religious doctrine was being actively challenged. New ideas posited that consciousness and mind were products of a physical organ of thought, challenging the dominant religious view that mental experience was a function of the soul and spirit.[19] If mind was a product of an organ of the body, then the cure for disordered thought lay in secular practices of medicine. If mind was the province of divine spirit – the soul – then the cure for disordered thought lay in rituals of moral purification. Adding to this were the relatively rapid advances in the physical sciences and their claims about the influence of unseen forces such as gravity, magnetism, and electricity. Ideas were in transition.

Gassner was a Catholic priest in eastern Switzerland who was afflicted with headaches and dizziness that appeared when he was conducting Mass. After concluding that he was being tormented by Satan, Gassner applied the church's ancient rituals of exorcism to cure himself and was successful. He then decided to use his talents as an exorcist to help others. In time, he gained fame for the effective cures his exorcisms could produce and was much sought after. (And understandably so, as most of what regular medicine had to offer at that time was blood-letting and induced vomiting.)

Gassner first required his patients to attest to their Christian faith. Then, he asked the patient for permission to execute a trial exorcism during which he would call upon the demon thought to be responsible for the disease to increase the symptoms. The idea was to see if he could establish a kind of dialogue with the demon. If the symptoms did increase, Gassner would conclude that the disease was indeed diabolical in origin, with the demon willing to engage, and so he would then proceed with a full ritual exorcism. If the presenting symptoms didn't increase during the trial exorcism, the patient was referred to a regular physician. Gassner's reputation grew, and his methods were copied by others. However, as this happened, he met with resistance from civil authorities. He was practicing exorcism in a time in which secular reason was being fore-grounded and superstition was gradually being rejected (earlier in the century, the practice of exorcism had been rejected by Protestants). Gassner's conception of what he was doing in his work was out of touch with the intellectual currents of the modernizing world, and several formal inquiries into his methods were conducted. Eventually, the controversy he aroused caused the Catholic establishment to direct Gassner to get out of the public eye by restricting his practice to cases referred to him through the church hierarchy.

Contemporaneous with Gassner, Franz Mesmer, a conventionally trained physician, was gaining fame for a method of healing that was similar to Gassner's. In both cases, the treatment protocol involved first attempting to establish an interpersonal rapport with the patient such that it was clear that the patient was open to the healer's influence. With this in place, Gassner and

From the basement up 199

Mesmer were able to use the power of suggestion to increase symptoms and also to cause them to go into remission. The center of the therapeutic method was the use of the healer's reputation and authority to place the disease in a conceptual frame in which the patient believed the healer had the power to effect a cure. Sometimes, in such circumstances, that may be all it takes: healing may indeed occur. This is understood today as the placebo effect, a phenomenon that neatly demonstrates the phenomenal power of human discourse to reconstruct the world right down to underlying body processes. The conceptualization that Mesmer offered patients was the idea that all life was interconnected with a physical force he called "animal magnetism." Mesmer and his patients believed that he was healing them as he passed his hands over them to manipulate this force. (On occasion, to increase the effect, he had patients swallow iron filings or sit in tubs of magnetized water.)

Mesmer was summoned to consult with one of the commissions investigating Gassner and, after studying Gassner's methods, reported that Gassner was indeed producing legitimate cures but was mistaken in attributing them to the expulsion of demons. Mesmer maintained that, without knowing it, Gassner was gifted with the ability to channel the patient's animal magnetism. Like Gassner, Mesmer attracted many adherents to his methods (and detractors: he too was eventually investigated by a committee that included Benjamin Franklin, then American ambassador to France, and the physician Joseph-Ignace Guillotin, inventor of the popular head-removal device), but, in the shifting philosophical framework of the modernizing world, methods based on religion and the authority of tradition were being replaced by secular practices, and so, despite its foundation in erroneous ideas, "Mesmerism" (the origin of our familiar word "mesmerizing") continued as a movement beyond Franz Mesmer's death, eventually, after many transformations, leading to modern dynamic psychiatry, whereas exorcism largely became an historical artifact.

Eventually, in the 1840s, an English practitioner named James Braid renamed Mesmer's method "hypnotism." And, although the idea of animal magnetism was abandoned, and acceptance of the practice of hypnotism has waxed and waned, by the late nineteenth century, hypnosis was understood as a method that could provide a way to demonstrate, probe, and influence the relatively newly discovered unconscious mind. Examples of this include the use of hypnotism to relieve hysterical symptoms or to explore repressed accounts of traumatic experience.

The essential common aspect of both Gassner's and Mesmer's methods was their use of interpersonal influence: the power of someone regarded as a credible authority to reframe a person's conception of reality (to cause fundamental changes to the fields of meaning that comprise the mind), even, in some cases, to the point of causing physical symptoms to come or go. Similar to other pseudoscientific methods (Reiki, emotional freedom technique (EFT), neurolinguistic programming, facilitated communication, past life therapy, astrology, etc.) and a cousin of shamanic healing and voodoo, hypnotism is simply suggestion and theater, providing an excellent demonstration of the power of

200 *The shape of the modern self*

belief and the potential of interpersonal persuasion, bolstered by ritual and by association with the authority of science and medicine.

A now classic study of the mid-twentieth century demonstrated that hypnotized students would comply when asked to perform a number of exotic and potentially dangerous behaviors, such as placing their hand in a cage with what they thought was a poisonous snake, or in a beaker that supposedly contained acid. As it turned out, however, a similar rate of compliance was obtainable among those who were merely asked to do the same apparently dangerous behaviors by someone they perceived to be a legitimate authority (a university scientist wearing a lab coat).[20] There are many accounts of the power of shamanic healing in non-Western societies and of the effectiveness of psychological suggestion and faith healing in our own.[21] Indeed, placebos are as effective as many psychiatric medications widely prescribed today.[22] The common element in all of these practices is a strong belief in the legitimacy of the prescribed cure and the authority of the healer. The healer's skill inheres in the ability to create this context, sometimes against resistance, and to make use of the aura of authority to implant helpful new beliefs in the mind of the patient.

Discredited by science, Mesmer nevertheless stimulated considerable interest in animal magnetism. Clearly, something important happened sometimes in these hypnotic sessions. In many places in Europe, adherents to Mesmer's ideas formed Societies of Harmony (the harmony part referring to the idea that mesmerism brought magnetic fields into harmonic alignment). Mesmer tried to maintain personal control over the movement he had stimulated, but was unsuccessful. The movement spread beyond his reach, and its modes of practice and conceptual trappings were modified. However, the key element of the practice remained the creation between the practitioner and the subject of what the magnetists called "the rapport" – the establishment of an unusually open receptivity of the mind of the patient to the ideas and the will of the mesmerizer. In other words, the essential elements are one person whose mind is fully open to influence and another who believes in their powers of influence. This is an unusual situation but one that is sensible within the mind – language framework presented in previous chapters. Mind is a social creation. Continuous interpersonal encounter is vital to the creation and maintenance of the myriad fields of meaning that constitute it. What mesmerism and its historical and cultural variants demonstrate is just how foundational and consequential this interdependence can be. No one has a mind on their own.

Psychiatrist R. D. Laing regarded hypnosis as a model for a common form of interpersonal influence in the family in which a parent makes attributions about a child in the child's presence, especially to a third person. The parent says to another adult about her child, who's present, "He's a quick learner." Structurally, this is similar to hypnotic suggestion insofar as the authority relationship between parent and child is of sufficient dimension to render impossible any discounting of the attribution by the child. As Laing put it, "a relationship . . . may be of such power that you become what I take you to be."[23] In this type of hypnotic attribution, foundational ideas in a child's emerging sense of self are

From the basement up 201

established interpersonally ("I'm a quick learner"). This happens in adult relationships too, and mutually so among long-term intimate partners who regard each other as uniquely credible and authoritative with respect to each other's self-identity.

As a formal practice, hypnosis played an important role in late nineteenth-century theorizing of the self and psychopathology. The technique helped to establish popular belief in the presence of the unconscious as an influential layer of mind. During this time, the French neurologist Jean-Martin Charcot (1825–1893), who pioneered work on a host of neurological disorders, lectured on the use of hypnosis to treat hysterical symptoms – maladies that occur without basis in any detectable physical defect, such as hysterical paralysis of a limb, or hysterical blindness or deafness. In these cases, a hypnotist could sometimes relieve symptoms. As there was nothing wrong with the body, the symptoms were real, and the patient wasn't in conscious control of them, this led to the hypothesis that hypnotic technique allowed the physician direct communication with a layer of unconscious mental process that was the site of the patient's malady (often thought to be repressed sexuality).

Charcot was a professor of pathological anatomy at the Sorbonne, and the physicians Joseph Breuer and Sigmund Freud attended his lectures and subsequently collaborated in theorizing the role of the unconscious in the psychodynamics of the mind, jointly preparing the way for Freud's massively influential psychoanalytic theories.[24] Freud believed that the only possible explanation for hypnotic phenomena was an unconscious layer of mind available for influence through suggestion, and he began to experiment with hypnotic technique. In time, however, experience demonstrated that some patients couldn't be hypnotized, and he abandoned hypnotism in favor of other methods for exploring the unconscious, such as free association and, particularly, the analysis of dreams.

Dreaming: unconscious tea leaves of the self

As with hypnotism, the story of the changing conceptualization of dreaming helps to illustrate the emergence by the early twentieth century of the unconscious as an established feature of the modern mind. Cross-culturally and historically, there's been great variability in the way that dreams have been regarded. Freud summed up his view of the history of dreaming when he wrote:

> During the epoch which may be described as prescientific, men had no difficulty in finding an explanation of dreams. When they remembered a dream after waking up, they regarded it as either a favorable or a hostile manifestation by higher powers, demonic and divine. When modes of thought belonging to natural science began to flourish, all this ingenious mythology was transformed into psychology, and today only a small minority of educated people doubt that dreams are a product of the dreamer's own mind.[25]

202 *The shape of the modern self*

As the field of psychology only came into being in the latter half of the 1800s (the American Psychological Association was founded in 1892), Freud's remarks, made originally about 1900, indicate how recently had been the switch in the conceptualization of dreaming from spiritual to secular. This is consistent with Charles Dickens's depiction of Ebenezer Scrooge on a mid-1800s Christmas Eve rejecting the idea that his dreaming vision of Jacob Marley's ghost was a spiritual visitation, dismissing the ghost as merely a consequence of indigestion ("There's more of gravy than grave about you, whatever you are!"). This idea was congruent with the science of that era, which held that what you ate could affect your dreams.[26]

In many cultures and times, dreaming has been viewed as a medium connecting the spiritual and material worlds. The Bible includes many instances in which people understood their dreams to be divinely inspired, and the Talmud cautions that an uninterpreted dream is like an unopened letter from God. So too, and particularly vividly, in Book II of Homer's *Iliad* (eighth century BCE), where the dream is not an event but a being, a kind of animate agent, something like a Western Union telegraph boy, that an Olympian god can send to deliver a message to the sleeping mind of a mortal. Jove dispatched such a dream messenger to King Agamemnon to tell him in his sleep that the gods were now unified in their view that it was time for Agamemnon to summon his soldiers to attack Troy. To maximize the persuasive effect, the dream messenger chose to appear in Agamemnon's sleeping mind in the form of Nestor, Agamemnon's most trusted councilor.

Between the classical Greeks and modern sleep science lies a diverse anthropological lore that includes the Native Australian belief that dreams are journeys that may include interacting with others, living or dead, and that may comingle with waking states,[27] and the American Indian belief that dreams represent an alternative reality as real as waking life.[28] Some cultures look to dreams for medical diagnosis, and many cultures ascribe to dreams the power of premonition. Some even believe that dreams can be influenced telepathically. Indeed, it's not uncommon for modern Americans to be able to recount a dream that seemed to be influenced by someone else's waking thoughts or to forecast an event of significance.[29] Although some of this lingers, much of it faded as modernity came on, the dream coming to be regarded as a means of communication between aspects of the conscious self and repressed cognitions and emotions. By 1900, it was no longer what you ate for dinner that determined your dreams, but experiences too traumatic for your mind to digest.

As noted in Chapter 2, Carl Jung regarded the mind as constituted not only of the data of day-to-day experience but also of built-in predispositions to respond to life situations in common ways. He referred to these as "archetypes" and believed that they originated in the multimillion-year history of human evolution, which left its traces on the structures and predispositions not only of the body, but also of the mind. Jung's archetypes are inherited aptitudes that prestructure cognition and emotional life, in their effect, defining common pathways for living.[30] The archetypes show up in universal dream symbolism

From the basement up   203

providing a vehicle for what Jung called the "collective unconscious" (the inherited wisdom of the human species) to convey information useful for navigating the challenges of personal development.

Freud and Jung parted ways over the idea of the collective unconscious. Freud's focus on dream symbolism was less about universal experience and self-actualization and more about the management of trauma. For Freud, the symbolism of dreams was the result of the mind's strategically obscured encoding of traumatic experience repressed into the unconscious. The imagery of the dream was assumed to stand in for latent cognitions or wishes. Thus, like all other symbolic experience, dream content is metaphoric. After her parents' divorce, a girl frequently dreams of earthquakes.[31] A man dreams of being harassed by a female drill sergeant, which, by analogy, represents his problems at work where he's felt ill used by female supervisors. Joseph Campbell recounts a dream about driving a car related by a young woman upset at the loss of her virginity: "A stone had broken my windshield. I was now open to the storm and rain. Tears came to my eyes. Could I ever reach my destination in this car?"[32] The metaphor is obvious, but often obscure to the dreamer. Traditional psychoanalytic theory holds that that's the essence of the protective function of the unconscious, as is the tendency to quickly forget dreams after waking. Not all dreams reflect potentially self-threatening material, but, still, the content fades. This suggests that the more general reason for this is that, as discussed in previous chapters, symbolic meaning that is constructed on one's own and not deployed in discourse with others tends to become obscure and unavailable for conscious recall.

Through the principle of metaphoric condensation, one element of the imagery of a dream might stand in as an amalgam of several aspects of latent content. For example, a man experiencing marital conflict also suffers foot pain. One day, he sees a podiatrist. Later in the day, the marital conflict resolves. That night he has a vivid dream of an old stone bridge with pronounced arches spanning a small creek in a wooded rural setting. An obvious interpretation is that the bridge is a condensed symbol representing both the reconciliation of his conflict and his foot problems, the presence of the bridge's arches representing the arches in his feet. Because symbols imply their differentia, which often stand in opposition (religion implies atheism, male implies female), some dream imagery may stand in antithetical relationship to its actual meaning.[33] But sometimes it's perfectly straightforward: a man, sensing his relationship has dead-ended because his partner has started to withhold sex, dreams that he's in a car that she's driving, and suddenly, without apparent reason, she turns the wheel and runs the car into a low wall of snow and ice where it comes to a halt.

Dream analysis has fallen off the scope of normal psychiatric practice. Mainstream psychiatry has shifted from its traditional concern with sorting meaning (assuming all behavior, dreaming included, is communicative, and the psychiatrist functions as an interpreter, helping make the meaning clear), becoming a biomedically oriented profession more concerned with the regulation of impulse and emotion using drugs (assuming that disordered behavior reflects problems in the workings of the material brain). Some believe that

204 *The shape of the modern self*

the dream is not a window to the unconscious mind but a more or less random byproduct of REM sleep. Yet Rosalind Cartwright, "the queen of dream research," reported that, in dream studies, subjects sleeping at home log more dream segments involving instances of sex and aggression than they do sleeping in a dream laboratory,[34] which suggests that dream content is not random, but rather that the mind remains interpersonally aware during sleep, and that repression and the management of self-presentation are ongoing even during dreaming. Regardless, there's no question that dreams provide vivid examples of insightful metaphoric symbolization and so can be useful in the exploration of the deeper aspects of self-identity.

Of course, all communication, whether produced by the waking or sleeping mind, is symbolic and so is always personal, to some degree metaphorically representational. When one speaks of love, or ambition, or family, or anything of significance, the meanings of our words bear the freight of our lives and distinguish us through their oppositional implications. They're laden with the condensed meanings that they have taken on as a result of our particular experience with them, and so, potentially, all discourse is deeply saturated with clues about life experience and issues of self. Sometimes, to see these clues and interpret them profitably, one needs to interpret normal interpersonal discourse in somewhat the same way that one interprets a poem or a dream: not literally or head-on, but sideways, so to speak.

The position of the unconscious in the conceptualization of interpersonal life has shifted since the early twentieth century and the heyday of psychoanalytic theory. This has been less apparent in the broad culture than in those areas of psychology and the brain sciences that discount ideas that can't be taken into the lab for experimental verification, which include much from psychoanalytic theory (and, for that matter, virtually all historical scholarship). However, psychoanalytic concepts and terminology remain indispensable in many fields and continue as basic elements of the working vocabulary of the analysis of everyday interpersonal life, particularly when trying to account for puzzling inconsistencies between aptitudes and behavior. One doesn't have to look far for examples: the soldier from a long-concluded war who continues to suffer severe social-emotional problems; the professional whose job is on the chopping block who claims that doesn't bother him but coincidentally develops a compelling belief in an imminent, world-ending nuclear war; or the young man of means repeatedly arrested for shoplifting small items he doesn't need. In such cases, the common assumption is that cognition, emotion, and behavior are driven by repressed or dissociated trauma, and that the individual's conscious awareness, conditioned response, and deliberate motivation aren't all that's in play.

Self-defense

Editing traumatic experience from conscious awareness through repression is a form of self-defense that may result in behavior that seems irrational. Ready examples involve cases of massive trauma, as in war experiences or

From the basement up   205

rape, so disruptive of the self-system that the result is PTSD. But, in modernity's fast changing circumstances of meaning, it is universally difficult to maintain secure personal identity. In a world mostly constructed in discourse, subject to the varying points of view of a highly segmented, super-diverse society, people more or less continually butt up against contrary ideas and shifting interpretations that have implications for the self, challenging presumptions about personal merit and undermining the viability of life plans and pathways. Being in the first place a socially constructed object, the self is highly vulnerable to shifting conditions of culture. Born in the understandings of gender that were current only decades ago, what happens when this foundational structure of self-identity is destabilized, expanded, revalued, disempowered, and dissociated from its traditionally rooted position in the culture? What happen are anxiety, insecurity of self, and, often, unconscious attempts at defense. Of course, this happens not only with respect to the dramatic uncertainty that has grown up around gender, but with respect to myriad other elements in the swirling universe of concepts of relevance to self-identity.

Hence, in the analysis of interpersonal behavior, the crown jewels of the psychoanalytic perspective are the "defense mechanisms," the range of common cognitive and interpersonal maneuvers that are unconsciously deployed to defend against threats to the sense of personal identity. These stratagems comprise a kind of interpersonal body armor that serves to deflect anxiety and insecurity.

Threats to personal identity are omnipresent, ranging from those as trivial as failure to perform an everyday behavior at a level of normal competence, as when one can't remember what one intended to say, to those of overwhelming emotional significance, such as an adolescent might experience coming home from school to find her single-parent mother had left town permanently, abandoning her and her siblings without apparent reason. The threat can be directly relevant to self-identity and self-esteem, as might occur when a small child is left out from play with others, or when one is rejected in an important intimate relationship. In other cases, the threat can target ideas that are foundational to one's vision of reality: one's understanding of the coherence, safety, and continuity of the features of everyday life. Examples of this latter type include continuing anxiety that may follow exposure to rape, violence, war, or sudden natural disasters such as having your town destroyed in violent weather, or from events that redefine the boundaries of the common-sense realm of the possible, such as the 9/11 destruction of the World Trade Center.

Threats can also originate internally, resulting from a powerful biological impulse that threatens one's vision of self as moral, as might occur in a fantasy of sexual interest in the context of a taboo family relationship. If the threat is directed at a particularly foundational idea ("I'm lovable," "I'm good," "I'm heterosexual," "My town will be here tomorrow," "Buildings are safe from suicidal terrorists piloting airplanes"), there may be severe distortion

206 *The shape of the modern self*

of perception in the service of the coherence and survival of the ego. Cramer defines the defense mechanisms as "unconscious mental mechanisms that are directed against both internal drive pressures and external pressures, especially those that threaten self-esteem or the structure of the self."[35] She believes that the function of the defense mechanisms is "to protect the individual from experiencing excessive anxiety, and to protect the integration of the self." Table 10.1, which is based on Laing's list,[36] provides definition for some of them.

Table 10.1 Common Defense Mechanisms

Defense Mechanism	Example
Denial: "this is the case" is changed to "this is not the case"	In war, a mother receives word that her son has been killed, but can't tolerate this reality and continues to set the table for him, keeping his room and clothes ready for his return
	At school, a student sees a grade of "C" next to his name and automatically assumes the professor made a grading error
	An alcoholic refuses to admit having a drinking problem, despite it being apparent to others
Splitting: a complex matter is broken into isolated parts	Under threat, a person divides the world artificially into "us" and "them." All Americans are good. All "them" are evil
	A woman who is having an affair regards her husband as all good but not fun and sexual, and her lover as all fun and sexual but not decent enough to be a candidate for marriage
	A soldier required to kill in the course of duty cannot morally integrate the experience after the war, and his self becomes fractured, the moral violations of war split off from day-to-day consciousness, but returning in nightmares
Identification: feeling anxiously inadequate or ill at ease in myself, I adopt the idea that I'm someone else	Adolescent adoption of the hairstyles, material appearance, and manners of media stars
	Wearing clothing with prominent corporate logos
Displacement: the unconscious transfer of intense feelings or emotions to a safer outlet	A man who feels threatened at work goes to the gym afterwards for a session with a punching bag
	A woman who receives news that her novel was rejected by a publisher belittles her husband
	According to Ernest Becker, Sigmund Freud suffered from a particularly severe fear of his own death but displaced it into an expressed concern that he not die before his mother in order to save her from the pain he imagined she would experience at losing him

(Continued)

From the basement up 207

Table 10.1 (Continued)

Defense Mechanism	Example
Projection: what I find anxiety-producing within myself I relocate externally (this may be the basis for scapegoating)	A corporate executive enjoys a multimillion-dollar salary but unconsciously feels anxious guilt for making 60 times the wages of the average worker in the United States. She projects this externally, speaking to others about the world being full of welfare cheats and low-income criminals
	As a spouse, I transform "I don't love myself" into "you don't love me"
	A child introjects the intense conflict between her parents that led to their hostile divorce. She expresses it at first in antisocial behavior, but in time, as an adult, becomes a fan of TV wrestling and demolition derby
	Feeling increasingly marginalized as a senior citizen, I become angry over what I contend is America's declining influence and prestige in world affairs
Regression: reverting to an earlier state of psychological development	An adult, in the face of stress becomes dependent and unable to take responsibility
	There's also the "benign regression" of some beginning intimate relationships. In a heterosexual couple, the theory goes, each partner may remind the other of the opposite sex parent (see transference below), and with this they may find themselves feeling and acting like children again with each other. It's fun, playful – a benign regression
Reaction-formation: I substitute an opposite feeling for the one that I would really have if it didn't make me so anxious	A 13-year-old boy aggressively pushes little girls on the playground, not because he doesn't like them but because his new feelings of sexual attraction to girls are not yet integrated into the self and make him anxious
	A man jokes at a funeral because to fully experience the sadness and grief feels like it risks a kind of psychological disintegration
Transference: bringing the unresolved issues of a previous relationship, particularly one from childhood, into a current relationship	A woman complains about the communication deficits of the men she's dated, yet selects men to date who seem remote and unreachable interpersonally. This allows the woman to replay the unresolved problems from her childhood in her relationship with her own communicationally remote, unavailable father

Conclusion

By the mid-nineteenth century, the intensifying psychic and interpersonal demands of the modernizing world had achieved force sufficient to bring the unconscious into visibility. In the deeper past, an unconscious dimension of mind, in the modern sense of a storage locker of repressed traumatic experience and censored impulse, wasn't much recognized. Americans only began to become aware of the unconscious simultaneously with their entry into the

208 *The shape of the modern self*

modern secular world (i.e., particularly since the late 1700s).[37] Whatever of the unconscious was in existence in earlier times, it appears to have remained undiscovered and unconceptualized, something like evolution before Darwin or gravitation before Galileo and Newton. However, it's important to appreciate the difference between discoveries such as evolution and gravitation versus the "discovery" of the unconscious. The two former processes were deduced in consideration of timeless patterns of physical evidence. Although evolution was only discovered in the nineteenth century and gravitation in the seventeenth, the traces of these forces span all history and presumably exist independently of human awareness of them.

In contrast to this, and in sympathy with the argument that consciousness of self, the Me, came into being as an adaptive response to the heightening sociological complexity of the Greco-Roman world,[38] it's possible that the unconscious mind was discovered only recently because its former influence was significantly diminished; in other words, its present distinctiveness is a relatively recent emergent of the modernizing world and its evolving psychic and emotional stresses. The complexities of both the public (work) lives and the private (intimate) lives of modern people have come to require such extensive management of self-expression that one must repress a great deal of experience, which means that these experiences impact beneath consciousness.[39]

This is important to appreciate, because there is no reason to think that the psychological demands that have so intensified the expression of the unconscious in everyday life will become lighter in the foreseeable future. Rather, the appearance of the unconscious marks the start point of a progression in which, like startled turtles, people in modern societies have withdrawn protectively into their shells, and, in our time, somewhat more than a century after the unconscious began to be broadly recognized and discussed, observers of interpersonal life continue to comment on *increasing* demands and complexities of social experience and on emerging forms of withdrawal.

These include signs of mounting interest in the possibility of substituting robots for live companionship;[40] the "absent presence" of the digitally connected;[41] the emotional absence of the pharmacologically withdrawn (594 million prescriptions for the top 25 psychiatric drugs were written in America in 2016 alone); rising rates of solo households; hookup culture; rising age of marriage; plunging remarriage rates; and, generally, the hesitation to expose oneself to the risks of committed intimacy. Seeing these phenomena as commonly reflective of a growing cultural current provides clues to the direction interpersonal life will track in the future.

Notes

1 Fuller, *Americans and the unconscious*, 11.
2 From *Il Galateo* by Della Casa (1609), an early manual on etiquette, quoted in Elias, *The history of manners*.
3 Nadel, *Social control and self-regulation*
4 Edelman, *The remembered present: A biological theory of consciousness*

From the basement up   209

5 Elias, *The history of manners*; Kasson, *Rudeness & civility: manners in nineteenth-century urban America.*

6 Elias, *The history of manners.*

7 Muchembled, *A history of violence: from the end of the Middle Ages to the present.*

8 Roth, *American homicide.*

9 Whyte, *The unconscious before Freud: a history of the evolution of human awareness*; Berlin, *The roots of romanticism* (2nd ed.); Csikszentmihali, *Flow: the psychology of optimal experience.*

10 Hofstadter, *I am a strange loop.*

11 Csikszentmihali, *Flow: the psychology of optimal experience.*

12 Sartre, *Being and nothingness: A phenomenological essay on ontology.*

13 *Ibid.*, 173.

14 Young, *The harmony of illusions: inventing post-traumatic stress disorder.*

15 Hacking, *Rewriting the soul: multiple personality and the sciences of memory.*

16 Whyte, *The unconscious before Freud: a history of the evolution of human awareness.*

17 Friedman, *The discovery of the unconscious reflected in changing word usage in the United States 1880–1980* (unpublished doctoral dissertation).

18 Ellenberger, *The discovery of the unconscious: the history and evolution of dynamic psychiatry.*

19 Makari, *Soul machine: the invention of the modern mind.*

20 Orne et al., Social control in the psychological experiment: antisocial behavior and hypnosis.

21 For example, Frank, *Persuasion and healing: a comparative study of psychotherapy.*

22 Whitaker, *Anatomy of an epidemic: magic bullets, psychiatric drugs and the astonishing rise of mental illness*; Slater, *Blue dreams: the science and the story of the drugs that changed our minds.*

23 Laing, *The politics of the family and other essays*, 79.

24 Robinson, *An intellectual history of psychology* (3rd ed.).

25 Freud, *On dreams*, 5.

26 Hobson, *Dreaming: a very short introduction.*

27 Moss, *The secret history of dreaming.*

28 Lincoln, *The dream in primitive cultures 1935.*

29 Van de Castle, *Our dreaming mind.*

30 Stevens, *The two million-year-old self.*

31 Catron, *How to fall in love with anyone: a memoir in essays.*

32 Campbell, *The hero with a thousand faces* (2nd ed.), 103.

33 Szasz, *The myth of mental illness: foundations of a theory of personal conduct* (revised ed.).

34 Cartwright, *The twenty-four hour mind: the role of sleep and dreaming in our emotional lives.*

35 Cramer, *Protecting the self: defense mechanisms in action*, 7.

36 Laing, *The politics of the family and other essays.*

37 Fuller, *Americans and the unconscious.*

38 Jaynes, *The origin of consciousness in the breakdown of the bicameral mind.*

39 Berger et al., *The homeless mind: modernization and consciousness.*

40 For example, Levy, *Love and sex with robots: the evolution of human – robot relationships*; Turkle, *Alone together: why we expect more from technology and less from each other.*

41 For example, Gergen, The challenge of absent presence; Turkle, *Reclaiming conversation: the power of talk in a digital age.*

11 And from the outside in

Influences of work, technology, and societal institutions

> Daisy, Daisy, who shall I be?
> And who will it be who will marry me?
> Rich man, poor man, beggarman, thief,
> Doctor, lawyer, merchant, chief?
>
> Traditional nursery rhyme

Societal roles and institutions

Basic role theory holds that society can be viewed at the macro level as a collection of institutions. Beneath this, at the micro level, are those who perform the role functions required by each institution: the politicians, technicians, and bureaucrats who comprise a government, the soldiers who comprise the military, the students and professors who comprise a university, the mothers, fathers, and children who comprise a family. In this view, the sense of self-identity is largely derived from the roles one occupies. If you think of society as a baseball game, then the pitcher's answer to the question of self-definition, "Who am I?" is "I'm a pitcher," and that perception brings with it the definitional force of all the traditions, lore, scripts, coveted meanings, and expectations associated with that profession. According to this elementary formulation, society is an aggregation of people who inhabit social roles and relate to each other within their conventions. Each role carries its own behavioral expectations, duties, and obligations. One learns these for each of the roles one assumes: the script for the role, the ways of behaving and thinking and the attributes of character that accompany the role (a cop should be honest, a priest should be self-sacrificing, an athlete should be aggressive, a therapist should be empathic). In the simplest conception of role theory, self-identity resides at the intersection of one's various role performances. For those who occupy more than one role (pitcher, church deacon, engineer, adjunct professor, father, officer in the National Guard), the sense of self may consist of a sort of amalgamation of the attributes of each role.

In this model, traditional social structure reaches from the past to mold personal identity and behavior in the present. The nursing school graduate steps into the world equipped with a new sense of identity to occupy an understood

DOI: 10.4324/9781003010234-14

And from the outside in   211

position in the social order. This is clear enough. However, this picture has become complex and cloudy as the evolving conditions of modern societies have increased the range, diversity, frequency of turnover, and degree of disconnection of role relationships. In consequence, role-related activity is now less binding and more frequently questioned. By the mid-twentieth century, Americans had come to experience themselves in their role-related activity in somewhat the same way actors experience the characters they portray – as a kind of performance-at-a-remove, with much less relevance for self-definition.

Gemeinschaft und Gesellschaft

Sociological discussion of the shifting relationship between the self-concept and role involvements can be traced to prominent social philosophers of the nineteenth century, among whom stood Ferdinand Tönnies, a foundational figure in sociology. Among Tönnies's most widely disseminated contributions was the analytical distinction between two types of social groups, which he referred to as Gemeinschaft and Gesellschaft.[1] This distinction is useful in the historical contrast of colonial – agrarian versus contemporary – urban – post-industrial American society. Sociologist Arlie Hochschild described the Gemeinschaft world of former times as one in which an American's life "begins and ends in one locale, in one occupation, in one household, within one world view, and [is lived] according to one set of rules."[2] Gemeinschaft is characteristic of communal life in families and small villages in which roles are concrete, consensually understood, and relatively simple in structure, which means that they tend not to produce competing demands.

In such circumstances people's sense of connection is accomplished within the context of these role functions by the close interpenetration of each other's self-concept (e.g., mother – child or master – apprentice, who define each other in their mutual and ongoing interaction in interdependent identities that tend to encompass much of the individual's sense of self). It is important to point out that these are also identities that are not in doubt or dispute. They are frequently influenced by the uncontested circumstances of birth (gender, race, social position) and reflect an ongoing and all-encompassing station of life: mother, baker, farmer, apprentice, daughter, and so on. In Gemeinschaft societies, interpersonal discourse doesn't bear the freight of negotiating answers to questions of self-definition. Externally defined, the self is a done deal. In Gemeinschaft, the answer to "Who am I?" is an obvious truth grounded in one's small set of relatively harmonious role involvements. In the distant past, in some cases, the relationship between self-identity and social role was so fundamental that, to this day, for many European-Americans, it may be memorialized in their family name.

Peter Laslett's vivid description of day-to-day life in Gemeinschaft preindustrial England attests to the degree to which members of a household dwelled and worked together in clear, all-encompassing role relationships that tended to be harmonious, mutually supportive, and life-long. The baker was a baker for his entire adult life, his trade performed in his own home, and the

212 *The shape of the modern self*

Table 11.1 Common English and German Role-Related Family Names

Abbott	Fischer	Richter
Archer	Fisher	Sawyer
Baker	Forester	Schmidt
Barber	Fowler	Schneider
Bauer	Gardner	Shepherd
Bishop	Glover	Shoemaker
Bowman	Goldsmith	Skinner
Carpenter	Hooper	Smith
Chandler	Joyner	Tanner
Chaplin	Keeler	Taylor
Clark	Mason	Thatcher
Cook	Miller	Wagner
Cooper	Miner	Wainwright
Crocker	Painter	Waterman
Draper	Parson	Weaver
Dresser	Plummer	Weber
Farmer	Potter	Yeager

great majority of his contacts were the members of his household: his wife, his children, and his apprentices. The purpose, value, and meaning of his work were tangible and self-evident. The members of the household ate together, worked together, and resided in the same building. The baker's marriage lasted until either he or his wife died, and, in the case that his wife died before him, a new occupant of that role might be quickly obtained. Outside of attendance at church, the women of the household might never leave it. "Few persons in the old world ever found themselves in groups larger than family groups, and there were not too many families of more than a dozen members."[3]

In contrast to this, Gesellschaft is characteristic of abstract modern organizations such as parent – teacher associations, corporations, tenants' associations, or political meetups. Connections between people in such organizations may not be ongoing and aren't likely to involve significant definition of self. In this type of association, role involvement is usually partial – the aspects of your self-narrative that you relate to others at a PTA meeting aren't the whole story, and your sense of personal identity isn't much subject to influence by other members of the organization. In Gesellschaft, the set of role involvements are complexly structured: that is, they tend to place people in frameworks of competing demands, not only for time but for investments much closer to the self, such as emotional energy and commitments to the particular beliefs and ethos of the role.[4] For example, the ethos of medical practice demands a primary commitment to the health of patients, but the nurse who is also a parent may have to choose between the primary obligations of both roles. The nurse-father, who is also a member of a community band, a scout leader, a member of his church board, and a team member of a bicycle racing club may have to struggle with conflicts arising from commitments to the roles he occupies in those groups as well.

And from the outside in   213

One of the characteristics of life in modern segmented societies is that these relationships tend to be widely dispersed across well-separated social networks, and even geographically distinct locations. When they come into conflict with each other, as they frequently do, one is forced to reflect on which role's commitments to honor. This type of conflict, which is a hallmark of modern societies, forces the question "Who am I?": "Am I a physician or am I a father?", "Am I a musician or am I a scout leader?", "Am I a mother or am I a business executive?" These conflicts are a defining characteristic of the era, resulting not only in a lower investment of self in each role, but also in many situations where one's subjectivity is located somewhere distant from where one is physically located (as exemplified by checking email while at the beach, texting family while on the job, listening to a work-related podcast while working out at the gym, interacting on Facebook during a course lecture, managing work duties from a cell phone while driving with the family, etc.).[5] Beyond this, as the configuration of significant values and beliefs will vary across different social contexts, a person who interacts within multiple segmented relationships must necessarily adopt a certain relativism and multi-perspectivism, an ability to rapidly switch in and out of perspectives. This will have the effect of reducing commitment to any single field of meaning, creating greater uncertainty and encouraging detachment, inward focus, and some degree of analytical distance from the surrounding world, and reducing the ability to ever feel fully committed to particular social relationships, even with primary partners.

One might expect that role functions related to family involvement would be protected from these issues; however, the modern family has become a considerably more abstract experience, with plenty of potential for the development of diverse role sets and their inherent conflicts. Today, the family of origin may be complexly structured owing to the divorce and remarriage of parents and siblings (recall that the U.S. is currently the world leader in the rate of termination and reconstitution of marital and non-marital intimate relationships). And the family created in one's own marriage (or cohabitation) may also have been reconstituted as a result of earlier divorce and, in some cases, might include children from multiple partners.

Then there are relations with the extended families of current and former partners. What rules of obligation, generational deference, and etiquette apply in interaction with your half-sister's second grandmother's significant other? Perhaps not that important, but the point is that, until recent times, such questions rarely came up. Often, the range of family involvements include members spread throughout the country. So holiday gatherings may present stressful logistical and relationship problems as one negotiates the complicated tangle of familial memberships and commitments and their competing moral and emotional demands.

In addition, in our time, it's not uncommon to hold more than one job at the same time (according to the U.S. Bureau of Labor Statistics, this is currently true of one in ten Americans),[6] to change lines of work as jobs come and go, and to maintain social ties with people in well-separated service or recreational

214 *The shape of the modern self*

groups (e.g., musical groups or sports organizations). Households comprised of spouses born in separate countries are now more frequent in the U.S.,[7] as are households with multidenominational religious affiliations (e.g., Jewish wife and Catholic husband).[8] Currently, 42 percent of American marriages are interfaith, and this may bring spiritual commitments into conflict as well, if not at the beginning of the relationship, then possibly later on.

In this fluid and complex social web, the gravitational forces that pull self-identity in one direction or another emanate from a wider range of situations and people than in any previous era, and so the sense of self is less likely to be related to any particular role, and sometimes is not cleanly embedded in a nuclear family structure that is all that stable. This forces people to form a sense of personal identity, if not independent of traditional institutional affiliations, then more loosely connected to them. In these circumstances, authorship of the biographical self-narrative is more likely to be an ongoing project situated within those few intimate relationships in which there *is* significant longevity and depth. It is in the situation of a modern Gesellschaft society that intimacy plays a greater role in the construction of the sense of self. Enduring close relationships become the principal location for the construction and validation of the broad arc of the life narrative. We take our role conflicts to our relationship partners for their analysis and input ("What do you think I should do: go to the meeting or go to the rehearsal? If I go to the rehearsal, what should I say if someone from work sees me there?"), for their reassurance ("Don't worry about it, you can say the internet was down and you never got the email"), and for their help in repairing the coherence of our self-narrative in the face of the frequent necessity of choosing to honor one set of competing commitments over another ("You did the right thing. The department meetings are mostly ritual, but the rehearsal couldn't go on without you").

Work

Considering America's history, it is likely that the vision of the self as a function of a small set of harmonious and more or less clearly understood social roles was more apt in earlier periods. Not only have Americans' involvements thinned out over a broader range of roles, but, as institutions have become more rationally structured, abstract, bureaucratic, and centered outside of the local community, jobs have diminished in their power to impart self-definitional meaning. Since the late nineteenth century, behavior in complex bureaucratic organizations is ever more a matter of following formalized institutional procedures and scripts. As this has come about, it has become common to feel some measure of alienation at work, which is to say that one may increasingly experience a disconnect between roles enacted on the job and core values and beliefs.

As well, this is now the "gig economy," where in some cases jobs have become more like hookups than marriages: temporary associations of convenience rather than long-term, committed, self-defining relationships. Today, in

And from the outside in 215

many industries, a growing proportion of the workforce consists of employees hired, let go, and rehired for indeterminate periods of time, or hired as freelancers, independent contractors, or contingency workers. There's been as much as a 30 percent increase in the proportion of these jobs in the American workforce since 2001.[9]

A vivid example of this is supplied by employment trends in universities, where, during the last 20 years, a shift has occurred such that a majority of faculty are now hired course-to-course, year-to-year, or on other limited contracts. Once the majority, faculty in full-time positions that carry tenure have become a minority.[10] This is likely to become even more pronounced as economic tensions are causing universities to scramble to reduce costs further. The university is being pushed by the forces of modernity in the direction of what Bauman called a "zombie institution"[11] and Giddens called a "shell institution."[12] By either name, these theorists refer to an organizational structure hanging on from the past whose core mission and values are eroding in the rapid currents of change in the modern world, including globalization and international competition, fast economic and technological change, and, particularly, the management of risk, which requires institutions to divert significant resources to activities such as self-surveillance, legal review, and public relations. People whose job activities constitute the core functions of the organization (e.g., teachers, doctors, police officers, line workers, scientists, etc.) are increasingly reined in and outnumbered by "the suits." Not surprisingly, the Gallup organization, which regularly surveys employee engagement, has, since 2000, consistently found that 70 percent of the American workforce feel alienated from their jobs.[13] And alienated externally as well: the flux in employment of the gig economy contributes to increases in generalized distrust of others.[14]

Deinstitutionalization

In many sectors, modernity has also resulted in a reduction in the moral authority of institutional life and, as a result, a weakening of claims that institutional roles can make on character and self-definition. The legitimacy of the military suffered from public disillusionment in the face of the contradictions and unclear purpose of the Vietnam and Iraq wars. As an institution, professional sports – even Olympic sports – has lost legitimacy in scandals involving performance-enhancing drugs, thrown games, bribery, sexual exploitation, and rigged judging. The Catholic Church has suffered diminished authority in its morally conflicted positions on gender equality and family issues and in its child-sex scandals and their institutional cover-up. Stories of institutional corruption in police departments make the news almost weekly. The legitimacy of the university has been diminished by its rampant inflation of grades, top-heavy layers of administration, corporate CEO-style salaries for college presidents, and subjugation of its core education mission in the pursuit of the profits of intercollegiate sports.

216 *The shape of the modern self*

The professional legitimacy of the American Psychological Association (APA) was degraded in the scandal over the its leadership's overt cooperation with the CIA's programs of torture. The American Psychiatric Association stands accused by professional insiders and outsiders alike of having been brought "to an unprecedented crisis of credibility"[15] in the widening public perception that the profession is riddled with conflicts of interest stemming from psychiatrists' financial involvement with the pharmaceutical companies that manufacture the psychiatric drugs psychiatrists ever more commonly prescribe.[16] In recent years, the predictable partisanship of the Supreme Court has left its credibility teetering, as did the FBI's partisan intervention in the 2016 presidential election. Other institutions suffered deflated moral legitimacy long before, including Congress and the political profession generally, law and law enforcement, finance, and banking. Possibly the last link to the days of naïve faith in the honor of the profession of broadcast journalism died with Walter Cronkite. And so on. Sociologist Alan Wolfe believes that, since the mid-1950s, America has had increasing trouble sustaining faith in the inherent honesty and credibility of its institutions,[17] and, although trust in some institutions does fluctuate (e.g., people usually feel confident in a new president during the first year of office), social scientists' repeated measurement of trust in American institutions since the 1970s reveals overall declines.[18]

Some scholars believe that America has entered a phase of "deinstitutionalization," which has brought in its wake an intensification of the experience of self as subjectively formed. This has happened as many people have lost the ability to define themselves satisfactorily in their external, role-related involvements. In a society in which spin and lobbying and economic self-interest are understood to universally pervade institutional behavior, there has come a disenchantment such that, "the identity-defining power of institutions has been greatly weakened."[19] In fact, not only have institutional roles diminished in their power of definition, for some, self-definition is actually now obtained in reverse: in the struggle *against* the institutional roles in which the individual's life is involved (think *M.A.S.H.*, the Bourne films, institutional whistleblowers such as Edward Snowden, or that virtually every politician now runs for office as an outsider). Institutional roles "cease to be the 'home' of the self; instead, in some cases, they become oppressive realities that distort and estrange the self."[20]

Emotional labor

America's service-oriented economy often demands that individuals detach themselves from fully authentic involvement with others in the work-related sector of their lives.[21] Today's jobs are more likely to require as a core accomplishment of work the achievement of a particular state of emotion between employee and client, usually positive (as reflected in the job title "Customer Happiness Coordinator"), but not always, as in the case of collections agents, police, drill sergeants, or school disciplinarians, who may attempt to manufacture fear, and so, commonly, the success of a business now depends more than in the past on its employees' skills in building positive relationships with clients, whether one actually has positive regard for the client or not. In our era, Spirit and Southwest Airlines staff sing and tell jokes during flights, stores position greeters at store entrances, grocery store staff are required to cordially greet customers at the checkout area and ask how they're doing, dental hygienists deliver massages to adults and distribute wash-off tattoos and cartoon stickers to children, and university instructors are evaluated on their students' emotional reactions to their courses, rather than on how much they actually learned.

As of the early 1980s, it was estimated that one-third of all U.S. jobs involved such emotional labor,[22] a proportion that is surely higher today. In a service economy, labor is performed in social activity, and the product of economic activity is relationships. The manipulation of emotion in the service of economic activity separates workers from an integrated and authentic life, contributing to a propensity for the subjective experience of self to be partitioned, such that one fabricates a persona for each job, for each distinct family group, and for other segmented areas of ongoing social experience. These persona, in their distinction, in their partial involvement, in their propensity to involve disingenuous interpersonal contact, and, as we'll explore later, in their multiplicity, tend to encourage reflexive questioning about where exactly the "real" self lies. And so we tend to look for it in our few significant (and genuine) interpersonal relationships.

Sociologist Eva Illouz describes how this represents a substantial alteration – almost an inversion – of the social practices of earlier times. In the nineteenth century and before, emotion, or "true feeling," was often suppressed in the service of marriage, at least in the ideal case, and in this the spouses performed a variety of emotional labor *at home* similar to what many in modern societies must now do *at work*. Illouz quotes from a letter from a woman who had traveled with her husband to the Colorado frontier in the 1800s: "I am ashamed to be so homesick . . . . I try to be cheerful for [her husband's] sake, for fear he might think I wasn't happy with him."[23] The idea that a good wife would suppress self in the service of her husband's emotional experience was common into the 1960s.[24] Wives were advised never to appear to know more than their husbands and, if they got angry, to make sure to display their anger in terms that flattered their husband's sense of masculinity (e.g., by stamping their feet and appearing childlike or, as Goffman documented, by intentionally appearing to know less than their partner).[25] As Illouz argues, today, a wife would be counseled not to engage in this kind of emotional labor, but to express their true feelings, and the husband would be counseled to validate them and be responsive. To do otherwise would abrogate the ethos of authenticity that has become characteristic of intimate relationships since the end of the era of separate spheres in the 1960s.

In previous times, in the ideal case, the institution of marriage may have rested more easily on the shoulders of men and women because its demands

218 *The shape of the modern self*

of self, of emotion and behavior, were framed externally, in the shared beliefs of the larger culture. A marriage's success wasn't dependent on sustaining authentic positive feeling states, which is difficult in the chaotic circumstances of meaning within fluid modernity. Like much work performed today, the management of emotional expression was an institutional duty (and, it should be noted, because of its patriarchal structure, not one that was particularly kind to the fate of women; hence, the famous advice to early twentieth-century British women, whose welfare was assumed to depend on their spouse's satisfaction with them, to "lie back, close your eyes and think of England" when having to endure episodes of unwanted sexual intimacy).

Reflexivity: producing the self on one's own

With sources of external self-definition weakened, personal identity is under continuous reflexive revision through ongoing consideration of the choices and circumstances of our lives. This is not an easy task. Nor is it something done once and finally, such that one can then move on. Even for those fortunate enough to escape the common challenges to self-identity posed by events such as divorce, job loss, and health difficulties, the fluid character of modernity renders self-identity a preoccupation that must be more or less continuously worked on, if only for the reason that it is never long before the various fields of meaning in which the self has been established change or realign.

In the nineteenth century and earlier, Americans navigated the world with a more encompassing and stable sense of themselves derived from occupational roles, community, and church. However, by the time of America's shift from a production-oriented economy to a consumer-oriented economy, which occurred in the mid-twentieth century, the influence of these external sources of identity was crumbling, leaving many with the problem of working out self on their own and, in the difficulty of that, vulnerable to stress and anxiety. Sociologists observed that Americans were increasingly retreating to the shallow sense of identity that inheres in social conformity.[26] According to Taylor, "talk about 'identity' in the modern sense would have been incomprehensible to our forebears of a couple centuries ago."[27]

Modernity diminishes connection to traditional knowledge and consensual social values and diminishes involvement in self-defining roles, institutions, and community associations. While the upside to this is unprecedented freedom to define self as desired, this task is confronted individually, and, in the churn of meaning in the mass culture and the fast-changing circumstances of work, personally crafted self-identity is more often disrupted. This may impact emotionally and spill into our social relationships, which is where we most often go to look for help with this problem. In some traditional societies, marriage may not involve free choice and may have relatively little bearing on personal identity, which to a great extent is defined in the circumstances of birth. But, in modernity's equality and freedom, the selection of a partner often involves searching for the one who will contribute significantly to the quest

And from the outside in 219

for security of self. Regardless of where one looks for support, today common role conflicts force questions of self-definition ("Am I committed to my job or committed to my family?", "Am I your teacher or am I your friend?", "Can I be feminine and a business leader at the same time?", "Am I a Catholic or am I a health professional?", "Am I your manager or am I your spouse?"). The solutions to these questions have become more complicated.

Modernity is inherently generative of novel situations (in Bauman's metaphor, formerly solid aspects of society that once provided stability and structure have become "liquid") and, because of this, the stances one takes on the job or in other contexts are no longer as easily incorporated in the kind of tradition- and identity-bearing packages that are usually associated with the concept of role. Reflexivity is forced upon everyone owing to the decreased basis of tradition and prior experience from which people can draw.[28] One must see one's way through questions regarding job behavior, appropriate gender relations, expectations for intimacy, shared parenting, and many other areas that are unique to this era. And the answers to these questions tend to be unstable and of limited generalizability. In the past, one might have consulted elders for guidance, but not so often today. The modern world has become so unprecedented that every segment of society, elders included, now gropes to find its way in the same dark woods. However, though many may be feeling their way along, the question most central to this era is not "where am I?" but rather "who am I?" To the extent that that question is not satisfactorily answered, to the extent that one cannot establish a stable structure of being, one becomes anxious, doubtful, and impulsive, the mind vulnerable to the currents of sham, fantasy, and contradictory belief inherent in unfiltered culture.

Technology

Most commonly, "technology" refers to inventions and innovation in materials, tools, and machinery that, although developed to solve practical problems, may lead to unexpected transformations in everyday life. But technology can also refer to social practices. Sociologist Jacques Ellul argued that one of the principal characteristics of mid-twentieth-century modernity was the technologizing of a great proportion of human activity.[29] Here, "technologizing" refers to the standardization of methods for accomplishing tasks – "techniques" – which is immediately visible in medicine, education, accounting, police work, and myriad other areas of organizational life (today's biz-speak for this is "best practices"). This is driven by the scientization of many areas of life, even marital and family relations, where spouses may be counseled by mental health professionals on the best techniques for listening, disclosing, having conflicts, and managing their children. As standardization, regulation, and routinization remove individual judgment and creativity from human activity, this tends to subtly chip away at the connection between what one does (working, managing, parenting, relating) and the benefits to the sense of being that inhere in work that permits individual judgment and expression.

220   *The shape of the modern self*

On the other hand, some technological impacts are anything but subtle, and this is particularly visible in the case of technologies of communication. Communication, after all, is the essence of consciousness, and whatever impacts communication practices will likely have consequences for the mind. Today, America is winding down its honeymoon with digital communication technologies and beginning to ask about their unintended impacts in many areas, including education, work, civic life, and politics, but especially in their degradation of the quality of social relationships through interference with empathy and rich dialogical connection.[30] Because communication is the vehicle through which mind forms and interconnects with others to create and stabilize meaning, innovations in methods of communication rarely leave adopters' psychology unaltered. The standard account of this extends backwards thousands of years to the invention of the alphabet, the standardization of written language, and the spread of literacy.

Narrative consciousness

In one of history's greatest moments of prophecy, 2,400 years before the invention of the Post-it, Plato warned that the invention of writing would eventually undermine the skill of memory. The spread of literacy did just that, and more.[31] Writing also turned social hierarchy on its head, disempowering older people whose long experience of the past had, in the days before books and libraries, been the best source of wisdom and practical knowledge in the family and the village. Writing is also isolating. We withdraw to write, and when people read in the same room, they become non-interactive and socially remote (as when spouses retreat into the newspaper during breakfast). Further, writing imposes a particular style of organization on narrative: written stories proceed in temporal sequence, arguments are expected to progress linearly, from premises to supporting points and analysis to conclusions. As literacy spread, it influenced how we think about ourselves and our personal relationships, tending to force accounts into the narrative forms that have come down to us as a result of our literacy.

We think of intimate relationships in terms of a linear developmental history combining the life stories of two separate people: the sources of initial attraction, the events of the early years, how they handled having and raising children, the issues of the retirement years. When something goes wrong, we look to the past for its sources and the logic of how that might have chained into the present to cause trouble. This way of thinking predominates in literate cultures, so much so that this account, which, intentionally or not, is frequently pursued in order to establish moral responsibility, often becomes embroiled in conflict.

But this isn't the only way. In oral cultures narratives tend to be formed of easily remembered phrases and clichés, are more likely to be rhythmic, less likely to progress linearly, and more likely to reference dramatic and vivid imagery than analytic detail or abstraction (in other words, a little more like dreams, raps, poems, or music videos). In an oral culture, when intimates are

And from the outside in 221

having difficulty with each other, the solution is less likely to involve history-taking and the analysis of responsibility, perhaps instead being sought in the performance of a transformational ritual in front of the village or clan. The Pirahãs, members of an oral culture who inhabit an area of the Amazonian jungle, handle instances of sexual infidelity through a ritual of atonement in which the man who strayed places his head in the lap of his partner and she whacks it with a stick for several hours. After this the couple's relationship returns to normal.[32]

New media

Now, writing competes with media that bias perception in their own new ways. Visual media, such as film, television, video, and still photography, favor brevity, emotional impact, and montage and sometimes distort linear time sequencing. The web's mixed media and hyper-media favor digression, mash-up, and a dream-like erosion of boundaries between otherwise isolated content. In an interesting example of the way that the narrative styles of new communication media can shape mental experience, psychological flashbacks were rarely reported in post-war experiences of soldiers before the mid-twentieth century, by which time they'd become common.[33] Following the Vietnam War, Americans understand that a PTSD-stricken vet hearing a car backfire may suddenly travel backward in time to re-experience a traumatic event. But this didn't happen before the mid-twentieth century, by which point flashback had become a narrative trope commonly employed in television and film. This is probably not the whole story, because, as we've seen, by the mid-twentieth century, the meaningful foundations of being were eroding in modernity's impacts, leaving people much more prone to anxiety and more easily influenced by consciousness-altering technologies.

Similarly, the growth of visual narrative cultivates particular types of self-awareness (Do I look the part?), as well as the theatrical framing of one's story of self (Am I convincing in the role? Is my life following the trajectory of stories that movies and TV suggest we should anticipate? Can I find an audience and be famous? Do I look like a leading man?). From YouTube, Vimeo, Snapchat, Instagram, and Tinder to the GoPro camera, the selfie stick (now also known as "the wand of narcissism" or the "narcissistick"), and the sophisticated photo and video production capabilities available on everybody's smartphones, America has become a culture that uses the lens as a tool of the self, particularly for telling stories to each other about personal identity. This has encouraged the self-absorption in personal image that has become a hallmark of the era (the *Oxford English Dictionary* proclaimed that "selfie" was the word of the year for 2013 and Twitter Inc. proclaimed 2014 to be "the year of the selfie").[34] Newly introduced technologies have often influenced the ways people connect, their conception of themselves, the range of possibilities in their lives, and the distribution of social power and status. The devices don't in themselves determine social practices, but they stimulate change.

222 *The shape of the modern self*

The story of the intersection of technological and interpersonal change tends to be clear in the historical record because it's often easy to link inventions to particular dates, and so it's tempting to use technology's timeline to index change in interpersonal life (e.g., family life before and after electric light, before and after television). One of the main insights revealed by a such review is that the rate of introduction of interpersonally relevant inventions has accelerated dramatically since the Industrial Revolution. In fact, today, in a sort of digital gold rush, software developers the world over are frantically rolling out new tools explicitly designed to alter interpersonal practices, each hoping their social platform will be the next big thing.

Unintended consequences

However, the social impacts of technologies are rarely direct, and rarely what their designers intended. No one imagined that the cell phone would lead to increased social isolation (Gergen's "absent presence,"[35] Conley's "elsewhere" society,[36] Turkle's "alone together")[37] or to pervasive surveillance; the automobile's back seat wasn't designed to undermine parental authority and fuel the sexual revolution;[38] and there's nothing in the circuits of a TV set that was put there to shake up political discourse[39] or stimulate fearfulness among viewers.[40] So there's no telling just what's ahead when a technological innovation begins to diffuse and be adopted. In many cases, technologies impact in unforeseen ways when the innovation awakens or accelerates economic or psychological potentials already latent in the culture.

The telephone was originally intended to be an assistive device for the deaf, and the phonograph was supposed to be a machine for recording telephone calls. But the telephone brought extensive secondary impacts, including the acceleration of population mobility, the dispersal of families, and the erosion of community. With the telephone's promise to provide a means to sustain connection with children who move far from home, more children moved far from home. The phonograph became one of the key inventions contributing to the evolution of consumer-driven youth culture, which, in its emphasis on shifting fashion, contributes significantly to the disembedding of the self from meaningful tradition. The polygraph and, more recently, the fMRI machine haven't had the same breadth of impact, but each has played an important role in promoting particular conceptions of self and other.

Technological innovation sometimes promotes change just by supplying new metaphors for imagining the self. Self-as-computer is the uber-metaphor of our age, promoted actively in the fields of cognitive neuroscience and artificial intelligence (as in Marvin Minsky's discussion of the self as a collection of software subroutines).[41] This has so run away with popular culture that some, like AI maven David Levy, envision the future as one in which human consciousness will be duplicated by computers, and human intimacy replaced by human – robot relationships.[42] Likely this persistently recurrent theme in film and literature expresses the greater complexity of interpersonal relationships in our time and the extent to which many may now yearn for more reliable and less complicated forms of intimacy. The robot motif attests to a widespread desire to reclaim something important that's fading in modern interpersonal experience.

Homo medicatus

Certainly what should top any list of interpersonally transformative technologies in America's history is the invention and dissemination of drugs affecting interpersonal experience. In addition to the introduction of the birth control pill, no list of interpersonally important technologies is complete that doesn't include several classes of psychiatric drugs, increasingly prescribed since the 1950s, whose purpose is to standardize psychological life and emotional experience. Psychiatry has "lost interest in the patient's inner life" and is now "in the grip of a pharmacological scientism," losing interest in the exploration of meaning and in consequence becoming "nearly mindless."[43] The first wave of the new psychiatric drugs included the blockbusters Miltown and Equanil, introduced shortly after World War II as mild tranquilizers, and marketed for a shifting range of lifestyle concerns, primarily of middle- and upper-class Americans who were more likely than others to be able to afford them.[44] The drugs offered the prospect of a chemically perfected life, dulling the anguish of women whose economic, marital, and political prospects were relegated to second-class status (these drugs were those "mother's little helpers," made famous, ironically, by the Rolling Stones, who surely rank among the world's most prominent ingesters of psychoactive compounds) and lowering the anxiety levels of urban-professional men, made jittery by the stressful requirements of modern economic life. These were the men who, a decade or two earlier, might have been diagnosed with neurasthenia (recall "NewYorkitis").

At first, marketed to the public in the same manner as automobiles and laundry soap, in ad campaigns that targeted people's sense of self, these drugs demonstrated that fortunes could be made in the pharmacological treatment of lifestyle issues. However, Miltown, Equanil, and their derivatives ran into trouble when, in time, it became apparent that they had undesirable side effects, including dependence. But the race was on. And, since the days of Miltown, drug companies have continually jostled for market share, repurposing old drugs and introducing new compounds that promise better performance or address newly created psychological concerns (e.g., ADHD) and evolving new methods of marketing them. Common psychiatric medications on the market today include lithium for bipolar disorder, the benzodiazepine drugs for anxiety (such as Xanax, Ativan, Valium, Librium), SSRI-class antidepressants (e.g., Prozac, Zoloft, Paxil), the antipsychotics (e.g., Thorazine, Risperdal), and stimulants for ADHD (e.g., Adderall, Ritalin). These drugs impact emotion, energy, mental focus, and sexual interest, and, through them, social experience and self-identity.

224   *The shape of the modern self*

The breadth of dissemination of psychiatric drugs challenges the imagination. As of 2011, more than one in ten teenage and adult Americans were taking antidepressant medications, up 400 percent from the 1980s,[45] and it's estimated that the rate of use today is nearly one in four among middle-aged women. U.S. doctors wrote 50 million prescriptions just for the anti-anxiety drug Xanax in 2010, or about one new prescription every second (and Xanax is just one of several competing anti-anxiety drugs).[46] Drugs for ADHD are now prescribed to 3.5 million American children, including 10,000 toddlers younger than 3.[47]

The National Institute of Mental Health estimates that, as of 2012, one in five Americans exhibits a mental disorder diagnosable according to the criteria of the American Psychiatric Association,[48] and, in many cases, treatment starts with the prescription pad. During the first 80 years of the twentieth century, before the pharmaceutical industry began promoting drugs to treat it, depression was considered a rare disease. But, since the 1980s, and the introduction of these drugs, the diagnosis of depression has jumped a thousandfold, with the disorder now judged second only to heart disease as a disability.[49] Americans spent $11 billion on antidepressant medications in 2010.[50]

The impacts of psychiatric drugs on interpersonal life are direct and intentional, but researchers are only beginning to probe the question of what this massive infusion of mood-altering chemicals into the American bloodstream has wrought, whether the drugs have performed as intended; what unforeseen secondary impacts are associated with their use; what it will ultimately mean for the future of American society to translate so many conditions of living, formerly regarded as normal, into pathologies; and whether the expansive claims of the NIMH and the APA about the breadth of mental illness in America make sense[51] or even represent a corruption of public trust.[52] The broad use of these drugs is changing the boundaries between normal and pathological in interpersonal experience, and our understanding of human agency and moral accountability (e.g., is your channel-surfing, poor-listening spouse simply self-absorbed, inconsiderate, or psychologically abusive? Or a pitiable victim of ADHD and, therefore, unable to do anything about it except take a pill?).

Communication theorist Neil Postman believed that, by the late nineteenth century, America had become a "technopoly," which he defined as a society dominated by science in which the pursuit of technology, standardization, and efficiency had become an ultimate cultural value.[53] Focusing on psychiatry's relentless medicalization of everyday experience, psychiatric critic Thomas Szasz believed that, as of the twenty-first century, America had become a "pharmocracy," which he defined as a society dominated by drug companies whose powerful economic influence significantly shapes government policy, the mass culture, and our conception of individual and interpersonal normal.[54] Part of our folk wisdom is that Americans have a knack for technological innovation and its commercialization. America has rarely turned away from the economic exploitation of a new process, gadget, or pill, regardless of what unforeseen changes that produces in the fabric of our lives.

And from the outside in   225

Insofar as technology's influences have tended to accelerate the large trends of modernity that have rendered the sense of self more precarious and social connections more vulnerable to disruption, and, given a growing concern that the overuse of psychiatric drugs may be doing significant harm,[55] one can imagine a benefit in trying to get some control over these processes. However, to do so means standing squarely in the path of the juggernaut.

A vivid contrast to mainstream America's runaway use of technology is apparent in the rich community and cultural stability of the Old Order Amish, who recognized long ago that new technologies carry social and spiritual consequences and have chosen to adopt very few of them, and then only after careful consideration of what secondary impacts those technologies bring along and whether they may be disruptive of the fields of meaning the Amish strive to preserve. As an example of particular relevance, there are no selfies among the Amish. In the late nineteenth century, the Amish decided to prohibit the use of cameras because they believe photographs tend to make the self an object of analytical focus, challenging the virtue of humility.[56] This may supply some context for understanding research that found that Amish women in Lancaster County, Pennsylvania, were far less likely to be concerned about appearance and weight than non-Amish women from the same area.[57]

Even among those deeply concerned about the runaway impacts of technology, few are likely to contemplate converting to the Amish religion. But this interesting subcultural group, voluntarily frozen in the technological past, with its strong, trusting communities, stable families, robust health, low rates of anxiety and depression, and security of self, provides insight into the relationship of technology (and other aspects of modernity) to the quality of interpersonal life and demonstrates that resistance to technology is, at least in principle, in reach of those who wish to live deliberately.

Notes

1 Tönnies, *Community and society.*
2 Hochschild, *The managed heart: commercialization of human feeling*, 21.
3 Laslett, *The world we have lost: England before the industrial age* (3rd ed.), 7.
4 Coser, *In defense of modernity: role complexity and individual autonomy.*
5 Conley, *Elsewhere, U.S.A.*
6 United States Bureau of Labor Statistics, Employment situation news release.
7 Larsen and Walters, Married-couple households by nativity status: 2011.
8 Riley, *'Til faith do us part: How interfaith marriage is transforming America.*
9 Scheiber, Rising economic insecurity tied to decades-long trend in employment practices.
10 Ginsberg, *The fall of the faculty: the rise of the all-administrative university and why it matters.*
11 Bauman, *Liquid times: living in an age of uncertainty.*
12 Giddens, *Runaway world.*
13 Gallup, State of the American workplace.
14 Lawrence, *(Dis)placing trust: the long-term effects of job displacement on generalised trust over the adult lifecourse.*
15 Fava, Financial conflicts of interest in psychiatry, 19.

226   *The shape of the modern self*

16 Davies, *Cracked: the unhappy truth about psychiatry*; Healy, *Pharmageddon*; Lane, *Shyness: how normal behavior became a sickness*; Schwarz, *ADHD nation: children, doctors, big pharma, and the making of an American epidemic*; Whitaker, *Anatomy of an epidemic: magic bullets, psychiatric drugs and the astonishing rise of mental illness*; Whitaker and Cosgrove, *Psychiatry under the influence*.
17 Wolfe, *Moral freedom: the search for virtue in a world of choice*.
18 Smith, Inappropriate prescribing.
19 Berger et al., *The homeless mind: Modernization and consciousness*, 93.
20 *Ibid.*, 93.
21 Hochschild, *The managed heart: commercialization of human feeling*.
22 *Ibid.*
23 Illouz, *Why love hurts: a sociological explanation*, 38.
24 Coontz, *A strange stirring: The Feminine Mystique and American women at the dawn of the 1960s*.
25 Goffman, *The presentation of self in everyday life*.
26 Riesman et al., *The lonely crowd*.
27 Taylor, *Sources of the self: the making of modern identity*, 28.
28 Archer, *The reflexive imperative in late modernity*.
29 Ellul, *The technological society*.
30 Turkle, *Reclaiming conversation: the power of talk in a digital age*.
31 Ong, *Orality and literacy: the technologizing of the word*.
32 Everett, *Don't sleep, there are snakes: life and language in the Amazonian jungle*.
33 Jones et al., Flashbacks and post-traumatic stress disorder: the genesis of a 20th-century diagnosis.
34 Ng, Twitter declares 2014 the year of the selfie.
35 Gergen, *The challenge of absent presence*.
36 Conley, *Elsewhere, U.S.A.*
37 Turkle, *Alone together: why we expect more from technology and less from each other*.
38 Bailey, *From front porch to back seat: courtship in twentieth-century America*.
39 Meyrowitz, *No sense of place: The impact of electronic media on social behavior*.
40 Shanahan and Morgan, *Television and its viewers: cultivation theory and research*.
41 Minsky, *The society of mind*.
42 Levy, *Love and sex with robots: the evolution of human – robot relationships*.
43 Modell, *Imagination and the meaningful brain*, 4–5.
44 Herzberg, *Happy pills in America: from Miltown to Prozac*.
45 Pratt et al., Antidepressant use in persons aged 12 and over: United States, 2005–2008.
46 Herper, America's most popular mind medicines.
47 Schwarz, The selling of attention deficit disorder; Schwarz, Thousands of toddlers are medicated for A.D.H.D., report finds, raising worries.
48 National Institute of Mental Health, Any mental illness (AMI) among adults.
49 Healy, *Let them eat Prozac: the unhealthy relationship between the pharmaceutical industry and depression*.
50 Smith, Inappropriate prescribing.
51 For example, Davies, *Cracked: the unhappy truth about psychiatry*; Frances, *Saving normal: an insider's revolt against out-of-control psychiatric diagnosis, DSM-5, Big Pharma, and the medicalization of ordinary life*; Whitaker, *Anatomy of an epidemic: magic bullets, psychiatric drugs and the astonishing rise of mental illness*.
52 Whitaker and Cosgrove, *Psychiatry under the influence*.
53 Postman, *Technopoly: the surrender of culture to technology*.
54 Szasz, *The medicalization of everyday life: selected essays*.

And from the outside in   227

55 Davies, *Cracked: the unhappy truth about psychiatry*; Lane, *Shyness: how normal behavior became a sickness*; Whitaker, *Anatomy of an epidemic: magic bullets, psychiatric drugs and the astonishing rise of mental illness*.
56 Kraybill et al., *The Amish*.
57 Miller et al., Health status, health conditions, and health behaviors among Amish women: results from the Central Pennsylvania Women's Health Study (CePAWHS).

12 We are each other

The dawn of the interpersonal self

Speaker and hearer, words
making a passage between them,
begin a community.

Two minds

in succession, grandfather
and grandson, they sit and talk
on the enclosed porch,

looking out at the town, which
recalls itself in their talk
and is carried forward.

Their conversation has
no pattern of its own,
but alludes casually

to a shaped knowledge
in the minds of the two men
who love each other.
Wendell Berry, from "The handing down" in "New Collected Poems"[1]

Theories of the interpersonal self

Social institutions, roles, and technological innovations are as much the children of language and discourse as are mind and culture. So, although it may be convenient for analytical purposes, carving up influences on behavior into internal and external factors is something like trying to understand *The Starry Night* in terms of the culture of post-impressionist art in which the work was situated and the brain abnormalities that were responsible for van Gogh's seizures, without reference to his biography, social relationships, and sense of himself. The minds of artists may be unusually permeable to the churn of unfiltered modern culture, but it was van Gogh who produced that painting, not just his body or the culture in which his life was embedded. The self-structure is the active, agentic uber-process that mediates between the body, the rest of mind,

DOI: 10.4324/9781003010234-15

We are each other 229

and the super-diversity of culture, but there's an indivisible wholeness to this. Mind, culture, and self are made of the same stuff. Self-identity is a structure of mind, and culture is the collective product of many minds networked in discourse. The self and culture have co-evolved with the changing circumstances of modernity. By our era, culture has become so full of diverse, ephemeral, false, and contradictory notions that to encounter it without the benefit of a strong and secure structure of self is to risk significant psycho-emotional distress. Culture and self are linked byproducts of language and human discourse. Both are ever present in conversation.

A family's discussion about where the daughter should attend college becomes heated precisely because each family member's sense of self-identity may be at stake on many levels ("I want my daughter to attend MIT like I did," "I don't want to go to college: I want to continue to pursue success with my acting career," "If we send her to the state university, we'll be better able to afford her education and I'll be able to take a sabbatical from work and finish writing my book"). That there's argument among family members and not simply an order from the head of the household, and that the argument is over selecting a university for a young woman, rather than locating a husband for her or sending her into service or to work in the mills, both reflect and reaffirm the cultural circumstances of this historical period. The culture in which people's lives are embedded is perpetuated in a continuous process of reaffirmation in ordinary conversation. This is a two-way process: our lives, directed in terms of our constructed sense of self-identity, reflect culture, and culture is reflected in our talk.[2] Over time, external institutions that once had a strong influence on personal identity have lost authority, and culture has become more complex, multivocal, and self-contradictory. In the face of these changes, personal identity has become difficult to sustain without strong support. And, in the decline of meaningful community, this support is now more difficult to find – it has to be actively and skillfully brokered on the interpersonal level. We are caught in the philosophically awkward situation of needing each other in order to sustain our sense of ourselves as autonomous.

As we've seen, the mass culture is all over this loop, employing the technologies of social science research to analyze our discourse, sniff out our desires and insecurities, amplify them, and then market products as solutions. There are countless examples, but the process is particularly vivid in a recent Google advertising campaign for its Android operating system, featuring the slogan: "Android: Be Together. Not the Same." Both the device and advertising message are cultural artifacts whose sensibility is situated within common concerns of interpersonal life in twenty-first-century America. The text of the ad, no doubt formulated in analysis of talk from ad agency focus groups, invites reflection on the widespread extent of social isolation and insecurity of self and proposes that using an Android cell phone can help with these issues. Note how weirdly the ad distorts the relationship between these concerns. As we've seen, the sense of community derives from immersing self in an ongoing social collective, which requires limitation and some degree of conformity. Nobody solves the problem of social isolation by making a point of being not

230 *The shape of the modern self*

the same. On top of this sits the irony that the Google corporation is the non plus ultra of an industry whose products, for all their wonders, have also accelerated community breakdown, superficial social connection, and insecurity of being. Unquestionably, these problems preceded the digital age, but, as a genre of mass culture, the most visible impacts of digital communication technologies have been their intensification of problems of community and self, not their resolution. When Google proposes that its products actually represent solutions to isolation and insecurity of identity, it's a case of the foxes selling chickens tickets to the banquet.

Culture is produced, reproduced, and reconfirmed in discourse and, as in the Google example, it reflects the collective experience of its constituents. In anticipation of later discussion, I'd like to point out here that the pop-science idea that culture is comprised of viral packets of meaning called "memes" that invade the mind in order to reproduce themselves misunderstands the mutually influential nature of symbols. Culture is built of symbols: it doesn't enter the mind unaffected, as if it was the bird flu or a set of signals. We will take a more detailed look at meme theory in Chapter 14.

Sometimes, we do think of language, which represents culture, as a kind of fixed code. Prepping for a trip to Paris, one looks up the French words for bread, hotel, and other concepts that might be needed to construct sentences that allow rudimentary discourse with the French. But language isn't just a way of representing preexisting meaning in order to engage in mechanical task-oriented encounters, such as checking in at a hotel or buying bread. As Edward Sapir asserted, a language isn't just a distinct code for identifying universal experience, "the worlds in which different societies live are distinct worlds, not merely the same worlds with different labels attached."[3] Because language is a system of symbols whose meanings are always colored by cultural circumstances as well as our own ideas and experience, whether we're conscious of using it in this way or not, language is a medium that conveys much more than the dictionary definitions of words. The words we use are a window into the deeply held presumptions, the "dark matter,"[4] of culture, and, too, they are a window into the foundational ideas that comprise our own subjectivity. Thus, coordinated with the fabric of cultural meaning that contextualizes everything we think, simultaneously in our talk, we cannot help but reveal ourselves. We continuously shed clues about the core organizing precepts that we live by. At the same time, provided we regard each other as equals, the structures of meaning that comprise our minds are reshaped in our encounter, moving toward a kind of blended consciousness, each mind comprised increasingly of meaning created together, coordinated with the presumptions of the culture but always our own. Culture and self are not fixed but endlessly reshaped in discourse. And, with the reduction in the influence of tradition, religion, and hierarchy, both have become more an interpersonal production than they were in the past.

The interpersonal perspective on the relationship between discourse, self, and culture belongs principally to post-mid-nineteenth century scholarship: that is, to our era and back roughly 100–150 years. There have been so many contributing currents that a thorough review is out of order here. However, a brief flyover is useful, because the progression of this body of thought serves as another indicator – like the emergence of the modern understanding of unconscious mental experience – of historical change in the relationship of inner being to social experience. Theories of the self are authored in light of the circumstances of the times and within the sensibilities and instrumentation of the historical period in which they were created. In other words, the way that the self was understood by a theorist from the past provides a kind of archeological data – a window into the period in which the theorist worked. So, it should come as no surprise that this is a predominantly Western (and, originally, predominantly American) body of theory. It was the transitions of the modernizing Western societies that created new difficulties for self-identity and psycho-emotional life. This complicated inner experience and brought the world of social relations to scientific scrutiny, and in few places as intensely as in the United States.

Principal credit for the view of the self as interpersonal – a product of discourse – belongs to four social philosophers of the late nineteenth and early twentieth centuries: philosopher and social psychologist George Herbert Mead, psychologist and philosopher Josiah Royce, Charles Cooley, who was one of the founding figures of the study of sociology in America, and William James, who influenced them all. Royce and James were friends and mutually influential (Royce described the mind as a stream of consciousness before James), and George Herbert Mead tutored James's children while Mead was a student in Boston.

Josiah Royce is now obscure among these figures. However, he was influential in his day and is appropriately credited for contributing key ideas about how self-identity is acquired. Royce's view was that the sense of self begins to coalesce as children interact with others and engage in imitative behavior.[5] If you wave to a 14-month-old baby, she's imitating when she waves back. You hide your head, then she does the same. The baby appears to delight in imitation; however, according to Royce, although imitation is a first step, she doesn't yet have a sense of self. That emerges later as a result of the contrasts the child perceives between her own behavior and the behavior of others.

The child also becomes aware of others' evaluative responses to her behavior and, through this, she develops an "ideal self," a vision of how she might be that would likely obtain the highest regard from others. Now the child's consciousness of self has taken a first step in becoming multiple – self versus ideal self – which represents an early movement toward the modern problem of needing to choose in any moment which of one's possible versions of self to enact. Royce's is a uniquely communal take on the concept of the ideal self, the self one strives to be or to be true to. One weaves a sense of personal morality in respect to this ideal. Assessments of right and wrong take shape in terms of this baseline vision of "best self," which is grounded in accumulated observations of others' reactions to one's own behavior. This is not an interpersonally negotiated process but a process of acquiring a vision of self shared by the external community.

William James's conception of the self was also not inherently interpersonal but, like Royce's, contained seminal ideas – in particular, the idea that the

232   *The shape of the modern self*

self-concept is influenced by our most important social relationships, and, as well, that a person may have multiple self-concepts. James believed that the self has several dimensions: (1) a "material self," constituted of possessions, property, and body; (2) a "social self," consisting of the recognition one receives from others; (3) a "spiritual self," comprised of one's inner or subjective being – feelings, will, psychic dispositions, moral sensibility, and conscience; and (4) the "pure ego," a more abstract idea by which James meant the principle of connection between all thought and sensation that imparts a sense of individual coherence.

It's the social self that is relevant to our discussion. James believed that a person has as many of them as there are "distinct groups of persons about whose opinion he cares," and, as we've seen, this is an important idea in light of the changing social conditions of the last 150 years. As the forces of modernity have acted upon interpersonal experience, they've tended to ever more finely segment it. The number of groups people typically need to sync with and the degree of distinctiveness between them have become pronounced. And so, following James, it is possible to imagine that the sense of self as fragmented into somewhat distinctive sub-identities might be increasingly evident in the experience of those in modern societies. There's no evidence that William James had changing historical conditions in mind in his conceptualization of the self. His focus was primarily psychological. And, indeed, when he wrote, many of the dimensions of change we've examined were only beginning to become evident and the subject of discussion among sociologically oriented theorists such as Ferdinand Tönnies and Emile Durkheim. However, as we'll see in the next chapter, James's idea of multiple selves was prescient in its anticipation of social and psychological phenomena of the mid-twentieth and twenty-first centuries.

The looking glass self

Cooley was a leading figure in early American sociology, now chiefly remembered for his formulation of the "looking glass self," which is the notion that the sense of self takes shape as we see how others react to us. We form our idea of who we are in accordance with the sense we get from interacting with others of how they regard us, what qualities and attributes they attach to us. The process is vividly exemplified by Erin White, writing about her relationship partner:

> Chris introduced me to myself. This is who you are, she seemed to say to me every time she touched me. At first I was startled; at first I demurred. Oh, no, I wanted to say. I think you are mistaken. But she wasn't.[6]

According to Cooley, one literally sees one's self in others, just as one might see one's face reflected in a mirror:

> As we see our face, figure, and dress in the glass, and are interested in them because they are ours, and pleased or otherwise with them according

We are each other   233

as they do or do not answer to what we should like them to be; so in imagination we see in another's mind some thought of our appearance, manners, aims, deeds, character, friends, and so on, and are variously affected by it.[7]

How do you know what your face looks like? Obviously, you see it every morning in the mirror. However, your perception is not direct; it is mediated by language – you see yourself as "ugly," "pretty," "old," "weathered," "beautiful," and so on. The meanings of these descriptive terms are established in social comparison and contextualized by the cultural circumstances of this historical period. What is beautiful today is not what was beautiful 200 years ago. At this time in Western societies, for a female, a conventionally attractive face – the kind likely to be seen in a cosmetics ad – is relatively thin, with smooth, unblemished skin, full lips, and symmetrically positioned eyes. The face in the mirror has either more or fewer of those qualities. The physical face has a physical reality, but we don't see it as such. We see a version of it filtered through the cultural meanings and values that frame the times. So, how do you know what your face looks like? A better answer than look in the mirror is that you know by looking into the minds of those around you, which reflect (and refract) the culture. That is, you interact with others and observe how they react to you and, from this, deduce how you might regard yourself in coordination with conventions of meaning. We know we are "pretty," "handsome," "young," or "old" not because we are in any objective sense, but in light of the cultural circumstances of the time, because people treat us as though we are. (Note, however, that this isn't always the one-way street that Cooley described: we also seek out those who are likely to see us in the ways we desire to be seen.)

Cooley's conception of the looking glass self helps us understand how social interaction may cause people to assume qualities that others project upon them. A team of workers talks among themselves about their perceptions of a new manager's personality characteristics and, by informal consensus, agree that the manager lacks leadership qualities, perhaps not so much because she does in any objective sense, but because this may be an effective form of censure among people who may dislike the newcomer for any variety of idiosyncratic reasons. While team members are unlikely to express this to the manager directly, she certainly notices how she's treated (for example, the team doesn't go to her for advice, doesn't ask for her approval of their work or keep her informed about progress, or speaks to her in meetings as though she's unlikely to understand). As a result, she grows insecure in her role and less able to lead and make decisions, becoming less effective and appearing less mentally adept. The team's perceptions become a self-fulfilling prophecy, their meanings for their manager herding the woman into a particular understanding of herself.

Symbolic interaction

Mead built on James's, Royce's, and Cooley's ideas in formulating the highly influential symbolic interactionist perspective on the social nature of the

234　*The shape of the modern self*

self-concept.[8] For Mead, the self emerges gradually in interaction beginning in infancy. Initially, the infant's vocalizations are idiosyncratic, but her maturing mind is gradually populated with words that label objects and experiences, which permits increasingly complex thought. Not only does language allow the child to incorporate names for things and ever more intricately model the world, the acquired words bring access to the mental perspectives of other people. To acquire a word is, at least at first, and especially for a child, to acquire some specific person's point of view. The child's discovery of the meaning of "love" is actually her discovery of what that symbol signifies for some particular person – initially, her primary caregiver. However, relatively quickly comes the understanding that love takes different associations when used with other adults, and that it also has a sort of non-specific general meaning applicable to one group or another. I write this sentence with a selection of words chosen on the basis of my assumptions of how they'll be understood by my reader. As I haven't interacted with any readers personally, my thought is of a generalized sense of anyone who might read this and their likely response to my language. Mead referred to this as "the generalized other" – the sense of the non-specific audience's perspective on our discourse.

When the audience is a specific person, language can be precisely adjusted in anticipation of that person's perspectives and reactions. In this way, the psychology of that individual enters the mind. When speaking with a relationship partner, we anticipate her style of thought, her sensitivities, how she's likely to react, the types of information that make her defensive or put her at ease, and the way she sees us. We carry within us a model of her mind. We anticipate each other's perspectives, and our minds intermingle. The more our interaction, the greater the intermingling and the richer our appreciation of each other's fields of meaning. In important relationships between those who regard each other as moral and intellectual equals, we lay down common values and mutually structure each other's minds and perceptions, which results in some degree of psychological convergence. The contents of our minds become interdependent.

These dynamics are specific to our historical context. Modernity shifts culture in the direction of greater diversity, from relatively consensual understanding to pluralism, privacy, and individualism, and from external to internal sources of knowledge. As a result, modern people sense that meaning is relative and subject to change. Thus, in this era, the system of shared meaning that is created in our intimate discourse has the opportunity to become more private, vivid, and distinctive. There is greater opportunity to create shared systems of meaning that are well differentiated from the meanings of the generalized culture, because the range of cultural meaning – the pool of concepts and distinctions we have to work with – is now far greater than in the past, and this provides resources to construct points of view that are uniquely ours.

By analogy, if you think of the cultural perspectives of Colonial Americans as having been constructed of the available building materials of that time – perhaps not much more than glass, simple metals, stone, bricks, and planks – then the range of structures that colonists could build was constrained

We are each other   235

by the limitations imposed by the physical characteristics of those few materials. By analogy, in our time, the available materials for building meaning in American culture consist as well of reinforced concrete, aluminum, glass block, tile, tar paper, adobe, carbon fiber, plaster, Plexiglas, plastic, fiberboard, tungsten cable, fiberglass, sheet rock, and many others. This diversity supports the construction of a significantly more differentiated and individualized range of structures. In this diversity, intimate relationships can become much more vivid centers of privately shared meaning than was the case before.

Social intelligence

Mead anticipated that some people would be better equipped to engage in the task of building meaning with others and spoke of "social intelligence" more than 80 years before the term was popularized. Mead's view was that,

> the whole nature of intelligence is social to the very core – that this putting of one's self in the places of others, this taking by one's self of their roles or attitudes, is not merely one of the various aspects or expressions of intelligence . . . but is the very essence of its character.[9]

Empathy, the ability to accurately assess the perspective of those with whom we are interacting, to understand what meaning they bring to a situation and what they'll likely take from it, is the essential prerequisite in building the shared fields of meaning that sustain high quality social relationships. It is the essential skill of modern interpersonal life, and Mead believed that children begin to acquire it in play, where they try on roles and experiment with how others might regard them. For example, when a child plays at being a mother and orders her toy dog to bed early for misbehaving, the child is trying on a mother's point of view. In modern parlance the child is acquiring a "theory of mind," an understanding of the individual nature of others' internal experience. Children's play is sometimes misunderstood as a diversional activity that occupies the child while he matures sufficiently to begin disciplined learning. Rather, play is an exercise of imagination that leads to the acquisition of increasingly complex and accurate mental and emotional maps of how the social and material worlds work.[10]

As the child ages, more complicated games, such as baseball, encourage a more skillful empathy because, there, thoughts and actions must be synced simultaneously with those of a range of others involved in interdependent activity. To play baseball well, each team player has to accurately and simultaneously apprehend in each moment in the game the way things look to all other players, each of whom has individual quirks and a role-related perspective that's unique to the position they play. This demands sophisticated empathic cognition.

This may be a good moment to recall that there is evidence of declining empathy among young Americans. Not only have bullying and self-focus been

236 *The shape of the modern self*

on the increase, but, in a meta-analysis, psychologist Sara Konrath and her colleagues also found significant declines between 1980 and 2010 on scales measuring "empathic concern" (emotional sympathy for others) and "perspective taking" (the core empathic skill of seeing the world as it's seen by someone else).[11] Konrath and her colleagues point to the rising use of social media such as Facebook and Twitter, the adoption of cell phones, and the replacement of face-to-face interaction with texting. Other scholars believe that the mass infusion of digital technologies has resulted in diminished capacities for focus and concentration, both of which play a role in effective interpersonal relations.[12]

Empathic perspective taking is undermined when conversation shifts online because, there, people aren't fully exposed to each other, impeding their ability to apprehend each other's systems of meaning. Empathy necessarily suffers when conversations don't occur in real time or when they are reduced to text exchanges, notes on Facebook walls, or emails. Emoticons and emojis are inadequate substitutes for the face-to-face display of emotion in real time (*New York Times* columnist Timothy Egan has called the emoji "the worst thing to happen to communication in our time").[13] We just can't read each other as well without the immediacy of physical presence. This leaves many device-enraptured Americans isolated within their own subjectivity, socially hamstrung by a diminished sense of the other. Happily, Turkle provides evidence that empathic skills can rebound when circumstances force people to return to face-to-face encounter.[14]

One criticism of symbolic interactionism is that, in setting its focus narrowly on individuals' discourse, the perspective has tended to ignore the other half of the conversation – culture loop: the influence of the institutions and institutional structures of meaning in which interpersonal interactions are embedded, as well as situations in which social power is unequally distributed.[15] The implications of this point have been underappreciated within the social sciences, which, as a whole, rarely concern themselves with influence that operates at the historical-cultural level.

As we've seen, modernity's progress has been defined in substantial shifts in the nature of people's institutional involvements and, particularly, in the relative social power of men and women. As institutions have decreased in their power to influence personal identity, particularly since the late nineteenth century when the interpersonal perspective on the self was taking hold, the site for the definition of self has shifted to social relationships. We can see this in the trajectory of theory from Royce and James (late nineteenth century) to Cooley and Mead (early twentieth century). Today, people aren't born into self-defining roles to the degree that they were in former times. At the same time, the size of the gap between the social power of men and women has narrowed, allowing intimate cross-sex relationships to evolve into a primary location for the construction and repair of self-identity.

While this plays out throughout the modern world, this is most vividly an American story. The historical and cultural conditions that shape interpersonal experience in the U.S. in this era gain their highest expression in America's exceptional diversity and mobility. Yet, even today, there is sufficient range among America's ethnic and religious subgroups that, in some cases, their social conditions may bear greater resemblance to Tönnies's Gemeinschaft society than Gesellschaft mainstream America. It would be difficult to imagine a social philosopher whose only exposure to American culture was limited to the Old Order Amish constructing a theory of interpersonal interaction, subjectivity, perspective taking, and the construction of meaning as did Mead, a man from Chicago, living in an historical period struggling to understand the relatively fresh impacts of mass society, diversity, immigration, urbanization, industrialization, and so on.

It's no coincidence that virtually all philosophical and scientific attention ever directed toward understanding interpersonal life kicked off at the same time that the social changes wrought by the Industrial Revolution began to accelerate and be broadly manifest, turning self-definition and intimate life upside down. It wasn't just the unconscious mind that came into prominence in the accelerating changes of modernity: these changes also made self-identity into a vivid and increasingly fragile life project and, for those with the skills, transformed marital intimacy into a protective communal partnership of binding secrets, private morality, and self-defining understanding.

Thus, the processes of communication that create and sustain intimacy, the self-concept, friendships, and the family are neither timeless nor universal. They rose to prominence in the changing social conditions of the modern world, particularly in the movement of conversation from something more like signal exchange to a process of negotiating symbolic meaning. Any theory of self, mind, intimacy, or interpersonal interaction that fails to take account of modernity's shifts – that fails to place itself within this flow of history – risks an increasingly rapid erosion of relevance as the social conditions in which the theory was founded will inevitably collapse from underneath it.

Synthesis

Mind and personal identity are brought into being in symbolic interaction. Without some form of language, and others to interact with, no one develops mind or a self-concept in any normal sense. Thought and identity are influenced by the facts of physical being, but the body doesn't generate mind or self-identity on its own. Language enables mind and serves as the medium for the construction of personal identity. This occurs in the interpersonal realm under the influence of culture. In conditions now historically distant, though not far from view in today's non-modern societies, the fields of meaning that constitute culture were so limited, self-consistent, broadly shared, and stable that communication then functioned more as a system of signal exchange: more transmission and reception than negotiation and persuasion. In such circumstances, notions of personal identity are embedded in broadly held perspectives derived from religion, tradition, and community. There, one becomes the person one was born to be, given the allowances of the culture. Non-modern people don't

238   *The shape of the modern self*

possess the freedoms of self-identity and lifestyle that characterize modern societies, but, precisely because more of life is predetermined, there is less of the insecurity of self that results from failure to actualize bespoke dreams and ambitions. Deep community limits life in many ways, but, in the shared values and beliefs of deep community, people are not burdened with the pernicious difficulty of brokering confirmation for their place in the universe.

Culture and mind are both constructed of symbols, with culture being the collective repository of the structures of symbolic meaning that individual minds have generated and shared. But, in modernity's extraordinary diversity and plurality of perspective, rapid shifts in belief and values, contradiction, spin, and sham, there has developed a gulf between mind and culture. As a system of meaning, mind is selective, personal, integrated, and ordered, and meaning is held with some degree of conviction, while, in highly modern societies, culture is a collection of meaning that tends to be indiscriminate, inconsistent, and chaotic, with much of it held in question. A mind that has to encounter and process culture directly, without the benefit of a strong filtering and organizing edifice of self, is easily overwhelmed, anxious, pushed toward protective withdrawal and, increasingly, toward the contorted modes of perception and thought that characterize mental disorders. More commonly, when the self-system is not so much in danger of obliteration as simply weakly formed, threatened, or otherwise overwhelmed, the result is anxiety, impulsive behavior, narcissistic self-concern, and the common distortions of neurotic defensiveness. Without a strong structure of self, there is no basis for directing behavior except in ad hoc efforts to protect whatever ideas of personal identity there may be against further dissolution. In the absence of a secure sense of personal identity, feelings of hopelessness inhere in the inability to effectively filter the confusion of culture, leaving one facing the dark conclusion that life is situated in a shifting matrix of such uncertain and complex meaning that it all may sum to nothing; that, in the end, everything is equally significant and equally insignificant. This renders selective, purposeful action impossible, as one direction of activity seems as valid as another. In the extreme, it may even seem that life and death are of equal value, save that death may seem to offer escape from these difficulties of being.

So, in modern America, the self-system functions protectively as we cope day to day with the overloaded semiotic condition of the era. Our ideas of who we are give direction to our behavior and habits of perception and provide a basis for agency and will. Right or wrong, people who know who they are know where they are going, what they value, and what they need to do. A strong structure of self functions like the heat shield on a space capsule, protecting the machine from friction and radiation as it plunges through the atmosphere. Without the shield of self-identity to protect against the semiotic maelstrom of modern culture, mind is overwhelmed. As the cultural conditions of modernity have gained force, for many people it has become much more difficult to construct and sustain a stable and effective foundation of self. This has become a critical difficulty in the United States and other modern societies.

We are each other 239

Fragility of self is the thread connecting many of the most prominent concerns about interpersonal experience in discussion today: declining empathy; high rates of relationship turnover; record-setting levels of anxiety, depression, and other psycho-emotional disorders; high rates of suicide and addiction; delayed marriage; high rates of solo living and other forms of interpersonal withdrawal; declining happiness; increasing narcissism; and so on.

As the great frameworks of tradition, religion, and community that once imparted identity and purpose have receded in influence, Americans have looked to their interpersonal relationships to supply what's been lost. Increasingly, it isn't enough to partner with someone just for economic or reproductive purposes. Most Americans also now pursue intimacy in hope of obtaining the support for self-identity that used to be provided externally. This makes partner selection more important and riskier, promotes caution about commitment, and encourages lengthy probationary periods for beginning relationships. Fortunately, another of the hallmark processes of modernity is rising egalitarianism, which in recent years has finally moved far enough along in respect of gender equality to create the potential for mutual influence and true communion in those heterosexual intimate couples that are able to take advantage of this new opportunity.

And none too soon. In the exhilarating new freedoms of self-definition in modern societies (in that same new egalitarianism), it is easier to experience oneself as highly differentiated. But the backside risk in living a vividly distinctive life is isolation and the anxiety that may result from the realization that the meaningful symbols that define one's life aren't shared and are, therefore, insubstantial and difficult to sustain (here again, this essential point: symbols that aren't shared lose meaning and fade). And, for many, this risk is amplified by the alienating qualities of ungenuine encounter in jobs in service-oriented bureaucratic organizations or institutions whose credibility has been compromised. These days, it's not uncommon to have little basis for connection with neighbors, who now come and go more frequently and differ from us on a dozen axes of belief and lifestyle. And, as family networks have become more prone to change, complicated in composition, and dispersed geographically, it's become more difficult to sustain a sense of rich connection with close kin. Hence, today, in these trend lines, many Americans may have an easier time fulfilling the "not the same" end of the crafty Android advertising oxymoron than the "be together" part. The perception of "not the same" comes naturally in the atomized circumstances of modernity. But selves crafted outside the supports (and constraints) of strong community tend to be less stable, and, as Jean-Paul Sartre argued, enhanced freedom of self-definition tends to generate anguish: over selves imagined that prove unsustainable, and over fantasies of identity promoted by the mass culture that actually lie beyond anyone's reach. Greenfeld contends that this doesn't just generate low-grade philosophical disquiet. This is the core phenomenon driving surging rates of psychiatric disorders in highly modern societies.[16] Without a strongly anchored foundation of self, we are inadequately protected from the buzzing diversity of modern culture. Our

240 *The shape of the modern self*

best defense is the self-nurturing, self-sustaining little cultures we weave in conversation in deeply connected, ongoing interpersonal relationships.

Notes

1 Copyright 2012, Wendell Berry, from "The handing down." Reprinted by permission of North Point Press.
2 Carbaugh, *Cultures in conversation.*
3 Sapir, The status of linguistics as a science, 209.
4 Everett, *Dark matter of the mind: the culturally articulated unconscious.*
5 Kegley, *Josiah Royce in focus.*
6 White, Her life. My life, 169.
7 Cooley, *Human nature and the social order*, 152.
8 Mead, *Mind, self, and society: from the standpoint of a social behaviorist.*
9 *Ibid.*, 141.
10 Gopnik, *The philosophical baby: what children's minds tell us about truth, love, and the meaning of life.*
11 Konrath et al., Changes in dispositional empathy in American college students over time: a meta-analysis.
12 Bauerlein, *The dumbest generation: how the digital age stupefies young Americans and jeopardizes our future*; Carr, *The shallows: what the internet is doing to our brains*; Jackson, *Distracted: the erosion of attention and the coming dark age.*
13 Egan, The eight-second attention span.
14 Turkle, *Reclaiming conversation: the power of talk in a digital age.*
15 Meltzer et al., *Symbolic interactionism: Genesis, varieties and criticism.*
16 Greenfeld, *Mind, modernity, madness: the impact of culture on human experience.*

13 Multi-Me

Self, intimacy, and loss

A multiple personality is in a certain sense normal.

G. H. Mead, *Mind, Self, & Society*[1]

Multiple selves

The opening of Chapter 8 raised a question about the extent of loss when *Titanic* sank on April 14, 1912. According to *The Washington Post*, 1,800 people perished, and, as there's just one soul per body, in the language of the times, the *Post*'s banner headline announced: "ONE THOUSAND EIGHT HUNDRED SOULS LOST." However, as we've seen, as modernity has come on, the spiritual/religious idea of the soul has tended to be displaced by the scientific/secular idea of the self. And now the math isn't as simple. As the twentieth century moved forward, so did the notion of multiplicity, the idea that a single body could be home base to a person with some number of more or less differentiated selves embedded within it.

According to various accounts, the extent to which this occurs may range from a minimal sense of personal inconsistency as we interact with people in dissimilar contexts, possibly adopting somewhat different styles of speech and emphasizing different values and interests (e.g., few adolescents represent themselves the same way to friends as they do to parents, few adults to bosses as they do to co-workers, only someone with loose screws presents authentically to the cop who just pulled them over, etc.); through the mild-to-profound dissociative psychological circumstances of PTSD, in which one may feel life flickering between a highly differentiated past and present self; all the way to full-blown dissociative identity disorder/multiple personality disorder (DID/MPD) in which some people appear to share their body among a group of utterly differentiated inhabitants. This extreme sense of multiplicity became a Hollywood fascination dramatized repeatedly since the book publication and film adaptations of Jackson's (1954) *The Bird's Nest* and Thigpen and Cleckley's (1957) *The Three Faces of Eve*. Intriguingly, cases of DID/MPD are much more commonly diagnosed in the United States than in other parts of the world, and,

DOI: 10.4324/9781003010234-16

242   *The shape of the modern self*

more intriguing still, the number of embedded personalities therapists discovered per individual increased dramatically as the twentieth century moved on.[2]

We can safely assume that there were no cases of DID/MPD on board *Titanic*. The farther back one looks, the less evidence there is of anything like a modern consciousness of self-identity, much less a sense of multiplicity. The DID diagnosis, even now controversial among experts,[3] didn't exist in *Titanic*'s time, and the medical record suggests that cases were scarce before our own era.[4] Indeed, DID/MPD is diagnosed more frequently among women than men, and, as *Titanic*'s women and children were more likely to have made it into the lifeboats, the probabilities are that, if there actually had been any cases of DID/MPD on board, they wouldn't have been included in the death tally. As for the more pedestrian sense of multiplicity linked to the range of differentiated social contexts in which one interacts, the highest rate of loss on *Titanic* occurred among the ship's crew and working-class emigrant passengers, groups whose life circumstances were then less likely to have yet been affected by the processes of social segmentation that were ramping up in the modernizing world. It's the pressures of social segmentation, one of modernity's hallmark conditions, that bring on multiplicity.

William James had written in 1890 that, "a man has as many social selves as there are individuals who recognize him and carry an image of him in their mind." But the examples James used to illustrate his theories about the self were of people (actually only men) with horse farms and yachts. So, although James may stand among the first to discuss the fragmentation of identity in the modernizing world, it's unlikely that the fragmented psychosocial circumstances of his privileged peers were yet reflected equally throughout the population. So, returning to our math problem, at least among *Titanic*'s crew and emigrant passengers, the number of souls might have been reasonably similar to the number of selves. Move forward 100 years to our time, however, and it's a different story. By the mid-twentieth century, eminent sociologist Erving Goffman had published his landmark book *The Presentation of Self in Everyday Life*.[5] This seminal work paints a vivid portrait of routine interpersonal encounters in mid-twentieth-century American society, which he depicted to be comprised of people performing arbitrary self-enactments with the overt cooperation of others who play along with them, and with the tacit cooperation of those observing as audience. For Goffman, everybody seems to be at least somewhat removed from the role identities they're performing. They're not the wife or the doctor or the student or the Shetland Island farmer he interviewed, but people consciously aware that their role – wife, doctor, student, or farmer – is to some degree an adopted persona, a performance, and not reflective of their core being. By the 1990s, the line from the television ad for cold remedies, "I'm not a doctor, but I play one on TV," had become a ubiquitous trope, heard over and over again, an emblem of the extensive degree to which, by then, Americans were experiencing a sense of separation between the requirements of their exterior role performances and their interior lives.

In Goffman's world, self-identity isn't stitched into us by society or by God, and it isn't a story about who we are that we struggle to be true to. Nor is it, like the soul, the project of a life's refinement of character. Rather, the self inheres in facade and performance, a matter of varying personae that are enacted across the range of segmented interpersonal contexts everyone navigates during the week. Goffman's view of self-identity is theatrical and wholly interpersonal: who you are isn't something defined internally, but is conscious performance in public, most often involving the spontaneous cooperation of others to stage effectively. This vision of self-identity as strategically crafted cooperative performance became so influential that it shifted understanding of severe psycho-emotional disorders, as is quite clear for those in the interactional school of psychotherapy.[6]

In the interactional view, psycho-emotional disorders aren't regarded as stemming from flaws of the brain. In fact, they may not be seen as appropriately attributed to the individual at all, but are rather regarded as an outcome of the group's process as a group. That is, they are in some way functional for the group (usually the family). For example, a therapist from the interactional school may entertain the hypothesis that a child's criminally aggressive and impulsive behavior is a projective representation of deep issues in the family unit – most likely, suppressed conflict between the parents. Continually diverting attention to the child helps the family avoid a possibly cataclysmic conflict between mom and dad.

Similarly, a schizophrenic's odd manner of talk isn't seen as the result of organic malfunction in the brain, but as a sensible attempt by a person with a failed structure of personal identity to avoid the normal stresses to self that inhere in routine conversation. According to R. D. Laing, behavior that gets labeled schizophrenic comprises "a special strategy that a person invents in order to live in an unlivable situation."[7] The schizophrenic isn't someone with a malfunctioning brain, but a vulnerable person coping with the excruciating mental disorganization that accompanies collapsed self-identity. The schizophrenic communicates using the same palette of cultural meanings as everyone else, but in defensive ways designed to keep the maddening contradictions of the culture at bay by short-circuiting conversational processes that normally connect us to each other and, through each other, to the psychically painful shams, deceits, and inconsistencies of the larger culture.[8]

The fantasy identities defensively enacted by psychotics aren't random, but are sensitive to cultural and historical circumstance. Psychiatrists no longer administer to patients pretending to be Napoleon Bonaparte or Jesus Christ. Now, it's likely to be some variation on Truman Burbank,[9] the character at the center of the 1990s science fiction film *The Truman Show*, who, as the unwitting focus of a reality TV production about his own life, was surrounded by people posing as neighbors and co-workers, who were in actuality members of the TV company. This is an apt metaphor for the existential circumstances of this era. Throughout the day, over and over again, one encounters people who, in all probability, would admit that they really aren't quite the person they feel they must present themselves to be. Of course, in bygone days, when life was embedded in close community, this common disparity would have been impossible.

The cooperative enactment of one self or another

As we saw in Chapter 11, there was nothing new in the idea that self-identity is related to role performance, but Goffman radically extended the idea of "performance" to include virtually all day-to-day encounters, related to formal roles or not, and his work emphasized that performances of self are not monologues, but rather are communication events involving cooperative meaning-making among groups of people. He pushed the idea of performance using the metaphor of the theater to encourage the analysis of any routine social situation in terms of staging (front- and back-stage regions where well-separated interactions may be pursued simultaneously – nowadays rather obvious in the common sight of people texting while in meetings, or out with the family, or at the theater, or in class, etc.), props and costumes (businessmen and -women who adorn themselves with conspicuous symbols of wealth, such as expensive watches, jewelry, and designer clothing), and the degree of cooperation that occurs as those involved in the scene being performed help each other stay in role using what Goffman termed "facework."

Imagine, for example, a man and a woman out to dinner at a restaurant. The man excuses himself, leaves the table, and walks into the women's bathroom by mistake. This produces some muffled sounds of female surprise from the bathroom, a quick exit by the man, and a small measure of shame and embarrassment, the social emotions that accompany failure to enact a role identity competently. When he returns, his date comments that the faded male/female figures on the doors are ambiguous, and she wouldn't know one from the other either and had herself almost entered the men's room. She's helped him save face – that is, to repair a damaged performance.[10] Meanwhile, others at the restaurant collude in the repair effort by pretending not to have noticed the episode, engaging in what Goffman called "civil inattention."

Your audience for a performed identity may be yourself or fantasized;[11] however, in general, Goffman's insight was that identities are social accomplishments, often impossible to sustain independent of the cooperation of those around us. It's very difficult to regard yourself as a great lover if you can't find anyone to agree to date you, as an effective teacher if your students sleep through your classes or don't show up, as a leader at work if no one takes your counsel, or as a valued spouse if your wife ignores you or cheats. Social cooperation is intrinsic to the performance of identity (recall philosopher Charles Taylor's argument that you can't be a self on your own).

As the twentieth century moved forward, the strategic management of public identity was no longer exclusively the problem of the politician and the corporation; role identity was experienced as an ever more complicated interpersonal accomplishment managed actively across the increasingly segmented terrain Americans navigate day to day. Because of this segmentation, modern life no longer provides a firm basis for the development of personal identity as a consistent principle.[12] Or, as Nobel poet Wisława Szymborska put it, in the circumstances of late modernity, identity has become "like a raincoat you

Multi-Me 245

button on the run";[13] in other words, something you grab and throw on quickly to get through an occasion, likely with a great deal of improvisation, because our social situations now are less scripted, more chaotic, and more subject to unforeseen influences.

In the emerging fluidity and complex segmentation of social life in the late twentieth century, scholars began to discuss the self as prone to dissociation, comprised of a composite of the perspectives that accrue as a result of enacting multiple separated *identities*. This flows seamlessly from the theoretical ideas discussed in previous chapters. As seen in Chapter 11, role theory links self-identity to social roles and their associated lore, scripts, and performance demands, and, for many Americans, the range and diversity of role involvements have increased. The shift to two-paycheck households provides a vivid case in point. This dramatic change of the 1970s and 80s introduced greater segmentation into women's lives and complicated notions of gender for men and women in ways that continue to reverberate. On the less scripted, interpersonal side, recall that, for Cooley and Mead, personal identity is strongly influenced by seeing how others react to us (see Chapter 12). It follows that the greater the diversity in the range of people with whom we interact, and the more diverse the occasions for our interaction, the more complicated our sense of who we are may become. Because of this, in our era, some degree of self-fragmentation may be common, and social scientists began to speak of "identities" to refer to the increasingly distinct multiple segments of a sense of self. As Mead said in the quotation at the opening of this chapter, in a sense, multiple personality has become a normal condition of American life, like so much else that we take in stride (but, cumulatively, strides that more frequently take us in the direction of the pharmacy or the divorce lawyer).

What are the psychological consequences of this mode of being? Ingmar Bergman's film *Persona* centers on the situation of Elisabet Vogler, an actress under a psychiatrist's care after she has become blunted, apathetic, and mute, having lost the ability to speak. The doctor confronts her,

> You think I don't understand? The hopeless dream of being. Not seeming to be, but being. Conscious and awake at every moment. At the same time, the chasm between what you are to others and what you are to yourself. The feeling of vertigo, and the constant hunger to be unmasked once and for all. To be seen through, cut down . . . perhaps even annihilated. Every tone of voice a lie, every gesture a falsehood.

The film was released in 1966, when the appearance of this quality of modern being was still recent enough to be vivid. One half-century later, it is almost too common to notice, but the result is the same: people in withdrawal, interacting less with others, turning ever inward.

Certainly, to an important extent, most of us are limited by our life circumstances in the set of identities we can take on. However, in principle, in the dramaturgical world described by Goffman and others of the symbolic

246 *The shape of the modern self*

interactionist tradition, you can be whoever you assert yourself to be, moving into and out of identities, provided only that you manage the performances convincingly and round up any necessary props and cast members, and a supportive audience. You don't need a release from tradition or a ticket from God.

Goffman provides numerous examples of people performing one social identity or another without apparent requirement that the identity performed connect to any continuous reality of being. The minimal requirement for self-identity is simply the successful performance of a scene. Translating this into the language of the street, for as long as you can manage to look to others like a duck and put out a convincing quack, then, regardless of your DNA, you're a duck (again, recall from Chapter 2, Rachel Dolezal, the biologically white woman who presented herself as black and became a leader in the Spokane chapter of the NAACP). In the shift from the self-stabilizing conditions of life in smaller and more intimate communities, where identities performed and available audiences were limited and continuous, to urban anonymity, and beyond to the utterly unverifiable personae of the internet, it's far easier now than in the past to experiment with identity and sustain highly complicated and fragmented identity sets. In fact, if you join an online world such as *Second Life*, you can even spend your evenings quacking about as an avatar duck.

Very clearly, the modern world has moved in a more Goffmanesque direction, and, as a result, there's less point in speaking of "true" or "core" selves. Where's the true self in a world of contrivance and theater, where the role of Hamlet can be performed by anybody who knows the lines, and where whoever is playing him, having finished his performance, walks away to begin portraying someone else? Hamlet comes into existence only in being enacted by a cooperating cast of players: he's real and alive only in the socially cooperative performance that brings him to life, and he's gone when the play ends. Within Goffman's theoretical frame, this is the case for all our identities, which leads to questions about the psychological and spiritual consequences of modern life in which, for many, the set of identities that comprise the self is dispersed across an unprecedented breadth of social situations, many of which are more vulnerable to turnover than in the past.

Screen actors who engage in a broad range of character performances strive to do so at a professional distance, without suffering any sense of inconsistency of self, even as they may encounter annoying fans who persistently treat them as though they are, in actuality, one of the characters they've portrayed. As was the case for Bergman's Elisabet Vogler, if they are unable to do so, the profession may become a kind of existential hell in which the actor risks becoming increasingly confused about the reality of who they are, the deeper into the career they go (and, given the seemingly high rates of divorce, substance abuse, and extreme behavior associated with the film acting profession, maybe some do suffer this). Yet, in our time, because most of us experience multiplicity to some degree, and we are not professional actors who realize that our performances are works-for-hire and not representative of our essential selves, it's possible to become preoccupied with the problem of authenticity. Mostly we take this in our stride, but, inevitably, this generates stress and contributes to anxiety about the fundamental location of the "true" and authentic self. Continually flipping in and out of various perspectives and idiomatic modes of expression is psychologically taxing, and it's difficult to sustain multiple story lines simultaneously. Further, as every self is a moral system, multiplicity necessarily generates moral contradiction and anguish. One may routinely sweep such difficulties under the carpet, but living as a complex self-contradictory multi-person takes its toll. Nobody enjoys internal inconsistency.

In an era in which many are involved in multiple and transitory role commitments, and in which, "duplicity has become a built-in feature of public life,"[14] relationships with friends and family acquire special importance, providing one of the only places where an authentic, deeply encompassing, and continuing sense of personal identity can be experienced and socially validated. This may be one reason why Americans have gradually been reducing interaction with middle-tier contacts, such as neighbors, while intensifying interaction with family and other genuinely close intimates.[15] A stable community of friendship and intimacy provides a shield and a haven from the alienation and anxiety that accompany lives spread out and, unavoidably, tinged with some degree of facade and contrivance. This is what T. S. Eliot was referring to in 1916 in his "Portrait of a Lady," in which he concludes that, in a life thinned out, "composed so much, so much of odds and ends," without high-quality friendships, life becomes "cauchemar" (a nightmare).

In addition to the existential unease that may result from living with the contradictions of segmented identities, the circumstances of fluid modernity tend to discourage a sense of historical place. The world Goffman described is one in which performances of self aren't connected to any overriding sense of plot.[16] Goffman's people seem to carry themselves without awareness of larger cultural values or traditions, or of the extent to which their lives reflect anything much beyond impression management and other concerns of the moment. This wasn't oversight on Goffman's part: he got it right. This is what happens in the decline of community, religion, and deep tradition. It becomes much more difficult to see why we're here and where we're going.

Like that of many other social theorists, Goffman's writing didn't connect the interpersonal phenomena that were the focus of his analysis to the larger cultural processes that frame them and that might provide insight, for example, for how it came to be that role distance and multiple identity came into focus only a little over 100 years ago, or why self-identity has become more fragile and difficult in the conditions of modernity, or why PTSD, characterized by the interiorization of highly dissociated and contradictory fields of meaning, has risen to the status of a signature psycho-emotional disorder of modern times. Possibly some amount of social life may have always been a matter of people moving in and out of roles and facades in the way that Goffman described, but it's unlikely that it was as much as now. Ours is the age of products such as Dermablend and Ferbs, which, among other uses, are marketed to help change the appearance of race or to conceal tattoos, the display of which could pose

248 *The shape of the modern self*

problems for those who also may sometimes need to pass as conventionally professional. The self *became* "homeless,"[17] "protean,"[18] "mutable,"[19] and, in general, shape-shifting as a required adaptation to the changing circumstances of modernity.

Fragmentation, anxiety, and alienation

Some believe that there has been a disjunction between the qualities of life under modernity and what is typically seen in the West today, commonly referring to the new situation as postmodernity, but, sometimes, with some differences among the terms: high modernity, hyper-modernity, late modernity, metamodernism, second modernity, or liquid modernity. Regardless of how one refers to the era, the thrust of the postmodern vision of the self is consistent with our discussion. Among the hallmarks of this new understanding of self-identity is the notion that it is now formed in a manner largely detached from formerly potent external influences, detached even from the normal constraints of narrative form, such as linear time sequencing and syllogistic reason. Some argue that, in the current age, the biographical self-narrative is a story that can be told virtually any way with equal validity, and thus notions of a "true self" have become obsolete. The person is a "social chameleon, constantly borrowing bits and pieces of identity from whatever sources are available."[20] The continuity of the self is "dissolved . . . by the fragmentation of experience,"[21] which renders our era notably schizoid in character.[22] The unleashing of multiple selves is a defining quality of a metamodernist age brought on by the internet.[23] The self has "retreated into nihilistic postmodern disarray," and, thus, "its compass spins wildly out of control . . . losing its ability to pick and choose its own moral course."[24]

I think it's a safe bet that most would regard such commentary on the status of their self-concept as somewhat exaggerated, if not hallucinatory. A stressed, fragmented, or liquid sense of identity is one thing, but a vaporized self without any internal consistency and moral structure takes this outside of normal experience and into the territory of psychiatric conditions such as borderline personality disorder, sociopathy, DID/MPD, and psychosis. As we've seen, there have been important historical impacts, but, like global warming, they've been so subtle and slow in coming that, even while the circumstances of interpersonal life have been changing at an ever accelerating pace, the common experience is of day-to-day coherence and stability. As it is with climate change, one gains a sense of perspective only by looking back over expanses of time measured in decades, and often in generations. There are a range of influences tracking through the history of modernity that have tended to isolate people from each other and destabilize the experience of self.

To cope, one may place distance between roles performed and the "real self" (i.e., we take the roles a little less seriously: while we may perform them conscientiously and competently, we're less likely to feel defined by them), and this may foster something like a sense of homelessness. Who wouldn't feel some degree of alienation after a day's highly compartmentalized work in a bureaucratically structured institution (a corporation, hospital, university, school system, government agency, the military, etc.) that requires one to represent abstract policies in which one may have little interest and with which one may have no personal connection, or perhaps with which one actively disagrees (likely a disagreement that can't be expressed without career risk)?

Today, a receptionist at a medical office routinely requires new arrivals to complete a clipboard full of medical history forms, waivers, and legal releases, the implications of which may be completely obscure. Probing this is likely to result in the receptionist disclaiming knowledge of the use or implications of the forms and just reiterating that they have to be completed. Here, no one in the encounter has any idea of why they're doing what they're doing. Questioning this exposes the sometimes surreal nature of bureaucratic activity in complex modern organizations.

Who wouldn't feel some degree of self-alienation if work requires engaging with segmented groups of people who have differing cultural priorities and values as though you shared them? Or, as per Hochschild's discussion of the growing proportion of emotional labor in many jobs,[25] who wouldn't feel some degree of self-alienation if your job requires more or less continuous ungenuine displays of emotion (e.g., perpetual cheerfulness, interest, energy, or enthusiasm)? These scenarios may not be universal, but they're common.

According to psychologist Kenneth Gergen, in postmodern life, with the ability to pick up and discard identities, "life becomes a candy store for one's developing appetites."[26] This statement, published in the early 1990s, likely reflected awareness of the utopian possibilities inherent in that time of a rising economy, easing of global communications and travel, and the emergence of the internet's new venues and methods of online interaction. However, with the benefit of additional perspective, it's clear this miscalculated the psycho-emotional impacts of identity flux. There is no evidence linking identity fragmentation or instability to happiness, but, rather, a growing appreciation that instability threatens mental health. It appears that, for many moderns, interpersonal life has become more isolated, stressful, insecure, depressed, and anxious than liberated, expressive, self-enhancing, and playful. As Maslow argued, to be experimental with identity requires a secure base,[27] and interpersonal/ontological security is not a notable feature of this period of history. Rather, ours is an era notable for retreat from involvement and commitment in intimacy (Americans are more likely to delay marriage, initiate divorce, avoid remarriage, live alone, etc.), setting records for the frequency of diagnosis of depression and anxiety disorders and the prescription of antidepressant and anti-anxiety drugs. According to Bauman, an essential fear of failed identity is projected into a culturally pervasive preoccupation with external threat, which shows up in fear of disease, terrorism, crime, second-hand smoke, immigrants, fatty food, high blood pressure, threat to our children, sexual predators, becoming ugly, memory lapse, bed bugs, people of other religions, aging, sharks at the beach, flabby abs, being sexually mundane, high cholesterol, and – most

250 *The shape of the modern self*

fittingly among these projective fears – identity theft.[28] All stand in for the anxiety of self-alienation that accompanies life in a time of high fragmentation where self-identity is less consistent and less stable.

Shared mind, partner loss, and loss of self

> Still today, months after his death, I go and sit at his grave, absent-mindedly stroking the grass as if it were his hair, talking to him using nicknames only he would understand.[29]

The candy store metaphor *is* apt in this sense: in childhood orgies of jelly beans and chocolate bars, many learn the miserable consequences and importance of self-protective limitation. Children learn the pain of failed bids at identity in the common little traumas that result from being cut from a sports team, turned down for a date, failing a test, blowing a musical audition, or losing composure delivering a speech to a class. A 5-year-old may confidently assert that she'll pursue a career as a race car driver, a veterinarian, a space ship pilot, or the president. Or she may not if she's already begun to learn that identity, easily imagined, isn't as easily obtained, and that failed bids at identity are painful and socially costly.[30] In an era in which self-identity isn't provided externally or shored up in close community with neighbors, unless we have built strong community on our own, each such blow is likely to chip a little piece from our sense of personal security and moral worth. We need the supports of interpersonal community in this age: deep, intimate relationships and strong friendships. And so, next to creating such relationships, among the greatest interpersonal challenges of this era is recovering from the termination of a long-term, self-stabilizing, symbolically interdependent relationship.

The depth of distress that can accompany the disruption of a such a relationship is illustrated in accounts of "magical thinking" following loss, which can involve denial and other defensive contortions of perception and logic. Especially, if the loss was sudden or unanticipated, as in an abrupt abandonment or accidental death, impacts can be similar to PTSD. Sleep is disrupted by nightmares and episodes of endless churning review. The survivor has to work through the profound existential difficulties that result from suddenly losing a primary source of support for life-defining values, routines, beliefs, and assumptions – for entire fields of meaning. It was that lost partner who had co-authored, validated, and stabilized the meaning that constituted the survivor's mind, including, especially, their sense of self. As an extreme expression of how deeply this loss can affect the mind, a recent UK study found that surviving spouses are more likely to be diagnosed with dementia in the months immediately following the death of a partner, but that this extra risk recedes in time.[31] Presumably, the mind returns to normal function as the survivor, gradually shifting to dialogue with others, establishes new social support for central fields of meaning.

In the survivor's new condition of pervasive upended meaning, there may be a sense of being perpetually liminal: endlessly pulled back and forth between the currents of the present and the past.[32] There may be an otherworldly quality about ordinary events, the perception of hidden significances, clues, and signs of higher meaning, all stemming from the need to somehow find sensibility for the disastrous sudden loss. There may be the adoption of a kind of desperate spirituality as the survivor struggles to comprehend and work through the raw emotional impact without being overwhelmed, to shelter from the anxious insecurity of the abrupt disruption of personal identity, and to find faith that rebuilding may eventually be possible. As the healing process moves forward, some of this may settle, and then depression is common.[33] C. S. Lewis's marriage to fellow author Joy Davidman ended in 1960 after just 4 years, when Davidman died of cancer. Their relationship had been highly collaborative. Lewis's *A Grief Observed* recounts his response to the loss, and, as he was deeply religious, much of the account relates his effort to work through the blow this loss represented to his faith. One can assume the marriage was symbolically interdependent, because Lewis and Davidman were literary collaborators and, according to their children, vigorously engaged each other in conversation as intellectual equals. Lewis related his frustration in his mind's habitual reaching out to her only to find her gone:

> Thought and thought, feeling after feeling, action after action, had H. [Joy Davidman] as their object. Now their target is gone. I keep from habit fitting an arrow to the string, then I remember and have to lay the bow down.[34]

And then his testament to the extent to which his understanding of his own narrative history was disrupted in her death, "Did you ever know, dear, how much you took away with you when you left? You have stripped me even of my past."[35] Lewis died of a heart attack at age 65, 3 years after his wife's death.

In speaking about the relationship between author Joan Didion and her husband John Gregory Dunne, writer Calvin Trillin described them in this way, "Among all the married couples I knew, they were the ones who were almost always together. I always said they're the sort of married couple that finish each other's sentences."[36] In Didion's account of her experiences in the year following the sudden death of her husband from a heart attack, she described one aspect of the shock to her sense of self:

> For forty years, I saw myself through John's eyes. I did not age. This year for the first time since I was twenty-nine I saw myself through the eyes of others. This year for the first time since I was twenty-nine I realized that my image of myself was of someone significantly younger . . . . when we mourn our losses we also mourn, for better or for worse, ourselves. As we were. As we are no longer.[37]

252   *The shape of the modern self*

Didion and Dunne's was certainly a highly symbolically interdependent relationship. Like Lewis and Davidman, both spouses were accomplished writers, and both worked at home, traveled together, and routinely consulted each other and collaborated on their creative projects. As she described, Joan Didion's sense of personal identity had become intricately transformed in the culture of shared meaning that she and her husband had created. Over time, her self had taken shape, and that shape was sustained in his looking glass.

So profound is the self-defining quality of symbolically interdependent relationships that the loss of the other is also a loss of self. There's no postmodern playfulness in this. At this level, the dissolution of self is revealed to be one of the worst experiences and greatest challenges of a life. To say of our era that the self has dissolved in the fragmentation of postmodernity is to fail to appreciate what the experience of the disruption of self-identity is actually like. To be sure, the impact of loss isn't always so extreme, but it's often significant and rarely pleasant. Pleasant is possible in cases where one has become alienated from a role-identity or social relationship. Examples could include when you're married to someone with whom you never became symbolically interdependent and no longer like and are finally able to leave; or when your job requires you to perform in a way that is contrary to your beliefs and values and you are able to resign. But, in these cases, the situation you're terminating had either failed to establish or had lost self-definitional importance.

A symbolically interdependent relationship is one in which partners have become primary points of reference for each other's meaningful interpretations of the world and themselves. When, in the course of normal affairs, partners are beset with doubt, they're most likely to turn to each other for support for their attitudes and ideas. When they have a novel experience, what they make of it is likely to form and solidify in discussion with each other.

As a sidebar, I want to revisit a point discussed in Chapter 9 for the sake of anyone who may be hesitating here, perhaps reflecting on your own intimate situation and your keen awareness of particular points of persistent disagreement between you and your partner. You've been together a long time but have an easier time seeing the differences between you than the extent of agreement and interdependence. So it may be. The dramatic changes in outlook that accompany couple members' reconstruction of self and world "remains, in bulk, unapprehended and unarticulated."[38] Recall that the mind becomes analytically active in the perception of difficulty; otherwise, consciousness simply flows. For this reason, it's not unusual to harbor awareness of points of persistent difference between self and partner, while failing to appreciate the vastly greater extent of interdependent meaning that you co-established over time. But that awareness surfaces quickly in the aftermath of the breakup, when the newly separated encounter the world without normal support for the myriad beliefs and values with which they had surrounded themselves and which gave definition and purpose to their psychological and emotional being.

As in the quotation that opens this section, commonly, widowed spouses continue an inner dialogue with the lost partner. It's estimated that this occurs for about 30 percent of the bereaved.[39] As an index of the strength of the desire to remain connected in dialogue, I recently spoke with a woman who uses a spiritualist medium to continue conversation with her deceased partner, a practice that may be more common than you think.[40] Indeed, British physician W. Dewi Rees performed a comprehensive survey of the impacts of spousal death in Mid Wales, finding that nearly half of the 227 widows and 66 widowers his team interviewed had experienced some form of hallucinatory contact with their dead partner. The likelihood of hallucination was greater the longer the couple had been together, and was more frequent among professional and managerial workers, people more likely to work with their minds than their hands, with talk and ideas.[41]

Even the separated and divorced, bound up in the confusion, conflict, and pain of the issues of their terminated relationship, may nevertheless continue to regard their former partner as a singularly important source of understanding and confirmation for the fields of meaning most central to their sense of themselves and the world. In light of this, it should be clear that psychological distress, not postmodern delight, is what results when people are thrown into circumstances that complicate their sense of self and worldview, either through loss, change of economic circumstance, or the common requirement of shifting in and out of segmented social relationships, each with its somewhat different complex of beliefs, self-definitions, and moral commitments. It is the psychological and emotional impacts that stem from identity stress that drive America's rising rates of mental disorders. Nowhere is this link more vivid than in the termination of a long-term self-defining intimate relationship, where, in some cases, the support for core identity is ripped away, leaving the former partner desperate for support and stability. Something of the same type of impact might occur for someone who has lost a self-defining job, such as a soldier whose sense of self was transformed in the stress and camaraderie of battle to such an extent that she feels alienated from her pre-military life, her civilian friends and family, only feeling comfortable and understood in the company of those she fought next to. This may be a part of the reason that the U.S. military is currently experiencing high rates of suicide among troops returned from service in battle zones in Afghanistan and the Middle East. Unlike the situation of the past, today's soldiers aren't returning to a society characterized by strong, self-defining community. Now, psychological support must come from intimate relationships that are much harder to establish and sustain, particularly so as war experiences – so central and self-defining – may be difficult to share or make sense of to outsiders, spouses included.

As we've seen, a stable sense of self became more difficult to achieve as a result of the transformations of the modernizing world. The institutional and social structures that once served to anchor identity no longer function in this way as effectively, and so we turn to our significant partners, seeking the security of mutual self-definition. Like boats on the lake, we moor to each other for the self-stabilizing rewards of community. This works well enough in calm waters, but not in turbulence, and, increasingly in our time, the waters aren't

254 *The shape of the modern self*

calm for long. Some of the same forces responsible for the world's escalating frequency of unstable weather (industrialization, globalization, etc.) are also generating social instability by upending long-term employment opportunities; intensifying migration, social mobility, and urbanization; depleting meaning from public life and occupational roles; and so on. As a result, the times strongly encourage multiplicity and adaptive self-definition: people who are able to change their sense of who they are to meet the shifting requirements of an increasingly fluid world. But fast-shifting definitions of self constitute a serious threat to intimate stability. What becomes of marriage when partners change identity?

The starting period of many intimate relationships is distinguished by a kind of fog of infatuation.[42] Interacting almost exclusively in restricted and positive situations, one sees in the other a relief from loneliness, an empowering partnership, a soulmate, the beginning of a meaningful new phase of life, the fulfillment of all sorts of desires and dreams, and this cake is often frosted with sexual delights. Trivial points of agreement ("We both like to go to the movies!") and superficial observations ("He's *so* loving to his cat!") are vastly overgeneralized ("I just know she's going to like the opera," "We'll have six children and he'll make a wonderful dad") to the point that it may seem to partners as though they were designed for each other. (Hence, Freud's quip that it's only love that can make a god or an angel out of a grocery store clerk.)[43] In truth, as new partners really aren't privy to much detail about each other, the situation is ripe for fantasy, projection, and transference. Often, this happens in both directions, creating a self-amplifying loop in which partners not only misattribute perfection to each other, but, in doing so, receive a reinforcing boost in self-esteem from the perception that the faultless new partner seems to regard them so positively. To be the recipient of the esteem of a perfect person will swell anybody's spirits. However, in the absence of actual detail, the being one has fallen for may be mostly a composite of projected desires and hopes.

In this misty period of narcissistic distortion, there's a tendency to gloss over signs of future difficulty. The feelings can be almost narcotic, and so one sweeps data under the carpet that might be disruptive of fantasies. Here lie the seeds of what can evolve into an implicit contract in which both couple members expect support to be continually forthcoming, and that the partner won't significantly change. Each assumes that the other won't just accommodate all their quirky inclinations, habits, neurotic tendencies, and identities (why shouldn't they? There was no indication otherwise at first), but that they'll actually support and celebrate them. Forever.

However, with the passing of time come the complications of integrating complexly structured selves, changing external demands, and shifting values and interests. In addition to whatever range of personal qualities and identities brought to the relationship at its inception, new identity demands are often thrust upon us (e.g., in losing a job or getting a new one that requires the performance of new dimensions of personality, perhaps extroversion required of a sales job in place of the quiet self-sufficiency of a technology contractor).

Multi-Me 255

Identities may also evolve and carry the self to new configurations that may not align as well with our partner. Here's the danger in putting your partner through professional school only to find that she emerges with a different sense of personal identity and fading interest in your relationship – perhaps, in fact, a sense that, in its tacit commitments to the continuation of obsolete notions of who she is, the relationship has become an obstacle to her new sense of self.

The degree to which gender roles have been redefined in the last 60 years, particularly for women, has certainly encouraged change in self-definition for many people, likely creating significant challenges in many intimate partnerships. Indeed, inevitably and universally, common events in the life cycle (e.g., aging, job changes, retirement, infirmity, etc.) and in the cycle of relationship development (e.g., moving in together, getting married, having a child, becoming a grandparent) generate new identity demands. Being a husband or wife isn't the same as being a boyfriend or girlfriend, and becoming parents propels us into new visions of self and a new set of moral and behavioral restraints. It's important to understand that identities, even informal ones that operate at the level of fantasy (e.g., whatever it might mean, I see myself as a "real man"), usually involve felt moral commitments, experienced as internal pressures to respond to life situations in particular ways consistent with the identity (e.g., it may perhaps be difficult to get a "real man" to agree to attend a baby shower), and are unlikely to be adopted or changed lightly. Hence, identity shifts can be a key trigger of intimate conflict.

Conflicts over identity shifts may be particularly difficult to manage as many couples lack a shared conceptual vocabulary that would permit them to recognize and discuss identity issues as they arise. As we saw in Chapter 9, language is everything: if you don't have the words, you can't have the thoughts, much less the discussion. Until they begin to use concepts such as the days of the week or the hours of the clock, young children are incapable of discussing the future or the past and so live more in the present. Similarly, couple members who have no familiarity with concepts relevant to identity and self may not be able to constructively discuss their relationship issues. When identity conflicts aren't seen and addressed for what they are, the result may include such phenomena as hostile humor, uncomfortable teasing, or acts of sabotage and resistance.

We may not like it, but, as the larger culture segments and realigns the economic, political, and religious currents, we have to shift to cope with them, and this pulls at the ropes that connect us to each other. We shouldn't be surprised, therefore, that our interpersonal relationships, whose intimacies center in the mutual definition of self, have become more difficult and fragile (nor should we be surprised at the extent to which issues of self-identity – projectively expressed in nationalism, xenophobia, and religious intolerance – have surfaced in the wake of modernity). Unfortunately, this has happened at the same time that we need those relationships the most. But – and this is no coincidence – it's exactly the demands of fluid modernity that have made the intimacies of our interpersonal relationships become so vivid and potentially

256 *The shape of the modern self*

fulfilling. The implication of this is that, if, as people sometimes wish, we were able to step back in time to the possibility of greater relationship stability, we'd forgo the opportunity to experience the joy and satisfaction of participating in symbolically interdependent intimacy in a continuing egalitarian framework characterized by ongoing support and a sense of deeply meaningful and self-sustaining community. It may be challenging to get there and difficult to sustain, but the payoff is unprecedented in history. And anyway, there's no way back.

Distributed intimacy

In a time of segmented social experience, Americans whose paths take them into many reasonably segregated interpersonal contexts throughout the week are more likely to experience some degree of fragmented self-identity, some sense in which they may feel freer to represent certain visions of self and accompanying notions of morality within these particular isolated social relationships. There may be a version of self shared with those on the job, a bit of a different one with your ex-spouse, another with your current partner, another with fellow crew members of the dragon boat squad, another with your parents, another enacted via your avatar in *Second Life*. In another common pattern, work life may require the enactment of ongoing positive interpersonal relationships across a range of clients, as may be the case for consultants, case managers, and service workers in many fields.

On the flip side of this, Americans now outsource many interpersonal functions that formerly were handled personally, or within the family unit: wedding planners, dating coaches, personal trainers, massage therapists, couple counselors, nannies, home health care aides, life coaches, and so on.[44] Many of these represent ongoing personal relationships that place us in conversations that address values and qualities of the self, even if indirectly. In other words, in modern America, to some degree, it isn't uncommon for self-identity to be "distributed." In each of these contexts, conversations occur that may create, to varying extent, bonds of friendship and intimacy grounded in their mutual support for assorted images of each other, for assorted identities. Each such relationship has a claim on some version of our self-narrative, and sometimes these varying selves and their accompanying value commitments may be sufficiently at odds with each other to foster embarrassment should these contexts become crossed. For example, members of the dragon boat squad may often bond by sharing stories about the degree to which their workplace managers are incompetent and their ex-spouses are unreliable. If so, they may prefer lunching with their manager or ex at a restaurant some distance from the boat launch.

At this point, it may be useful to emphasize something that's been implicit but should now be on the table: that marriage (or any of its variants) is neither a necessary nor sufficient condition for the experience of intimacy. To be intimate is to be a participant in an interpersonal relationship in which conversation is ongoing and tends to influence each partner's vision of self and identity, and in which there's joint buy-in to a somewhat unique construction of values and beliefs about the world, creating a distinctive culture of meaning. Clearly, in this sense, although symbolic interdependence might represent an ideal for marriage, it isn't required for marriage and may frequently be absent, even in otherwise happy relationships. On the other hand, the potential for intimacy and symbolic interdependence is inherent to ongoing friendship. Meaningful friendships are *always* founded in an assumption of mutual equality, but marriages are only sometimes so, and, as the perception of equality is a precondition for mutual influence, we may be surer to find symbolic interdependence within deep, active friendships than with long-term marital partners. However, when symbolic interdependence is found within long-term marriages, it's likely to be more encompassing, as the normal structure of marriage exposes a much wider range of experience to mutual interpretation.

As we've seen, prior to recent progress in leveling the power and status relationship between men and women, it may have been uncommon for heterosexual marital partners to achieve the type of mutual persuasion required of symbolic interdependence. Marriages founded in a structure of inequality may be happy, committed, and profoundly affectionate, but, unless partners regard each other as equally credible, they can't influence each other's minds to the same degree. You can be happy in your subordinate position at work and enjoy working with your boss, but, because the distribution of authority is unequal, at best, you can be a highly valued team member or a sidekick, but you can't be an equal co-author of the meaningful routines, concepts, assumptions, and values that constitute the workplace. Thus, the structure of patriarchal marriage rules out symbolic interdependence. In the case that the patriarchal couple has achieved highly consensual beliefs and values over time, it's because the less powerful partner has shifted to either accommodate or introject the beliefs and values of the more powerful partner. In the case of plural marriage, extramarital involvement, or "simultaneous multipartnerships,"[45] though relationships involve multiple partners, as one might imagine, that does not mean that the addition of marital crew members multiplies the degree of self-defining intimacy available to the spouses. The reverse seems much more likely as – with, perhaps, the fascinating exception of the mid-nineteenth-century communal marriage practices of the Oneidans of central New York[46] – plural marriage is never a marriage among social equals.

In her analysis of the changing historical circumstances of Western culture that have left intimate male – female relationships more emotionally risky and fraught, undermining early-to-mid-twentieth-century models of marriage, sociologist Eva Illouz grapples with the question of what's at stake for men and women in marriage that might account for the dynamics we see in our era of delayed marriage, reluctance to commit, frequent divorce, declining rates of remarriage, solo living, and so on. She examines, and discards as inadequate, explanations based on evolutionary genetics (e.g., that evolution shaped male behavior to favor strategies of low commitment and broad access

258   *The shape of the modern self*

to reproductive partners while encouraging women to seek committed partnership[47] – see next chapter), differences in male/female psychology (e.g., Chodorow – see Chapter 3), and economic exchange (e.g., male's power at home being displaced by rising economic empowerment of women). She argues that the first part of the answer to this question lies in the rise of individualism and the recasting of the world of heterosexual intimacy as a marketplace, driven by quickly changing notions of value and so vast that it cripples our ability to choose with confidence.[48] That seems correct, but only addresses the external circumstances of relationships. It doesn't address the question of what's at stake in intimacy. That, for Illouz, is that, in modernity, the sense of self-worth has been disconnected from its former, less troubled dependence on social position and, instead, must be continually replenished in ongoing interaction in social relationships (particularly love relationships). This is an important insight, but it's still a partial answer: it's more than self-esteem. Our intimate interpersonal relationships are core sites for self-definition, for the construction of a stable and relevant system for understanding the world and our place within it, and for a sense of community that shores up notions of morality and our ideas about where we've come from and where we're going. In a world that's displaced most people from the secure position of their forebears in religion's frameworks of morality and meaning, that for many has rendered work abstract and impersonal, that bombards us with the often predatory codswallop of commercial and political culture, more than ever men and women struggle to answer the existential questions: "Who am I?", "Why am I alive?", and "How should I live?" The answers we live by are created in our interpersonal relationships (and, thus, as Eliot said, life without them – "*cauchemar!*"). That's what we seek in intimacy.

In an ahistorical fashion common in interpersonal scholarship, in recent decades many communication theorists have asserted that people are motivated in their particular interpersonal interactions to adopt communication practices that reduce uncertainty about what to expect from each other.[49] There is no doubt that this is the case, but this is regarded as a universal social-psychological process. Instead, this principle should be focused much more broadly and wired back up to the greater historical situation: in former times, life was embedded in extra-individual structures of meaning and action and appeared to offer greater certainty. Life in our time is infused with uncertainty about core aspects of existence, and we all struggle to reduce the insecurity that this generates. The site where this happens is our intimate interpersonal relationships, either inside marriage or irrespective of it.

Thus, as day-to-day experience has spread out across an expanding range of segmented social contexts, as innovative digital communications have increased the possibility of sustaining many isolated relationships simultaneously, and as additional factors of modernity have tended to render the long-term prospects of any marriage-type relationship more risky, a new possibility has been created for managing the need for intimacy, one that might contribute to Illouz's search for an explanation for low levels of commitment within existing proto-marital relationships and reduced interest in forming them. Simply put, in the current context of interpersonal life, one might reasonably hesitate to invest all oneself in a single, potentially volatile relationship and opt instead, as in stock investing, for the relative safety of a diversified portfolio, especially so in a time in which intimacy, like so much else, has become infused with the rationalities of the marketplace.

Perhaps this is what drives some portion of the singles dating scene, and some of what drives those who pursue extramarital affairs. However, this need not have anything to do with patterns of sexuality. Under pressures of modernity, and indeed throughout history, it's always been possible for sexuality and intimacy to function as isolated venues for interpersonal activity (hence, the logic of that most infamous line, "But darling, she didn't mean anything to me!"). Rather, I'm speaking here of the range of intimate sites where one may find self-definition and support. One might seek support for identities A and B here, and identity C there, and so on. This is particularly easy since the advent of digital communication via the internet and mobile technologies, which, in their global reach and privacy, virtually beg the creation of segmented relationships.

Of course, interpersonal relationships characterized by significant intimacy can also be distributed across time, as in the case of a person who has a series of intimate marital relationships. However, there are two problems with this. The first is that no truly intimate relationship ends without significant emotional fallout and anguish, and so serial relationships may be exhausting. Moreover, those who index the success of marriage against its ability to sustain the experience of romantic involvement will recognize that the idea of serial marriage is anathema to classical romantic love and its notion of an exclusive investment of the emotions, the soul, and one's future.[50] What flights of passion are possible when you're on your fifth marriage, or cohabiting with your tenth boyfriend? In the tradition of romantic passion, love that's not unconditional and eternal is not love at all. Classical romantic love is something that, when it exists, can only be given once or it's something else, for you can't dedicate true love to more than one person without depleting the idea of its meaning and lowering your standard of experience. But many probably accept this. With America leading the world in the rate of turnover in marital and nonmarital relationships, it's easy to see how a traditional, all-encompassing giving of self to other might seem rash in our time, and how this encourages the replacement of the classical association of unconditional love within a marriage by a framework of reward – cost analysis and provisional contracting, either implicitly or explicitly, as in the idea of short-term "renewal" marriage commitments or in the drawing up of prenuptial agreements. There are choices for how to accomplish intimacy, and, under different historical circumstances, people have pursued this problem along different pathways. You might imagine that a majority would prefer the traditional standard: a sustaining commitment to a single individual, where the depth and breadth of the couple's constructed culture has had time to become sufficiently intimate and comprehensive to satisfy the search for self-definition and the security of community. The members of

260 *The shape of the modern self*

such a relationship are each other's principal intimate partners and find in their intimacy a majority of what they require. This is an accomplishment of broad-ranging discourse between partners who regard each other as equally credible and who sustain a shared orientation to morality, derivative of their ongoing conversation.

Notes

1 Mead, *Mind, self, and society: from the standpoint of a social behaviorist*, 142.
2 Kihlstrom, Dissociative disorders.
3 Gillig, Dissociative identity disorder: a controversial diagnosis.
4 Hacking, *Rewriting the soul: multiple personality and the sciences of memory.*
5 Goffman, *The presentation of self in everyday life.*
6 For example, Watzlawick et al., *Pragmatics of human communication: a study of interactional patterns, pathologies, and paradoxes.*
7 Laing, *The politics of experience*, 115.
8 See Haley, *Strategies of psychotherapy.*
9 Gold and Gold, *Suspicious minds.*
10 See Goffman, On face-work.
11 Schlenker, Identities, identifications, and relationships.
12 Luckmann, Personal identity as an evolutionary and historical problem.
13 Szymborska, Life while you wait, 169.
14 Wolfe, *Moral freedom: the search for virtue in a world of choice*, 100.
15 Dunkelman, *The vanishing neighbor: the transformation of American community.*
16 Sennett, *The fall of public man: on the social psychology of capitalism.*
17 Berger et al., *The homeless mind: modernization and consciousness.*
18 Lifton, *The protean self: human resilience in an age of fragmentation.*
19 Zurcher, *The mutable self: a self-concept for social change.*
20 Gergen, *The saturated self: dilemmas of identity in contemporary life*, 150.
21 Giddens, *The consequences of modernity*, 150.
22 Sass, *Madness and modernism: insanity in the light of modern art, literature, and thought.*
23 Weil, What do teens learn online today? That identity is a work in progress.
24 Holstein and Gubrium, *The self we live by: narrative identity in a postmodern world*, 222.
25 Hochschild, *The managed heart: commercialization of human feeling.*
26 Gergen, *The saturated self: dilemmas of identity in contemporary life*, 150.
27 Maslow, *Toward a psychology of being.*
28 Bauman, *Liquid times: living in an age of uncertainty.*
29 Kalanithi, My marriage didn't end when I became a widow, n.p.
30 See, for example, Nesdale and Zimmer-Gembeck, Peer rejection in childhood: social groups, rejection sensitivity, and solitude.
31 Forbes et al., Partner bereavement and detection of dementia: a UK-based cohort study using routine health data.
32 See Morris, *The evil hours: a biography of post-traumatic stress disorder.*
33 Stroebe and Stroebe, *Bereavement and health: the psychological and physical consequences of partner loss.*
34 Lewis, *A grief observed*, 47.
35 *Ibid.*, 61.
36 Dunne, *Joan Didion: The center will not hold.*
37 Didion, *The year of magical thinking*, 197–198.

Multi-Me   261

38 Berger and Kellner, Marriage and the construction of reality: an exercise in the microsociology of knowledge, 16.
39 Bonanno, *The other side of sadness: what the new science of bereavement tells us about life after loss.*
40 Chase, Losing my husband – and finding him again through a medium; Smith, *After this: when life is over, where do we go?*
41 Rees, The hallucinations of widowhood.
42 Murray and Holmes, The construction of relationship realities.
43 Freud, *Psychopathology of everyday life.*
44 Hochschild, *The outsourced self: intimate life in market times.*
45 See Druckerman, *Lust in translation: infidelity from Tokyo to Tennessee.*
46 Klaw, *Without sin: the life and death of the Oneida Community.*
47 Trivers, Parental investment and sexual selection.
48 Illouz, *Why love hurts: a sociological explanation.*
49 Berger and Calabrese, Some explorations in initial interaction and beyond: toward a developmental theory of communication.
50 Bauman, *Liquid love: on the frailty of human bonds.*

14 Mini-Me

Wrong ideas about communication, self, and intimacy

> Action is to motion as mind is to brain.
> Kenneth Burke, *The Rhetoric of Religion: Studies in Logology*[1]

Action and motion

As modernity loosened the reins of external authority, the function of intimate discourse gradually shifted from something more like data exchange (which, in the case of marriage, occurred between partners of unequal status) to a dialogue of equals in which the open-ended but sticky nature of symbolic language builds interdependent community of mind. Conversation acquired the potential to function as a kind of social glue gradually bonding partners in a mutually cultivated vision of each other and the larger world. Gradually, talk became the nexus of existential being.

Though the mid-twentieth-century communication philosopher Kenneth Burke demonstrated no awareness of this aspect of the history of social discourse, and he wasn't concerned with the transformations of intimate life that accompanied the shifting status of talk, he was an important pioneer in the question of what it means that minds are built of symbols, and that, consequently, one never knows the world directly, but always through fields of agreed-upon ideas, meanings, values, and presumptions knitted together in interaction with others. For Burke, that we think and speak using symbols conveys freedom and agency: the ability to construct the world as we wish, to lead lives of choice and conscious action, to be the directors of our own experience and responsible for the consequences of our conduct. The alternative, the situation of animals without language whose brains run on signals rather than symbols, is not a life of choice and action, but one of motion, determined by reflex, operant conditioning, brain chemistry, emotional equilibrium, and other factors beyond conscious control.

Like Freud, Mead, and Goffman, Burke's ideas reflected the conditions of America at the time he worked. Had he lived in the seventeenth century, it's not likely he'd have penned a vision of language-as-symbolic-action, because language wasn't as visibly functioning in that way at the time. Similarly, Sartre wrote about existentialism in the mid-twentieth century, but he wouldn't have done so 200 years earlier either, because it wasn't until his

DOI: 10.4324/9781003010234-17

Mini-Me 263

time – which was also Burke's time – that the processes of modernity were visibly loosening meaning, altering the function of conversation, and complicating inner experience in Western societies. The modern world has gradually become a world of communication, meaning making, and reflexivity, but also one in which many have difficulty with the psychological burden that it has created. In the new uncertainty of meaning and increased frequency with which one experiences doubt and the anguish of choice, some retreat into themselves, or into ill-fitting stock identities offered by the mass media, sheltering in conformity, as had become common in America by the mid-twentieth century.[2]

I've referred to aspects of Burke's vision from time to time in the preceding chapters, but now I'm going to move the core of it center stage to use as a fixed point of contrast. This will make it easier to discuss the implications of several current alternative scientific perspectives that are substantially out of sync with the facts of this period of history and its unprecedented freedom of agency: freedom to personalize meaning, to define self in one's own creative terms, to engage with others under the presumption that all are fully capable moral agents. Taking these perspectives into account is not merely an academic exercise: failure to place early twenty-first-century experience in its proper frame is an invitation to mystification and suffering.

There are four currently influential areas in the sciences with discourses that fail to appreciate the issues at play in this era of elevated existential freedom. Each of them promotes a deterministic vision of consciousness, the self, and intimate experience that's out of alignment with the historical record. They misunderstand interpersonal life and so can't account for its contemporary dynamics (which, as we've seen, include elevated rates of relationship disruption, narcissism, solo living, declining trust and empathy, disconnection from community and neighbors, etc.). It's worth taking a close look at these four because understanding results not only from coming to grips with what something is, but also from coming to appreciate how it differs from the alternatives; therefore, in our effort to appreciate the relationships between language, mind, culture, intimacy, and self, these four areas supply useful points of contrast. Review of them provides a look at where one can end up when attempting to account for interpersonal life without adequately comprehending the history of modernity, or the symbolic nature of mind and language. Our four philosophical suspects are evolutionary psychology, meme theory, cognitive science/neuroscience, and medical psychiatry (or, in the terms of three of their critics, Raymond Tallis, Mary Midgley, and Thomas Szasz: "Darwinitis," "phlogiston," "neuromania," and "pseudology").[3] These perspectives (collectively, the "life-as-motion" perspectives) have in common that they're universalist, claiming equal validity across all times and cultures, which is a sure sign of trouble for any theory that has anything to do with language, the self-concept, or intimacy. They also share a facile understanding of communication, regarding discourse not as an active process of mutual influence, but as a mechanical system of signal exchange.

264 *The shape of the modern self*

The belief that conscious thought is beside the point, that motivation is biologically programmed, that the sense of self is an illusion produced in a computer-brain, and that discourse is the kind of information transfer that takes place between machines is incorrect. Broad acceptance of these ideas about interpersonal life leads, without much stretch, to the nightmare world of human – robot friendships and sexual relationships described by enthusiasts as a near-term inevitability,[4] an alluring vision frequently explored in literature and film (*Adventures of the Artificial Woman, Metropolis, Blade Runner, The Stepford Wives, A.I. Artificial Intelligence, Robot and Frank, Her, Ex Machina*, etc.).

Consider the idea that the ultimate basis for your loyalty to your spouse and your investment in your children is not that you believe in them and love them in appreciation of their minds, their morals, their creative spirit, the fields of meaning that you've cultivated together, and your shared history, but rather is biological; that your attraction to your spouse is "chemistry" – based in genetically controlled hormones and neurotransmitters; that your loyalty stems from the presence of the hormone vasopressin in your body and your feelings of care for your children from oxytocin; that you and your spouse aren't responsible for your own choices or behavior; indeed, that even your thoughts are not your own, but are either the direct result of "memes," implanted in you by communication processes in the external culture, or the indirect result of genetic programming. These ideas lie at the heart of the life-as-motion sciences, various ones promoting one or another aspect of this desolate vision.

The contrast with Burke could scarcely be stronger, as can be seen in his "Definition of Man," which summarizes the key ideas in his perspective.[5] According to Burke, the human being is:

> *the symbol-using (symbol-making, symbol-misusing) animal*
> *inventor of the negative (or moralized by the negative)*
> *separated from his natural condition by instruments of his own making*
> *goaded by the sense of hierarchy (or moved by the sense of order)*
> *and rotten with perfection.*

Except for the last clause, we've visited all of these ideas in previous chapters.

Symbol-using means social and connected in meaning

Consistent with our central thesis, Burke's first point is that humans communicate, not with signals, but with symbols whose meanings are dynamic and determined in use (in "conventional relation," recall from Chapter 3). To be precise, the part that constitutes our humanity communicates with symbols; the animal part runs on signals. When the doctor taps your knee with her mallet, the reaction is not an interpreted matter subject to cultural variation and historical influence. It's a reflex (in fact, it's that master metaphor for mindlessness: the "knee jerk reaction"). The communication between the brain and the muscles of the leg is accomplished using signals that travel through the central nervous system. But the mind is a symbol-using organ. And so we're more or less continually making what we will of each other and the events around us. But not on our own: we do this together.

Symbols are *shared* elements of meaning. Words, sounds, or visual elements whose meanings you construct on your own but do not successfully share and establish in the consciousness of others have no currency or staying power. In fact, the only way you can understand a word that you make up on your own is in terms of conventional language, the meanings of which *are* socially negotiated.[6] And so, as we acquire language, we become linked, dependent on each other to confirm and sustain our idiosyncratic interpretations of ourselves and the world. In this way, symbols extend our minds beyond our own bodies, joining them to the minds of others in interdependent structures of socially agreed-upon meaning.

The signal is impersonal and indiscriminate: the electrical impulse that runs from your brain to your knee could accomplish the same result running in someone else's brain or knee. But the symbol is inherently connective and relational: you can't have a meaning by yourself. Language (and other visual and audible symbols such as flags, logos, styles of dress, guitar phrases, etc.) functions as an externalized lattice of meanings describing points at which your mind and the minds of particular other people intersect. It's likely that your understanding of "family" is saturated with a considerable amount of personal meaning and associated in particular ways and strengths with specific other feelings and concepts that you've shared with certain other people. Part of your conceptual-emotional map for the word "family" is shared uniquely with other members of your family of origin, certain aspects perhaps with just one specific member, and other aspects with other subsets of people – some may be shared with everyone. Other links of your meaning map for family are shared with the members of other groups with whom you've joined and had family experiences. Others derive from your education, the media, or other cultural experiences. Without ongoing engagement with those who co-authored our meaningful symbols and their interconnections (including, perhaps, by talking over old times with family, friends and colleagues, or by re-experiencing influential books or film), particular understandings may become vague and fade.

Without continuing social interaction, the mind loses its ability to hold on to idiosyncratic structures of meaning, memory blurs, and, in the extreme, our ability to make sense of the world frays. Helen Keller described her mental world before language as akin to drifting at sea enclosed in a thick bank of fog, without any sense of orientation.[7] Holding that in mind, as a thought experiment, imagine running your life backwards so that, as you regress in age, with each year you give up all the meaning that you had acquired that year: the new words, nuances, stories, distinctions, theories, concepts, and insights gradually peel away and are gone. With each year, you recede past people you met who introduced you to new understandings, experiences, and vocabulary. All of these, too, fall away as you regress into times before you met these people. You notice that, by age 10, there are aspects of life you can no longer describe

266 *The shape of the modern self*

because you no longer have the concepts. By about age 6, you're losing core language. By age 2, you're drifting, like Helen Keller, in a dense fog of undifferentiated sensation and emotion. We have no memory of this because, as toddlers, we have such limited command of language. Without language, much of experience is undifferentiable, unclassifiable, and inexpressible, and, recalling from Chapter 9 Ludwig Wittgenstein's assertion that, "The words with which I express my memory are my memory," that which can't be expressed in language can't be retained as memory, which is why we can't remember our pre-linguistic experience as infants. Of course, we aren't toddlers and we have full use of language, but still, as adults, if we can't engage each other to refresh and reconfirm our particular abstractions, distinctions, and their interconnections into accounts and stories – our meanings – there's a tendency for them to decay and for memory to distort and fade.

Isolation and the social connectome

It's well known that social isolation carries significant risk to health,[8] but isolation also carries the potential to erode meaning, and, if the isolation involves lengthy separation from significant social partners, it has the potential to erode core meanings related to our personhood. The circumstances of modernity – the press of anonymous social relations in the city, the struggle to manage the competing demands of widely dispersed social relationships and roles, the anxieties that accompany rapid change and economic instability, and so on – promote social withdrawal. Inward focus and solitude can provide relief from the stress and uncertainty of the era, and so, today, people withdraw in many ways, including escape into work, sports, computer games and media experiences, online worlds, music, alcohol, meditation, and so on. (As this goes to press, there's palpable excitement over two new of paths of escape from the psychological difficulties of modernity: one route involves emerging home-use virtual reality technologies that promise a new means to exit complicated lives in favor of simulated three-dimensional worlds that include visceral sensation. The other involves liberalized use of psychedelics.)[9]

American culture celebrates the self-sufficient individual, mythically epitomized in philosopher Henry David Thoreau's retreat in 1845 to a period of solitude, simplicity, and contemplation in his determination to live "deliberately," confronting "only the essential facts of life" in his rustic cabin at Walden Pond. So goes the story. In fact, Thoreau's cabin was less than 2 miles from the town of Concord, Massachusetts, and he received many visitors, including his mother, who brought things to eat, and he often walked to town to see family and friends and drink at the local pubs.[10] So much for the mythical rewards of a life of deliberate solitude.

Intimate partners may benefit by taking time apart from each other, but ongoing disruption of normal communication erodes the basis of a relationship in the same way that extreme social isolation of the elderly is visibly destructive of self-identity. The partner or partners who previously confirmed your sense of self and world are gone, and, in their absence, meaning that you established together may begin to fray. The wife whose husband is afflicted with progressive memory loss must not only watch his appreciation of important aspects of their shared world fade, but to a degree these meanings will erode for her too as they are no longer refreshed in use and become unconfirmable.

As in sensory deprivation experiments performed in university psych labs in the mid-twentieth century, which demonstrated that sensory depletion can lead to madness, the long-term solitary confinement of prisoners is a literally dehumanizing form of punishment: "Without the concrete experience of other [people] oriented toward common objects in a shared world, my own experience of the boundaries of those perceptual objects begins to waver,"[11] leading in some cases to vivid hallucinations and "a living death." This does not result merely from the torment of having one's freedom limited or from sensory deprivation by itself. It comes about as we lose contact with others whose perspectives provide a basis of confirmation for the perception of our own meaningful existence in the world. We know ourselves and our world in relation to others and their reactions to us and the world. How well we understand this when, camping in a tent in the wilderness forest in the blackness at midnight, we anxiously turn to each other and, whispering carefully, discuss what to make of that fluttering, rustling sound. Was it the sound of snapping twigs? Was that a snort? Could it have been approaching paws? Are we in danger? We work this out together, offering alternatives and eventually establishing a shared point of view. But we don't do this just when we camp out. This process is continuous in conversation: we do this as we discuss items from the news, or talk about our neighbors and friends, or what happened at work, or what to make of that change in our body, or our children, and on and on. Meaning – what we make of ourselves and the world around us – is created socially, as George Herbert Mead made clear. The contents of our minds result from the use of symbols whose meanings are established and sustained *interpersonally*, and more so now in the turbulence and uncertainty of modernity where meaning is to a greater extent up for grabs than in any other historical period.

In contrast to this, the neuroscientist Sebastian Seung has recently described progress in the appreciation of the way in which the brain's neurons intercommunicate through particular routes and pathways. He coined the term "connectome" to describe the brain's huge route map of such connections.[12] According to this account, every memory we have (and each memory's map of associated memories) is represented in the propensity of the brain to transmit signals through one patterned route of connected neurons over another. There are some 100 billion neurons in the adult brain, each sporting between 1,000 and 10,000 synaptic connections, and so the brain contains many trillions of neuronal pathways.[13] This is the connectome.

Seung believes that, if science had the skill to surgically alter aspects of the brain's connectome, this would be reflected in what we think. Neuroscientists see support of this in the action of hallucinogenic drugs, which are believed to have the effect of temporarily rearranging neural pathways, resulting in visions

268   *The shape of the modern self*

and altered states of consciousness as the brain's signaling system operates outside of its normal route map. And – no surprise to anyone who has tried to learn a musical instrument – there's evidence that deliberately practiced behavior can physically increase the strength of particular neural pathways, perhaps eventually allowing a virtuoso performance of *The Flight of the Bumblebee* from memory.

This is an interesting perspective, but it's important to appreciate that the connectome is not an adequate model of the mind. It is a model of memory and reflex that applies equally well to non-social and social organisms. It's a model of the material brain, which operates on neural signals. But the conscious mind is built of fields of symbols the meanings of which are established and sustained socially. This makes it possible to understand how a virtuoso musician can stand onstage at Carnegie Hall and perform *The Flight of the Bumblebee* from memory, all the while mentally rehashing aspects of her role in the back and forth of last night's tiff with her lover. If she's sufficiently well practiced, the musical performance may be accomplished by rote or reflex, leaving the mind free to contemplate what it will. Because the connectome is a model of reflex, it can't account for the social nature of meaning or for our intentionality, our choice making and moral agency, all of which lie at the core of conscious life. Animals too have connectomes and are capable of all sorts of rote performances, but, without language, they have no capacity for abstract and creative thought, no narrative construction of self, no mutual persuasion or moral discrimination; in short, they have no possibility of a life of choice and action.

However, taking the symbolic nature of interpersonal communication seriously, the connectome's idea of pathways of meaning is useful as a metaphor. The unique meanings that make us who we are don't originate in the neural pathways of the brain, though they may be inscribed there; they originate in the *social* pathways of our life, where intentionality and conscious choice are responsible for the patterns of discourse and human association in which we engage to make meaning and reconfirm it. The meanings that are the substance of thought are the outcome of choice making regarding the symbols and social situations we expose ourselves to – the vocabulary of concepts that we master, and the relationships we form and attend to, which sustain those symbols and the particular meanings that we create for them with our partners (this understanding is implicit in every parent's concern that their children select their friends carefully). The center of this decision making is located in our active symbol-processing mind, not in the signaling neural fibers of the material brain. The death of the body shuts down every neural connection of the brain, but, at least for as long as we're remembered, we live on in the minds of our significant social partners, influencing their thinking because, to an important degree, we *are* their thinking. Douglas Hofstadter stands out among others in the cognitive science/neuroscience field in his conceptualization of the self as arising in interpersonal interaction in a fashion sympathetic to the ideas explored in this book. He was brought to that position in significant degree as a result of the tragic, sudden loss of his wife, which sensitized him to many aspects of the process. He provides a vividly poignant account of the extent to which he felt he and his wife had fused into one consciousness, and how her values and hopes had not died when her body died but "lived on very determinedly in my brain."[14] The philosopher Derek Parfit anticipated this type of fusion of selves in marital partners in his groundbreaking paper on the nature of personal identity. For Parfit, it is sensible to speak of the self as distributed across social partners.[15] Self lives on, certainly, in one's most meaningful relationships.

Sebastian Seung suggests that the neuroscientist's electron microscope could be the right tool for tracing the neural patterns of the material brain's connectome, but the right tool for tracing the patterns of conscious thought and the sources of the meaning we make of the world is not the electron microscope, it's the sociogram: the social scientist's map of who we talk to and how frequently and how expansively (extended to include what we read and watch).

Historically, there's been a lively, ongoing current of debate about the relationships between mind, self, soul, and body that extends to the roots of Western philosophy. For all this, it's very odd to read today of the notion that the material brain somehow constitutes the conscious mind, such that some scientists have the expectation that, eventually, people will be able to achieve immortality by copying and preserving the neural patterns of the brain, so that, as the body wears out, they will be able to download their neural patterns into new bodies, or perhaps into machines, and awake to continue their sense of being. The belief that the self is inscribed in the electrical flows of the material brain is analogous to the idea that you can see a broken heart with an echocardiogram.

Mechanism and life as motion

The idea of the symbol is lost in the mechanistic vision of the life-as-motion sciences. This is obviously so in the case of neuroscience, which views the brain as a kind of signal-processing computer that creates the mind by accident, but also in evolutionary psychology, meme theory, and post-1980s medical psychiatry. So it might be useful at this point to briefly review what mechanism is about and what consequences follow if we make the error of thinking of human beings as machines.

Philosopher Steven Pepper argued that the historical gamut of approaches for understanding ourselves and the world sort into a set of four core conceptions, among which is mechanism.[16] The root metaphor of mechanism is captured by the mechanical clock and by the lever. The action of one component of the machine (a cogwheel in the clock or, in the lever, a board resting on a fulcrum) activates another component through a transfer of energy. While the idea of energy transfer is clear in the case of cogs, gears, springs, and levers (and cleverly illustrated in Rube Goldberg cartoons), it may also be that they occur through other means – for example, through signals transferred from one component to another by changes in electrical or chemical fields (as occurs

270   *The shape of the modern self*

between neurons in the brain) or in the detection of a change in temperature, sound, pressure, luminance, motion, weight, pattern, and so on. Digital computers are mechanical devices that operate in this way. Most of them have power switches and keyboards, but some have no traditionally mechanical moving parts at all, so that all of their activity is determined through other types of signals. Still, the computer is a mechanical thing, which means that its mode of communication is signal-driven, not symbol-driven, and so its behaviors (outputs) are completely determined by internal and external stimuli (inputs). There is no possibility of meaning making in a determinate mechanical system.

In exceedingly complex mechanical systems, signal-based mechanisms of feedback and control can provide the appearance of intelligent and purposive behavior.[17] A recent exhibit at New York City's National Museum of Mathematics named *Robot Swarm* featured two dozen small, illuminated crab-like robots that move under a glass floor, reacting to their perception of the location of the people on the floor above them. In one condition, the herd of little robots appear to run away as they are approached overhead; in another, they spin in whatever direction the viewer turns; and, in another, they move to optimize their distance from each other. The behavior of the swarm is interactive and interdependent and appears purposive, but it is governed by mathematical rules and communication signals broadcast wirelessly to and from each of the robots. Their appearance of conscious intelligence is intriguing, but the robot swarm is a mindless machine.

The natural world may also seem to exhibit intelligence and purpose. Like our ancestors, we may be tempted to think of the weather as a conscious agency that becalms the ships of arrogant sailors and punishes the unworthy with droughts, floods, and tornadoes. However, today, most understand that weather phenomena result from mechanical transfers of energy, in principle reducible to a set of mathematical functions. Modern science gradually stripped Mother Nature of her conscious agency as her habits became increasingly well known, and the probabilities of her behavior mathematically deducible with greater precision. Conceptualized in this way, nature no longer has free choice and so can no longer be invoked as a divine or moral force. To do so today sounds romantic, primitive, or crazy (as in the claim that Hurricane Katrina's destruction of New Orleans was nature's retribution for the city's culture of liberal sexuality).

This is an instance of the familiar story of science displacing mysticism and religious belief. In the case of weather prediction, most would think this a good thing. Air travel is uncertain enough: who would get on a plane under the presumption that safe passage through bad weather was reserved for the worthy? Having transformed Mother Nature from a conscious moral instrument into a mindless, amoral machine, in certain corners of science where theories bear on communication, self, and intimacy, scientists have been advocating ideas the effect of which would do the same to the rest of us, not only demoting Mother Nature to the status of a machine, but your mother too. The connecting vision of the life-as-motion sciences is that the human is a kind of signal-processing biological machine, essentially monadic and self-contained, yet, like the *Robot Swarm*, capable of intricate and complexly coordinated behavior. Richard Dawkins, a leading figure in both evolutionary psychology and meme theory, put it this way: "We are survival machines – robot vehicles blindly programmed to preserve the selfish molecules known as genes."[18]

Darwinitis

This vision is center stage in evolutionary psychology's account of male – female intimate relationships, where attraction is viewed as a gene-driven process that causes people to engage in patterns of behavior that maximize reproductive success, passing along copies of DNA through their children. Here, ordinary conversation is understood to be driven by biological prerequisites established in the mists of evolutionary history. For example, the claim has been made that the conversation of adult males has been shaped by evolution to be more self-promotional than the conversation of females, and this serves the purpose of attracting mates by putting reproductively relevant accomplishments and advantages on display for choosy females to evaluate.[19] It's thought that the female is programmed to be choosy because she can bring considerably fewer offspring into the world than a male, and so, with more at stake in the act of reproduction, females may be genetically predisposed to take steps to equalize their partner's investment before embarking on a reproductive program with him. Those who don't may be victimized by under-committed males who reproduce with them and then run off to reproduce elsewhere. Should that happen, the abandoned woman is more likely to exhaust her limited resources in the care of the philanderer's child and, thus, less likely to reproduce again, and so, the story goes, genes for female choosiness will tend to proliferate in the gene pool, while males are driven to engage in acts that advertise the resources that they bring to the table as tokens of their investment in reproduction. This is the "standard narrative" of evolutionary psychology.[20]

However, nature displays an enormous variety of animal and insect mating practices, ranging from beetles that eat their mates to fish that simply spew their eggs and sperm into the water indiscriminately.[21] And, as regards human mating and the standard narrative, consider the practice of multiple accumulative fertilization of some South American societies, in which cultural beliefs hold that, once pregnant, a woman can bestow additional benefits on her child by continuing to have intercourse with other men, the sperm from each bestowing additional qualities on the developing fetus.[22] So the idea that there is a kind of genetic necessity to human patterns of mating behavior is not so clear. Indeed, the notion that partners might take time to get to know each other or seek evidence of commitment prior to having children has no need of biological science for explanation. America's grandmothers have been recommending as much since the inauguration of free-choice mate selection in the late eighteenth century.

The most commonly referenced sources for the standard narrative are Richard Dawkins's selfish gene theory[23] and Robert Trivers's theory of parental

272 *The shape of the modern self*

investment.[24] Together, they've been used by evolutionary psychologists to promote a vision of the human as a genetically programmed reproduction machine whose communication practices, functioning as signal systems, operate in the service of genetic self-interest. For evolutionary psychology, there's no point to human intimacy beyond reproduction and the successful rearing of children who pass along parents' DNA. Attraction is based on the mutual perception that each partner represents the best opportunity possible as regards fecundity and reproductive fitness. However, as one might imagine, there's considerable dissent over this perspective, and not only from humanists, philosophers, and social scientists. Yale ornithologist Richard Prum believes that the perspective is flatly wrong and, in fact, ignores Darwin's own ideas.[25] According to evolutionary theorist Niles Eldridge, humans

> are so atypical, so fundamentally *not* subject to the biological rules that still guide the lives of all other species that to reduce our existence in this manner, to see ourselves as mere shells being marched around by our inner genes, is not just bad biology. It verges on being a willfully stupid joke or, even worse, a malevolent political doctrine.[26]

As for Eldridge's comment about lame humor, consider the conceptualization of the function of communication in a dating situation offered by two evolutionary psychologists in their recent book *Mating Intelligence Unleashed*: "Under the mating intelligence framework, opening gambits can be conceptualized as a form of courtship display that signals various traits."[27] The authors follow this with a discussion of pick-up lines that men use to display their reproductively useful attributes. Here's one of their examples of a pick-up line that reveals a man's wealth and, hence, his ability to materially match the female's initially greater biological level of investment in reproduction: "Hi, my name's William, I'm one of the owners here, would you like to dance?" And, for a pick-up line that reveals potential reproductive potency: "Well, hey there, I may not be Fred Flintstone, but I bet I can make your Bed Rock!" Following this is a discussion of the way in which conversation in a dating environment functions as a code of "honest signals" whose purpose is similar to that of the enormous, sweeping, but otherwise useless and genetically costly, tail feathers of the male great argus pheasant – a way of demonstrating reproductive fitness to choosy females and, in general, sorting through the probabilities of reproductive success.

For these authors, the brain is an array of switches, something like the gates, posts, bumpers, and baskets of a pinball machine. Conversation is a matter of shooting the right messages through the brain's receivers to stimulate the target response. The bumpers and other obstacles are constituted of psychology's mid-twentieth-century catalog of proposed personality components, such as IQ, introversion/extraversion, attachment style, psychoticism, self-esteem, internal/external locus of control, and so on. The intelligence in "mating intelligence" is knowing your target well enough to be able to spin your courtship

Mini-Me 273

message in the way that will have the desired impact on a person of the personality configuration with whom you're conversing. To be clear, in this vision, "conversing" means engaging in verbal and nonverbal exchanges whose clandestine purpose is to signal your interest in acts of sexual reproduction motivated by the selfish and tyrannical demands of your genes that you get off your duff and get them propagated. Obviously, overt and covert interest in sex is at play in a great deal of human social behavior. But the idea that social motives are genetically driven and aimed at reproduction of DNA, that communication behavior is more under the influence of biology than consciously agentic, is egregiously reductive, akin to asserting that World War II was a test of species fitness, or dining at Manhattan's Four Seasons is about acquiring protein.

Eldredge raised the possibility of evolutionary psychology representing a "malevolent political doctrine." The basis for this is the tendency of advocates to grab onto current normative social practices and then, using chains of retrospective logical analysis, proclaim them to be the genetically based outcome of evolution. In this way, the perspective often seems to its critics to serve as a rationale for status quo cultural practices, including many that are politically fraught. Commonly, the claim is made that some quotidian item of social behavior originated as a genetically controlled adaptive response to the social or material environment affecting our hominid ancestors. In this sort of retrodictive science, it's almost impossible to separate bias from fact.

According to anthropologist Helen Fisher, who is a leading proponent of this perspective and often reasons this way, even occupational choices are genetically programmed, and love is a mindless, universal, genetically triggered evolutionary strategy that occurs in all animals, producing pairs who are more likely to bring offspring to the point that they can survive on their own.[28] The point at which this happens in a human relationship, according to Fisher, is at about 4 years, which she reasons is the time at which the genetically controlled chemicals that are responsible for intimate bonds begin to fade, leaving relationships at risk of dissolution and divorce. David Buss, another prominent voice in the application of evolutionary psychology to intimate relationships, believes that humans are programmed by evolution to leave a deficient partner because "staying with a bad mate does not help a person successfully pass on their genes."[29]

As one might imagine, cultural and historical variability challenges the ideas of evolutionary psychology. Is human heterosexual intimacy primarily about sexual reproduction? It's hard to see it that way. Innovations in fertility control have been actively pursued throughout recorded history. Books providing information on the subject were in circulation in the U.S. since at least the nineteenth century.[30] The invention of the birth control pill in the mid-twentieth century ushered in massively positive changes in the quality of life for women and the ability of husbands and wives to interact on equal terms. And, contrary to the view of human sexuality as driven by a genetic imperative to reproduce one's DNA as often as one can, provided adequate possibility of survival, the number of children born to couples has recently

274 *The shape of the modern self*

dropped below replacement level in several of the world's most affluent societies,[31] indicating a complex and possibly inverse relationship between couples' material resources and their motivation to reproduce and rear children. In addition, the foundational premises of the "standard narrative" – that evolution shaped males to be motivated to pursue strategies of prolific reproduction – turn out to be wrong. Mathematically, the surest strategy for obtaining the greatest number of offspring is continuing reproduction with the same partner.[32] Buss's idea that patterns of couple dissolution are driven by genetics is difficult to reconcile with the historical record of the overwhelming influences of factors such as law, urbanization, economics, and religion on patterns of divorce. The Old Order Amish have pretty much the same genetics as everyone else, but a divorce rate of zero. Fisher's idea that the bond that human parents share is of a kind with the bonds shared by mating ducks is similarly difficult to reconcile with all that we know about the history of modernity and the evolution of the psychodynamic mind and its influences on perception and attraction. As regards the marital bond, historians attest that, for most of time, its basis has been economic alliance[33] and began with the advent of agricultural society some 10,000 years ago, which reorganized human patterns of mating to accommodate new ideas about property and its inheritance.[34] To be sure, the intimate relationship has an important sexual aspect in many cases, but not in all cases, and the reproductive function of sex figures in only a minuscule proportion of sexual encounters. Just as obviously, intimacy need not be heterosexual.

What *is* so consequential to intimacy is social equality, which is a matter of law, prejudice, and normative belief – mind and culture, not genes. Ironically, if the evolutionary psychology account of intimacy has had any actual influence, it has most likely been to reinforce ideas of gender inequality, which, as we have seen, undermines the basis for actual intimacy. The cover art for *Mating Intelligence Unleashed*, published by a leading academic press, depicts a curvaceous young woman preening in front of five male students who are clearly enraptured with her appearance. The men have books. The woman doesn't.

There is, in fact, practically no aspect of interpersonal behavior that is not culturally and historically specific. As with all other animals, evolution has been responsible for the form of our bodies, but, unlike any other animal, humans broke free of nature with the invention of language and culture. We are, as Burke put it, separated from our natural condition by instruments of our own making: symbols. Genetically controlled impulses drive the sensation of hunger and the urge to eat. No doubt they act in the case of sexual desire as well. But how we satisfy our appetites – in what rhythms, under what circumstances, in what proportion, with what meaning and significance, and with what variety of partners – are questions that lead to the analysis of language, mind, identity, and culture, to the realm of consciously motivated symbolic action. Richard Dawkins to the contrary, we may be the vehicles of genes, but, because we are symbol users, we are no longer their robot slaves.

Phlogiston

Let us now turn to a brief consideration of meme theory, first proposed by Dawkins to deal with the problems that human mind and culture pose for the idea of genetic evolution as a universal account for the behavior of all life forms. If, as it seems, so much of human behavior is actually accountable in terms of our conscious mind, our will, and our culture, the role of evolution in the explanation of human behavior, while not completely sidelined, is certainly diminished. As we've seen, evolutionary psychology's idea that much of what we do and say to each other is actually held over from genetic programming is unconvincing. Whatever variability in human behavior can be traced back to evolution is dwarfed by the degree of influence of historical/cultural context and our own conscious agency. This has created theoretical difficulties for those who seek a universal account of life that fits it all into a common program. Enter the meme.

The idea of meme theory is to identify a unit of culture that is analogous to the gene insofar as these cultural units, like genes, will be selected for or extinguished depending on the degree to which they confer survival benefits on the minds they inhabit. Dawkins's original examples include tunes, catchphrases, clothing fashions, and the idea of God. He proposed that human culture is reducible to packets of meaning that function like viruses, jumping from brain to brain, infecting and controlling our thoughts. He quotes N. K. Humphrey: "When you plant a fertile meme in my mind you literally parasitize my brain, turning it into a vehicle for the meme's propagation in just the way that a virus may parasitize the genetic mechanism of a host cell."[35] The meme idea first appeared in a short final chapter to Dawkins's (1976) *The Selfish Gene*, as a speculative extension of the theory of evolution to deal with the problem of human mind and culture.

According to Dawkins, memes are spread by imitation. We observe and copy, and so the meme proliferates in the population. Susan Blackmore argues that language evolved in order to make meme transmission more efficient and effective. According to her, in the same way that, when we sneeze, we transmit viruses, when we speak, we transmit memes. And, when we listen, we are contaminated by them. Considering her meme theory of language against an account based on evolutionary psychology, Blackmore believes people talk not because it confers survival advantage to our DNA (recall those cringy pick-up lines that evolutionary psychologists believe function as signals of our reproductive viability), but rather, "the reason we talk so much is . . . to spread our memes."[36] She argues that the human brain evolved its large capacity under the control of memes. The more memes a brain can store, the more the individual is likely to thrive, passing along both genes for large brains and memes for culture. Cognitive scientist and philosopher Daniel Dennett has argued that the human mind is nothing but memes, and the self-concept, therefore, is an illusion: a meme that is a product of your memes.[37]

276 *The shape of the modern self*

The idea of the meme as an element of culture that is passed along has entered everyday speech, to a limited degree becoming what it describes. On the street, "meme" loses its connection with particular theories of evolution, language, and mind and functions like a synonym for "fad" that's been dressed up in a lab coat, and, in a recent twist, "meme" has also come to refer to digital pictures that are sent around the internet, each picture inscribed with text intended to demonstrate the sender's wit. "Fad" is similarly scientized in saying that something has "gone viral."

But Dawkins, Blackmore, Dennett, and other memists mean something more radical in their understanding of the meme. They believe the memetic elements of culture literally control the human mind. Here is the strange upside-down quality to the meme idea. Most people would think it very odd if someone suggested that an orchestra was a chord's way of being reproduced, or a driver was a car's way of moving around, or, as per Dennett, a scholar was a library's way of reproducing itself, but that's meme theory. Meme theory proposes a mechanical conception of human communication running merely as a process of imitation, as signal reception and reproduction – as we'll see shortly, the monkey-see-monkey-do world of mirror neurons. The meme perspective asserts that people pursue the ideas, values, and life programs that they do not because they decide to, but because their brains are invaded by virus-like agents that take over and run them around.

Where do ideas like this come from? Raymond Tallis believes that meme theory has become important to those who think that evolution operates at the level of the gene, and that gene selection is the process responsible for human evolution.[38] The trouble is that evolution at the level of the gene is extremely slow, whereas human evolution, driven by cultural change, has been exceptionally fast. Thus, for the selfish gene idea itself to survive as an account of human behavior, it's required the invention of a complementary replicator that operates on culture. Tallis regards meme theory as a futile attempt at "filling in the ditch" that separates the evolution of other life forms from the human situation.[39]

Meme theory supplies a handy example of the "rotten with perfection" clause of Burke's definition, in which he speaks to the human tendency to become committed to the implications of ideas, sometimes blinded to where that may lead. Burke believed that "there is a kind of 'terministic compulsion'"[40] to carry out the implications of one's ideas and rhetoric, perhaps even to one's own destruction. Most of us are familiar with "ideology" carrying people along in this way. This is that notion stated more generally: after strongly espousing a program of belief and publicly committing to it, it may be extremely difficult to back away or offer qualification, even when that leads straight off a cliff.[41]

Philosopher Mary Midgley believed that the idea of memetic evolution benefits from a tendency to associate atomistic explanation with understanding and truth. To be sure, a simple theory describing the relations between a few clearly differentiated concepts makes for a more easily comprehensible story and clear directions for research (students of science know this as "Occam's

Razor" – the idea that, given choice between two theories that account for the same thing, most of the time the simpler theory is preferred over the more complicated one). But neither mind nor culture divide sensibly into discrete building blocks, and so, according to Midgley, meme theory "is an excellent illustration of the mess that tends to result when models drawn from the physical sciences are drafted in without good reason to explain human behavior."[42] Midgley compares the meme idea to the mistaken eighteenth-century notion of "phlogiston," a substance then thought to be released as a material burns. But probably a more apt comparison is to animal magnetism, the eighteenth-century belief we visited in Chapter 10 that held that one person could influence another by passing their hands over the magnetic fields of the body. Animal magnetism, phlogiston, and the meme are all superfluous concepts that resulted from incorrect understanding of the processes they were coined to explain. As Midgley further points out, an additionally baffling aspect of meme theory is that, by the time it was originated in the 1970s, the social sciences had honed methods for understanding social influence for decades. In the humanities, the roots of the study of social influence extend right the way back to Aristotle's publication of *The Rhetoric* in the fourth century BCE. It's not as if scholars didn't already possess sophisticated theories for conceptualizing persuasion and social influence and refined methodologies for their study. But one might never guess that from the biologists and their theory of the meme.

Mirror neuromania

In light of meme theory, it's important now to mention the discovery of the mirror neuron. The relatively recent identification of this brain mechanism has caused considerable excitement. Some view the mirror neuron as providing a kind of built-in capacity for social imitation that chains up to constitute a biological basis for empathy.[43] Others regard the mirror neuron as no less than the basic engine of all human civilization and cultural evolution.[44] And, indeed, the mirror neuron has been implicated in a sweep of phenomena including lip reading, phantom limbs, obesity, mass hysteria, the contagion of the yawn and laughter, emotional recognition in the face, sexual orientation, stuttering, business leadership, and self-awareness in dolphins.[45]

The mirror neuron was discovered at the beginning of the 1990s at the University of Parma. There, researchers studying hand movement in monkeys noticed a set of neurons that became active both when the monkey engaged in an action itself as well as when the monkey observed another monkey (or a human) engaging in the same action.[46] Monkey A observes Monkey B reach for a raisin, and brain scans indicate that that registers neurologically in A in the same way that it does in B. This seems to provide a biological basis for some type of cognitive and emotional synchrony, which may play a role in the imitative learning of animals without language, including preverbal infants. Before language forms, infants have already engaged for months in increasingly complex interpersonal exchange and coordination with their caregivers.

278　*The shape of the modern self*

With nearly 2 years of practice in interpersonal coordination, language's conceptual structures and its apparatus for rich subjective interconnection may be readily overlaid on a brain/mind in which behavioral synchronization, emotional resonance, and imitative sociality are already well established.[47]

That sounds good. However, the role of mirror neurons in human cognitive development and intersubjectivity hasn't been established beyond controversy,[48] and the relevance of this biological mechanism to symbolic interconnection in the mental process of adult humans seems likely to be remote. Moreover, the frequent suggestion that mirror neurons represent a basis for the kind of intelligent, nuanced, deliberately conscious consideration and insight into the cognitive and emotional experience of someone else that we think of when we speak of empathy as a key interpersonal skill is egregiously reductive,[49] at its worst suggesting that, if your spouse fails to appreciate your point of view, the problem is in her material brain – in her "monkey-see-monkey-do" circuits – rather than in anything she could and should do something about.

There's quite a gap between one monkey having a synchronous neural reaction in the brain while watching another monkey grasp a raisin and a wife reflecting on the way in which her husband might feel about the loss of his job, and how that might ramify throughout his meaningful construction of self and world, his plans for the future, his emotions and moral commitments, and so on. And, as a mechanism for the transmission of cultural memes, the mirror neuron makes the idea of the meme even more unlikely. The notion that Shakespeare's Sonnet 116 ("Let me not to the marriage of true minds admit impediments") can be traced back to the mechanism of memes and mirror neurons involves a chain of causality that's not just thin, it is invisible. Taken for more than what the mirror neuron actually is – a simple mechanism for imitation in lower animals – this line of theory sidelines what makes us who we are. Lots of animals have mirror neurons, but not language. And, without language, they can't have empathy, art, intellectual accomplishment, heroism, or morality in any sense relevant to the discussion of the normal human experience.

Inventor of the negative means actively agentic

Now to burrow a little more deeply into the diminished moral universe of the life-as-motion sciences. It should be apparent that it's difficult to conceptualize a basis for morality in a biologically determined world in which the self-concept and free will are illusions, but some attempt this by arguing that behavior that might look like it was morally motivated may actually be under genetic control, selected by evolution, and coded into the neural structures of the human brain (see, for example, Patricia Churchland,[50] a neuro-philosopher who Raymond Tallis has crowned "the Queen of Neuromania").[51] In such a view, morality is more a matter of genes than conscious choice. For example, behavior that appears altruistic, in that it confers advantage to the group while being costly to the individual, might be bred in because it favors the survival of others with similar genes (close relatives especially).

Pete, the sentinel prairie dog who alerts his colony to the presence of a threatening predator, increases the odds of survival of his relatives in the colony at his own expense because he's more likely to be noticed and attacked by the predator. However, there's nothing morally laudable about Pete's behavior because he didn't agree to take on the sentinel function as a result of conscious deliberation: Pete's life is under genetic control. And his behavior isn't self-sacrificing because prairie dogs don't have selves to sacrifice. Without language, which confers mind, free will, the self-concept, and morality, behavior is neither good nor bad; it just is. As Burke argued, in a world without language, there's no way to conceptualize alternatives, and so there's no confrontation with questions of right and wrong, and no basis for praising right decisions or condemning wrong ones. This is what he meant in saying that we are the "inventor of the negative" *and moralized by it*. Because of language, we can imagine the consequences of doing X and of not doing X. Questions of morality and social responsibility stem from this capability to think through alternative futures and freely choose between them.

To be moral requires mind, free choice, and self-control, and they only exist because of language. But the life-as-motion scientists clamor to convince us that the brain makes our decisions for us before our mind is conscious of them,[52] that our awareness of self is a peculiar illusion created by the physical brain, and our sense of possibility in the world reduces to questions of what behavior confers the best advantage to our DNA and which memes have infected us. This vision negates the possibility of morality because it leaves no conscious self that is responsible for anything much beyond post game analysis.

In a court of law, diminished mental capacity is a legal defense that can make it possible to get away with quite a bit, and, clearly, diminished mental capacity is what's being dealt out by the life-as-motion sciences. Among them, the topper award must surely go to medical psychiatry where, having come to believe in the neuroscience idea that the character of mental experience is largely a matter of chemical balance and genetics, with increasing frequency, medical psychiatrists don't bother to try to convince you your mind is beside the point – they simply drug it until it is. Compared with medical psychiatry, which has extensive social and cultural influence and, through the prescription pad, immediate impacts on interpersonal experience, evolutionary psychology and meme theory are relatively harmless academic perspectives. On the other hand, here in the twenty-first century, it's very likely that each of us is routinely in contact with (working or socializing with, dating, married to, parenting, or related to) people whose minds, emotions, and interpersonal experiences are under the influence of prescription psychoactive drugs.

Pseudology: the medicalization of normal interpersonal experience

The psychotherapy industry began to coalesce into its current form not much before the mid-nineteenth century, by which time the juggernaut of modernity

280 *The shape of the modern self*

was proceeding at full steam. Around that time, new "nervous conditions," particularly neurasthenia in men (recall "NewYorkitis" from Chapter 6) and hysteria in women, were appearing with increasing frequency, and, in part, modern psychotherapy grew out of efforts to conceptualize and treat them. In a relatively short span of time, the therapy industry became huge, diverse, and influential in interpersonal life in both formal/public as well as private/intimate contexts. Psychological, psychoanalytic, and psychiatric concepts have pervaded life in the modern era, reshaping the common understanding of self and other and promoting standards for interpersonal conduct in the workplace, the school, and the home.

Illouz traces the beginning of these changes to Freud's lectures at Clark University in 1909, which expanded the domain of psychiatric practice in America from its previously restricted focus on significant pathology to include virtually all of ordinary life.[53] As related in Chapter 10, this was the beginning of a change in outlook in which an unconscious layer of mental experience was not so much objectively discovered as argued into existence by Freud, Breuer, Charcot, Jung, Janet, and others, so effectively that the assumption that there is an actively influential unconscious at work behind the personae that we present to ourselves and to each other has become a feature of ordinary interpersonal life that is now taken for granted.

Classically, in the practice of psychotherapy, it is assumed that the sources of "nervous disorders" can be traced to unresolved traumatic experience that has been dissociated and relegated to the unconscious in protection of the self. Exposing, interpreting, and integrating that material is the general goal of the therapeutic program, and so, high among the qualifications for an effective psychotherapist is advanced sensitivity to the symbolic nature of what we say and how we behave – an ability to translate and place in context the meaning of the experiences and behaviors that drive people to the therapist's office.

This is why Thomas Szasz argued that, properly understood, psychotherapy ought to be regarded as a clinical extension of the communication field.[54] With the exception of a handful of organic diseases that affect the brain, such as Alzheimer's, Huntington's disease, and epilepsy, the conditions that lead people to seek psychiatric treatment have no basis in any detectible dysfunction of the physical body. For Szasz, as in the case of the interpersonal maneuvers commonly used in defense of the self (the defense mechanisms discussed in Chapter 10), psychiatric symptoms stand in for problems in the coherence of the self-narrative and are, therefore, a kind of metaphoric code that requires interpretation.

Today, professionals train as psychotherapists through a variety of disciplines including clinical psychology, psychoanalysis, medicine, social work, pastoral training, and counseling psychology in education. And, within these approaches, there are many distinctive schools of practice. Therefore, seeing a psychotherapist can mean seeing someone from a broad range of training backgrounds and any number of conceptual orientations. Initially, the common thread connecting most of these approaches to healing was talk, or, as it

Mini-Me 281

was once called, "abreaction." Abreaction refers to the cathartic exposure of repressed traumatic experience in conversation with an analyst, who serves as a supportive guide to reintegration of the dissociated material as it is brought to the surface. My point of emphasis is that psychotherapy originated as a talking craft that took the symbolic nature of mental experience very seriously, and, in many cases, this is still what goes on in psychotherapy; however, as we'll see, uniquely among the various schools of therapy, as the twentieth century progressed, the mainstream of medical psychiatry diverged and turned away from the talking cure, and many believe that that has had grievous consequences.

Medical psychiatry not only abandoned its focus on talk and the interpretation of symbolic meaning, it actually stood its former skill set on its head, kicking talk-based therapy out of the office and adopting new protocols of professional practice based on symptom checklists, the prescription pad, and the premises of a biological disease model of the mind grounded in the rhetoric of neuroscience and genetics,[55] a model that specifically confuses that which is of the mind and symbolic (unusual emotion, hearing voices, social withdrawal, suicidal thoughts) with that which is of the signaling brain (i.e., structural or chemical faults in the material brain, such as occur in a genuinely organic disease of the brain such as epilepsy). This confusion, the cultural influence of which has been amplified by a drug industry that profits from the promotion of a biological model of mental illness, has tended to undermine Americans' appreciation of their own range of moral agency, resulting in an increase in the likelihood that people regard themselves and those around them who behave in ways that cause concern as victims of brain disease rather than agentic human beings struggling to cope with the challenging semiotic conditions of life in this difficult period of history.

Children of a lesser god

Before 1950, if you sought help from a medical psychiatrist because you were having difficulty with motivation, or your social life, or anxiety, or other emotion, the doctor's response would center on the exploration of how your experience might be understandable in the context of your childhood history, your immediate social situation, your self-perceptions, your ambitions, and your unfolding life narrative. As these were brought to light, the focus of treatment would be to help you reshape your self-narrative in such a way that these factors might operate for you with happier consequence (using an essentially rhetorical approach characterized by psychotherapist Paul Watzlawick and his colleagues as "the gentle art of reframing").[56] By the 1950s, however, a range of new drugs such as Thorazine and Miltown, the smash-hit anti-anxiety drug, were transforming psychiatric practice. Despite the fact that the new psychotropic drugs only targeted symptoms, offered no cures for underlying problems, and often had significant undesirable side effects, these drugs were highly successful commercial products. They were marketed to doctors with aggressive tactics that included free gifts, free samples, and even

282 *The shape of the modern self*

"bonus points" that doctors could accumulate based on the number of prescriptions they wrote, which allowed them to select items for themselves from gift catalogs.[57]

Between the early 1950s and 1980, psychoanalytic treatment models still dominated the field of medical psychiatry, and the new drugs were seen as adjunctive therapies that could reduce symptoms so that talk therapy could have a better chance. But, in the early 1980s, medical psychiatry abruptly abandoned talk therapy-based approaches grounded in psychodynamic theory in favor of a biological model of mental illness. Many critics believe that this change was more the result of drug company influence and blind faith than convincing scientific evidence. Thus, today, if you bring your life difficulties to a medical psychiatrist, the treatment program often starts and stops with the prescription pad. The assumption is that your problems originate in faults in your brain's system of neuronal signaling. Such scientific support for this position as there is is not based on direct tests of critical tenets of the biological model of mental disorders, but on the effects of drugs on cognitive or emotional states. Critics charge that, as a body, this work tends to be contaminated by methodological flaws (e.g., cherry-picking subjects for experimental and control groups), as well as conflict-of-interest issues that include the suppression of studies with unsupportive findings, the repackaging and republication of findings from supportive studies (creating the impression of a broader basis of research support than actually exists), and significant direct and indirect payouts from drug companies to the psychiatrists and researchers who publish drug evaluation studies.[58] In former times, the therapeutic framework assumed that the psychiatrist functions as a special type of wise and supportive partner, an interpreter, an intimate, a counselor and guide, but that, ultimately, the patient is responsible for the impact of their behavior on others. Getting past difficulties requires a gradual reconceptualization of self and subsequent changes in behavior. As insight is gained, the patient changes and grows, and becomes less anxious and more adaptive. But the current framework of psychiatry assumes that the doctor is a medical specialist concerned with disease in the signaling material brain, and so matters of mind, insight, and self-definition, if not irrelevant, are no longer of primary importance.

As is common in cognitive neuroscience, this model reduces human agency by removing the rationale for believing you can exercise conscious control over your condition. You're thought to have a disease of the brain, and so, as for a disease of the thyroid gland or the heart, treatment is a course of medications, perhaps for the rest of your life. In assigning a disease name to your problems and persuading you that they are based in faulty brain chemistry, the psychiatrist absolves you of responsibility for your condition and, thus, for your impact on others (provided you take your pills), and so medical psychiatry may now function as a secular moral authority where, as in religion, individuals may go to receive a kind of absolution.

Unlike religion, which promotes the belief that a moral life requires active control of choice and limitations of self, the price extracted by medical psychiatry's conceptualization of your difficulties (e.g., for your marital problems that stem from your inattention to your spouse) is acceptance of a model that contends that you actually don't have the capacity for choice. You've been afflicted with an odd type of disease, one that doesn't have any indicators in the material body (perhaps ADHD or dissociative identity disorder). Now, believing that you're behaving as you are because of influences beyond your control, you needn't feel guilt. However, your human agency has been diminished. Insofar as the medical authority has informed you that you have a disease, it may not be reasonable for your spouse to continue to blame you for your inattention, but, unless the drugs actually turn your behavior around, she's no more likely to enjoy your company and, either way, she's less likely to regard you as an inspirational life partner.

The Book of Woe

Freud, Charcot, Breuer, and others among the founding figures of psychoanalysis had degrees in medicine, and so, from the onset, medical psychiatry has enjoyed an advantage in the prestige hierarchy of therapeutic practice. In court, a psychiatrist's testimony normally carries greater prestige than the testimony of a therapist from a competing discipline such as clinical psychology or social work. The authority of medical psychiatry also benefited significantly when, in 1951, the U.S. government assigned the medical profession a monopoly to authorize access to therapeutic drugs through the prescription process. In addition, medical psychiatry has come to dominate in diagnostic authority. It is the primary professional organization of medical psychiatry, the American Psychiatric Association (APA), that is the arbiter of the legal nosology of psychiatric disorders detailed in its *Diagnostic and Statistical Manual of Mental Disorders* (DSM), the highly influential, but equally controversial, bible of diagnosis for psychiatric disorders, referred to recently as "The Book of Woe."[59]

This manual, first published in 1952, was created in an effort to establish scientifically reliable and valid criteria for deciding if someone is normal or if their behavior signals a pathology of the mind and is treatable, in the manner of a physical disease such as tendinitis, through an established protocol. As, in extreme cases, the treatment for psychopathology may include involuntary incarceration, surgical or chemical lobotomy, electric shock, or a lifetime course of mood-dulling drugs that bear significant secondary health risks such as obesity, lethargy, alteration to the brain, persisting personality changes, and even heightened risk of suicide,[60] most people would not want to find their personal quirks or lifestyle choices listed in the DSM (unless, perhaps, having them there is valuable for some economic or strategic purpose such as obtaining disability payouts or avoiding family or legal responsibilities). However, it has become more difficult to dodge the DSM's net because the range of experience the DSM classifies as falling in the domain of psychiatric illness has been expanding like yeast in a damp closet.

284   *The shape of the modern self*

The first edition of the DSM identified 108 types of mental illness. The second edition identified 185, the third 265, and the fourth 354.[61] DSM-5, published in 2013, didn't expand in the manner of the previous editions, but, according to Allen Frances, who directed the creation of the fourth edition, DSM-5 significantly loosened the diagnostic criteria for many existing categories.[62] At the beginning of the twentieth century, the rate of incidence of mental disease was estimated by various sources to be approximately 1 in 1,000 Americans.[63] By the mid-twentieth century, in the wake of the first edition of the DSM, the rate had advanced to 1 in 100. The newly founded National Institute of Mental Health was then operating with an annual budget of about $86.5 million at today's value (roughly one-fifth the level of funding of New York City's Department of Parks and Recreation). Now, incredibly, the National Institute of Mental Health, which operates today with a budget of $1.4 billion, estimates the rate of mental disorders at about 1 in 5 Americans.[64]

As we've seen, there are good reasons to believe that challenges to self-identity that accompany modernity are the causative factors in America's rising rates of interpersonal difficulty and psycho-emotional distress. However, the value of this insight has been blunted by trends in psychiatric theory and practice that are out of sync. As noted, beginning the early 1980s, medical psychiatry replaced psychoanalytically based therapies grounded in discourse, insight, and self-repair with drug therapies grounded in the broken-brain model. It is hard to imagine two more incompatible theoretical perspectives, with one contending that social conditions that destabilize symbolic structures of mind are the problem, and the other contending that the trouble is in the mechanical signal-processing human body.

There are two other influential factors adding mud to these waters, making it difficult to achieve consensus about how to respond effectively to rising rates of psycho-emotional distress. The first of these, as noted, is the disproportionate influence of the pharmaceutical industry on mental health research, theory, and practice. The second stems from the gradual shift of state-level moral enforcement away from its traditional basis in law and the courts. State enforcement of moral control is now increasingly staged within the framework of the mental health professions. Mostly this is a subtle process, reflected in the broadening of the DSM to such an extent that it now seems to critics to serve as much as a book on right living as a nosology of disease. It is certainly ever more difficult for normal Americans to escape its reach. Indeed, to do so could mean living in a manner so colorless, safe, and conforming that many would not want to.

Today, you can be diagnosed with a DSM mental disorder if you crave your cigars more than the APA thinks you should (tobacco use disorder), like to drink in excess of their sense of what you should (alcohol use disorder), or smoke too much pot (cannabis use disorder), make foolish financial investments or engage in sexual indiscretions (symptoms of bipolar disorder), don't listen well or greet people properly (social communication disorder), are too thin (anorexia nervosa) or too fat (obesity), are preoccupied with the possibility that your partner is cheating on you (obsessional jealousy), grieve a dead relative longer than the APA thinks you should (persistent complex bereavement disorder), are female and don't have orgasms or they aren't sufficiently intense (female orgasmic disorder), or are male and have them more quickly than you or your partner would like (premature ejaculation), pick your skin too much (skin picking disorder), fail to throw things away that others believe have no value (hoarding disorder), spend more time than they think you should worrying about the way you look (body dysmorphic disorder), get irritable when you're having a period (premenstrual dysphoric disorder), spend too much time playing games on the internet (internet gaming disorder), or refuse to take the meds that your psychiatrist prescribed (nonadherence to medical treatment).

Obviously, these are not symptoms of disease in any normal sense of disease. They are indicators of values, lifestyle, and choices in interpersonal conduct. In their extremes, they may be things we regret or don't like about each other. Either way, to the extent that they are matters of choice, they are moral matters, and so, if they are to be evaluated, the relevant considerations are ethical, not biological. The categories for male and female orgasmic behavior might come closest to being something of the body, beyond conscious control, but, regardless of what else they might be, there is no basis for thinking of them as diseases of the mind. As the Mayo Clinic defines it, premature ejaculation occurs when the male ejaculates sooner than he or his partner would like. In other words, it's like the rest, a matter of values and preference.

Thus, the DSM has become a kind of secular "Ten-Commandments-times-35," dissolving boundaries that once differentiated medical practice, religion, social mores, and law. Historian and philosopher Michel Foucault believed that a blurring between psychiatry and law enforcement occurred as modernizing societies sought more humane methods of social control, but also methods that were more penetrating and far-reaching.[65] This is particularly clear in the case of suicide, which, in many places until recent times, was classified as a felony crime for which you could be held in jail. In most places, the statutes that criminalized suicide have been rescinded; nevertheless, today, if you attempt to murder yourself, you may still be incarcerated involuntarily in a locked psychiatric facility.

The blurring between psychiatry, public morality, and social control is in evidence as well in the history of psychiatry's regrettable involvement with sexual practices. Richard von Krafft-Ebing's influential 1886 medical text *Psychopathia Sexualis* transformed virtually every form of non-procreative sex into a category of mental disease, essentially allowing psychiatry to take the leading position in moral crusades previously championed in nineteenth-century America by oddball prudes such as John Harvey Kellogg, Sylvester Graham, and Anthony Comstock.[66] According to Krafft-Ebing, masturbation is a causative factor in neurosis and insanity and, therefore, a medical matter. This baton has now been passed to the DSM, where, for example, "voyeuristic disorder" (DSM-5 code 302.82) is assigned when (1) an individual is aroused by observing someone else naked, or taking their clothes off, or performing

286 *The shape of the modern self*

sex; (2) this interest is either the basis for attempting sexual contact with a non-consenting person, or the interest interferes with work; and (3) the individual experiencing the arousal is over 18. Considering that the Nielsen research firm recently reported that, in any given month, 30 percent of the American workforce uses a workplace computer to view pornographic websites,[67] it isn't easy to understand voyeuristic disorder as a medical concern so much as a common matter of personal interest and workplace focus.

And, as for attempting sexual contact with a non-consenting person, in this, what was historically regarded as a criminal offense – rape, at the extreme – is transmuted by the DSM into a psychiatric matter, the idea grounded in unsubstantiated assumptions about neurotransmitters and the material brain. Rutgers Professor of Law Margo Kaplan recently argued in the *New York Times* that pedophilia is not a moral or cultural matter but a neurological disorder of the brain and should, therefore, be treated with psychiatric medication and cognitive-behavior therapy rather than criminal law.[68] On the flip side of this, sociologist Viviana Zelizer discusses the case of a Kansas lawyer disbarred for seducing one of his clients. The lawyer attempted to defend himself during the disbarment procedure by arguing that he was a victim of "hypersexuality" (sex addiction), a condition for which he claimed he was being treated by a mental health professional.[69] (Sex addiction was included in the third edition of the DSM, but was voted out of the fourth edition.)

Voting mental disorders into and out of existence

Prior to its revision in 1974, the DSM included homosexuality as a category of mental illness. It was removed in response to social pressure from the gay rights movement, which, in the wake of successes of the civil rights movement, was gaining a national voice at that time. Incredibly, the decision about whether to sustain homosexuality as a category of disease or to kick it out of the DSM and return it to normality was not made in reference to any body of objective scientific data, but by taking a vote among members of the American Psychiatric Association (the tally was 5,854 for removing it and 3,810 for keeping it).[70] Though the regulation of social behavior via politics and law is almost always accomplished by vote, to say the least, it's difficult to imagine any legitimate branch of medical science establishing its fundamental claims about whether or not something is a disease by means of the ballot. Yet this is a standard methodology of the DSM.

PTSD was not included in the DSM until the 1980 edition, and this happened as a result of significant political pressure from Vietnam War vets. The history of revision of the DSM through the most recent edition has been one of polling, lobbying, and voting, which suggests that DSM categories have a sufficiently unusual relationship to the real world to raise questions about how behaviors come to be included, what it means for something to be listed, and what it means that a disorder previously included can suddenly be withdrawn. (If only diseases such as polio, COVID-19, or cancer could be eradicated by doctors voting against them.) The process casts doubt on the claim that medical psychiatry deals with physical disorders treatable by drugs that correct problems in neurotransmitters within the brain. Critics argue that medical psychiatry has little foundation in scientific fact and attempts to position itself as the arbiter of matters of civil life and morality. Its medications work by brute force, not actually correcting anything at all. It distinguishes normal from abnormal using procedures similar to those used by the Vatican to distinguish sin – deliberation at the top of the profession. This is not the method of science and is why Thomas Szasz referred to medical psychiatry as "pseudology."[71] There's no question that modernity destabilizes self-identity, exacting a heavy toll in anxiety, depression, and other severe forms of psycho-emotional trouble. Many believe that mainstream medical psychiatry errs in conceptualizing these problems as problems of the body, and that, in doing so, it just treats symptoms instead of their underlying causes. The unsupported idea that psycho-emotional disorders originate in malfunctions of the material body impedes progress in addressing the true causes of suffering in our era, which lie in the complex interplay of mental, social, and cultural experience.

Burke argued that, of the qualities that set humans apart from other animals, none is as important as the use of symbols. But we also misuse them. Obviously, we do so when we act in bad faith, deliberately misleading ourselves or each other. But also when we misinterpret, when we take as metaphor that which is literal (e.g., seeing your partner's genuine headache as a psychosomatic tactic for avoiding sex), or as literal that which is metaphor (e.g., regarding your partner's promise to love you forever as a proclamation of fact rather than a poetic expression of positive feeling). This confusion is the basis for a core criticism of modern medical psychiatry. In its shift to the brain disease model and a system of diagnosis guided by symptom checklists, comprised in many cases of ordinary experiences of ambiguous significance, medical psychiatry created a process in which it's too easy for a diagnostician to miss the unique situational influences of behavior or the possibility that behavior is symbolic – for example, that the feeling of panic in public places is not a sign of a broken brain, but a sensible symbolic reaction to the stresses of urban life and dissipated community that have made self-identity into a weaker and more vulnerable structure of mind and have amplified the risk of exposure to deceit and sham in public spaces.

This has been made worse by the dispersal of a great deal of psychiatric diagnosis and treatment to the offices of general practitioners who may have minimal training in mental health, likely even less exposure to sociological, historical, and anthropological theory, and very little time to spend with patients. Today, diagnoses of psychiatric disorders such as depression, social anxiety disorder, and ADHD are more likely to be made by family doctors who are guided by the DSM's checklists and who treat by prescription. And so we've entered an age characterized by epidemic-level administration of psychiatric drugs and by the reduced vision of human agency that the brain dysfunction model encourages. In 2016, 594 million prescriptions were written

288 *The shape of the modern self*

by American physicians for just the 25 top-selling psychiatric drugs,[72] (up from 429 million in 2013),[73] all with potential consequences for interpersonal behavior.

Conclusion

An evolutionary psychologist, a cognitive scientist/neuroscientist, a medical psychiatrist, and a meme theorist walk into a bar. The bartender says to the evolutionary psychologist, "What'll it be?" Noticing a picture of the bartender's family on the wall, the evolutionary psychologist says, "Four years with your fine looking daughter ought to be just about right!" The bartender frowns, then turns to the cognitive scientist/neuroscientist: "How about you ma'am? What can I bring you?" An utterly blank look on her face, the cognitive scientist/neuroscientist says, "Gosh I really don't know what I want, and I can see that that's a relevant question. Do you have a fMRI scanner?" Starting to be concerned, the bartender turns to the medical psychiatrist, "And you sir, what can I get for you?" The medical psychiatrist smiles and replies, "Wow, I could *really* go for a double martini!", then, suddenly, gasping in horror, exclaims, "DSM code 303.90! I've contracted a case of alcohol use disorder!", whips out a prescription pad, writes himself scripts for Topamax and Prozac, and bolts from the bar in search of a pharmacy. Now seriously befuddled, the bartender steadies himself, takes a deep breath, again plants a smile on his face, and turns to the meme theorist: "And how about you sir? What'll it be?" The meme theorist steadies himself, takes a deep breath, smiles back, and says, "And how about you sir? What'll it be?"

Alas, the loss of mind is really nothing to laugh about, and so neither are the theoretical positions reviewed in this chapter. All four reduce the function of talk to mechanical signal exchange, relegating mind and will to a mostly irrelevant sideshow, envisioning the basis for our involvements with each other in chemical terms, and substituting a kind of non-conscious informatics for the human ability to reason and choose. In the framework of the life-as-motion sciences, we're left without opportunities for personal growth and dignity that occur as humans confront their difficulties as conscious, free agents and work their way through them in conversation with others. For Sartre, the attraction in this is the possibility of avoiding existential anguish. As he noted, "we are always ready to take refuge in a belief in determinism if . . . freedom weighs upon us or if we need an excuse,"[74] but denying your own freedom is no solution because it places you in a condition of bad faith in relation to yourself.

Reacting to the uprooted qualities of Western civilization wrought by the great transformations of modernity and, especially, in the wake of the senseless and horrific calamity of World War I, T. S. Eliot penned his 1922 masterwork *The Wasteland*. It describes a fracturing world of broken images and unreal cities and asks, "what branches grow out of this stony rubbish?" That's a big question. Here may be part of the answer: taxed by the chronic psychic malaise that is the cost of life in a world of fast-changing truth, uncertain meaning,

Mini-Me 289

and unprecedented choice, many experience anxiety and depression, and some may respond to the attraction of a worldview that diminishes their responsibilities. There can be a kind of relief in the idea that our social involvements aren't our responsibility, but are controlled by genetics, that the brain makes our choices for us independent of conscious consideration, that self-identity is a biological artifact of the brain, and that it's a waste of time to work through the complicated issues of modern intimacy because, you believe, your intimate destiny is determined by the luck of the draw in a mechanical process of partner selection or by the chemical processes of the body.

So here may be the origin of our common nostalgia for the simpler situation of distant times, which Jaynes believed were happier and less troubled. Then, the human mind *was* more of a signal-processing system, less aware of itself, guided not as much by interior reason as by biology, the needs of the moment, and primitive emotional signals. Though traces of this linger in the deeper recesses of our psychology, that was long ago. There is no route back to the primitive world of signal, and we will find no salvation in an imagined future of robot relationships. Complicated, lonely, and anxious as our lives may be, we have to deal with the world as it is. As Sartre wrote, we may choose to regard ourselves as other than we now are, but such a choice is made in bad faith in the reality of human consciousness and will: "Whatever our being may be, it is a choice; and it depends on us to choose ourselves."[75] With better understanding of how the challenges and opportunities that modernity sets up for us originated, we are better prepared to choose to live smartly and deliberately, to engage in social practices that counteract and minimize the problems that modernity creates.

Notes

1 Burke, *The rhetoric of religion: studies in logology*, 39.
2 Riesman et al., *The lonely crowd*.
3 Tallis, *Aping mankind: neuromania, Darwinitis, and the misrepresentation of humanity*; Midgley, *Science and poetry*; Szasz, *Psychiatry: the science of lies*.
4 Levy, *Love and sex with robots: the evolution of human – robot relationships*.
5 Burke, *Language as symbolic action: essays on life, literature, and method*, 17.
6 See Wittgenstein, *Philosophical investigations*.
7 Keller, *The story of my life*.
8 Heffner, Isolation, health effects; Holt-Lunstad et al., Loneliness and social isolation as risk factors for mortality: A meta-analytic review; Valtorta et al., Loneliness and social isolation as risk factors for coronary heart disease and stroke: systematic review and meta-analysis of longitudinal observational studies; Yang et al., Social relationships and physiological determinants of longevity across the human life span.
9 Pollan, *How to change your mind: what the new science of psychedelics teaches us about consciousness, dying, addiction, depression, and transcendence*.
10 Klinenberg, *Going solo: the extraordinary rise and surprising appeal of living alone*.
11 Guenther, *Solitary confinement: social death and its afterlives*, 35.
12 Seung, *Connectome: how the brain's wiring makes us who we are*.

290   *The shape of the modern self*

13 Whitaker, *Anatomy of an epidemic: magic bullets, psychiatric drugs and the astonishing rise of mental illness.*
14 Hofstadter, *I am a strange loop*, 228.
15 Parfit, Personal identity.
16 Pepper, *World hypotheses: a study in evidence.*
17 Wiener, *The human use of human beings: cybernetics and society.*
18 Dawkins, *The selfish gene*, ix.
19 Dunbar et al., Human conversational behavior.
20 See Ryan and Cacilda, *Sex at dawn: how we mate, why we stray, and what it means for modern relationships.*
21 See Judson, *Dr. Tatiana's sex advice to all creation.*
22 Ryan and Cacilda, *Sex at dawn: how we mate, why we stray, and what it means for modern relationships.*
23 Dawkins, *The selfish gene.*
24 Trivers, Parental investment and sexual selection.
25 Prum, *The evolution of beauty: how Darwin's forgotten theory of mate choice shapes the animal world – and us.*
26 Eldredge, *Why we do it: rethinking sex and the selfish gene*, 27.
27 Geher and Kaufman, *Mating intelligence unleashed*, 35.
28 Fisher, *Why we love: the nature and chemistry of romantic love.*
29 Buss, *The evolution of desire: strategies of human mating*, 11.
30 D'Emilio and Freedman, *Intimate matters: a history of sexuality in America.*
31 Cherlin, *The marriage-go-round: the state of marriage and the family in America today.*
32 Fine, *Testosterone Rex: myths of sex, science, and society.*
33 Coontz, *Marriage, a history: how love conquered marriage.*
34 Ryan and Cacilda, *Sex at dawn: how we mate, why we stray, and what it means for modern relationships.*
35 Dawkins, *The selfish gene*, 207.
36 Blackmore, *The meme machine*, 84.
37 Dennett, *Consciousness explained.*
38 Tallis, *Aping mankind: neuromania, Darwinitis, and the misrepresentation of humanity.*
39 Tallis, *Reflections of a metaphysical fl'aneur and other essays.*
40 Burke, *Language as symbolic action: essays on life, literature, and method*, 19.
41 See Festinger Riecken, *When prophesy fails: a social and psychological study of a modern group that predicted the destruction of the world.*
42 Midgley, *Science and poetry*, 106.
43 Goleman, *Social intelligence: the new science of human relationships*; Frith, *Making up the mind: how the brain creates our mental world.*
44 For example, Ramachandran, Mirror neurons and imitation learning as the driving force behind the great leap forward in human evolution.
45 Hickok, *The myth of mirror neurons: the real neuroscience of communication and cognition.*
46 Rizzolatti and Fabbri-Destro, *Mirror neurons: from discovery to autism.*
47 Hobson, *Dreaming: a very short introduction.*
48 Graziano, *Consciousness and the social brain*; Hickok, *The myth of mirror neurons: the real neuroscience of communication and cognition*; Satel and Lilienfeld, *Brainwashed: the seductive appeal of mindless neuroscience*; Tallis, *Aping mankind: neuromania, Darwinitis, and the misrepresentation of humanity.*
49 *Ibid.*
50 Churchland, *Touching a nerve: the self as brain.*

51 Tallis, *Aping mankind: neuromania, Darwinitis, and the misrepresentation of humanity*, 317.
52 For example, Bergen, *Louder than words: the new science of how the mind makes meaning*; Wegner, *The illusion of conscious will*.
53 Illouz, *Cold intimacies: the making of emotional capitalism*.
54 Szasz, *The myth of mental illness: foundations of a theory of personal conduct* (revised ed.).
55 See, for example, Kupfer and Regier, Neuroscience, clinical evidence, and the future of psychiatric classification in DSM-5.
56 Watzlawick et al., *Change: principles of problem formation and problem resolution*.
57 Herzberg, *Happy pills in America: from Miltown to Prozac*.
58 Davies, *Cracked: the unhappy truth about psychiatry*.
59 Greenberg, *The book of woe: the DSM and the unmaking of psychiatry*.
60 Whitaker, *Anatomy of an epidemic: magic bullets, psychiatric drugs and the astonishing rise of mental illness*.
61 Blashfield, *Diagnostic models and systems*.
62 Frances, *Saving normal: an insider's revolt against out-of-control psychiatric diagnosis, DSM-5, Big Pharma, and the medicalization of ordinary life*.
63 See, for example, Davies, *Cracked: the unhappy truth about psychiatry*.
64 National Institute of Mental Health, Any mental illness (AMI) among adults.
65 Foucault, *Discipline and punish: the birth of the prison*.
66 See D'Emilio and Freedman, *Intimate matters: a history of sexuality in America*.
67 Monitopoli, 29% accessed porn on work computers last month.
68 Kaplan, Pedophilia: a disorder, not a crime.
69 Zelizer, *The purchase of intimacy*
70 Davies, *Cracked: the unhappy truth about psychiatry*.
71 Szasz, *Psychiatry: the science of lies*.
72 Grohol, Personal communication.
73 Grohol, Top 25 psychiatric medication prescriptions for 2013.
74 Sartre, *Being and nothingness: A phenomenological essay on ontology*, 82
75 *Ibid.*, 607.

References

Ackerman, Diane (2011). *One hundred names for love: a memoir*. New York: W.W. Norton.

Alexander, Marc (2018). Patchworks and field-boundaries: visualising the history of English. Retrieved Jan 17, 2018 from www.slideshare.net/marcgalexander/patchworks-and-fieldboundaries-visualising-the-history-of-english

Altman, Irwin, and Taylor, Dalmas (1973). *Social penetration: the development of interpersonal relationships*. New York: Holt.

Alwin, Duane F. (1988). From obedience to autonomy: changes in traits desired in children, 1924–1978. *Public Opinion Quarterly*. 52, 33–52.

Amato, Paul R., Booth, Alan, Johnson, David R., and Rogers, Stacy J. (2007). *Alone together: how marriage in America is changing*. Cambridge, MA: Harvard University Press.

Andersen, Kurt (2017). *Fantasyland: how America went haywire, a 500-year history*. New York: Random House.

Ansari, Aziz, and Klinenberg, Eric (2015). *Modern romance*. New York: Penguin Press.

Archer, Margaret S. (2012). *The reflexive imperative in late modernity*. Cambridge: Cambridge University Press.

Baggini, Julian (2011). *The ego trick: what does it mean to be you?* London: Granta.

Bailey, Beth L. (1988). *From front porch to back seat: courtship in twentieth-century America*. Baltimore, MD: Johns Hopkins University Press.

Barkan, Steven E., Rocque, Michael, and Houle, Jason (2013). State and regional suicide rates: a new look at an old puzzle. *Sociological Perspectives*, 56, 287–297.

Bateson, Gregory, Jackson, Don. D., Haley, Jay, and Weakland, John (1956). Toward a theory of schizophrenia. *Behavioral Science*. 1, 251–264.

Bauerlein, Mark (2009). *The dumbest generation: how the digital age stupefies young Americans and jeopardizes our future*. New York: Penguin.

Bauman, Zygmunt (2003). *Liquid love: on the frailty of human bonds*. Malden, MA: Polity Press.

Bauman, Zygmunt (2007). *Liquid times: living in an age of uncertainty*. Malden, MA: Polity Press.

Bauman, Zygmunt (2012). *Liquid modernity*. Malden, MA: Polity Press.

Baumeister, Roy F. (1986). *Identity: cultural change and the struggle for self*. New York: Oxford University Press.

Baym, Nancy K. (2010). *Personal connections in the digital age*. Malden, MA: Polity Press.

References 293

Beck, Ulrich, and Beck-Gernsheim, Elisabeth (1995). *The normal chaos of love.* Cambridge, UK: Polity Press.

Becker, Ernest (1973). *The denial of death.* New York: The Free Press.

Bellah, Robert N., Madsen, Richard, Sullivan, William M., Swidler, Ann, and Tipton, Steven M. (1985). *Habits of the heart: individualism and commitment in American life.* New York: Harper & Row.

Bem, Sandra L. (1981). Gender schema theory: a cognitive account of sex typing. *Psychological Review.* 88, 354–384.

Bender, Thomas (1978). *Community and social change in America.* Baltimore, MD: Johns Hopkins University Press.

Beniger, James R. (1986). *The control revolution: technological and economic origins of the information society.* Cambridge, MA: Harvard University Press.

Bergen, Benjamin K. (2012). *Louder than words: the new science of how the mind makes meaning.* New York: Basic Books.

Berger, Charles R., and Calabrese, Richard J. (1975). Some explorations in initial interaction and beyond: toward a developmental theory of communication. *Human Communication Research.* 1, 99–112.

Berger, Peter, and Kellner, Hansfried (1964). Marriage and the construction of reality: an exercise in the microsociology of knowledge. *Diogenes.* 12, 1–24.

Berger, Peter, Berger, Brigitte, and Kellner, Hansfried. (1973). *The homeless mind: modernization and consciousness.* New York: Vintage.

Berlin, Isaiah (2013). *The roots of romanticism* (2nd ed.). Princeton, NJ: Princeton University Press.

Bernard, Jessie (1972). *The future of marriage.* New York: Bantom Books.

Bernstein, Basil (1964). Elaborated and restricted codes: their social origins and some consequences. *American Anthropologist.* 66(6), 55–69.

Berry, Wendell (1984). The handing down. In *Collected poems.* New York: North Point Press.

Berry, Wendell (1998). Window poems. In *The selected poems of Wendell Berry.* New York: Counterpoint.

Berry, Wendell (2012). The loss of the future. In *The Long-Legged House.* Berkeley, CA: Counterpoint Press.

Bessant, Kenneth C. (2010). Authenticity, community, and modernity. *Journal for the Theory of Social Behavior.* 41(1), 2–32.

Black, Donald W. (2007). A review of compulsive buying disorder. *World Psychiatry.* 6(1), 14–18.

Blackmore, Susan (1999). *The meme machine.* New York: Oxford University Press.

Blashfield, Roger K. (1998). Diagnostic models and systems. In A. S. Bellack and M. Hersen (Eds.). *Comprehensive clinical psychology.* New York: Pergamon, pp. 57–80.

Blom, Philipp (2008). *The vertigo years: Europe, 1900–1914.* New York: Basic Books.

Bonanno, George A. (2009). *The other side of sadness: what the new science of bereavement tells us about life after loss.* New York: Basic Books.

Bonomi, Patricia U. (2003). *Under the cope of heaven: religion, society, and politics in colonial America* (updated ed.). New York: Oxford University Press.

Bruess, Carol J. S., and Pearson, Judy C. (1997). Interpersonal rituals in marriage and adult friendship. *Communication Monographs.* 64 (March), 25–46.

Burke, Kenneth (1945). *A grammar of motives.* Berkeley, CA: University of California Press.

Burke, Kenneth (1966). *Language as symbolic action: essays on life, literature, and method.* Berkeley, CA: University of California Press.

294 *References*

Burke, Kenneth (1969). *A rhetoric of motives*. Berkeley, CA: University of California Press.

Burke, Kenneth (1970). *The rhetoric of religion: studies in logology*. Berkeley, CA: University of California Press

Burke, Peter (1992). *History and social theory*. Ithaca, NY: Cornell University Press.

Burke, Peter (1993). *The art of conversation*. Ithaca, NY: Cornell University Press.

Bushman, Richard L. (1981). Family security in the transition from farm to city, 1750–1850. *Journal of Family History*. 6, 238–256.

Buss, David M. (2003). *The evolution of desire: strategies of human mating*. (revised ed.). New York: Basic Books.

Butler, Jon (1990). *Awash in a sea of faith: Christianizing the American people*. Cambridge, MA: Harvard University Press.

Calhoun, Arthur W. (1917). *A social history of the American family from colonial times to the present: Volume 1: colonial period*. Cleveland, OH: Arthur H. Clark.

Calvert, Karin (2001). Children in American family portraiture, 1670–1810. In Joseph M. Hawes and Elizabeth I. Nybakken (Eds.). *Family & society in American history*. Chicago, IL: University of Illinois Press, pp. 113–137.

Campbell, Joseph (1968). *The hero with a thousand faces* (2nd ed.). Princeton, NJ: Princeton University Press.

Caplow, Theodore, Bahr, Howard, M., Chadwick, Bruce A., Hill, Reuben, and Williamson, Margaret Holmes (1982). *Middletown families: fifty years of change and continuity*. Minneapolis, MN: University of Minnesota Press.

Carbaugh, Donal (2005). *Cultures in conversation*. New York: Routledge.

Carr, Nicholas (2011). *The shallows: what the internet is doing to our brains*. New York: W. W. Norton.

Carruthers, Peter (1996). *Language, thought, and consciousness: an essay in philosophical psychology*. New York: Cambridge University Press.

Carruthers, Susan L. (2018). When Americans were afraid of being brainwashed. *New York Times*, January 18. Retrieved January 21, 2018 from www. nytimes.com/2018/01/18/opinion/sunday/when-americans-were-afraid-of-being-brainwashed.html

Cartwright, Rosalind D. (2010). *The twenty-four hour mind: the role of sleep and dreaming in our emotional lives*. New York: Oxford University Press.

Catron, Mandy Len (2017). *How to fall in love with anyone: a memoir in essays*. New York: Simon & Schuster.

Celello, Kristin (2009). *Making marriage work: a history of marriage and divorce in the twentieth-century United States*. Chapel Hill, NC: University of North Carolina Press.

Chabris, Christopher F., and Simons, Daniel J. (2009). *The invisible gorilla: how our intuitions deceive us*. New York: Random House.

Charmody, Deirdre (1994). Hearst finds unexpected success in a magazine for dreamers. *New York Times*, September 12. Retrieved August 15, 2016 from www.nytimes.com/1994/09/12/business/the-media-business-hearst-finds-unexpected-success-in-a-magazine-for-dreamers.html

Chase, Lisa (2016). Losing my husband – and finding him again through a medium. *Elle*. Retrieved December 25 from www.elle.com/life-love/news/a30986/losing-my-husband-and-finding-him-through-a-medium

Cherlin, Andrew J. (2009). *The marriage-go-round: the state of marriage and the family in America today*. New York: Vintage Books.

References 295

Chetty, Raj, and Hendren, Nathaniel (2015). The impacts of neighborhoods on intergenerational mobility: childhood exposure effects and county-level estimates. Retrieved September 16, 2015 from www.equality-of-opportunity.org/images /hbhds paper.pdf

Chodorow, Nancy (1976). Oedipal asymmetries and heterosexual knots. *Social Problems*. 23, 454–468.

Chodorow, Nancy (1978/1999). *The reproduction of mothering: psychoanalysis and the sociology of gender*. Berkeley, CA: University of California Press.

Christensen, Kate (2016). Second time around. In Cathi Hanauer (Ed.) *The bitch is back: older, wiser, and (getting) happier*. New York: William Morrow, p. 251.

Churchland, Patricia (2013). *Touching a nerve: the self as brain*. New York: W. W. Norton.

Cigna Corporation. (2018). Cigna U.S. Loneliness Index: survey of 20,000 Americans examining behaviors driving loneliness in the United States. Retrieved May 1, 2018 from www.cigna.com

Clarke, Tainya C., Black, Lindsey I., Stussman, Barbara J., Barnes, Patricia M., and Nahin, Richard L. (2015). Trends in the use of complementary health approaches among adults: United States, 2002–2012. National Health Statistics Reports, p. 79.

Collins, Randall (2004). *Interaction ritual chains*. Princeton, NJ: Princeton University Press.

Conley, Dalton (2009). *Elsewhere, U.S.A.* New York: Vintage.

Cooley, Charles Horton (1902). *Human nature and the social order*. New York: Charles Scribner's.

Coontz, Stephanie (1988). *The social origins of private life: a history of American families 1600–1900*. New York: Verso.

Coontz, Stephanie (1992). *The way we never were: American families and the nostalgia trap*. New York: Basic Books.

Coontz, Stephanie (2005). *Marriage, a history: how love conquered marriage*. New York: Penguin Books.

Coontz, Stephanie (2012). *A strange stirring: The Feminine Mystique and American women at the dawn of the 1960s*. New York: Basic Books.

Coser, Rose Laub (1991). *In defense of modernity: role complexity and individual autonomy*. Stanford, CA: Stanford University Press.

Cox, Daniel, Jones, Robert P., and Navarro-Rivera, Juhem (2014). *I know what you did last Sunday: measuring social desirability bias in self-reported religious behavior, belief, and identity*. Washington, D.C.: Public Religion Research Institute.

Cozolino, Louis (2014). *The neuroscience of human relationships: attachment and the developing social brain* (2nd ed). New York: W. W. Norton.

Cramer, Phebe (2006). *Protecting the self: defense mechanisms in action*. New York: Guilford Press.

Csikszentmihali, Mihaly (2008). *Flow: the psychology of optimal experience*. New York: Harper Perennial.

Curtin, Sally C., Warner, Margaret, and Hedegaard, Holly (2016). Increase in suicide in the United States, 1999–2014. National Center for Health Statistics. Retrieved April 22, 2016 from www.cdc.gov/nchs/products/

D'Emilio, John, and Freedman, Estelle B. (1988). *Intimate matters: a history of sexuality in America*. New York: Harper & Row.

Damasio, Antonio (1994). *Descartes' error: emotion, reason, and the human brain*. London: Penguin Books.

296   References

Damasio, Antonio (2010). *Self comes to mind: constructing the conscious brain*. New York: Vintage.

Damasio, Antonio (2018). *The strange order of things: life, feeling, and the making of cultures*. New York: Pantheon Books.

Daniels, Roger (2002). *Coming to America: a history of immigration and ethnicity in American life* (2nd ed.). New York: Harper.

Darnton, Robert (1984). *The great cat massacre and other episodes in French cultural history*. New York: Basic Books.

Davies, James (2013). *Cracked: the unhappy truth about psychiatry*. New York: Pegasus Books.

Davis, Murray S. (1973). *Intimate relations*. New York: The Free Press.

Dawkins, Richard (1976). *The selfish gene*. New York: Oxford University Press.

de Tocqueville, Alexis (1966). *Democracy in America* (translated by George Lawrence and edited by J. P. Mayer). New York: Harper & Row.

Degler, Carl N. (1980). *At odds: women and the family in America from the Revolution to the present*. New York: Oxford University Press.

Demos, John (1986). *Past, present, and personal: the family and the life course in American history*. New York: Oxford University Press.

Dennett, Daniel C. (1991). *Consciousness explained*. New York: Back Bay Books.

Didion, Joan (2005). *The year of magical thinking*. New York: Vintage.

Division of Clinical Psychology (2014). *Understanding psychosis and schizophrenia*. Leicester, UK: British Psychological Society.

Donald, Merlin (1991). *Origins of the modern mind: three stages in the evolution of culture and cognition*. Cambridge, MA: Harvard University Press.

Donald, Merlin (2001). *A mind so rare: the evolution of human consciousness*. New York: W. W. Norton.

Druckerman, Pamela (2007). *Lust in translation: infidelity from Tokyo to Tennessee*. New York: Penguin Books.

Dunbar, R. I. M., Duncan, N. D. C., and Marriott, Anna (1997). Human conversational behavior. *Human Nature*. 8(3), 231–246.

Duncan, Hugh Dalziel (1968). *Symbols in society*. New York: Oxford University Press.

Dunkelman, Marc J. (2015). *The vanishing neighbor: the transformation of American community*. New York: W. W. Norton.

Dunne, Griffin (2017). *Joan Didion: the center will not hold*. Netflix.

Durkheim, Émile (1893/1997). *The division of labor in society*. New York: The Free Press.

Edelman, Gerald M. (1989). *The remembered present: a biological theory of consciousness*. New York: Basic Books.

Egan, Timothy (2016). The eight-second attention span. *New York Times*. Retrieved February 5, 2016 from www.nytimes.com/2016/01/22/opinion/the-eight-second-attention-span.html

Ehrenreich, Barbara (1990). *Fear of falling: the inner life of the middle class*. New York: Harper Perennial.

Ehrenreich, Barbara, and English, Deirdre (2005). *For her own good: two centuries of the experts' advice to women* (revised ed.). New York: Anchor Books.

Einstein, Mara (2016). *Black ops advertising*. New York: OR Books.

Eldredge, Niles (2004). *Why we do it: rethinking sex and the selfish gene*. New York: W. W. Norton.

Elias, Norbert (1978). *The history of manners*. New York: Pantheon Press.

Eliot, T. S. (1915). The love song of J. Alfred Prufrock. *Poetry: A Magazine of Verse.* June, 130–135.

Ellenberger, Henri F. (1970). *The discovery of the unconscious: the history and evolution of dynamic psychiatry.* New York: Basic Books.

Ellin, Abby (2015). After full lives together, more older couples are divorcing. *New York Times.* Retrieved October 31, 2015 from www.nytimes.com/2015/10/31/your-money/after-full-lives-together-more-older-couples-are-divorcing.html

Elliot, Anthony (2008). *Concepts of the self.* Malden, MA: Polity Press.

Ellul, Jacques (1964). *The technological society.* New York: Vintage Books.

Ellwood, Mark (2017). These luxury home mainstays may be gone in 20 years. *Bloomberg News.* Retrieved November 26, 2018 from www.bloomberg.com/news/articles/2017-01-23/these-luxury-real-estate-staples-may-be-gone-in-20-years

Erikson, Erik H. (1968). *Identity: youth and crisis.* New York: W. W. Norton.

Everett, Daniel L. (2008). *Don't sleep, there are snakes: life and language in the Amazonian jungle.* New York: Vintage.

Everett, Daniel L. (2016). *Dark matter of the mind: the culturally articulated unconscious.* Chicago: University of Chicago Press.

Ewing, Jack, and Davenport, Coral (2015). Volkswagen to stop sales of diesel cars involved in recall. *New York Times*, September 21, 2015. Retrieved September 20, 2015 from www.nytimes.com/2015/09/21/business/chief-apologizes-for-breach-of-trust-after-recall.html

Fava, Giovanni A. (2007). Financial conflicts of interest in psychiatry. *World Psychiatry.* 6, 19–24.

Fels, Anna (2014). Should we all take a bit of lithium? *New York Times*, September 13. Retrieved July 13, 2018 from www.nytimes.com/2014/09/14/opinion/sunday/should-we-all-take-a-bit-of-lithium.html

Ferrie, Joseph P. (2005). The end of American exceptionalism? Mobility in the .S. since 1850. *The Journal of Economic Perspectives.* 19(3), 199–215.

Festinger, Leon, and Riecken, Henry W. (1956). *When prophesy fails: a social and psychological study of a modern group that predicted the destruction of the world.* Minneapolis, MN: University of Minnesota Press.

Fine, Cordelia (2017). *Testosterone Rex: myths of sex, science, and society.* New York: W. W. Norton.

Fischer, Claude S. (2010). *Made in America.* Chicago: University of Chicago Press.

Fisher, Helen (2004). *Why we love: the nature and chemistry of romantic love.* New York: St. Martin's Griffin.

Flaherty, David H. (1972). *Privacy in colonial New England.* Charlottesville, VA: University Press of Virginia.

Flitter, Emily (2020). The price of Wells Fargo's fake account scandal grows by $3 billion. *New York Times*, February 21. Retrieved June 19, 2021 from www.nytimes.com/2020/02/21/business/wells-fargo-settlement.html

Foa, Uriel, G., Converse, John, Jr., Törnblom, Kjell Y., and Foa, Edna B. (1992). *Resource theory: explorations and applications.* Bingley, UK: Emerald.

Forbes, Harriet J., Wong, Angel Y., Morton, Caroline, Bhaskaran, Krishnan, Smeeth, Liam, Richards, Marcus, Schmidt, Sigrun A., Langan Sinead M., and Warren-Gash, Charlotte (2019). Partner bereavement and detection of dementia: a UK-based cohort study using routine health data. *Journal of Alzheimer's Disease.* 72, 653–662.

Foucault, Michel (1995). *Discipline and punish: the birth of the prison.* (2nd ed.). New York: Vintage Books.

298   *References*

Fraley, R. Chris, and Shaver, Phillip R. (2000). Adult romantic attachment: theoretical developments, emerging controversies, and unanswered questions. *The Review of Psychology*. 4, 132–154.

Frances, Allen (2013). *Saving normal: an insider's revolt against out-of-control psychiatric diagnosis, DSM-5, Big Pharma, and the medicalization of ordinary life.* New York: Harper Collins.

Frank, Jerome D. (1973). *Persuasion and healing: a comparative study of psychotherapy.* Baltimore, MD: Johns Hopkins University Press.

Frankl, Viktor E. (1984). *Man's search for meaning: an introduction to logotherapy* (3rd ed.). New York: Touchstone Books

Freitas, Donna (2013). *The end of sex: how hookup culture is leaving a generation unhappy, sexually unfulfilled, and confused about intimacy.* New York: Basic Books.

Freud, Sigmund (1914/1952). *On dreams*. New York: W.W. Norton.

Freud, Sigmund (1915). *Psychopathology of everyday life*. New York: Macmillan.

Freud, Sigmund (1930/1961). Civilization and its discontents. New York: W.W. Norton.

Friedman, Richard A. (1988). The discovery of the unconscious reflected in changing word usage in the United States 1880–1980 (Unpublished doctoral dissertation). Rutgers University, New Brunswick, NJ.

Friedman, Richard A. (2015). Infidelity lurks in your genes. *New York Times*, May 22. Retrieved June 27, 2016. from www.nytimes.com/2015/05/24/opinion/sunday/infidelity-lurks-in-your-genes.html

Frith, Chris (2007). *Making up the mind: how the brain creates our mental world.* Malden, MA: Blackwell.

Fuller, Robert C. (1986). *Americans and the unconscious*. New York: Oxford University Press.

Gaite, Carmen Martin (1991). *Love customs in eighteenth century Spain*. Berkeley, CA: University of California Press.

Gallup Inc. (2013). State of the American workplace. Retrieved August 30, 2015 from www.gallup.com/file/service of the American workplace report 2013.pdf

Gardinier, Bob. (2000). Priest told parishioners of plans for sex change. *Albany Times Union*. Retrieved August 30, 2014 from http://alb.merlinone.net/mweb/wmsql.wm/request?oneimage&imageid=6066791

Geertz, Clifford (1975). On the nature of anthropological understanding. *American Scientist*, 63, 47–53.

Geher, Glenn, and Kaufman, Scott Barry (2013). *Mating intelligence unleashed*. New York: Oxford University Press.

Gergen, Kenneth J. (1991). *The saturated self: dilemmas of identity in contemporary life.* New York: Basic Books.

Gergen, Kenneth J. (2000). The challenge of absent presence. In J. E. Katz and M. Aarkus (Eds.). *Perpetual contact: mobile communication, private talk, public performance.* Cambridge: Cambridge University Press, pp. 227–241.

Giddens, Anthony (1990). *The consequences of modernity*. Stanford, CA: Stanford University Press.

Giddens, Anthony (1991). *Modernity and self-identity: self and society in the late modern age.* Stanford, CA: Stanford University Press.

Giddens, Anthony (1992). *The transformation of intimacy: sexuality, love & eroticism in modern societies.* Stanford, CA: Stanford University Press.

Giddens, Anthony (2000). *Runaway world*. New York: Routledge.

References 299

Gillig, Paulette Marie (2009). Dissociative identity disorder: a controversial diagnosis. *Psychiatry*. 6, 24–29.

Gillis, John R. (1996). *A world of their own making: myth, ritual, and the quest for family values*. Cambridge, MA: Harvard University Press.

Ginsberg, Benjamin (2011). *The fall of the faculty: the rise of the all-administrative university and why it matters*. New York: Oxford University Press.

Gleick, James (2013). Total noise, only louder. *New York Magazine*, April 20. Retrieved April 24, 2013 from http://nymag.com/news/intelligencer/boston-manhunt-2013-4/

Goffman, Erving (1959). *The presentation of self in everyday life*. New York: Anchor Books.

Goffman, Erving (1966). *Behavior in public places: notes on the social organization of gatherings*. New York: Simon & Schuster.

Goffman, Erving (1967). On face-work. In *Interaction ritual*. New York: Anchor Books, pp. 5–45.

Gold, Joel, and Gold, Ian (2014). *Suspicious minds: how culture shapes madness*. New York: The Free Press.

Goleman, Daniel (2006). *Social intelligence: the new science of human relationships*. New York: Bantam Books.

Gopnik, Alison (2009). *The philosophical baby: what children's minds tell us about truth, love, and the meaning of life*. New York: Picador.

Gottlieb, Lori (2010). *Marry him: the case for settling for Mr. Good Enough*. New York: New American Library.

Graziano, Michael S. A. (2013). *Consciousness and the social brain*. New York: Oxford University Press.

Greenberg, Gary (2013). *The book of woe: the DSM and the unmaking of psychiatry*. New York: Blue Rider Press.

Greenfeld, Liah (2013). *Mind, modernity, madness: the impact of culture on human experience*. Cambridge, MA: Harvard University Press.

Greenfield, Susan (2008). *ID: the quest for meaning in the 21st century*. London: Sceptre.

Grohol, John M. (2015). Top 25 psychiatric medication prescriptions for 2013. Retrieved May 1, 2015 from http://psychcentral.com/lib/top-25-psychiatric-medication-prescriptions-for-2013/00019543

Grohol, John M. (2019). Personal communication.

Grotstein, James S. (1985). *Splitting and projective identification*. Northvale, NJ: Jason Aronson.

Guenther, Lisa (2013). *Solitary confinement: social death and its afterlives*. Minneapolis, MN: University of Minnesota Press.

Hacking, Ian (1995). *Rewriting the soul: multiple personality and the sciences of memory*. Princeton, NJ: Princeton University Press.

Haley, Jay (1963). *Strategies of psychotherapy*. New York: Grune & Stratton.

Halpern, David (2005). *Social capital*. Malden, MA: Polity Press.

Harari, Yuval Noah (2015). *Sapiens: a brief history of humankind*. New York: HarperCollins.

Harcourt, Felice (Ed.) (1971). *Memoirs of Madame de La Tour de Pin*. New York: Harcourt.

Harré, Rom (1998). *The singular self*. London: Sage.

Healy, David (2004). *Let them eat Prozac: the unhealthy relationship between the pharmaceutical industry and depression*. New York: New York University Press.

300 References

Healy, David (2012). *Pharmageddon*. Berkeley, CA: University of California Press.

Hedegaard, Holly, Curtin, Sally, and Warner, Margaret (2018). Suicide mortality in the United States, 1999–2017. NCHS Data Brief No. 330. National Center for Health Statistics. Retrieved January 7, 2020 from www.cdc.gov.nchs/products/databriefs/db330.htm

Heffner, Kathi L. (2009). Isolation, health effects. In Harry T. Reis, and Susan Sprecher (Eds.). *Encyclopedia of human relationships*. Thousand Oaks, CA: Sage, pp. 933–936.

Henderson, John M. (2014). Eye-tracking technology aims to take your unconscious pizza order. *Scientific American*. Retrieved September 3, 2015 from www.scientificamerican.com/article/eye-tracking-technology-aims-to-take-your-unconscious-pizza-order/

Herman, Judith L. (1992). *Trauma and recovery*. New York: Basic Books.

Hermans, Hubert J. M., and Gieser, Thorsten (2012). History, main tenets and core concepts of dialogical self theory. In H. J. M. Hermans and Thorsten Gieser (Eds.). *Handbook of dialogical self theory*. Cambridge: Cambridge University Press, pp. 1–22.

Herper, Matthew (2010). America's most popular mind medicines. *Forbes*. Retrieved March 25, 2015 from www.forbes.com/2010/09/16/prozac-xanax-valium-business-healthcare-psychiatric-drugs.html

Herzberg, David (2009). *Happy pills in America: from Miltown to Prozac*. Baltimore, MD: Johns Hopkins University Press.

Hewett, John (1989). *Dilemmas of the American self*. Philadelphia, PA: Temple University Press.

Hickok, Gregory (2014). *The myth of mirror neurons: the real neuroscience of communication and cognition*. New York: W. W. Norton.

Hoagland, Tony (2018). Data rain. In *Priest turned therapist treats fear of God*. Minneapolis, MN: Graywolf Press.

Hobson, J. Allan (2002). *Dreaming: a very short introduction*. New York: Oxford University Press.

Hobson, Peter (2004). *The cradle of thought: exploring the origins of thinking*. London, Pan Books.

Hochschild, Arlie Russell (1983). *The managed heart: commercialization of human feeling*. Berkeley, CA: University of California Press.

Hochschild, Arlie Russell (2012). *The outsourced self: intimate life in market times*. New York: Metropolitan Books.

Hofstadter, Douglas (2007). *I am a strange loop*. New York: Basic Books.

Holstein, James A., and Gubrium, Jabbar (2000). *The self we live by: narrative identity in a postmodern world*. New York: Oxford University Press.

Holt-Lunstad, Julianne, Smith, Timothy B., Baker, Mark, Harris, Tyler, and Stephenson, David (2015). Loneliness and social isolation as risk factors for mortality: a meta-analytic review. *Perspectives on Psychological Science*. 10(2), 227–237.

Illouz, Eva (2007). *Cold intimacies: the making of emotional capitalism*. Malden, MA: Polity Press.

Illouz, Eva (2012). *Why love hurts: a sociological explanation*. Malden, MA: Polity Press.

Jackson, Maggie (2009). *Distracted: the erosion of attention and the coming dark age*. New York: Prometheus Books.

James, William (1890/1981). *The principles of psychology, Volume 1*. Cambridge, MA: Harvard University Press.

Jaynes, Julian (1990). *The origin of consciousness in the breakdown of the bicameral mind*. New York: Houghton Mifflin.

References 301

Jensen, Christopher (2015). Essential part of the Volkswagen diesel repair is the owner. *New York Times*, October 19. Retrieved October 18, 2015 from www.nytimes.com/2015/10/19/business/the-owner-has-a-crucial-part-in-volkswagen-diesel-repair.html

Johnson, Frank (1985). The Western concept of self. In A. J. Marsella, G. DeVos, and F. L. K. Hsu (Eds.), *Culture and self: Asian and Western perspectives*. New York: Tavistock, pp. 90–138.

Jones, Edgar, Vermaas, Robert Hoogins, McCartney, Helen, Beeh, Charlotte, Palmer, Ian, Hyams, Kenneth, and Wessely, Simon (2003). Flashbacks and post-traumatic stress disorder: the genesis of a 20th-century diagnosis. *British Journal of Psychiatry*. 182, 158–163.

Jones, Louis C. (1992). The evil eye among European-Americans. In Alan Dundes (Ed.). *The evil eye: a casebook*. Madison, WI: University of Wisconsin Press, pp. 150–168.

Judson, Olivia (2002). *Dr. Tatiana's sex advice to all creation*. New York: Henry Holt.

Julian, Kate (2018). Why are young people having so little sex? Despite the easing of taboos and the rise of hookup aps, Americans are in the midst of a sex recession. *The Atlantic*. Retrieved November 27, 2018 from www.theatlantic.com/magazine/archive/2018/12/the-sex-recession/573949/

Kalanithi, Lucy (2016). My marriage didn't end when I became a widow. *New York Times*, January 6. Retrieved from https://opinionator.blogs.nytimes.com/2016/01/06/my-marriage-didnt-end-when-i-became-a-widow/

Kaplan, Margo (2014). Pedophilia: a disorder, not a crime. *New York Times*, October 6. Retrieved May 1, 2015 from www.nytimes.com/2014/10/06/opinion/pedophilia-a-disorder-not-a-crime.html

Kaplan, Robert D. (2017). *Earning the Rockies: how geography shapes America's role in the world*. New York: Random House.

Kasson, John (1991). *Rudeness & civility: manners in nineteenth-century urban America*. New York: Noonday Press.

Kegley, Jacquelyn Ann K. (2008). *Josiah Royce in focus*. Bloomington, IN: University of Indiana Press.

Keller, Helen (1903). *The story of my life*. New York: Doubleday, Page.

Kessler, Ronald C., Amminger, G. Paul, Aguilar-Gaxiola, Sergio, Alonso, Jordi, Lee, Sing, and Ustan, T. Bedirhan (2007). Age of onset of mental disorders: a review of recent literature. *Current Opinion in Psychiatry*. 20(4), 359–264.

Key, Wilson Bryan (1974). *Subliminal seduction*. New York: Signet.

Kihlstrom, John F. (2005). Dissociative disorders. *Annual Review of Clinical Psychology*. 1, 227–253.

Klaw, Spencer (1993). *Without sin: the life and death of the Oneida Community*. New York: Penguin Books.

Klinenberg, Eric (2012). *Going solo: the extraordinary rise and surprising appeal of living alone*. New York: Penguin Press.

Kolata, Gina, and Cohen, Sarah (2016). Drug overdoses propel rise in mortality rates of young whites. *New York Times*, January 17. Retrieved January 17, 2016 from www.nytimes.com/2016/01/17/accelerating overdoes-propel-rise-in-mortality-rates-among-young-whites.html

Konrath, Sara H., Chopik, William J., Hsing, Courtney K., and O'Brien, Ed (2014). Changes in adult attachment styles in American college students over time: a meta-analysis. *Personality and Social Psychology Review*. 18(4), 326–348.

302 *References*

Konrath, Sara H., O'Brien, Edward H., and Hsing, Courtney (2011). Changes in dispositional empathy in American college students over time: a meta-analysis. *Personality and Social Psychology Review*. 15(2), 180–198.

Kraybill, Donald B., Johnson-Weiner, Karen M., and Nolt, Steven M. (2013). *The Amish*. Baltimore, MD: Johns Hopkins University Press.

Kreider, Rose M. (2006). Remarriage in the United States. Presented at the annual meeting of the American Sociological Association. Montreal, Canada, August 10–14.

Kupfer, David J., and Regier, Darrel, A. (2011). Neuroscience, clinical evidence, and the future of psychiatric classification in DSM-5. *The American Journal of Psychiatry*. 168(7), 672–674.

Laing, R. D. (1967). *The politics of experience*. New York: Ballantine Books.

Laing, R. D. (1971). *The politics of the family and other essays*. New York: Vintage.

Lakoff, George (2012). Foreword. In Benjamin K. Bergen, *Louder than words: the new science of how the mind makes meaning*. NY: Basic Books, pp. ix – xi.

Lakoff, George, and Johnson, Mark (1980). *Metaphors we live by*. Chicago: University of Chicago Press.

Lamb, Kate (2018). "I felt disgusted": inside Indonesia's fake Twitter account factories. *The Guardian*. Retrieved July 29, 2018 from www.theguardian.com/world/2018/jul/23/indonesias-fake-twitter-account-factories-jakarta-politic

Lane, Christopher (2007). *Shyness: how normal behavior became a sickness*. New Haven, CT: Yale University Press.

Lane, Robert E. (2000). *The loss of happiness in market democracies*. New Haven, CT: Yale University Press.

Langer, Susanne K. (1957). *Philosophy in a new key: a study in the symbolism of religion, rite, and art* (3rd ed.). Cambridge, MA: Harvard University Press.

Lantz, Herman R., Keyes, Jane, and Schultz, Martin (1975). The American family in the preindustrial period: from base lines in history to change. *American Sociological Review*. 40(February), 21–36.

Larkin, Jack (1988). *The reshaping of everyday life 1790–1840*. New York: Harper & Row.

Larsen, Luke J., and Walters, Nathan P. (2013). Married-couple households by nativity status: 2011. Retrieved October 18, 2016 from www.census.gov/prod/2013pubs/acsbr11-16.pdf

Lasch, Christopher (1977). *Haven in a heartless world: the family besieged*. New York: W. W. Norton.

Lasch, Christopher (1979). *The culture of narcissism: American life in an age of diminishing expectations*. New York: W.W. Norton.

Lasch, Christopher (1993). The culture of consumption. In Mary K. Cayton, Elliot J. Gorn, and Peter W. Williams (Eds.), *The encyclopedia of American social history: Volume II*. New York: Scribners, pp. 1381–1390.

Laslett, Peter (1984). *The world we have lost: England before the industrial age* (3rd ed.). New York: Charles Scribner's.

Lawrence, James (2015). (Dis)placing trust: the long-term effects of job displacement on generalised trust over the adult lifecourse. *Social Science Research*. 50, 46–59.

Lehrer, Jonah (2016). *A book about love*. New York: Simon & Schuster.

Leonhardt, David, and Quealy, Kevin (2015). How your hometown affects your chances of marriage. *New York Times*. Retrieved May 15, 2015 from www.nytimes.com/2015/05/15/upshot/the-places-that-discourage-marriage-most.html

References 303

Levy, David (2008). *Love and sex with robots: the evolution of human – robot relationships*. New York: Harper Perennial.

Lewis, C. S. (1961). *A grief observed*. New York: Harper Collins.

Lifton, Robert Jay (1993). *The protean self: human resilience in an age of fragmentation*. New York: Basic Books.

Lincoln, Jackson Steward (1935/2010). *The dream in primitive cultures 1935*. Whitefish, MT: Kessinger.

Luckmann, Thomas (1979). Personal identity as an evolutionary and historical problem. In M. von Cranach, Foppa, W. Lepenies, and D. Ploog (Eds.). *Human ethology: claims and limits of a new discipline*. London: Cambridge University Press, pp. 56–74.

Lyons, John O. (1978). *The invention of the self: the hinge of consciousness in the eighteenth century*. Carbondale, IL: University of Southern Illinois Press.

Main, Gloria (2001). *Peoples of a spacious land: families and cultures in colonial New England*. Cambridge, MA: Harvard University Press.

Makari, George (2015). *Soul machine: the invention of the modern mind*. New York: W. W. Norton.

Mank, Russell Walter Jr. (1975). Family structure in Northampton, Massachusetts, 1654–1729 (doctoral dissertation). University of Denver.

Mansfield, Nick (2000). *Subjectivity: theories of the self from Freud to Haraway*. New York: New York University Press.

Marchand, Roland (1985). *Advertising the American dream: making way for modernity 1920–1940*. Berkeley, CA: University of California Press.

Marsden, Peter V., and Srivastava, Sameer B. (2012). Trends in informal social participation, 1974–2008. In Peter V. Marsen (Ed.). *Social trends in American life: findings from the General Social Survey since 1972*. Princeton, NJ: Princeton University Press, pp. 240–263.

Maslow, Abraham (1968). *Toward a psychology of being*. New York: John-Wiley.

McCall, George J., McCall, Michal M., Denzin, Norman K., and Kurth, Suzanne (1970). *Social relationships*. Chicago: Aldine.

McCall, George, and Simmons, J. L. (1978). *Identities and interactions: an examination of human associations in everyday life* (revised ed.). New York: Free Press.

Mead, George Herbert (1934/1962). *Mind, self, and society: from the standpoint of a social behaviorist*. Edited by Charles W. Morris. Chicago, IL: University of Chicago Press.

Meads/Wilson Collection (nd). Correspondence. Albany Institute of History and Art.

Meltzer, Bernard N., Petras, John W., and Reynolds, Larry T. (1975). *Symbolic interactionism: genesis, varieties and criticism*. Boston, MA: Routledge & Kegan Paul.

Merleau-Ponty, Maurice (1962). *Phenomenology of perception*. London: Routledge & Kegan Paul.

Metzinger, Thomas (2009). *The ego tunnel: the science of the mind and the myth of the self*. New York: Basic Books.

Meyrowitz, Joshua (1985). *No sense of place: the impact of electronic media on social behavior*. New York: Oxford University Press.

Midgley, Mary (2002). *Science and poetry*. New York: Routledge.

Miller, Kirk, Yost, Berwood, Flaherty, Sean, Hillemeier, Marianne M., Chase, Gary A., Weisman, Carol S., and Dyer, Anne-Marie (2007). Health status, health conditions, and health behaviors among Amish women: results from the Central Pennsylvania Women's Health Study (CePAWHS). *Women's Health Issues*. 17(3), 162–171.

304 *References*

Minsky, Marvin (1986). *The society of mind*. New York: Simon & Schuster.

Mintz, Steven, and Kellogg, Susan (1988). *Domestic revolutions: a social history of American family life*. New York: Free Press.

Modell, Arnold H. (2003). *Imagination and the meaningful brain*. Cambridge, MA: MIT Press.

Molloy, Raven, Smith, Christopher, L., and Wozniak, Abigail (2011). Internal migration in the United States. *Journal of Economic Perspectives*. 25(3, Summer), 173–196.

Monitopoli, Brian (2010). 29% accessed porn on work computers last month. Retrieved May 1, 2015 from www.cbsnews.com/news/20-accessed-porn-on-work-computers-last-month

Monkkonen, Eric H. (1985). *America becomes urban: the development of U.S. cities & towns 1780–1980*. Berkeley, CA: University of California Press.

Monto, Martin A., and Carey, Anna G. (2014). A new standard of sexual behavior? Are claims associated with the "Hookup Culture" supported by General Social Survey Data? *Journal of Sex Research*. 51, 605–615.

Moore, Thomas J., and Mattison, Donald R. (2016). Adult utilization of psychiatric drugs and differences by sex, age, and race. *Journal of the American Medical Association – Internal Medicine*. Published online December 12. Retrieved December 13, 2016 from http://jamanetwork.com/journals/jamainternalmedicine/fullarticle/2592697

Morgan, Edmund S. (1966). *The Puritan family: religion and domestic relations in seventeenth century New England*. New York: Harper & Row.

Morris, David J. (2015). *The evil hours: a biography of post-traumatic stress disorder*. New York: Houghton Mifflin Harcourt.

Mosbergen, Dominique (2014). Man posing for gun selfie dies after firearm goes off: report. *Huffington Post*. Retrieved February 22, 2015 from www.huffingtonpost.com/2014/08/04/man-gun-selfie-oscar-aguilar/_n/_5647947.html

Moss, Robert (2009). *The secret history of dreaming*. Novato, CA: New World Library.

Muchembled, Robert (2012). *A history of violence: from the end of the Middle Ages to the present*. Malden, MA: Polity Press.

Murray, Sandra L, and Holmes, John G. (1996). The construction of relationship realities. In Garth J. O. Fletcher and Julie Fitness (Eds.). *Knowledge structures in close relationships*. Mahwah, NJ: Lawrence Erlbaum, pp. 91–120.

Nadel, S. F. (1953). Social control and self-regulation. *Social Forces*. 31, 265–273.

National Geographic Society (1988). *Historical atlas of the United States*. Washington, D.C.: National Geographic Society.

National Institute of Mental Health (2015). Any mental illness (AMI) among adults. Retrieved March 27, 2015 from www.nimh.nih.gov/health/statistics/prevalence/any-mental-illness-ami-among-adults.shtml

Nesdale, Drew, and Zimmer-Gembeck, Melanie J. (2014). Peer rejection in childhood: social groups, rejection sensitivity, and solitude. In Robert J. Coplan and Julie C. Bowker (Eds.). *The handbook of solitude: psychological perspectives on social isolation, social withdrawal, and being along*. Chichester, UK: John-Wiley, pp. 129–149.

New York City Department of City Planning (2012). NYC total and foreign-born population 1790–2000. Retrieved September 28, 2012 from www.nyc.gov/html/dcp/pdf/census/1790-2000nyctotalforeignbirth.pdf

Ng, Naomi (2014). Twitter declares 2014 the year of the selfie. Retrieved March 27, 2015 from www.cnn.com/2014/12/12/techtwitter-selfie-trend/

References 305

Nisbet, Robert (1953/2010). *The quest for community: a study in the ethics of order and freedom*. Wilmington, DE: Intercollegiate Studies Institute.

NORC (2015). General social survey: trends in psychological well-being, 1972–2014. Retrieved January 7, 2016 from www.norc.org/PDFs/GSS

O'Connor, Anahad (2015). New York Attorney General targets supplements at major retailers. Retrieved February 3, 2015 from http://well.blogs.nytimes.com/2015/02/03/new-york-attorney-general-targets-supplements-at-major-retailers

Oliver, Mary (1997). Stars. In *West wind: poems and prose poems*. New York: Houghton Mifflin, p. 13.

O'Malley, Michael (1990). *Keeping watch: a history of American time*. New York: Viking.

Ong, Walter J. (1982). *Orality and literacy: the technologizing of the word*. New York: Routledge.

Orne, M. T., and Evans, F. J. (1965). Social control in the psychological experiment: antisocial behavior and hypnosis. *Journal of Personality and Social Psychology*. 1, 189–200.

Packard, Vance (1959). *The hidden persuaders*. New York: Pocket Books.

Packard, Vance (1974). *A nation of strangers*. New York: Pocket Books.

Paoletti, Jo B. (1997). The gendering of infants' and toddlers' clothing in America. In K. Martinez and K. Ames (Eds.)., *The material culture of gender: the gender of material culture*. Hanover, NH: University Press of New England, pp. 27–35.

Parfit, Derek (1971). Personal identity. *Philosophical Review*. 80(1), 3–27.

Parrillo, Vincent N. (2009). *Diversity in America* (3rd ed). Thousand Oaks, CA: Pine Forge Press.

Pepper, Steven C. (1970). *World hypotheses: a study in evidence*. Berkeley, CA: University of California Press.

PerryUndem Research Communication (2017). The state of the union on gender equality, sexism, and women's rights: results from a national survey conducted by PerryUndem. Retrieved April 30, 2020 from www.scribd.com/document/336804316/PerryUndem-Gender-Equality-Report

Pew Center for Research on Social and Demographic Trends (2008). American mobility: who moves? Who stays put? Where's home? Washington, D.C.: The Pew Research Center.

Pew Forum on Hispanic Trends (2015). Modern immigration wave brings 59 million to U.S., driving population growth and change through 2065. Views on immigration's impact on U.S. society mixed. Washington, D.C.: The Pew Research Center.

Pew Forum on Religion and Public Life (2008). U.S. religious landscape survey: religious affiliation: diverse and dynamic. Washington, D.C.: The Pew Research Center.

Pew Forum on Religion and Public Life (2012). "Nones" on the rise: one-in-five adults have no religious affiliation. Washington, D.C.: The Pew Research Center.

Pew Forum on Religion and Public Life (2015). A closer look at America's rapidly growing religious "nones." Washington, D.C.: The Pew Research Center.

Pew Forum on Social and Demographic Trends (2010). *The decline of marriage and the rise of new families*. Washington, D.C.: The Pew Research Center.

Pew Forum on Social and Demographic Trends (2014). *Millennials in adulthood: detached from institutions, networked with friends*. Washington, D.C.: The Pew Research Center.

Pollan, Michael (2018). *How to change your mind: what the new science of psychedelics teaches us about consciousness, dying, addiction, depression, and transcendence*. New York: Penguin Press.

306 References

Postman, Neil (1993). *Technopoly: the surrender of culture to technology.* New York: Vintage.

Pratt, Laura A., Brody, Debra J., and Gu, Quiping (2011). Antidepressant use in persons aged 12 and over: United States, 2005–2008. National Center for Health Statistics Data Brief. No. 76. Retrieved March 25, 2015 from www.cdc.gov/nchs/data/databriefs/db76.pdf

Presser, Stanley, and Stinson, Linda (1998). Data collection mode and social desirability bias in self-reported religious attendance. *American Sociological Review.* 63(1), 137–145.

Prewitt, Kenneth (2013). *What is your race? The census and our flawed efforts to classify Americans.* Princeton, NJ: Princeton University Press.

Prum, Richard O. (2017). *The evolution of beauty: how Darwin's forgotten theory of mate choice shapes the animal world – and us.* New York: Doubleday.

Putnam, Robert D. (2000). *Bowling alone: the collapse and revival of American community.* New York: Simon & Schuster.

Putnam, Robert D. (2007). E pluribus unum: diversity and community in the twenty-first century. *Scandinavian Political Studies.* 30(2), 137–174.

Rahula, Walpola (1974). *What the Buddha taught* (2nd ed.). New York: Grove Press.

Ramachandran, Vilayanur (nd). Mirror neurons and imitation learning as the driving force behind the great leap forward in human evolution. Retrieved February 25, 2015 from https://edge.org/conversation/mirror-neurons-and-imitation-learning-as-the-driving-force-behind-the-great-leap-forward-in-human-evolution

Rees, W. Dewi (1971). The hallucinations of widowhood. *British Medical Journal.* 4, 37–41.

Reynolds, Peter H. (2009). *The north star.* Somerville, MA: Candlewick Press.

Riesman, David, Glazer, Nathan, and Denney, Reuel (1961). *The lonely crowd.* New Haven: Yale University Press.

Riley, Naomi Schaefer (2013). *'Til faith do us part: how interfaith marriage is transforming America.* New York: Oxford University Press.

Ritzer, George (1996). *The MacDonaldization of society* (revised ed.). Thousand Oaks, CA: Pine Forge Press.

Rizzolatti, Giacomo, and Fabbri-Destro, Maddalena (2010). Mirror neurons: from discovery to autism. *Experimental Brain Research.* 200(3–4), 223–237.

Roberts, Sam (2010). Listening to (and saving) the world's languages. *New York Times,* April 28, 2010. Retrieved November 28, 2013 from www.nytimes.com/2010/04/29/nyregion/29lost.html

Robinson, Daniel N. (1995). *An intellectual history of psychology* (3rd ed.). Madison, WI: University of Wisconsin Press.

Robinson, Marilynne (2010). *Absence of mind: the dispelling of inwardness from the modern myth of the self.* New Haven, CT: Yale University Press.

Robinson, Robert V., and Jackson, Elton F. (2001). Is trust in others declining in America? An age-period-cohort analysis. *Social Science Research.* 30, 117–145.

Rose, Nikolas, and Abi-Rached, Joelle M. (2013). *Neuro: the new brain sciences and the management of the mind.* Princeton, NJ: Princeton University Press.

Rosenberg, Morris (1989). Self-concept research: a historical overview. *Social Forces.* 68(1), 34–44.

Roth, Randolph (2009). *American homicide.* Cambridge, MA: Belknap Press of Harvard University Press.

Rozhon, Tracie (2007). To have, hold and cherish, until bedtime. *New York Times,* March 11. Retrieved April 27, 2018 from www.nytimes.com/2007/03/11/us/11separate.html

References 307

Rubin, Lillian Breslow (1976). *Worlds of pain: life in the working-class family*. New York: Basic Books.

Rubin, Lillian Breslow (1983). *Intimate strangers: men and women together*. New York: Harper Perennial.

Rusbult, Caryl E., and Righetti, Francesca (2009). Investment model. In Harry T. Reis and Susan Sprecher (Eds.). *Encyclopedia of human relationships*. Thousand Oaks, CA: Sage, pp. 928–931.

Ryan, Camille (2013). Language use in the United States: 2011. American Community Survey Reports. United States Census Bureau. Retrieved November 28, 2013 from www.census.gov/prod/2013pubs/acs-22.pdf

Ryan, Christopher, and Jeth'a, Cacilda (2010). *Sex at dawn: how we mate, why we stray, and what it means for modern relationships*. New York: Harper Perennial.

Sapir, Edward E. (1929). The status of linguistics as a science. *Language*. 5(4), 207–214.

Sartre, Jean-Paul (1943/1986). *Being and nothingness: a phenomenological essay on ontology* (translated and with an introduction by Hazel E. Barnes). New York: Washington Square Press.

Sass, Louis (2017). *Madness and modernism: insanity in the light of modern art, literature, and thought* (revised ed.). New York: Oxford University Press.

Satel, Sally, and Lilienfeld, Scott O. (2013). *Brainwashed: the seductive appeal of mindless neuroscience*. New York: Basic Books.

Sato, Toru, Harman, Brittany, A., Donohoe, Whitney, M., Weaver, Allison, and Hall, William A. (2010). Individual differences in ego depletion: the role of sociotropy-autonomy. *Motivation and Emotion*. 34(2), 205–213.

Scheiber, Noam (2015). Rising economic insecurity tied to decades-long trend in employment practices. *New York Times*, July 13. Retrieved July 13, 2015 from www.nytimes.com/2015/07/13/rising-economic-insecurity-tied-to-decades-long-trend-in-emploment-practices.html

Schlenker, Barry R. (1984). Identities, identifications, and relationships. In Valerian J. Derlega (Ed.). *Communication, intimacy, and close relationships*. New York: Academic Press, pp. 71–104.

Schnabel, Landon (forthcoming). Religion and gender equality worldwide: a country-level analysis. *Social Indicators Research*. 1–15.

Schwartz, Barry (2004). *The paradox of choice: why more is less*. New York: Harper Collins.

Schwarz, Alan (2013). The selling of attention deficit disorder. *New York Times*, December 14. Retrieved December 15, 2013 from www.nytimes.com/2013/12/15/health/the-selling-of-attention-deficit-disorder.html

Schwarz, Alan (2014). Thousands of toddlers are medicated for A.D.H.D., report finds, raising worries. *New York Times*, May 16. Retrieved August 12, 2014 from www.nytimes.com/2014/05/17/us/among-experts-scrutiny-of-attention-disorder-diagnoses-in-2-and-3-year-olds.html

Schwarz, Alan (2016). *ADHD nation: children, doctors, big pharma, and the making of an American epidemic*. New York: Schribner.

Seife, Charles (2014). *Virtual unreality: just because the internet told you, how do you know it's true?* New York: Viking Penguin.

Sennett, Richard (1976). *The fall of public man: on the social psychology of capitalism*. New York: Vintage Books.

Sennett, Richard (2012). *Together: the rituals, pleasures and politics of cooperation*. New Haven, CT: Yale University Press.

308 *References*

Seung, Sebastian (2013). *Connectome: how the brain's wiring makes us who we are.* New York: Houghton Mifflin.

Shanahan, James, and Morgan, Michael (1999). *Television and its viewers: cultivation theory and research.* London: Cambridge University Press.

Shils, Edward (1981). *Tradition.* Chicago: University of Chicago Press.

Slater, Lauren (2018). *Blue dreams: the science and the story of the drugs that changed our minds.* New York: Little, Brown.

Smith, Brendan L. (2012). Inappropriate prescribing. *Monitor on Psychology.* 43(6), 36.

Smith, Claire Bidwell (2015). *After this: when life is over, where do we go?* New York: Penguin Random House.

Smith, Shannon (2009). Bank account model. In Harry T. Reis and Susan Sprecher (Eds.). *Encyclopedia of human relationships.* Thousand Oaks, CA: Sage, pp. 148–149.

Smith, Tom W. (1998). A review of church attendance measures. *American Sociological Review.* 63(1), 131–136.

Stevens, Anthony (1993). *The two million-year-old self.* College Station, TX: Texas A&M University Press.

Stevenson, Betsey, and Wolfers, Justin (2009). The paradox of declining female happiness. National Bureau of Economic Research (NBER) Working Paper No. 14969. Retrieved March 2, 2016 from www.nber.org/papers/w14969

Stone, Lawrence (1977). *The family, sex and marriage in England 1500–1800.* London: Penguin.

Strand, Oliver (2016). Is the world's best croissant in Australia? *New York Times,* April 11. Retrieved April 17, 2016 from www.nytimes.com/2016/04/11/t-magazine/food/lune-croissanterie-melbourne-croissants.html

Streitfeld, David (2013). Give yourself 5 stars? Online, it might cost you. *New York Times.* Retrieved April 23, 2018 from www.nytimes.com/technology/give-yourself-4-starts-online-it-might-cost-you.html

Stroebe, Wolfgang, and Stroebe, Margaret S. (1987). *Bereavement and health: the psychological and physical consequences of partner loss.* New York: Cambridge University Press.

Szasz, Thomas (2007). *The medicalization of everyday life: selected essays.* Syracuse, NY: Syracuse University Press.

Szasz, Thomas S. (1974). *The myth of mental illness: foundations of a theory of personal conduct* (revised ed.). New York: Harper & Row.

Szasz, Thomas S. (2008). *Psychiatry: the science of lies.* Syracuse, NY: Syracuse University Press.

Szymborska, Wisława (1995). *View with a grain of sand: selected poems.* New York: Houghton Mifflin Harcourt.

Szymborska, Wisława (1998). Life while you wait. In *Poems new and collected 1957–1997.* New York: Harcourt.

Tallis, Raymond (2004). *Why the mind is not a computer: a pocket lexicon of neuromythology.* Exeter, UK: Imprint Academic.

Tallis, Raymond (2011). *Aping mankind: neuromania, Darwinitis, and the misrepresentation of humanity.* Durham, UK: Acumen.

Tallis, Raymond (2013). *Reflections of a metaphysical flâneur and other essays.* Durham, UK: Acumen.

Tavernise, Sabrina (2016a). Sweeping pain as suicides hit a 30-year high. *New York Times.* Retrieved April 22, 2016 from www.nytimes.com/2016/04/22/health/us-suicide-rate-surges-to-a-30-year-high.htm

References 309

Taylor, Charles (1989). *Sources of the self: the making of modern identity*. Cambridge, MA: Harvard University Press.

Taylor, Charles (1991). *The ethics of authenticity*. Cambridge, MA: Harvard University Press.

Taylor, Charles (2007). *A secular age*. Cambridge, MA: Belknap Press of Harvard University Press.

Taylor, Charles (2016). *The language animal: the full shape of the human linguistic capacity*. Cambridge, MA: Belknap Press of Harvard University Press.

Taylor, Robert J. (Ed.) (1979). *The Adams papers, papers of John Adams, Vol. 4, February – August 1776*. Cambridge, MA: Harvard University Press, pp. 208–213.

The Harris Poll (2013). Americans' belief in God, miracles and heaven declines: belief in Darwin's theory of evolution rises. Retrieved June 28, 2021 from https://theharrispoll.com/new-york-n-y-december-16–2013-a-new-harris-poll-finds-that-while-a-strong-majority-74-of-u-s-adults-do-believe-in-god-this-belief-is-in-decline-when-compared-to-previous-years-as-just-over/

Thibaut, John, and Kelley, Harold (1959). *The social psychology of groups*. New York: John Wiley & Sons.

Todd, Arthur J. (1916). Primitive notions of the "self." *American Journal of Psychology*, 27(2), 171–202.

Trans-Atlantic Slave Trade Database. (2016). Trans-Atlantic slave trade – estimates. Accessed May 9, 2016 from www.slavevoyages.org/tast/assessment/estimates.faces

Triandis, Harry C. (1989). The self and social behavior in differing cultural contexts. *Psychological Review*. 96(3), 506–520.

Trivers, Robert L. (1972). Parental investment and sexual selection. In Bernard Campbell (Ed.). *Sexual selection and the descent of man*. Chicago, IL: Aldine, pp. 136–179.

Tuan, Yi-Fu (1982). *Segmented worlds and self: group life and individual consciousness*. Minneapolis, MN: University of Minnesota Press.

Turkle, Sherry (1995). *Life on the screen: identity in the age of the internet*. New York: Simon and Schuster.

Turkle, Sherry (2011). *Alone together: why we expect more from technology and less from each other*. New York: Basic Books.

Turkle, Sherry (2015). *Reclaiming conversation: the power of talk in a digital age*. New York: Penguin Press.

Twenge, Jean M., Konrath, Sarah, Foster, Joshua D., Campbell, W. Keith, and Bushman, Brad J. (2008). Egos inflating over time: a cross-temporal meta-analysis of the Narcissistic Personality Inventory. *Journal of Personality*. 76, 4, 875–901.

Tönnies, Ferdinand (1887/2011). *Community and society* (Translated by Charles P. Loomis). Mineola, NY: Dover.

United States Bureau of Labor Statistics (2013). Employment situation news release. Retrieved March 25, 2013 from www.bls.gov/news.release/empsit.htm

United States Census Bureau (2007). Statistical abstract of the United States: 2008. Washington, D.C.: U.S. Government Printing Office.

United States Census Bureau (2014). America's families and living arrangements: 2013: Households (H table series). Retrieved September 29, 2014 from www.census.gov/hhes/families/data/cps2013H.html

Valtorta, Nicole K., Kanaan, Mona, Gilbody, Simon, Ronzi, Sara, and Hanratty, Barbara (2016). Loneliness and social isolation as risk factors for coronary heart disease and stroke: systematic review and meta-analysis of longitudinal observational studies. *Heart*. 0, 1–8.

310 *References*

Van de Castle, Robert L. (1994). *Our dreaming mind*. New York: Ballantine.

Vassos, Evangelos, Pedersen, Carsten B., Murray, Robin M., Collier, David A., and Lewis, Cathryn M. (2012). Meta-analysis of the association of urbanicity with schizophrenia. *Schizophrenia Bulletin*. 38(6), 1118–1123.

Viney, Linda (1969). Self: the history of a concept. *Journal of the History of the Behavioral Sciences*. 5(4), 349–359.

Walster, Elaine, Walster, G. William., and Berscheid, Ellen. (1978). *Equity: theory and research*. New York: Allyn & Bacon.

Wang, Wendy (2013). For young adults, the ideal marriage meets reality. Pew Research Center "FactTank." Published July 10. Retrieved November 28, 2013 from www.pewresearch.org/fact-take/2013/07/10/for-young-adults-the-ideal-marriage-meets-realty

Wang, Wendy, and Parker, Kim (2014). Record share of Americans have never married as values, economics and gender patterns change. Pew Research Center. Published September 24, 2014. Retrieved September 30, 2014 from www.pewresearch.org/social-trends/2014/09/24/record-share-of-americans-have-never-married

Warner, Kimberly, Lowell, Beth, Disla, Carlos, Ortenzi, Kate, Savitz, Jacqueline, and Hirshfield, Michael (2015). Oceana reveals mislabeling of iconic Chesapeake Blue Crab. Oceana. Retrieved October 29, 2015 from http://usa.oceana.org/sites/default/files/crab-testing-report-final-3.27.15.pdf

Warner, Kimberly, Timme, W., Lowell, B., and Hirshfield, Michael (2013). Oceana study reveals seafood fraud nationwide. Oceana. Retrieved October 29, 2015 from http://usa.oceana.org/reports/oceana-study-reveals-seafood-fraud-nationwide

Watts, Alan (1951/2011). *The wisdom of insecurity: a message for an age of anxiety* (2nd ed.). New York: Vintage.

Watzlawick, Paul, Beavin Bavelas, Janet, and Jackson, Don (1967). *Pragmatics of human communication: a study of interactional patterns, pathologies, and paradoxes*. New York: W. W. Norton.

Watzlawick, Paul, Weakland, John H., and Fisch, Richard (1974). *Change: principles of problem formation and problem resolution*. New York: W. W. Norton.

Wegner, Daniel M. (2002). *The illusion of conscious will*. Cambridge, MA: Bradford Books, MIT Press.

Wegner, Daniel M., Giuliano, Toni, and Hertel, Paula T. (1985). Cognitive interdependence in close relationships. In W. J. Ickes (Ed.). *Compatible and incompatible relationships*. New York: Springer-Verlag, pp. 253–276.

Weigel, Moira (2016). *Labor of love: the invention of dating*. New York: Farrar, Straus & Giroux.

Weil, Elizabeth (2019). What do teens learn online today? That identity is a work in progress. *New York Times*. Retrieved November 15, 2019 from www.nytimes.com/interactive/2019/11/13/magazine/internet-teens.html

Whitaker, Robert (2010). *Anatomy of an epidemic: magic bullets, psychiatric drugs and the astonishing rise of mental illness*. New York: Random House.

Whitaker, Robert, and Cosgrove, Lisa (2015). *Psychiatry under the influence*. New York: Palgrave Macmillan.

White, E. B. (1949/1976). *Here is New York*. New York: The Little Bookroom.

White, Erin (2016). Her life. My life. In Cathi Hanauer (Ed.). *The bitch is back: older, wiser, and (getting) happier*. New York: William Morrow, pp. 167–178.

Whyte, Lancelot Law (1960). *The unconscious before Freud: a history of the evolution of human awareness*. New York: Basic Books.

References 311

Wiener, Jon (2014). What makes Ohio State the most unequal public university in America? *The Nation.* Retrieved June 18, 2015 from www.thenation.com/blog/179920/what-makes-ohio-state-most-unequal-public-university-america

Wiener, Norbert (1954). *The human use of human beings: cybernetics and society.* Boston, MA: Houghton Mifflin.

Winterson, Jeanette (2011). *Why be happy when you could be normal?* New York: Grove Press.

Wittgenstein, Ludwig (1953/2009). *Philosophical investigations* (translated by G. E. M. Anscombe, P. M. S. Hacker, and Joachim Schulte; revised 4th ed. by P. M. S. Hacker and Joachim Schulte). Malden, MA: Wiley-Blackwell.

Wolfe, Alan (2001). *Moral freedom: the search for virtue in a world of choice.* New York: W. W. Norton.

Wolin, Steven J., and Bennett, Linda A. (1984). Family rituals. *Family Process.* 23, 401–420.

Woolf, Virginia (1929/2013). *A room of one's own.* New York: Snowball.

Wright, Thomas (1871). *The homes of other days: a history of domestic manners and sentiments in England.* London: Trübner.

Wu, Tim (2016). Mother Nature is brought to you by . . . *New York Times.* Retrieved December 4, 2016 from www.nytimes.com/2016/12/02/opinion/sunday/mother-nature-is-brought-to-you-by.html

Wuthnow, Robert (2013). *Small-town America: finding community, shaping the future.* Princeton, NJ: Princeton University Press.

Yang, Yang Claire, Boen, Courtney, Gerken, Karen, Li, Ting, Schorpp, Kristen, and Harris, Kathleen Mullan (2016). Social relationships and physiological determinants of longevity across the human life span. *Proceedings of the National Academy of Sciences.* Published online January 4, 2016, doi:10.1073/pnas.1511085112

Yeginsu, Ceylan (2018). U.K. appoints a minister for loneliness. *New York Times.* Retrieved January 17, 2018 from www.nytimes.com/2018/01/17/world/europe/uk-britain-loneliness.html

Young, Allan (1995). *The harmony of illusions: inventing post-traumatic stress disorder.* Princeton, NJ: Princeton University Press.

Yurchisin, Jennifer, Watchravesringkan, Kittichai, and McCabe, Deborah Brown (2005). An exploration of identity re-creation in the context of internet dating. *Social Behavior and Personality.* 33(8), 735–750.

Zeldin, Theodore (1996). *An intimate history of humanity.* New York: Harper Perennial.

Zelizer, Viviana A. (2005). *The purchase of intimacy.* Princeton, NJ: Princeton University Press.

Zerubavel, Eviatar (1990). *The fine line: making distinctions in everyday life.* Chicago, IL: University of Chicago Press.

Zurcher, Louis A. (1977). *The mutable self: a self-concept for social change.* Beverly Hills, CA: Sage.

Index

abandonment of self 80
abreaction 281
academic journals, rate of appearance of
 articles about the self 164
accelerated feedback loops,
 psychological consequences 143
Ackerman, Diane 56, 182
acquired memory 172, 196
active symbol-processing mind 268
actors (film and stage) and problems of
 self 246–7
Adams, John 95
addictive behavior 42, 70, 105, 112, 239,
 286
ADHD 3–4, 224
adolescence 36, 132, 170
advanced social coordination 29–30
advertising 111–12, 159–60; *see also*
 dark communications industries
advice columns 193
affectionate relationships 46–7
agoraphobia, coincident with the rapid
 onset of urbanization 126
agrarian society declines resulting in
 restructuring of family life, sex roles,
 and personal identity 145
Albany, New York 111
alienation 17, 111, 117, 146, 214, 248–50
alternative/new partners 15, 56, 78, 254
Altman, Irwin 80
Alzheimer's disease (see dementia and
 memory loss)
Amazon: fraudulent product reviews
 109; displacement of local businesses
 111
America: analysis of trends 1–3, 8;
 areas of change **69**; communication-
 as-symbol 45–6; "culture of
 narcissism" 7; current of restlessness

70; declining empathy 235–6;
 diagnosable psychiatric disorders 4;
 escape in fantasy 41–2; interpersonal
 experiences 236–7; languages
 spoken in households 118; mental
 disorders 284; modern children 82;
 presidents 90; psychological and social
 difficulties 8; sense of self 13; white
 males 90
American economy: national economy
 displacing local economy 107–8
American Linguistic Association and
 gender neutral language and Sapir
 Whorf hypothesis 34
American Psychiatric Association (APA)
 224, 283, 284–5, 286
American Psychological Association
 (APA) and endorsement of methods of
 torture in the war on terror 216
American society: major directions of
 change 68–9
analog I (Jaynes) 33
anatta (Buddhist idea that the self is an
 illusion) 167
Andersen, Kurt 9–10
Android operating system paradoxical
 advertisement 229
anguish 195–6, 247
anguish-of-being 42
anguish-of-decision 42
animalis loquentes (the talking animal)
 25
animal magnetism (Mesmer) 199,
 200, 277; *see also* mesmerism, and
 hypnotism
animals: cognitive capabilities and social
 behavior 27; self and language 183;
 signal communication 26–7, 28,
 176–7, 264–5; vocalization 28

Index 313

animistic spirituality 98
anomie (Durkheim) 117, 161
anonymity of urban life, impacts of 125, 138
anti-anxiety drugs 281; *see also* Equanil, Miltown, Xanax
anxiety: originating in the acquisition of symbolic language 30, and from loss of control of the self-narrative 195, and from rapid cultural change 205, 218, and from the decline of tradition 104, and from trauma 205; self-identity as protection from 35; absent in episodic culture 31; higher frequency among adolescents 36; attempts at management through classic mechanisms of psychological defense 206, and through aggression, hostility, scapegoating, and bullying 9, 107, 249–50, and through alignment with contrarian ideas 42, and through addictive, compulsive, or ritualized behavior 102, 105, and through drugs and alcohol 42, and through compulsive shopping 112, and through social conformity 218; lower rates among the Old Order Amish 225, and among members of non-modern Amazonian tribes 16; linked to impulsive behavior 238, and to poorly formed self-identity 7, 158, 238–9, and to increased autonomy and freedom of self-definition 13, 38, 239, and to social segmentation and psychological fragmentation 247–50, and to high speed information flows 40, and to the threat of economic decline 91, and to instability of meaning created by commercial and political codswallop 111 258, and to geographical relocation 120, and to psychological fragmentation and social segmentation 144, 248, and to social isolation 169, 239, and to memory loss 171; as a basis for the emergence of unconscious mental operations 189
aphasia: and limbic speech 29; and spouse of stroke victim functioning as a spare mind 182
archetypes (Jungian) as cultural templates for self-identity 202–3
architecture of the house 134–5, 148–9
Aristotle 163, 277

Arrival (science fiction film) 34
artisan foods 110
artisans 106
Associated Press 142
associational learning 180
associational meaning 47
atomization 121
attachment 85, 184–185
attachment theory 80
attraction (interpersonal) 80, 220, 264, 271–2, 274
attractive faces in history 233
autobiographical/narrative self 33–4
automobile manufacturers and fraud 160
autonomy 37, 59–62, 81, 105, 123, 134, 138, 150, 159
awareness of self 132, 157–9; *see also* self-identity
Azusa, California 121

babies 177–8, 234; *see also* infants
Bailey, Beth 79
bank account model of relationships 80
Baron Cohen, Sacha 124
Baroque era music 76, 102
Bauman, Zygmunt 104, 108, 127, 215, 249
Becker, Ernest 59, 61, 166, **206**
Beck-Gernsheim, Elisabeth 106
Beck, Ulrich 106
Bedrooms (see architecture)
belief consensus declining with increasing sociological diversity 118
Bellah, Robert 123
Bell Labs 49
Bem, Sandra 54–5
Berger, Peter 120
Bergman, Ingmar 245, 246
Berlin (city) 47, 134
Berlin, Isaiah 175
Bernard, Jessie 84
Bernstein, Basil 56
Berra, Lawrence Peter ('Yogi') 39
Berry, Wendell 171, 228
Berscheid, Ellen. 80
bicameral mind (Jaynes) 32–3
Big Bang 23–5
biographical self-narrative 173, 179, 214, 248
biological theory of depression 7
The Bird's Nest (Jackson) 241
birth control pill and gains in women's equality 223

314 *Index*

Blackmore, Susan 275
body dualism 167
Bolero (Ravel) 15
bonds 274
Borat (film) 124
borderline personality disorder 16, 36, 41, 138
Boston Marathon bombing and high speed information flows 142
Braid, James 199
brain functions and the self 180–1
brainwashing, mid-twentieth century fascination with 159
Brandenburg (German city) 47
branding people through product choices and corporate logos 111–12
Breuer, Joseph 201
broadcast journalism, fading trust in 216
Buddhism 175–6
bureaucracy 55, 146–7
bureaucratically structured institutions 249
Burke, Kenneth 46, 91, 182, 262–3, 264, 276, 279, 287
Burke, Peter 17
Bush, Jeb 143
Buss, David 273, 274

Calhoun, Arthur 72–3
Cambridge Analytica 160
camera as a tool of the self 221
Campbell, Joseph 203
Cartesian mind 167, 168
Cartesian split 166, 170
Cartwright, Rosalind 204
Catholic Church 55, 99–100, 108, 215
causa sui project (Becker): the inevitably futile search for autonomy 59
Celello, Kristin 96
Chabris, Christopher 24
characterological templates (Carl Jung's archetypes) 24–5
Charcot, Jean-Martin 201
chemically perfected lives 223
Chesapeake Bay blue crab, marketing fraud 110
childhood, history of 80–81
childhood dress, history of 146
children 80–2, 231, 235, 250, and the hypnotic acquisition of identity 200; as miniature adults 80–81
Chodorow, Nancy 61, 258
choice 39–40, 57, 72–4, 78, 90, 93, 104, 118, 161–2, 168, 183, 218, 262–3, 268, 270–1, 273, 278–9, 282–3, 285, 289
cholera epidemic of 1832 99

A Christmas Carol (Dickens) 202
The Chronicles of Narnia 111
church attendance, declining 99–100
Churchland, Patricia 278
Ciccone, Madonna Louise (Madonna) 23
Cincinnati, rapid population growth 128
Citi Field (Shea Stadium) and the commercial takeover of public symbols 111
civil inattention (Goffman) 125, 244
Civilization and Its Discontents (Freud) 95
civil rights movement contributing to restructuring of power relationships and social equality for women 96
Classical Greek civilization 176
Cleckley, Hervey M. 241
Clemens, Samuel (Mark Twain) 73
climate change 1–19, 70, 117, 248
clothing, styles of 39, 145–6
club membership, declining 122
code of "honest signals" used to convey reproductive potential 272
codes of conduct and the suppression of impulse 192
co-evolution of consciousness 62
cognitive interconnections in intimacy 40
cognitive neuroscience 3, 6–7, 179, 263, 282
cognitive revolution in human prehistory 25
cognitive science 178, 179, 182–3, 263
Colonial America (1600s and 1700s) 10–11; areas of change 68, **69**; childhood dress 146; children 80; cohesive world 149; communication and courtship 71–7; communities 74; communities of similarly minded people 75–6; consensual uniculture 118; "coverture" 82–3; cultural perspectives 234–5; houses 134–5, 148; intimate life 12–13, 79; marriages 72–3, 82–3; natural world 145; occult and magical explanations 99; patriarchal society 82–3; religion 97, 119; self-identity 57; stationary population 119; unconscious mind 197
color perception and the brain 180
commercial corruption of meaning 109
commitment in intimacy: difficult in conditions of abundant choice 57–8; asking for 62; as a commodity partners bring to relationships 80; confirmed in relationship micro-traditions 106; difficulty in complexly blended

Index 315

modern families 213; caution toward in modern relationships 239, 249; in standard narrative of evolutionary psychology 257, 271; in distributed intimacy 258–9

common sense as a binding and stabilizing cultural fabric of meaning 86, 89, 101, 122, 149, 188, 192–3, 205

communal experience 123, 136–7

communication: affectionate relationships 46–7; animals 177; appraisal of quality 48; appreciation of interaction 45; bypassing 5; as a catchword 96; connectome 268; and courtship 71–7; defining socially and morally 184–6; husbands and wives 83–4; inner experience 2–3; metaphorically representational 204; and modes of mental experience 28–9; neurons 51; and personal identity 2–3; ranking as a problem area in surveys of marital complaints, 96; schematic descriptions 49; understanding of self 7

communication as signal *see* signal communication

communication-as-symbol *see* symbolic communication; symbols

communication breakdowns 96

communication technologies 141, **141**, 149

communities: disordered and alienated life 117; emancipation from traditions 161–2; small towns 128; requirement of shared meaning, history, and memory at the expense of personal autonomy 122

compulsive routines 105–6; *see also* anxiety, and addictive behavior

computers 46, 49–50

Comstock, Anthony 285

con artists thriving in the anonymity of nineteenth century urbanization 125–6

conceptual-emotional maps 265

conflict as a tonic for those with deficits of self identity 42; *see also* anxiety

connectome (Seung) 267–8

conscious awareness in the moment (the I) 174–5, 180, 195

conscious experience, as per Descartes 166

consciousness 9, 166–7, 171, 263

consensual social values 218

consensual unicultures 118

consubstantial (Burke) 182

consumerism 79, 112–13

content holism, theory of consciousness 171

controlling impulses 192–3

conversation and the realignment of symbols 47–8; and the creation of reality 54; constrained in former times by rules of form 76–7; as a process that co-conditions the minds of partners 117; perceived in evolutionary psychology to be no more than the exchange of genetically programmed signals 272–3

Cooley, Charles 231, 232–3, 236, 245

Coontz, Stephanie 92, 94, 95

cooperative self-construction 173

Coser, Rose 11, 12, 137

couple dissolution 274; *see also* divorce, and loss of partner

courtly love and the sacrifice of self 80

courtship 71–7, 79, 272–3

coverture 82–3

COVID-19 xi–xii

Cozolino, Louis 51

Cramer, Phebe 206

Cronkite, Walter 216

cross-sex relationships and friendship in history 43

cultural change 14, 35, 42–3

cultural-level systems 53, 55

culture: American 9, 162, 266; as collective experience 230; collective expression of mind 168; constructed of symbols 34–5, 230, 238; digital 2, 8–9; language-equipped minds 238; and mind 5, 7, 34–6, 238; and modernity 234; and perception 54; and self 229, 230

Culture of Narcissism (Lasch) 7

culture wars 54, 55

Damasio, Antonio 167, 178, 183

Damasio, Hanna 183

dance, as pre-linguistic memetic communication 29; shift from structured to freeform, 77; traditional ethnic dance 103

dark communications industries (advertising and public relations) 93

Darnton, Robert 77

Darwin, Charles 26

dating 58, 73–4, 78, 79, 259, 272

Davidman, Joy 251, 252

Dawkins, Richard 271–2, 275

dead partners (continued communication with) 253; *see also* hallucinations

316 *Index*

deceit, increased potential for in the anonymity of urban environments 125

decision stress 40; *see also* choice

Declaration of Independence, speed of distribution of the news of 141

defense mechanisms for protection of the self narrative 206–7, as interpersonal body armor 205

Definition of Man (Burke) 264

deinstitutionalization 215–16

delaying marriages *74*, 257–8; *see also* marriages

dementia 170, 171, 180, 185, 250 (see also memory loss and Alzheimer's disease)

Democracy in America (de Tocqueville) 88–9

denial (defense mechanism) **206**, 250

Dennett, Daniel 181, 183, 275

dependency experienced as a threat in intimacy 60

depression 4, 6, 7, 13, 14, 16, 25, 30, 40, 70, 90, 92–3, 107, 111, 156, 158, 161, 167–8, 177, 224–5, 239, 249, 251, 287, 289

Dermablend 247–8; *see also* Ferbs

Descartes, René 5, 164, 166

despair (see anguish)

deterministic vision of consciousness 263

de Tocqueville, Alexis 88–90, 94

Diagnostic and Statistical Manual of Mental Disorders (DSM, DSM-5) 34, 283–7

Dickens, Charles 202

Didion, Joan 251–2

dietary and health supplement industry and fraud 109–10

differentiating processes 68, **69**, 116–29

digital age 2, 75

digital culture 2, 8–9

digital detox policies in organizations 52

diminished mental capacity and the life-as-motion sciences 279

disconnection from political and community involvement 123

disembedding processes 68, **69**, 88–112

Disney corporation 111, 156, 161

displacement (defense mechanism) **206**

dissociation of self 245

dissociative identity disorder/multiple personality disorder (DID/ MPD) 241–2

dissolution of self 80, 238, 252, 273

distributed intimacy (multiple partnerships) 256–60

distribution of information, accelerated 141–2

divorce 8, 57, 70, 85, 92, 96, 106, 143, 203, 207, 213, 218, 245–6, 249, 257, 273–4

Dolezal, Rachel 54

Donald, Merlin 27–31

double bind as a condition of life for women in mid-twentieth century U.S., 92

Douglas, Mary 91

dreaming 201–4

dream symbolism 203

drum circles and stress reduction through retreat to non-linguistic consciousness 29–30

Duncan, Hugh 55

Dunne, John Gregory 251–2

duplicity as a feature of modern life 247

Durkheim, Émile 117, 232

early language users, pre-symbolic communication, and greater certainty of meaning 32

Ebenezer Scrooge (*A Christmas Carol*) 202

Edelman, Gerald 178

egalitarianism 83, 91, 94, 96, 97

Ehrenreich, Barbara 145

Eldridge, Niles 272, 273

Eliot, T. S. 134, 247, 288

Ellul, Jacques 219

email 52, 120, 127, 143, 146, 160, 170, 192, 213–14 236

emoticons and emojis ("the worst thing to happen to communication in our time") 236

emotional immaturity as a reason for failed marriage 96

emotional labor 216–18, 249

emotion, inauthentic displays of 249

emotions 4, 23, 27, 29, 30, 53, 132, 138, 166, 175, 177, 192, 202, 206, 244, 259, 278–9

empathy 8, 40, 85, 121, 161, 165, 172, 220, 235–6.239, 263, 277–8

English, Deirdre 145

English language, growth of 38

enterprise culture, meritocracy as a more anxious form of hierarchy 91

entertainment media 148–9

Index 317

episodic culture (first stage of Merlin Donald's evolution of language and mind) 28
equality 13, 84, 89, 94, 97, 218–19
Equanil (tranquilizer) 5, 223
equity theory (Walster, Walster, and Berscheid) 80
Erikson, Erik 155
eroding community 121
escape in fantasy 41–2
Eternal Sunshine of the Spotless Mind (film) 171
etiquette books 191–2
Everett, Daniel 16, 34
evolutionary psychology 3, 263, 272–3
exchange theory (Thibaut and Kelley) 79–80
existential anxiety, 69, 109, 288
existential being, 12–3, 15–6, 41, 172, 262
existential definition 258
existential difficulty, 197; and segmentation 247, and partner loss 250
existential dread 39
existential freedom 263
existential hell (for actors) 246
existential insecurity, 116, 119, 122
existential pain 42
existential challenges 123
existential crisis 50, 86, 88–152
extended families 213
external frameworks of meaning 36, *see also* social imaginaries, paternalism, hierarchy and religion
exorcism (see Gassner)
extramarital affairs 88–9, 257, 259; *see also* marriages, and distributed intimacy

Facebook 52, 55, **141**, 236
faces, modern and historical descriptions of attractive and unattractive features 233
failed identity 249–50
Falklands War 142
fantasy identities 243
feedback loops 52
The Feminine Mystique (Friedan) 92
Ferbs 247–8; *see also* Dermablend
fidgety persons 3–4; *see also* ADHD
fields of meaning 13, 38, 43, 47–8, 52–3, 55, 199, 200, 218, 225, 234–5, 237, 247, 250, 253, 264

Fisher, Helen 273, 274
fish labeling, fraudulent 110–11
flashbacks 221
flight from conversation (Turkle) 9
flow, psychological state 174–5
fMRI brain scans 6–7, 222, 288
fog of infatuation 254
fog of news and the Boston Marathon bombing (Gleick) 142
Foucault, Michel 285
fragmentation of self 1, 15, 41, 149–50, 167, 242, 245, 248–50, 252
Frances, Allen 284
franchise operations and the loss of the sense of local 108
free-form language-as-private-symbol 77
Freudian psychoanalysis 159
Freud, Sigmund 95, 159, 171, 201–2, 203, **206**, 280
Friedan, Betty 92
Frost, Robert 39
Fuller, Robert C. 189
Full Metal Jacket (film) 132

Garciaparra, Nomar 105
Gassner, Johann Joseph 197–9
Geertz, Clifford 162
Geher, Glenn 272, 274
Gemeinschaft 211–14, 237
gender identity: rapid and dramatic expansion of options 54–5; and intimate connection 61–2
gender-inappropriate clothing 89
gender roles 10, 97, 255
Gergen, Kenneth 140, 249
Gesellschaft 211–14, 237
ghost marriage as a means of obtaining social identity 163
Giddens, Anthony 15, 57, 60, 94, 105, 112, 120, 215
gig economy 40, 214–15
Gillis, John 84
Gleick, James 142
Glen, New York 100
Glens Falls, New York 121
globalization 71, 107, 215, 254
global warming 248; *see also* climate change
Goffman, Erving 125, 217, 242–7, 262
Google 56, 71, 97, 229–30
Gottlieb, Lori 78
GPS tracking 160

318   *Index*

Graham, Sylvester 285
Graziano, Michael 181, 183
Green, Bernard 96
Greenfeld, Liah 5, 7, 14, 16, 97, 239
Greenfield, Susan 174
greenwashing (fraudulently associating
    marketed goods with ecologically
    positive symbols) 110
A Grief Observed (Lewis) 251
Groupthink, shared mind, and mental
    health 122
Gruen effect in marketing and shopping
    mall design 113
Grymes children 80, *81*

habitus (the common sense) 188
Hacking, Ian 158
hallucinations 38, 171, 253, 266
Henriette-Lucy, Marquise de La Tour du
    Pin Gouvernet 135–6
heterosexual intimacy 258, 273–4
Het Nieuwsblad 12
Hewett, John 14
The Hidden Persuaders (Packard) 159
hierarchy 13, 88–97
historical dramas in the media and the
    appeal of the past 10
Hoagland, Tony 140
Hobson, Peter 9, 176, 177–8, 179
Hochschild, Arlie 108, 211, 249
Hofstadter, Douglas 180, 195, 268–9
Homer 37, 176, 202
home thermostats and heat pumps as
    examples of signal communication 46
Homo erectus 29
Homo medicatus 223–5
Homo sapiens 24, 25
homosexuality 286
house design and privacy 134–5; *see also*
    architecture of the house
house of mirrors as metaphor for
    modernity 144
human prehistory 27–8
Humphrey, N. K. 275
husbands and wives: communication
    83–4; and industrialization 145;
    male–female intimate relationships
    271; nineteenth century 84; roles 157;
    separated and divorced 253; sharing
    minds 181–3; widowed spouses
    252–3; wives suppressing feelings
    217; working-class 83; *see also*
    marriages; men; partners; women

hypersexuality (sex addiction) 286
hypnotism 199–201; *see also* animal
    magnetism, and hypnosis

I and the Me 174–6
ideal self 231
identification (defense mechanism) 85,
    206
identity 16, 56–7, 124–5, 255
identity fragmentation (see fragmentation
    of self)
identity shifts 255
identity theft 249–50
idiolect 55; *see also* restricted code, and
    private language
Iliad (Homer) 37, 202
Illouz, Eva 78, 217, 257–9, 280
immigration 118, 160–1
impulse, regulation of 191, 193–4
incomprehensibility between modern
    and historical modes of consciousness
    81–2
individualism 37, 132, 258
industrialization 79, 127, 145–6
Industrial Revolution 95, 106–7, 237
infants 36, 61, 85, 177–8, 190, 231, 234,
    266, 277; *see also* babies
infatuation period in new relationships
    (see fog of infatuation)
information flows 11, 140–1, 146
initial awareness of self ("analog I") 33
insecure interpersonal attachments 8
Inside Out (film) 156
instability and mental health 249
institutional involvements 236
interactional school of psychotherapy
    243
interdependencies of meaning 180–1
internal migration 119–20
internet 2; civic influence 122; intimate
    partnerships online 121; self-
    referential information flows 144;
    social resources 121
internet dating 15, 39, 58, 79
interpersonal climate change 1
interpersonal experiences 14–15, 236–7
interpersonal influence 199–201
interpersonal loss 172–3
interpersonally relevant drugs 5
interpersonal perspectives 230–1
interpersonal self 228–32
interpersonal skills 106; *see also*
    empathy, and self disclosure

interpsychic bonds 97
intimacy 36–40; cognitive interconnections 40; and dependency 60; and individualism 37; modern theories 77–82; "particularized knowledge" 53; and privacy 37, 39; psychological experience 139; reluctance to commit to 57; and self-identity 239; social equality 274; unique historical calendar 56
intimate conflict conceptualized as signal exchange 51
intimate connections and male and female dynamics of self definition 60–3
intimate partners: interdependencies of meaning 180–1; microcultures 56; online 121; taking time apart 266–7
intimate relationships 5; Colonial America 12–13, 79; definition and stability 59; emotional fallout and anguish 259; evolutionary psychology 273; fog of infatuation 254; gene-driven process 271–4; inwardly generated identity 56–7; linear developmental history 220; marital and nonmarital 259; micro-traditions 106; minds mutually cultivated 53; orgasmic behavior 285; realignment of consciousness 62; self-definition 58, 184, 253, 258; stable communities of friendship 247; see also marriages; partners
inventions of relevant communication technologies 141–2
investment model of relationships 80
I (primary consciousness) 176–7, 190
isolation 60, 78, 116, 125–7, 131–151, 161, 173, 177, 189, 193, 222, 229, 230, 239, 266

Jackson, Shirley 241
James, William 166–7, 175, 176, 231–2, 236, 242
Jaynes, Julian 31–3, 125, 169, 176, 191, 289
Johnson, Mark 171
J. Peterman company as iconic marketer of clothing as props of the self 112
juggernaut (modernity as) 15, 105, 108, 225, 279
Jung, Carl 24–5, 202–3

Kalanithi, Lucy 250
Kaplan, Margo 286
Kaplan, Robert 108
Kaufman, Scott Barry 272, 274
Keller, Helen 265, 266
Kelley, Harold 79
Kellogg, John Harvey 285
Key, Wilson 159
kinship as bond 85
Knickerbocker Arena (Pepsi Arena) 111
Konrath, Sara 236
Koyaanisqatsi (film) 70
Krafft-Ebing, Richard von 285
Kubrick, Stanley 132

Laing, R. D. 200, 243
Lakoff, George 170, 171
Langdon, Olivia 73
language: abstracts from direct experience 190; adjusted for perspectives and reactions 234; classifying experiences 195; conventional symbols 178; courtship 76; determining reality 34; externalized lattice of meanings 265; as a fixed code 230; and human experience 180; interiorization 138; intimate medium 53; inventory of word types 35; meme transmission 275; and memory 172; organizing the world 53; origins and development 25–6; and personal identity 237; and self 181, 186; *shared* meanings 181; as signal 31–4; system of symbols 230; working differently in the past 82
language-as-signal-constrained-by-structure 77
language-as-symbolic-action 262–3
language-based communication 5
languages, number of spoken in New York City 118
Lasch, Christopher 7–8, 143
Laslett, Peter 12, 211
law enforcement versus psychiatric treatment 285
Lehrer, Jonah 184
Levy, David 222
Lewis, C. S. 251, 252
life-as-motion sciences 269, 278–9; *see also* evolutionary psychology, meme theory, mirror neurons, medical psychiatry, and psychiatry-as-pseudology
limbic speech 28–9

320　*Index*

limbic system 28, 183, 185
linguistic culture 24
local culture 108–9
loneliness 16–7, 62–3, 123–4, 134, 137, 184, 254
looking glass self 232–3
loosening of meaning in modernity 15
loss of language 180; *see also* aphasia, Alzheimer's disease, and dementia
loss of memory 170–3, 267; *see also* Alzheimer's disease, and dementia
loss of partner, psychological impact 46, 157, 180, 184, 185, 250–3, 268
loss of self as cataclysmic trauma motivating modern anxiety 42, 250–3, 268
love 80, 178, 184–5, 234, 254, 259, 273
The Love Song of J. Alfred Prufrock (Eliot) 134
Luckmann, Thomas 108
Lyons, John 163

MacDonaldization 108
machine communication as signal exchange 50
machines as metaphor for humans 269; *see also* self-as-computer
The Madness of King George (film) 197–8
Madonna (Madonna Louise Ciccone) 23
magical thinking 42, 250
The Manchurian Candidate (film) 159
The Man in the Gray Flannel Suit (film) 47
manners: role in the evolution of unconscious experience 190–3
manufactured past (as refuge from stress and anxiety) 9–10
marital bonds versus animal bonds 274
marital secrets 52–3; *see also* secrets as the essence of intimacy
marketing and advertising 109–10, 111–12
marriages 8; American and European 88–9, 94–5; Colonial marriages 72–3, 82–3; Colonial period 72–3; creation and maintenance of ideas 157; delaying *74*, 257–8; economic convenience 12–13; economic ties 85; egalitarian model 94, 96; emotional labor 217–18; equality 84; extramarital affairs 88–9, 257, 259; and intimacy 57, 256–7; loyalty to spouse and

children 264; and modernity 47; multiple partners 257; parental consent 73; paternalism 94; patriarchal couples 257; pragmatic rationality 73; private bedrooms 148; renewal of commitments 259; *see also* husbands and wives; intimate relationships
Marry Him (Gottlieb) 78
masculinity 54–5, 61
Maslow, Abraham 249
mass communication systems 161
mass culture 106–11, 113, 229
mass marketers 111–12
mass media 143
masturbation, and psychiatry as enforcer of prudish morality 285; *see also* homosexuality
material self (James) 232
material world versus symbolic world 23
Mather, Cotton 98
mating intelligence 272–3
Mating Intelligence Unleashed (Geher and Kaufman) 272, 274
McCall, George 75
MDA 5
Mead, George Herbert 231, 233–5, 236, 245, 267
meaningful communion 137
meaningful community 229; *see also* communities
meaningful friendships 257, 269
meaning maps 265
meanings 25, 32, 59, 177–84, 264–9; *see also* symbols
mechanical clock metaphor for mechanism as a world view 269–70
mechanical transfers of energy 51, 270
media 51–2, 143, 221–2
medical psychiatry 3, 4, 263, 281–3, 287
mediation, stress reducing benefits in retreat to episodic consciousness 29, 175
Meigs, Charles 95
Melville, Herman 135
meme theory 263, 275–7
memory 170–2, 179–80, 220
men: intimate connections 60–2; styles of clothing 145–6
mental disorders: digital connectivity 121; mid-to-late teens 36; rate of 40, 174, 284; types of 34; *see also* Diagnostic and Statistical Manual of Mental Disorders (DSM)

Index 321

mentalese 178
mental health: and instability 249; and
  social isolation 43
meritocratic enterprise cultures,
  precarious nature of the self in 92
Me (second dimension of awareness)
  176, 195
Mesmer, Franz Anton 197–200
mesmerism 199, *see also* hypnotism, and
  animal magnetism
metaphoric condensation in dreams 203
metaphors 171
Metaphors We Live By (Lakoff and
  Johnson) 171
Metzinger, Thomas 6, 167
microcultures 56
micro-traditions as symbols of
  connection 106
Middle Ages 192
middle classes 92, 121
middle-tier contacts 247
Middletown studies of early twentieth
  century American family life 83–4
Midgley, Mary 276–7
military, and information control during
  operations 141–2, socialization of
  soldiers through breakdown of identity
  132, recruiting adolescents 36
Miltown (tranquilizer) 5, 223, 281
mimesis 29–30
mimetic culture (second stage of Merlin
  Donald's evolution of language and
  mind) 29
mind: boundary with body 166; cognitive
  science/neuroscience 179; constructed
  of symbols 238; and culture 5, 7, 34–6,
  238; as culture-in-the-head 7, 35;
  interdependencies of meaning 180–1;
  and self 170; symbol-using organ 265
mirror neurons 277–8
mirrors: increasing frequency in
  historical household inventories 148
misattributing perfection to partner
  in infatuation 254; *see also* fog of
  infatuation
mixophobia (Bauman): fear of social
  diversity 127
Moby Dick (Melville) 135
model of the material brain, connectome
  as 268
models of unrealistic perfection in the
  media ("abundant flawlessness") 78
modern consciousness 11–12

modernist art as reflecting psychological
  difficulties accompanying modernity
  98; *see also* Sass, Louis
modernity xi–xii, 11; boundaries 137;
  codes of conduct 192; and culture 234;
  defining 16; equality and freedom
  218–19; foundation of self 238–9;
  institutional involvements 236; as
  "the juggernaut" (Giddens) 15; novel
  situations 219; privacy 133–4; and
  problems of self 16; self-identity
  218, 284; social withdrawal 266;
  symbolic communication 49; and the
  unconscious mind 188–90; world of
  communication 263
modern self, origins of 163
modern societies and novelty and the
  absence of traditional influence 103–5
morality: origin of in language and the
  capacity for choice 183–6
moral clarity as attractive part of the
  fantasized past 10
moral contradictions in multiplicity of
  identity 247
morality and the life-as-motion sciences
  279
Morgan, Edmund S. 72, 82–3
multidenominational religious affiliations
  214
multiple accumulative fertilization and
  the standard narrative of evolutionary
  psychology 271
multiple jobs 147; *see also* gig economy
multiple personality disorder/dissociative
  identity disorder (DID/ MPD) 241–2
multiple separated identities 245
multiplicity of identity 241–2, 245–7
Muncie, Indiana 83–4
music 76–7, 102–3, 268
mutual influence requiring social
  equality 84–5
mysticism, displaced by science 270
mythic culture (third stage of Merlin
  Donald's evolution of language and
  mind) 31

names and qualities of things 54
narcissism 7–8, 16, 36, 40, 85, 101, 121,
  138, 155, 221, 239, 254, 263
narcissistick ("selfie stick") 155, 221
narrative consciousness 220–1
National Institute of Mental Health
  (NIMH) 4, 174, 224, 284

322   *Index*

National Museum of Mathematics (New York) Robot Swarm exhibition 270
Nation of Strangers (Packard) 121
nation-states as religious organizations 100
Native American religions 98
Native Australians and dreams 202
nature/nurture debate as spurious 170
neural pathways 267–9
neurasthenia (shattered nerves) 126–7, 280; *see also* NewYorkitis
neuroscience 6, 158, 170, 178, 182–3
neurotransmitters 7–8, 264, 286–7
new/alternative partners 15, 56, 78, 254
new communication and entertainment technologies 14–15
new words experiment 37
New York and modern mate selection 75, and nineteenth century cholera epidemic 99, and number of languages spoken 118, and psychological stress (see NewYorkitis), and rapid population growth 118, and loneliness 124
NewYorkitis (shattered nerves) 127, 223, 280; *see also* neurasthenia
New York State Attorney General 109, 110
nineteenth century: advertising 159; art 98; courtship 73; duties and powers of people 89; estate houses 10; home dwellings 134; husbands and wives 84, 145; industrialization 145; scientific interest in self-concept 163; urbanization 123–4, 125; women 95
Nisbet, Robert 1–2, 4
non-modern cultures 11, 12, 162, 237–8
noon: varying definition of prior to the imposition of time zones 145
Northampton, Massachusetts and Colonial Era mate selection 71–2, 81
The North Star (Reynolds) 161
nostalgia 11, 289

occult and magical explanations 99
Oceana Research Group and exposure of fraudulent marketing of seafood 110
Ohio State University and growth of bureaucracy 147
Old Order Amish 11, 80, 100, 225, 237, 274
Oneida religious community and communal marriage 95

online dating 78, 79
online fraudulent product reviews 109
operant conditioning 177, 183, 185, 262
oral cultures 220–1
ordering food subconsciously 5
orgasmic behavior as a psychiatric concern 285
outsourcing interpersonal functions 256

Packard, Vance 121, 159
Pakistan 12
parental consent for marriage 73
parental investment theory (Trivers) 271–2
Parfit, Derek 269
partners: constructing world together 58–9; deficits of 15; fields of meaning 185; new/alternative 15, 78, 254; *see also* husbands and wives; intimate relationships
partner selection, difficulty of in modern society 75
past, knowledge of as essential for understanding the present 11
paternalism (see patriarchy)
patriarchy 24, 38, 42, 88–97, 131, 257
pedophilia as criminal behavior versus psychiatric disorder 286
Pepper, Steven 269
Pepsi Arena (Knickerbocker Arena) 111
performance of self, self as performance 244
Persona (film) commentary on the psychological difficulty of multiplicity of identity 245, 246
personal identity 1, 2–3, 5–6; anxious uncertainty 8; cooperative construction 173; disembedded and free-form 172; freedom to construct 168; how others react 245; and intimate relationships 58; and marriage 57; and mind 237–8; nonrational influences 188; stability 49; threats to 205–6
personal meaning 43, 106, 157
personal privacy 80, 131, 133
personal vocabularies 56
perspective taking (empathy) 236
pets 28, 46, 84, 156, 183
pharmaceutical industry 284
pharmocracy, America as (Szasz) 224
philosophers of language 111
phlogiston (meme theory) 277
phonographs, unintended consequences of 222

Index 323

physical boundaries, sex, and intimacy 139

physical seclusion and the sense of self 132

Pirahãs people (Amazonia) 16, 156, 221

Pizza Hut and mindless choice 5

placebos 199–200

Plato cave allegory 23–4, warning about literacy undermining the skill of memory 220

plural marriage 257; *see also* distributed intimacy

political communication 142–3

polygraph as a technology of the self 222

population mobility 120, 160–1

pornography as psychological escape 41; as an addictive behavior 105; viewing pornography at work 286

Portrait of a Lady (Eliot) 247

Post-it notes, literacy, and the loss of memory skills 220

Postman, Neil 224

postmodernity 248

post-traumatic stress disorder (PTSD) 196, 221, 286

post-war American economy 96

prenuptial agreements and commitment 259

prescriptions for psychiatric drugs 4, 287–8

The Presentation of Self in Everyday Life (Goffman) 242

primary consciousness (the I) 176–7, 190

primitive vocalized signals 26–7

The Principles of Psychology (James) 175

privacy 37, 39, 131–9, 161

private language 55; *see also* idiolect, and restricted code

private meanings 55–6, 138

problem solving and awareness of self 175

program-to-program communication in computers as signal exchange 49–50

projection (defense mechanism) **207**

protective inward withdrawal 124

Protestant denominations and the relativization of religious experience 99

Prufrock, J. Alfred 134, 148

Prum, Richard 272

psychiatric drugs 4, 223–5, 287–8

psychiatry: dream analysis 203; and law enforcement 285; as pseudology 28737

psychoanalysis 148, 159, 280, 283

psychoanalytic treatment models 282

psychodynamic theory 282

psycho-emotional disorders 36, 243, 287

psycho-emotional distress 284

psychological distress 253

psychological profiles 160

Psychopathia Sexualis (Krafft-Ebing) 285

psychotherapy 280–1

psychotic disorders and urban living 127

psychotropic drugs 281–2

psych-speak and the sense of self 138

public and private spheres 132–3, 145

public relations (see dark communications industries)

public trust, erosion of, and high speed information flows 142–3

pure ego (James) 232

pure relationships (Giddens), absence of external factors holding intimate relationships together 57, 60

Puritans 72–3, 83, 98, 145

Putnam, Robert D. 119, 122

race-based hierarchy 90

rape as criminal behavior versus mental illness 286; and the social repair of personal identity 173; and trauma, 205

Rath, Betsy 52–3

Ravel, Maurice 15

reaction-formation (defense mechanism) **207**

Real Estate Subdivision Name Generator as example of public meaninglessness in the service of commercial gain 109

real self (see true self)

reasoning by transferred epithet (Tallis) 50; (*see also*, self-as-computer)

reciprocity 80, 155

reconciling disparate versions of self 41

Reddit 142

Rees, W. Dewi 253

reflex 24, 180, 193, 262, 264, 268

reflexivity 35, 143, 218–19

Reggio, Godfrey 70

regression (defense mechanism) **207**

reincarnation as a source of self identity 162

relabeling food and the deliberate fabrication of meaning for commercial gain 110–11

324 *Index*

relationships: affectionate 46–7; "bank account model" 80; deep intimacy 139; deep relationships 40, 117, 169; dissolution/terminating 57, 170, 253; interpersonal 239, 255–6; "investment model" 80; new/alternative 15, 56, 78, 254; self-defining 184, 253
relationship stability 255–6
relative and diverse knowledge and the loss of authority of all competing perspectives 100
religion 97–101, 119, 158–9, 214
REM sleep and dreaming 204
renaming sports stadiums and the management of meaning for commercial gain 111
Rensselaer Polytechnic Institute and the marketing of identity 112
repetitive behavior, addiction, and the management of anxiety 105; *see also* anxiety
repressing reflex-like responses 191
repression 188–9, 193–4, 197, 204, (as defense mechanism, 204)
resource theory of relationships 80
restricted code (Bernstein) 56; *see also* idiolect, and private language
Reynolds, Peter 161
The Rhetoric (Aristotle) 277
rites of passage and the sense of personal identity 103
ritualized behavior, addiction, and the management of anxiety 105–6; *see also* anxiety
Robot Swarm 270–1
role of the body in formation of self identity 169–70
role-related family names 211–12, **212**
role theory and personal identity 210–11, 245
romantic love 37 259
romantic passion 259
Romney, Mitt 143
roses, color and the neurological construction of the real world 180
rote performance as a function of brain rather than mind 268
rotten with perfection clause of Burke's "Definition of Man" 276
Royce, Josiah 231, 236
Rubin, Lillian 61, 83

Sapir, Edward 230
Sapir – Whorf hypothesis 34

Sartre, Jean-Paul 49, 138, 165, 181, 196, 239, 288, 289
Sass, Louis 42, 98, 138
schizophrenia 14, 35, 243; *see also* double bind
science: mysticism and religious belief 270; and the self-concept 163
second dimension of awareness (Me) 176, 195
Second Life online environment 246, 256
second-order consciousness and psychological flow 175
secrets as the essence of intimacy 37, 39, 52–3, 132–3, 237
secularism 98, 99–101
segmentation, of social and personal experience 100, 145, 146, 148–50, 213, 256, 258
self: abandonment and dissolution 80; American culture 162; animals 183; and the body 170; characterological templates 24–5; conscious awareness 174–5; and culture 229; defining 138, 156, 184–5; and dissociation 245; evolving throughout life 7; historically emergent structure 169; as an illusion 167; as interpersonal 231; and language 181, 186; mind's stream of consciousness 166–7; and modernity 238–9; nature of 156, 164; as private 148; protective shield 36; reconciling disparate versions 41; shadows 162; and soul 157–8; theories of 231; twentieth century 164; understanding 7; validating and revalidating 38
self-alienation and segmented work 249–50; *see also* segmentation
self-as-computer 222–3
self-awareness 175, 194, 195, 221
self-concept (the Me) 6; academic journal articles 164; animals 183; biological and culture 158; biological/neuroscience 158; non-modern people 162–3; protective filter 35; scientific interest 163; second-order awareness 195; secular/scientific discussion 158; and self-awareness 196–7; soul and self 157–8; verifiable phenomenon 168
self-defense 204–6, **206–7**
self-definition 56, 157; advertising 111–12, 160; born to a station in life 93; freedoms in modernity 239; gender roles 255; heightened as a

Index 325

result of interpersonal conflict 42; hierarchically structured societies 88; important relationship partners 184; independent of others 59–60; intimate relationships 58, 184, 253, 258; secularism 101
self-differentiation, privacy, and living alone 135
self-disclosure 75, 126, 133, 155, 161
self-expression in rural and urban environments 124–5
self-fragmentation 1, 15, 41, 149–50, 166, 242, 245, 248–50, 252
self-identity 6, 14; clothing companies 112; communal validation 137; cultural-historical processes 172; defining 57, 157; and despair 195; fantasized past 10; foundations of 92; fragmentation 15; freedom to craft 137; and hierarchies 89–93; impulse management 193–4; and interpersonal dynamics 9; and intimacy 239; mass culture 113; minimal requirement 246; modern culture 35; and modernity 284; and morality 186; multiple jobs 213–14; and "performance" 244; perpetual state of revision 196; postmodernity 248; role functions in society 210; social and moral processes 184; socially constructed 7, 137; structure of mind 228–9; theatrical and interpersonal 242–3; twenty-first century 155; universities 112; *see also* awareness of self
selfies 155, 221
selfie sticks 155, 221
The Selfish Gene (Dawkins) 275
selfish gene theory (Dawkins) 271–2, 276
self-knowledge and high speed information flows 143–4
self-narrative 195, 256, 281
self-observations and personal identity 194
self-presentation 75, 149–50, 217
self-referential information flows 144
self-reflection 195
self-revelation 75
self-revision 196
self-stabilizing conditions of community 246, 253–4
self-sufficient individuals (*see also* autonomy) 266

self-threatening information (*see also* repression, and defense mechanism) 191
Sennett, Richard 76, 78, 82, 133
sensory deprivation experiments and the decay of meaning 267
separated spouses continuing to function as vital anchors for each others' meanings and sense of identity 253
separate spheres, period in American history 95–6
serotonin and depression 7
Seung, Sebastian 267–8, 269
seventeenth century: etiquette books 191–2; home dwellings 134; language and mind 34; public life and family life 133; waterways *68*
sex change and moral redefinition of a Catholic priest 55
sex-differentiated parenting, impacts of 61
shadows as part of self identity 162
shamanic healing 200; *see also* placebos
shared conceptual vocabulary 255
shared *internal* privacy 139
shared meaning 3, 51, 116, 150, 181, 234–5, 252
shared memory/morality 123
shared understandings 55–6
Shea Stadium (Citi Field) 111
shell institutions (Giddens) 215; *see also* zombie institutions
shopping and the management of anxiety 112–13; *see also* anxiety
signal communication: becoming a symbolic process 176; interpersonal interaction 58; language as 31–4; between machines 49; neuronal synapses 48; signal-to-symbol shift 45–6; social coordination 191; and symbolic language 24; and symbols 46, 264–5; unidirectional messages 48–9
Simmons, J. L. 75
Simons, Daniel 24
simultaneous multipartnerships 257
singles dating scene 259
Slater, Lauren 5
sleeping arrangements, marital 135
small towns versus cities and effects on self definition 128
social bonds 85
social capital 121
social connections 121, 123

326 *Index*

social equality 90–1, 274
social ethics and advice columns 193
social experience 52, 179–80
social imaginaries (Taylor) 24, 38, *see also* external frameworks of meaning
social imitation and mirror neurons 277
social inequality 84–5
social insecurity 159–62
social intelligence 235–7
social isolation 43, 266
social mobility 121
social penetration theory (Altman and Taylor) 80
social roles and the sense of self identity 210
social self (James) 232
social withdrawal and isolation effects on mind 266
Societies of Harmony and mesmerism 200
sociograms, as representation of networks of shared meaning 269
sociotropy 59
soldiers returning from battle zones and elevated rates of suicide 253
solo living, increasing preference for 8, 98, 135, 239, 256
Somalia, live coverage of U.S. Marines landing 141–2
soul 7, 156, 158, 166–7, 183, 198, 241–2, 258, 269
soulmate 72, 254; *see also* yokemates
source → message → receiver model of human communication 50–1
Southwest Airlines and emotional labor 217
Spain, eighteenth century and restricted martial conversation 76
Spanish American citizens and immigration 118
spare mind (spouse functioning as in global aphasia) 182
Spirit Airlines and emotional labor 217
spiritualist mediums and continued conversation with deceased partners 253
spiritual self (James) 232
splitting (defense mechanism) **206**
state-level moral enforcement and psychiatry 284
Stone, Lawrence 133
strange loops (Hofstadter) 195
strokes, cognitive and communication deficits, and partner as spare mind 182

subliminal persuasion 159
Subliminal Seduction (Key) 159
suicide 4, 7, 14, 120, 126, 183, 238, 253, 283–4
surviving spouses (widows and widowers) and the recovery of disrupted meaning 250–3
symbolically interdependent relationships 58, 252
symbolic communication 48–9, 177
symbolic exchange 48
symbolic interactionism 233–5, 236, 245–7
symbolic interdependence 58–9, 60, 62, 83, 96, 182, 257
symbolic language 24, 26–7, 30–1, 177–8, 190–1
symbolization 60, 176–8, 204
symbols 45–52, 264–6; associational meanings 47; cognitive science/neuroscience 179; and conscious thought 59; conveying freedom and agency 262; defining 47; dynamic meaning 264; humanity 264; instruments of social connection 37–8; mind-bridges 38; neuronal interconnections 179; *shared* elements of meaning 265; *see also* meanings
symbol templates 178–9
synchronous neural reactions 277–8
synthesis of theoretical perspective 237–40
Szasz, Thomas 224, 280, 287
Szymborska, Wisława 53, 244–5

talk therapy 4, 280–1
Tallis, Raymond 49, 50, 276, 278
Target 111
TargetPoint 160
Taylor, Charles 8, 16, 24, 30, 38, 56, 92, 98, 99, 100, 184, 185–6
Taylor, Dalmas 80
technological innovation 222
technologies of social saturation (Gergen) 140–1
technology 219–20, 222, 225
technopoly (Postman) 224
teen years, see adolescence
telephone answering machines 52
telephones, unintended consequences of 222
television channels, proliferation of 117–18

Index 327

terminating relationships 57, 170, 253
terministic compulsion (Burke) 276
terministic screens (Burke) 182
texting 2, 9, 52, 120, 141, 146, 189, 213, 236, 244
Thibaut, John 79
Thigpen, Corbett H. 241
This American Life 172
Thorazine (anti-psychotic medication) 223, 281
Thoreau, Henry David 266
The Three Faces of Eve (Thigpen and Cleckley) 241
Tidewater region and Colonial American architecture 134
time as defined in pre-modern and modern societies 145
Titanic, RMS and the loss of souls versus selves 156–7, 241, 242
Tönnies, Ferdinand 211, 232, 237
traditional goods, marketing of 104–105
traditional knowledge 218
traditional practices 102–5
traditional societies 105
tradition, receding influence of 101–6, 111, 161–2
transference (defense mechanism) **207**
transnational markets and the decline of the local 107; *see also* globalization
transoceanic voice communications cables 141
trauma 13, 42, 57, 173, 175, 184–5, 196, 203–4,
Trillin, Calvin 251
Trivers, Robert 271–2
true self 156, 246, 248
The Truman Show (film) 243
Tuan, Yi-Fu 9, 144
Turkle, Sherry 2, 8–9, 236
Twain, Mark (Samuel Clemens) 73
twentieth century: advertising 159; modernist art 98; "permanent identity crisis" 92; self-concept 164
twenty-first century: advertising 160; self-identity 155
Twitter **141**, 142
two-paycheck homes as a factor in rising social equality 96, 245

U-Haul stories as part of the common narrative of social mobility 120
uncertainty 258
unconditional love 259

unconscious awareness 180
unconscious influences 188
unconscious mind 40–1, 188–90, 197, 280
unfocused awareness of the unfolding present 175; *see also* primary consciousness, and episodic culture, and meditation, and drum circles
unidirectional messages 48–9
unintended consequences of new technologies of communication 222–3
unique historical calendars shared by intimate partners 56
universal civil rights as a factor in the demise of hierarchy 89
universities, and identity 112, and bureaucratic complexity 147, as shell institution 215
unmediated expression of base impulses 193
unsatisfactory lives, personal responsibility for in modernity 93
unverifiable information in high-speed information flows 142
urban anonymity 125, 138
urbanization 123–9; density and diversity 124–5; geography of isolation 127; identity and self-expression 124; and internet dating 78; marital relationships 127; marrying 74, *74*; mental experiences 126–7; psychotic disorders 127
urban population 128, *128*
U.S. Constitution: 14th and 15th Amendments 89; 19th Amendment 89
U.S. government, growth of size and bureaucratic complexity 146
U.S. Supreme Court and eroding credibility 216

van Gogh, Vincent 228
vervet monkeys and animal signal communication 177
Victoria Magazine and escape into a fantasized past 10
visualization 180
visual narratives 221
vocabulary and the possibility of conceptualization 26, and moral development 268
vocalized signals 26–7, 28
Volkswagen Corporation diesel emissions fraud 110
voyeuristic disorder (DSM-5) 285–6

328 Index

Wales 253
Walmart 108, 109, 110–11,
Walster, Elaine 80
Walster, G. William 80
wand of narcissism (selfie stick) 155, 221
Washington, George 146
The Washington Post 241
The Wasteland (Eliot) 288
waterways' influence on patterns of
    settlement and consciousness 67, *68*
Watts, Alan 167
weather, as expression of divine will
    versus scientifically predictable
    physical force 270
Weber, Max 99
West, Paul 56, 182
White, Erin 232
widowed spouses 252–3
Wilson, Henrietta 99
Winthrop, John 83, 94, 98
Wittgenstein, Ludwig 180, 266
Wolfe, Alan 216
women: autonomy and connection
    62; choosiness in evolutionary
    psychology account of mate selection
    271; Colonial marriages 72–3, 82–3;
    demand for equality 60; economic
    and political power 96; femininity
    54–5; gender identity 61–2;
    independent means 131; intimate

connections 60–2; legal status 94–5;
    nineteenth-century 10, 95; personal
    significance 92; self-as-connected 61;
    social equality 93–4; social status 83,
    94; styles of clothing 145–6; suffrage
    89; suppressing feelings 217; work
    and marriage 85; *see also* husbands
    and wives
women's movement 96
Woolf, Virginia 131
words 47–8, 54, 265
work 106–7, 214–15, 257; *see also* gig
    economy
working-class husbands and wives
    and communication deficits in early
    twentieth century America 83
writing, early and lack of reference
    to interior states 31, and narrative
    consciousness 220
Wuthnow, Robert 124

Xanax 4, 17, 70, 223–4

yokemates 72
Yosemite National Park 111

Zelizer, Viviana 286
zombie institutions (Bauman) 215; *see
    also* shell institutions
Zootopia (film) 161